**PETROGRADSKAYA**
*See pp64–73*
*Street Finder maps 1, 2*

**PALACE EMBANKMENT**
*See pp74–95*
*Street Finder maps 2, 5, 6*

**GOSTINYY DVOR**
*See pp96–113*
*Street Finder maps 2, 6*

Bol Nevka    Бол Невка

Petrogradskaya

Neva    Нева

Palace Embankment

Gostinyy Dvor

D0229789

| 0 metres | 600 |
| 0 yards | 600 |

# EYEWITNESS TRAVEL
# ST PETERSBURG

MAIN CONTRIBUTORS:
CATHERINE PHILLIPS
CHRISTOPHER AND MELANIE RICE

LONDON, NEW YORK,
MELBOURNE, MUNICH AND DELHI
www.dk.com

PROJECT EDITOR Anna Streiffert
ART EDITOR Marisa Renzullo

EDITOR Ella Milroy
DESIGNERS Gillian Andrews, Carolyn Hewitson,
Paul Jackson, Elly King, Nicola Rodway
VISUALIZER Joy Fitzsimmons
MAP CO-ORDINATORS Emily Green, David Pugh
PICTURE RESEARCH Brigitte Arora
DTP DESIGNERS Samantha Borland, Sarah Martin, Pamela Shiels

MAIN CONTRIBUTORS
Catherine Phillips, Christopher and Melanie Rice

PHOTOGRAPHERS
Demetrio Carrasco, John Heseltine

ILLUSTRATORS
Stephen Conlin, Maltings Partnership, Chris Orr & Associates,
Paul Weston

Reproduced by Colourscan, Singapore
Printed and bound by South China Printing Co. Ltd., China
First published in Great Britain in 1998
by Dorling Kindersley Limited, 80 Strand, London WC2R 0RL

Reprinted with revisions 2000, 2001, 2004, 2007, 2010

A CIP CATALOGUE RECORD IS AVAILABLE FROM THE BRITISH LIBRARY.

ISBN 978 1 4053 5197 3

FLOORS ARE REFERRED TO THROUGHOUT IN ACCORDANCE WITH EUROPEAN
USAGE; IE THE "FIRST FLOOR" IS THE FLOOR ABOVE GROUND LEVEL.

*Front cover main image: Golden cupolas at Tsarkoe Selo*

**The information in this
DK Eyewitness Travel Guide is checked regularly.**
Every effort has been made to ensure that this book is as up-to-date as
possible at the time of going to press. Some details, however, such
as telephone numbers, opening hours, prices, gallery hanging
arrangements and travel information are liable to change. The
publishers cannot accept responsibility for any consequences arising
from the use of this book, nor for any material on third party websites,
and cannot guarantee that any website address in this book will be
a suitable source of travel information. We value the views and
suggestions of our readers very highly. Please write to: Publisher,
DK Eyewitness Travel Guides, Dorling Kindersley, 80 Strand,
London WC2R 0RL, Great Britain.

◁ **The grand façade of the Hermitage in winter sunlight**

# CONTENTS

Bronze model of ship, a symbol
of St Petersburg

## INTRODUCING
## ST PETERSBURG

Petersburgers enjoying the snow
outside the Admiralty

## ST PETERSBURG
## AREA BY AREA

Little Stable Bridge crossing the Moyka river

## TRAVELLERS' NEEDS

## SURVIVAL GUIDE

15th-century icon of St George and
the Dragon, Russian Museum

Golden statues of the Grand
Cascade at Peterhof

St Isaac's Cathedral, lavishly decorated inside with more than
40 different stones and minerals

# HOW TO USE THIS GUIDE

This guide will help you to get the most from your visit to St Petersburg, providing expert recommendations as well as detailed practical information. *Introducing St Petersburg* maps the city and sets it in its geographical, historical and cultural context, with a quick-reference time-line on the history pages giving the dates of Russia's rulers and significant events. *St Petersburg at a Glance* is an overview of the city's main attractions. *St Petersburg Area by Area* starts on page 54 and describes all the important

sights, using maps, photographs and illustrations. The sights are arranged in two groups: those in the central districts and those a little further afield. The guided walks reveal three characteristics of the city – the canals, the Neva and the islands. *Beyond St Petersburg* describes sights requiring one- or two-day excursions. Hotel, restaurant, shopping and entertainment recommendations can be found in *Travellers' Needs*, while the *Survival Guide* includes tips on every-thing from transport and telephones to personal safety.

## FINDING YOUR WAY AROUND THE SIGHTSEEING SECTION

Each of the seven sightseeing areas is colour-coded for easy reference. Every chapter opens with an introduction to the area it covers, describing its history and character. For central districts, this is followed by a Street-

by-Street map illustrating a particularly interesting part of the area; for sights beyond the city limits, by a regional map. A simple numbering system relates sights to the maps. Important sights are covered by several pages.

**1 Introduction to the area**
*For easy reference, the sights are numbered and plotted on an area map, with metro stations shown where helpful. The key sights (great buildings, museums and open-air sights) are listed by category.*

**A locator map** shows where you are in relation to other areas of the city centre.

**Each area** has colour-coded thumb tabs.

**Locator map**

**The area shaded in pink** is shown in greater detail on the Street-by-Street map.

**2 Street-by-Street map**
*This gives a bird's eye view of interesting and important parts of each sightseeing area, with accurate drawings of all the buildings within them. The numbering of the sights ties in with the preceding area map and with the fuller descriptions on the pages that follow.*

**A suggested route** for a walk is shown in red.

## ST PETERSBURG AREA MAP

The coloured areas shown on this map *(see pp14–15)* are the five main sightseeing areas into which central St Petersburg has been divided for this guide. Each is covered in a full chapter in the St Petersburg Area by Area section *(pp54–131)*. They are also shown on other maps throughout the book. In St Petersburg *at a Glance (pp32–49)*, for example, they help you locate the most interesting museums and palaces or where to see the city's many delightfully designed bridges. The maps' coloured borders match the coloured thumb tabs on each page of the section.

---

**Numbers** refer to each sight's position on the area map and its place in the chapter.

**Practical information** lists all the information you need to visit every sight, including a map reference to the Street Finder maps *(pp238–45)*.

**3 Detailed information on each sight**
All the important sights are described individually. They are listed to follow the numbering on the area map at the start of the section. The key to the symbols summarizing practical information is on the back flap.

**A Visitors' Checklist** provides the practical information you will need to plan your visit.

**Story boxes** highlight unique aspects or historical connections of a particular sight.

**4 St Petersburg's major sights**
These are given two or more full pages in the sightseeing area in which they are found. Buildings of interesting architecture are dissected to reveal their interiors; museums and galleries have colour-coded floorplans to help you find important exhibits.

**Stars** indicate the best features or works of art.

# INTRODUCING
# ST PETERSBURG

# FOUR GREAT DAYS IN ST PETERSBURG

In just 300 years St Petersburg has had many faces. Peter the Great's folly, built on a swamp and intended to turn Russia's face towards the West, soon became a magnificent city reflecting the majesty of the Russian Empire. Then it was the "cradle of the Revolution", where Lenin came to power. During the Second World War it became a symbol of national pride. Today it is Russia's cultural capital, with a wonderfully preserved heritage and an international arts programme. Taken together, these four itineraries encompass the city's sight-seeing highlights. Individually, they show the influences that shaped the city: imperial, Russian and Soviet. The price guides include the cost of travel, food and admission.

*The Victory Monument*

Rastrelli's masterly main staircase at the Winter Palace

## IMPERIAL CITY

• Art and opulence
• Grand squares and views
• Remembering Rasputin

**TWO ADULTS** allow at least US$200

### Morning
The day starts at the centre of the city with the Baroque **Winter Palace** *(see pp92–3)*, once the official residence of the imperial family and now the heart of the **Hermitage** museum *(see pp84–93)*. Concentrate on the magnificent state rooms, where the Tsars received important guests. Do not miss the view over vast **Palace Square** *(see p83)*, which incorporates the glorious sweep of the General Staff Building, formerly home to the state ministries and now part of the museum. Relax with a leisurely walk along the embankment to **Krokodil** *(see p186)* for a light lunch.

### Afternoon
Head back along Galernaya ulitsa to **Decembrists' Square** *(see p78)* – the **Bronze Horseman**, a statue of Peter the Great, rears up at its centre. There are fine views across the river to Vasilevskiy Island, lined with rich mansions and handsome institutions.

Turn round, and take in **St Isaac's Cathedral** *(see pp80–81)*, topped by a gilded dome. It took from 1818 to 1858 to construct this colossal structure, which, since the Soviet era, has been designated a museum.

Under 1 km (half a mile) west, the **Yusupov Palace** *(see p120)* has an exhibition on Grigoriy Rasputin, the "holy man" murdered here by Prince Felix Yusupov. Dine in the garden pavilion of the palace at **Noble Nest** *(see p188)* or, for a more modest outlay, at **1913** *(see p186)* – the year the Romanovs celebrated 300 years on the throne.

## RUSSIAN CITY

• Icons and incense
• A traditional lunch
• Shopping for souvenirs

**TWO ADULTS** allow at least US$160

### Morning
This itinerary leads you to the best traditional Russian sights of St Petersburg, a city where European influences can be more evident then Russian. Start at the **Russian Museum** *(see pp104–7)*, the world's finest collection of Russian art. Marvel at the **Church on Spilled Blood**'s *(see p100)* glittering interior, then head to **Kalinka-Malinka** *(see p187)* for a traditional Russian lunch.

The Russian Revival-style Church on Spilled Blood

---

◁ *St Petersburg – View of the Troitskiy Bridge*, by 19th-century artist J Schroeder

## Afternoon

Inspired by the morning's sights, nip across to the **Souvenir Market** *(see p199)*, which sells everything from icons to fur hats.

Then take the green metro line from Gostinyy Dvor to Ploshchad Aleksandra Nevskovo to **Alexander Nevsky Monastery** *(see pp130–31)*. Many of Russia's notables, including Tchaikovsky and Dostoevsky, are buried here. As the afternoon fades, you may like to attend a magical candlelit choral service at the Church of the Annunciation.

Round off the day with a visit to nearby **Slavyanskiy stil** *(see p199)*, a shop selling wonderful Russian linen.

In the evening, visit the ballet *(see pp202–3)* or dine among folk dancers at **St Petersburg** *(see p188)*. For both, book ahead.

## A FAMILY DAY OUT

- Awesome views
- Gruesome specimens
- Food in a forest
- Skating or the circus

**FAMILY OF 4** allow at least US$150

## Morning

The day starts with a stiff climb up to the colonnade of **St Isaac's Cathedral** *(see pp80–81)* for panoramic city views. Then cross the Neva to the **Strelka** *(see pp58–9)* of Vasilevskiy Island to take in one of the museums there *(see p60)*: the **Zoological**, the **Naval** or – if your family likes pickled freaks and weird wonders – the **Kunstkammer**.

A pleasant walk across the river takes you to Petrogradskaya *(see pp64–73)*. Head to the inexpensive **Pelmeni Bar** for a filling lunch or, for something lighter, try vegetarian Troitskiy Most *(see p193)*.

## Afternoon

The focus of Petrogradskaya is the **Peter and Paul Fortress** *(see pp66–7)*, with its opulent cathedral and grim history. Attractions include the tombs of the Romanovs, prison

The still-operational mint at Peter and Paul Fortress

cells, displays on the history of the city, Peter the Great's rowing boat, and a rampart climb. In summer, the park surrounding the fortress has all kinds of family attractions.

Also in the park is **Zver** *(see p185)*, a restaurant surrounded by trees where adults can relax while their children run around.

After supper, take the metro to Krestovskiy Ostrov, then a short walk to the western spit of **Yelagin Island** *(see pp136–7)*, where there are fine sunsets and an ice rink in winter. Or, if it is too cold, how about a visit to the **Circus** *(see p201)*?

## SOVIET CITY

- Revolutionary heritage sites
- Monuments to the People
- Soviet-themed dining

**TWO ADULTS** allow at least US$90

## Morning

To indulge a fascination for Leningrad, "Cradle of the Revolution," start at the city centre's edge at the **Smolnyy Institute** *(see p128)*, home of the Revolution and later of the Communist Party. Opposite, catch bus No. 46 or No. 136 and ride past the monument to Dzerzhinsky, father of the Soviet secret police, past the **Field of Mars** *(see p94)* where the dead of the Revolution are buried, and across the river to the **Museum of Russian Political History** *(see p72)*. The **Cruiser Aurora** *(see p73)*, whose guns

sounded the 1917 Revolution, is moored a short distance away. For lunch, Georgian **Salkhino** *(see p185)* is nearby.

## Afternoon

A little further north, the small **Kirov Museum** *(see p72)* is devoted to the head of the city's Communist Party, Sergey Kirov, whose assassination in 1934 prompted a wave of executions.

To appreciate the Soviet glorification of the People's achievements, take the metro to Moskovskaya and the **Victory Monument** *(see p131)*, whose awesome underground Memorial Hall shows life during the Siege of Leningrad. Then take the metro back to Tekhnologicheskiy Institute and ride the red line between Avtovo and Ploshchad Vosstaniya, where each station tells a part of the history of the city *(see p222)*. Finally, dine at **Lenin's Mating Call** *(see p188)* or **Russian Kitsch** *(see p184)*.

The Avtovo metro station celebrating post-war car production

# Putting St Petersburg on the Map

The Russian Federation, or Russia as it is usually known, is the world's largest country, covering an area of 17.4 million sq km (6.7 million sq miles). Situated in its north-west corner, St Petersburg is Russia's second city, with a population of just under five million. Once Russia's capital and known as its "Window on the West" *(see pp20–21)*, the city was built on the marshy lands where the Neva joins the Gulf of Finland. Of the 12 countries bordering Russia, Estonia and Finland are St Petersburg's closest neighbours.

**KEY**

| | |
|---|---|
| | Motorway |
| | Major road |
| | Minor road |
| | Railway |
| | Country boundary |

0 kilometres  180

0 miles  180

## ST PETERSBURG AND ENVIRONS

Pechora

Ukhta

Kotlas

Kirov

Primore

Sosnovo

Ladoga

Vaskelovo

Novaya
Ladoga

A125

M10

A129

Gulf of Finland

A123

Sosnovy
Bor

Schlüsselburg

M18

A121

Pulkovo

Gatchina

Tosno

Kirishi

Volosovo

M11

M10

Vyritsa

A115

M20

**St Petersburg and Environs**
*St Petersburg has good rail links
to many interesting sights in the
vicinity (see pp228–9).*

**RUSSIAN
FEDERATION**

Ufa

Magnitogorsk

Ural

Orsk

Turgay

Tolyatti

Samara

Orenburg

Chelkar

Saratov

**KAZAKSTAN**

Volgograd

Volga

Astrakhan

Rostov-na-Donu

Donets

Mariupol

Krasnodar

*CASPIAN SEA*    **TURKMENISTAN**

Infrared satellite image of St Petersburg, Russia

## PUTTING RUSSIA ON THE MAP

*Arctic
Ocean*

NORWAY

SWEDEN

FINLAND

St Petersburg

**RUSSIAN
FEDERATION**

ESTONIA
LATVIA
LITHUANIA

UNITED
KINGDOM

REP OF
IRELAND

POLAND

BELARUS

GERMANY

UKRAINE

CZECH

HUNGARY

ROMANIA

FRANCE

ITALY

BULGARIA

*Bering
Sea*

SPAIN

GEORGIA

UZBEKISTAN

KAZAKSTAN

MONGOLIA

PORTUGAL

GREECE

TURKEY

KYRGYZSTAN

TURK
MENISTAN

TAJIKISTAN

CHINA

N KOREA

S KOREA

JAPAN

*Pacific
Ocean*

MOROCCO

TUNISIA

SYRIA
IRAQ

IRAN

AFGHAN
ISTAN

ALGERIA

LIBYA

EGYPT

SAUDI
ARABIA

PAKISTAN

NEPAL

INDIA

BURMA

# Central St Petersburg

St Petersburg's five central areas described in this book each have their own character, reflecting different sides of the city's past. The southern bank of the Neva, Palace Embankment, is lined with glorious, stately palaces. Gostinyy Dvor, to the east, has always been the commercial hub of the city with shops, bars and restaurants lining Nevskiy prospekt. To the west lies Sennaya Ploshchad, a mixture of romantic, tree-lined canals and reminders of the 19th-century low life of Dostoevsky's novels. Vasilevskiy Island, the city's largest, combines a naval heritage with scholarly institutions and museums. Petrogradskaya, to the north, is dominated by the Peter and Paul Fortress.

**Vasilevskiy Island**
*Adorned with figures representing four great Russian rivers, the Rostral Columns (see p60) stand on the eastern tip of the island. From here there are sweeping views of the Neva and its embankments.*

**Petrogradskaya**
*Burial place of the Romanov tsars, the Cathedral of SS Peter and Paul (see p68) stands in the fortress where Peter the Great began building the city in 1703. Its gilded spire dominates the skyline of Petrogradskaya, an area otherwise characterized by many splendid Style-Moderne buildings.*

**Gostinyy Dvor**
*Nevskiy prospekt, the city's main artery, is crossed by waterways such as Moyka river (see p36), shown here. These intersections are bustling in the summer, with cafés on river boats and by the water's edge.*

**Palace Embankment**
*Part of the Hermitage, the former imperial Winter Palace (see pp92–3), dominates this grand waterfront with a burst of Baroque splendour. The embankment is lined with monuments from the famous Bronze Horseman (p78) to Peter the Great's modest Summer Palace (p95).*

**Sennaya Ploshchad**
*Yusopov Palace (see p120) has ornate interiors and houses an exhibition on Gregory Rasputin. The surrounding area, with quiet streets lining its canals, is perfect for walks during the atmospheric White Nights.*

0 metres       600

0 yards       600

**KEY**

| | |
|---|---|
| ■ | Major sight |
| ■ | Main sight |
| Ⓜ | Metro station |
| 🚢 | River boat pier |
| 🚓 | Police station |
| ✚ | Orthodox church |

*Map labels:* SKAYA, PETROGRADSKAYA MOST, SAMPSONIEVSKIY MOST, Cruiser Aurora, Kshesinskaya Mansion, PETROVSKAYA NAB, Нева, Trinity Bridge, TROITSKIY MOST, NAB KUTUZOVA, Summer Palace, SUVOROVSKAYA PLOSHCHAD, NAB LEBYAZHEVO KANALA, Field of Mars, Church on Spilled Blood, Engineers Castle, Russian Museum, GRIBOEDOVA, INZHENERNAYA ULITSA, ITALYANSKAYA ULITSA, KLENOVAYA ULITSA, ITALYANSKAYA, Nevskiy Prospekt 2, Nevskiy Prospekt 1, НЕВСКИЙ ПРОСПЕКТ, Gostinyy Dvor, PER KRYLOVA, KARAVANNAYA UL, NABEREZHNAYA REKI FONTANKI, LOMONOSOVA, TORGOVYY PER, KSTIN PEREULOK

# THE HISTORY OF ST PETERSBURG

*F*ounded in 1703, within ten years St Petersburg had become capital of the vast Russian empire and quickly gained a reputation as one of Europe's most beautiful cities. In the 20th century it underwent three name changes, three revolutions and a 900-day siege. For a city less than 300 years old, it has an amazing history.

Some 850 years before St Petersburg became capital of Russia, local Slavic tribes invited the Viking chieftain Rurik to rule them. His successor founded Kiev, which grew into a great princedom. In 988 Grand Prince Vladimir adopted Orthodox Christianity with profound consequences; Orthodoxy was to become a cornerstone of Russian identity. Paradoxically, Russia only emerged as a united entity during the 250-year domination of the Muslim Mongols. In 1237 these fierce tribes conquered all the principalities except Novgorod. In the 14th century the Mongols chose Moscow's power-hungry grand prince, Ivan I (1325–40), to collect tribute from other subjugated principalities. This sealed the fate of the Mongols for, as Moscow thrived under their benevolence, she also became a real threat.

Ivan IV "the Terrible"

Mongol warriors in a 14th-century manuscript illustration

Within 50 years, an army led by Moscow's Grand Prince Dmitriy Donskoy won a first victory over the Mongols, and the idea of a Russian nation was born.

During the long reign of Ivan III (1462–1505) the Mongols were finally vanquished and Moscow's prestige increased. Ivan the Terrible (1533–84) was the first to be called "Tsar of All the Russias". Yet his reign, which began in glory, ended in disaster. Ivan killed his only heir, and the so-called Time of Troubles followed as Russia came under a succession of weak rulers and Polish usurpers invaded Moscow.

## THE FIRST ROMANOVS

To end this strife, in 1613 the leading citizens chose Mikhail Romanov to be tsar, thus initiating the 300-year Romanov rule. Under Mikhail, Russia recovered from her upheavals, but his greatest legacy was his son Aleksey. Intelligent and pious, Aleksey modernized the state, encouraging an influx of foreign architects, codifying laws and asserting the power of the state over the church.

## TIMELINE

| 800 | 1000 | 1200 | 1400 | 1600 |
|---|---|---|---|---|
| | **862** Rurik establishes Viking stronghold at Novgorod | **1147** Moscow is founded | **1480** Ivan III stops paying tribute to Mongols | **1605–13** Time of Troubles |
| | **863** Cyril and Methodius create early version of Cyrillic | **1462–1505** Reign of Ivan III | | *Boris Godunov* |
| **988** Prince Vladimir converts to Orthodox Christianity | **1108** Town of Vladimir is founded | **1223** First Mongol raid | **1242** Alexander Nevsky defeats the Teutonic Knights | **1533–84** Reign of Ivan IV the Terrible | **1613** Mikhail Romanov becomes first tsar of the Romanov dynasty |
| | **1240** Mongol rule established in Rus | **1598** Boris Godunov claims title of tsar after 12 years as regent | |

◁ **Peter the Great instructing his workers during the building of St Petersburg (Alexander von Kotzebue, 1862)**

## PETER THE GREAT

In the transition from a medieval to a more modern state, the future Peter the Great, founder of St Petersburg, was born. After his father Aleksey's death, Peter's childhood was overshadowed by severe rivalry between his mother's family, the Naryshkins, and that of his father's first wife, the Miloslavskiys. At the age of ten Peter ascended the throne, but the Streltsy Guards, influenced by the Miloslavskiys, started a bloody revolt. As a result his sickly half-brother Ivan became his co-tsar, and Ivan's sister Sophia their regent. The memory of seeing his family brutally killed caused his hatred of Moscow and distrust of its conservative, scheming society.

**Peter the Great (1682–1725)**

When Ivan died in 1696, the 24-year-old Peter had grown to a giant of a man with a tempestuous combination of willpower and energy. Long hours spent drilling toy soldiers as a child developed into a full-scale reform of the Russian army. But Peter's dream was of a Russian navy. In 1697, he went on a European tour to study shipbuilding and other wondrous achievements. To everyone's dismay the young tsar spent more hours working at the docks than socializing at court. On his return to Russia he lost no time in enforcing westernizing reforms.

### A NEW CAPITAL

It was Peter's determination to found a northern port with an unrestricted passage to the Baltic that led to war with Sweden, at the time one of the strongest countries in Europe. By May 1703 Peter had secured the Neva river and began to build the Peter and Paul Fortress and a shipyard opposite *(see pp20–21)*. Only an autocrat with Peter's drive could have succeeded in building a

**View of St Petersburg in the early 17th century, with the Admiralty shipyard to the left**

## TIMELINE

*Sophia, regent 1682–9*

| 1672 Birth of Peter the Great at Kolomenskoe Palace, Moscow | 1689 Peter banishes Sophia to Novodevichy Monastery, Moscow | 1697–8 Peter tours western Europe | 1698 Peter destroys the Streltsy Guards *(see p20)*. | 1703 St Petersburg is founded  1712 Seat of government moves to St Petersburg |
|---|---|---|---|---|
| **1680** | | **1690** | **1700** | **1710** |
| 1682 The Streltsy rebellion. Peter becomes co-tsar with half-brother Ivan V, under regency of his half-sister Sophia | | 1696 Ivan V dies; Peter becomes sole ruler. | 1700 Start of Northern War against Sweden  1709 Victory over Charles XII of Sweden at Battle of Poltava | 1714 Peter forbids the use of stone in buildings, except in St Petersburg |

## LIFE AT ELIZABETH'S COURT

When Elizabeth was not busy looking over architectural plans, she would lie around on her bed, gossiping with a group of ladies whose chief task it was to tickle her feet. Her restless nature meant that her courtiers had to endure endless hunts and skating parties, and were required to keep her company at all hours. Her riotous cross-dressing masquerades were notorious, as was her vast wardrobe, allegedly containing over 15,000 dresses.

Tsarina Elizabeth going for a stroll at Tsarskoe Selo, surrounded by eager courtiers

## THE PETTICOAT PERIOD

For most of the rest of the 18th century Russia was ruled by women, whose taste did much to set the celebrated architectural tone of St Petersburg.

During the brief reigns of Peter's wife Catherine I (1725–27) and his grandson Peter II (1727–30), the court abandoned this frontier city for the more comfortable life in Moscow. But when the throne passed to Anna, daughter of Peter's co-tsar Ivan, she decided to create a recognizably European court in St Petersburg. Anna was 37 at the time, and had spent most of her life in Germany. This was obvious in her choice of ministers and favourites, of whom many were German. Fashion and style, however, were imported from France and opera from Italy. Though she herself was serious, plain and somewhat cruel, Anna did much to put the court on a footing with the most frivolous in Europe, as well as encouraging a flowering of civilization.

Tsarina Elizabeth, daughter of Peter the Great, was the ideal successor to this twittering court. Elizabeth was attractive, energetic and cheerful, a combination that endeared her to almost everyone, especially the Guards who helped secure her place on the throne. She left the affairs of state to a series of well chosen advisors. The only element of seriousness lay in Elizabeth's perhaps surprising piety, which at times led her to retire temporarily into a convent. Her chief legacy is the splendid Baroque architecture she commissioned, mainly designed by her favourite architect Rastrelli (see p93).

city on this fetid bogland, where daylight and building materials were in short supply and disastrous floodings regular. More than 40,000 Swedish prisoners-of-war and peasants laboured and perished here, their bones contributing to the city's foundations.

Whether or not it was always Peter's intention to make this his new capital, it only became possible after his decisive victory at Poltava in 1709 put an end to the Swedish threat. St Petersburg was named capital of Russia in 1712 and, by Peter's death in 1725, there were 40,000 inhabitants in the city and many more in the surrounding labour encampments.

Elizabeth (1741–61)

# A Window on the West

Determined to drag his country out of the medieval period, and inspired by the few Westerners he met in Moscow, Peter the Great was the first tsar to travel to Europe. He returned with many ideas for reforms and architectural novelties which he put into practice in his new city. In 1710, when the Swedish threat was over, the reluctant imperial family and government were moved to this chilly, damp outland. But Peter was adamant and soon a rational street plan, stone buildings and academies made St Petersburg a thriving capital in which fashions and discoveries from Europe were tried out before filtering through to the rest of Russia.

**EXTENT OF THE CITY**

☐ *1712*   ☐ *Today*

## PLAN OF THE NEW CITY

This map of 1712 shows Peter's original plan for his capital, with Vasilevskiy Island as centre. This was abandoned due to the hazards of crossing the Neva, and the city spread out around the Admiralty instead.

**The Carpenter Tsar**
*During his 1697–8 tour of Europe, Peter (to the left in this picture) spent months at the Deptford Docks, labouring with his men to learn the basics of ship building.*

**Based on Amsterdam**, the original city grid was meant to follow a strict network of canals but this had to change *(see p57)*.

**Menshikov palace**

**New Fashions**
*Peter's desire to Westernize Russia led to a rule forcing his courtiers to have their bushy beards shaved off.*

## THE STRELTSY REBELLION

As a result of a malicious rumour that Peter's relatives planned the murder of his half-brother Ivan, in 1682 the Streltsy Guard regiments invaded the Kremlin. A horrifying massacre took place in front of the 10-year old Peter who saw his adviser and members of his family murdered. This traumatic event is probably what caused Peter's facial tic and certainly his wish to build another capital city. In 1698 he took a terrible revenge by torturing over a thousand Streltsy Guards to death.

**Brutal murders in the Kremlin, 1682**

**The Battle of Poltava**
*The struggle with Sweden for control over the Baltic led to the Great Northern War. Nine years after the embarassing defeat at Narva, Peter the Great's army reforms bore fruit. In 1709 he won a decisive battle over Charles XII at Poltava, and thereby Russia's first victory over a major European power.*

## WHERE TO SEE PETER THE GREAT'S CITY

Some of the buildings from the early St Petersburg still exist in the city centre, including the rustic Peter the Great's Cabin (p73), the Summer Palace (p95) and the Baroque Menshikov Palace (p62). Much of Peter and Paul Fortress (pp66–7) also dates from this time. It is also well worth visiting Monplaisir, Peter's first home at Peterhof (p150).

Peter the Great's workshop, the Summer Palace

Kronwerk (outer defence walls)

Peter and Paul Fortress

**The port** was here until the 1880s.

Admiralty

Summer Palace

**Wine Goblet**
*The tsar, who could hold his drink, enjoyed pressing alcohol on his guests until they passed out. This elegant crystal goblet belonged to his close friend Alexander Menshikov and is engraved with his coat of arms.*

**Marshy soil** and a lack of local stone made construction difficult. Thousands of labourers died during the first stages.

**Catherine I**
*After an unsuccessful first marriage, Peter was drawn to a Lithuanian girl who had followed the army back from the wars in 1704. Her healthy good looks were brought to the tsar's attention by Alexander Menshikov (see p62). Although only two daughters survived, their marriage was happy and Catherine succeeded Peter as the first woman on Russia's throne.*

**Mice Bury the Cat**
*Coloured woodcuts, lubki, served as political cartoons in Peter's day. The tsar was always portrayed as a cat on account of his moustache.*

## CATHERINE THE GREAT

Catherine, a German princess, was chosen by Elizabeth as wife for her successor, the petty-minded Peter III. When Peter ascended the throne in 1761 Catherine had resided in Russia for 18 years and was fully fluent in Russian. She had made it her duty to steep herself in the Russian culture which she later came to adore. Six months into Peter's reign, Catherine and

Catherine the Great in 1762

her allies in the Imperial Guard deposed the tsar. He was assassinated within days and she was crowned Catherine II.

By Catherine's death at the age of 67, her reputation as an enlightened leader *(see p24)* had been overshadowed by her illiberal reaction to the news of the French Revolution in 1789 and by scandalous rumours concerning her later love-affairs. However, she left a country vastly enlarged after successful campaigns against Turkey and Poland.

## WAR AND PEACE

During the Napoleonic Wars, under Catherine's grandson Alexander I, Russia finally took her place alongside the other great European powers.

Despite his part in the murder of his father Paul, much was expected of the handsome new tsar who was infected by the ideals of enlightened government. Russia was by now desperately in need of reform. Of particular concern was the plight of the peasantry, who were tied to the land in serfdom.

However, the necessities of war subsumed everything, and no inroads were made against the Russian autocracy during Alexander I's reign.

Determined to harness the wave of Russian patriotism, Alexander joined Britain and marched against Napoleon in Austria in 1805. After the crushing defeat at the battle of Austerlitz, however, the inexperienced tsar retreated, his army having lost 11,000 men.

At the Peace of Tilsit, signed in 1807, Napoleon divided Europe into French and Russian spheres, lulling Alexander into a false sense of security. In 1812 the French emperor invaded Russia, but was defeated by its size and climate. The Russian army followed his forces to Paris, taking part in the allied campaign which led Napoleon to abdicate in 1814. In celebration, Alexander commissioned a series of imposing public edifices in a fitting Empire style.

Murder of Paul I, 1801. Despite all his precautions, Catherine's unstable, paranoid son was murdered in a coup in his own fortified palace *(see p101)*

## TIMELINE

**Decembrist rebels defeated by tsarist troops, 1825**

## THE DECEMBRIST REBELLION

Officers of the Russian army who had witnessed the freedoms of democratic Europe were frustrated by Alexander's failure to consider constitutional reform. When his stern brother Nicholas was declared tsar in 1825, these liberals rallied their soldiers to support the older brother Constantine, who had given up his rights to the throne, in the hope that he would be more open-minded. They made a stand on 14th December on what is now Decembrists' Square *(see p78)*. Troops loyal to the tsar were instructed to fire on the rebels, killing hundreds before the leaders surrendered. The new tsar, Nicholas I, treated them with the severity which was to become the hallmark of his reign. Five leading figures were hanged, and over a hundred exiled to Siberia.

## A CITY OF RICH AND POOR

For much of the 19th century, a walk along Nevskiy prospekt offered a microcosm of an increasingly divided society. Striding past drunks, beggars and prostitutes, the city's courtiers, cocky young officers and leading citizens headed for shops selling imported fashionable accessories, or to the distinguished delicatessen Yeliseev's to buy caviar and champagne. They often lived above their means, mortgaging their serfs and lands to keep up with the astronomical costs of their luxurious lives. This was also a city in which the salary of a low ranking government clerk was never sufficient to feed a family. In the countryside, tension was growing among the serfs tied to the large estates of the aristocracy. With such blatant inequality, growing pressure for political reform was inevitable.

After the unrelenting autocracy of Nicholas I, the "Iron Tsar", liberals welcomed the reign of his fair-minded son Alexander II. In 1861, the tsar passed the Edict of Emancipation, abolishing serfdom, but requiring peasants to buy their land at far from advantageous terms. Thus industrialization finally took off as peasants flocked to the big cities to work in factories, only to be met by even worse living conditions.

## THE NAPOLEONIC INVASION

Napoleon's Grand Army of 600,000 men reached Moscow in September 1812, after the victory at Borodino, but was defeated by the tactics of non-engagement devised by the great Russian hero General Kutuzov. Finding himself in a city abandoned by its rulers and set on fire by its people, and with the Russian winter ahead, Napoleon was forced into a retreat over the frozen countryside. He eventually reached the border, with only 30,000 men left alive.

**French army retreating from Moscow 1812**

| 1822 Abolition of Masonic and secret societies | 1833 Pushkin publishes *The Bronze Horseman* | 1855 Death of Nicholas I; Alexander II succeeds him  1853–6 Crimean War | *Leo Tolstoy* | 1865–9 Tolstoy writes *War and Peace* |
|---|---|---|---|---|

**1820**  **1840**  **1860**

| 1825 The Decembrist Rebellion. Nicholas I becomes tsar | 1851 The "Nicholas Railway" opens between Moscow and St Petersburg | 1861 Emancipation of serfs  1864 Reforms in local government, law and education |
|---|---|---|

818 Construction of St saac's Cathedral starts

# The Enlightened Empress

Born a minor German princess, Catherine II was a
learned and energetic woman. She recognized the
importance of the great Enlightenment philosophers
Voltaire and Diderot, with whom she corresponded.
She bought impressive collections of European art
for the Hermitage *(see pp84–93)*, libraries for Russia's
scholars and talked much about reducing the burden
on Russia's serfs. However, a peasant uprising in the
1770s and news of the French Revolution in 1789 put
paid to her liberal notions and, when she died, the
majority of Russians were just as badly off as before.

**EXTENT OF THE CITY**

■ *1790*     ☐ *Today*

**The Temple** alludes to
Catherine's passion for
Neo-Classical
architecture.

**The medal** is
presented to
Count Orlov
for his
victory over
the Turks
at Chesma
in 1770.

**Royal Guards Swear Allegiance**
*On 28 June 1762, Catherine usurped the throne
of her unpopular husband Peter III in a palace
coup. The guards regiments flocked to support
her and the tsar was assassinated on 6 July.*

## CATHERINE THE GREAT

Catherine II "the Great" (1762–96) pursued an
expansionist foreign policy. Russia's first naval
victory, leading to the annexation of the Crimea,
is commemorated allegorically on this fabric.

**Count Alexey Orlov**, brother
of Catherine's one-time lover
Grigoriy, played an important role
in her takeover of the throne.

**Catherine's Instructions**
*In 1767 the 36-year-old
Catherine published her
22-chapter* Great Instruction
(Bolshoy Nakaz). *The book
is a collection of ideas on
which a reform of Russia's
legal system was to be based.*

**Pretender Pugachev**
*The greatest threat to
Catherine's reign was
caused by the Cossack
Pugachev who claimed
to be Peter III. He was
arrested, but escaped
to lead a widespread
peasant uprising which
broke out in 1773 and
only ended with his
execution in 1775.*

### The New Academy of Sciences

*Catherine, who founded over 25 major academic institutions in Russia, also commissioned new buildings for those already existing. Quarenghi built the Neo-Classical Academy of Sciences in 1783–5.*

**Catherine** is portrayed as Pallas Athena, goddess of wisdom and warfare, with her attributes of a shield and helmet.

## WHERE TO SEE THE NEO-CLASSICAL CITY

Catherine had the Marble Palace *(see p94)* and the Tauride Palace *(p128)* erected for two of her lovers, and added the Small and Large Hermitage and the theatre *(p84)* to the Winter Palace. Her architect Cameron designed the Cameron Gallery and the Agate Pavilion at Tsarskoe Selo *(p150)* and Pavlovsk Palace *(pp158–61)*.

Grecian Hall at Pavlovsk, created by Charles Cameron in 1782–6

### Empire-Style Vase (1790)

*Porcelain was much prized at court. In 1744 the first Russian producer, the Imperial Porcelain Factory, opened in St Petersburg.*

**The fabric,** used for a screen, was made by the Pernons factory, Lyons, in 1770.

### Mikhail Lomonosov

*A philosopher, historian, linguist and scientist, Lomonosov (1711–65) personified the intellectual enlightenment of 18th-century Russia (see p61). This sculpture of him as a boy by the seashore refers to his fisherman origins.*

### Grigoriy Potemkin (1739–91)

*Of all her lovers, Catherine respected and admired Prince Potemkin the most. He was a successful general and an influential counsellor. They remained friends until his death.*

Alexander II was murdered by a revolutionary group in 1881. Tragically, he is said to have had the plans for a Russian parliament in his pocket

## THE DEATH OF TSARIST RUSSIA

Pressure for reform had built up such a head of steam that in 1881, when still no radical changes had taken place, a revolutionary group murdered Alexander II. The reign of Alexander III was one of rabid reaction. The press was under strict censorship and the secret police more active than ever. But workers began to get organized and opposition was growing. Nicholas II took over a country on the verge of breakdown, in spite of the rapid industrialization of the 1890s. The unsuccessful war with Japan (1904–5) was followed by "Bloody Sunday". On 9th January 1905 a peaceful demonstration carried a petition to the tsar only to be met by bullets. News of the massacre spread like wildfire and the 1905 Revolution broke out with strikes all over Russia. To avert further disaster, Nicholas II promised basic civil rights and an elected Duma (parliament) with the right to veto legislation. However, the tsar simply dissolved the parliament whenever it displeased him. This high-handed behaviour, along with the royal family's unpopular intimate friendship with Rasputin (see p121), further damaged the Romanovs' reputation.

The outbreak of World War I brought a surge of patriotism which the tsar sought to ride. But, by late 1916, Russia had lost three and a half million men, morale at the front was low and food supplies at home scarce.

Red Army badge

## WORLD OF ART MOVEMENT

Costume design by Leon Bakst, 1911

The oppressive political climate at the turn of the century did not prevent art from flourishing. A small group of St Petersburg artists, including Bakst and Benois, grew into an influential creative movement under the inspired leadership of Sergey Diaghilev. Western art was introduced in their stylish *World of Art* magazine, while their stage designs and costumes for the Ballets Russes (see p118) brought Russian culture to the west.

## REVOLUTION AND CIVIL WAR

In February 1917 strikes broke out in the capital, now renamed Petrograd. The tsar was forced to abdicate, his family put under arrest and a Provisional Government set up. But revolutionaries returning from exile organized themselves and, in October, an armed revolution overthrew the government (see pp28–9).

## TIMELINE

The Romanov family in 1913

**1881** Alexander II is assassinated by the "People's Will" group. Alexander III becomes tsar.

**1902** Lenin publishes *What is to be Done?*

**1898** Social-Democratic Workers' party is founded. Russian museum opens

**1913** 300t anniversa Romanov

**1880**

**1900**

**1881–2** Anti-semitic pogroms

**1887** Lenin's brother is hanged for attempt on the tsar's life

**1894** Alexander III dies, Nicholas II accedes

**1903** Pro-violence Bolsheviks (under Lenin) secede from Social-Democratic Workers' party

**1904–5** Russo-Japanese War

**1905** The 1905 Revolution is followed by the inauguration of the first Duma in 1906

**1914** Outbreak of WWI; St Petersburg changes name to Petrograd

The leading Bolshevik party proved to be as careless of democracy as the tsar but, in March 1918, they kept their promise to take Russia out of the war. The army was desperately needed at home to fight the developing civil war. The Bolsheviks (Reds) found themselves threatened by a diverse coalition of anti-revolutionary groups which came to be known as the "Whites", initially supported by foreign intervention. It was the threat of the Whites rallying opposition around the royal family that led to their execution in July 1918. But the Whites were a disparate force and, by November 1920, the last troops had abandoned the struggle, leaving a devastated Soviet Russia to face two years of appalling famine. To manage, Lenin had to revise his aggressive "War Communism" nationalization project. His slightly milder New Economic Policy allowed for private enterprise.

**The imperial palaces around St Petersburg were totally destroyed by the Germans in World War II. This photo shows Pavlovsk *(see pp156–9)* in 1944**

### THE STALIN YEARS

In the five years after Lenin's death in 1924, Joseph Stalin used his position as General Secretary of the Communist Party to eliminate all rivals. He then established his long dictatorship.

The terror began in earnest with the collectivization of agriculture which forced the peasants to give up all livestock, machinery and land to collective farms. During this time, and in the ensuing famine of 1931–2, up to 10 million people are thought to have died.

**Joseph Stalin on a propaganda poster from 1933**

A first major purge of intellectuals took place in urban areas in 1928–9. Then, in December 1934, Sergey Kirov, the party leader in Leningrad, was assassin-ated on the secret orders of Stalin *(see p72)*. Blamed on an anti-Stalinist cell, the assasination was used as the catalyst for five years of purges throughout the country. By the time they were over, some 15 million people had been arrested, many sent to the Gulag (labour camps) and over a million executed.

Stalin's purge of the Red Army boded badly for World War II, for he had got rid of three quarters of his officers. When the Germans invaded Russia in 1941 they cut off Leningrad in less than three months, subjecting the city to a 900-day siege *(see p131)* which left more than two million people dead, half of them civilians. Leningrad came to be known as a "Hero City".

The Germans were eventually defeated, but the Russian people, who lost 20 million souls to the war, were subjected to a renewed terror by Stalin, which lasted until his death in March 1953.

# The Russian Revolution

St Petersburg is known as the cradle of the Russian Revolution, a central event in the history of the 20th century. After the 1917 February Revolution which led to the abdication of Tsar Nicholas II, the Provisional Government declared a political amnesty. Exiled revolutionaries such as Lenin and Trotsky flooded into the city. By setting up a network of Workers' and Soldiers' Soviets, representative councils elected by the people, they established an alternative government. In October, when soldiers had deserted from the front in droves, the revolutionary leaders decided on an armed uprising which brought the Communists to power.

**EXTENT OF THE CITY**

■ 1917      ☐ Today

**The Ex-Tsar**
*Nicholas II, seen here clearing snow at Tsarskoe Selo during his house arrest in March 1917, was later taken with his family to Yekaterinburg where they were murdered.*

**Soldier of the Red Guard**

**Looting** was tempting for the mob of sailors and soldiers, especially in the palace's well-stocked wine cellars.

## STORMING THE WINTER PALACE
Late on the evening of 25 October 1917 the battleship *Aurora (see p73)* fired some blank shots at the Winter Palace. The Red Guard, trained by Trotsky at the Smolnyy Institute, stormed the palace. Their aim was the arrest of the Provisional Government, unsuccessfully defended by 300 Cossacks.

**The Cossacks**, who defended the palace with some cadets and members of the Women's Battalion, were too few to offer any serious resistance.

**Lenin, Leader of the People**
*A charismatic speaker, as shown in this painting by Victor Ivanov, Lenin returned from exile in April to lead the Revolution. By 1918, his Bolshevik faction had shown their determination to rule.*

**Revolutionary Plate**
*Various ceramics with revolutionary themes, mixed with touches of Russian folklore, were produced to celebrate every occasion, in this case the Third International.*

### Leon Trotsky
*The intellectual Trotsky played a leading military role in the Revolution. In 1927, during the power struggle after Lenin's death, he was exiled by Stalin. In 1940 he was murdered in Mexico by a Stalinist agent.*

### Propaganda
*One hallmark of the Soviet regime was its propaganda. Artists were employed to design posters spreading its message through striking graphics. War Communism during the Civil War (1918–20) was encouraged by posters such as this one, extolling the "Workers' and Peasants' Defence".*

### Avant Garde Art
*Even before 1917, Russia's artists had been in a state of revolution, producing the world's first truly abstract paintings. A great example of this new movement is* Supremus No. 56, *painted in 1916 by Kazimir Malevich.*

**Ministers** of the Provisional Government tried to keep order but were arrested.

### New Values
*Traditions were radically altered by the Revolution; instead of church weddings, couples exchanged vows under the red flag. Loudly trumpeted sexual equality meant that women had to work twice as hard – at home and in the factories.*

---

## TIMELINE

| 1917 The February Revolution | **March** The tsar is persuaded to abdicate. Provisional Government is led by Prince Lvov | **October** Bolsheviks storm Winter Palace after signal from *Aurora* and expel Provisional Government | **March** Bolsheviks sign Brest-Litovsk peace treaty with Germany. Capital is moved to Moscow |
|---|---|---|---|

| 1917 | | 1918 | |
|---|---|---|---|
| **July** Kerensky becomes Prime Minister of Provisional Government | | **1918 January** Trotsky becomes Commissar of War | **July** Start of Civil War. Tsar and family are murdered in prison at Yekaterinburg |
| | | **December** Lenin forms the CHEKA (secret police) | |

*Cruiser* Aurora

The Washington Dove of Peace, a Russian caricature (1953) from the days of the Cold War

## THAW AND STAGNATION

Three years after Stalin's death his successor Nikita Khrushchev denounced Stalin's crimes at the Twentieth Party Congress and the period known as "The Thaw" began. Political prisoners were released, and Solzhenitsyn's *One Day In the Life of Ivan Denisovich,* about life in the Gulag, was published.

In foreign affairs, things were not so liberal. Soviet tanks invaded Hungary in 1956 to prevent the country seceding from the Warsaw Pact and, in 1962, Khrushchev's decision to put nuclear missiles on Cuba brought the world to the brink of nuclear war.

When Leonid Brezhnev took over in 1964, the intellectual climate froze once more and the persecution of political dissidents was stepped up. The first ten years of his regime were a time of relative plenty. But beneath the surface a vast black market and network of corruption was growing. The party apparatchiks, who benefited most from the corruption, had no interest in rocking the boat. When Brezhnev died in 1982, the politburo was determined to prevent the accession of a younger generation. He was followed by 68-year-old Yuriy Andropov and, when he died, 72-year-old Chernenko.

## GLASNOST AND PERESTROIKA

When 53-year-old Mikhail Gorbachev announced his policies of *glasnost* (openness) and *perestroika* (restructuring), when he took over in 1985, he had no idea what would follow. By the end of 1991 the Soviet Union and its empire were no more.

For the first time since 1917 the elections to the Congress of People's Deputies in 1989 contained

Mikhail Gorbachev and George Bush

an element of genuine choice, with rebels such as Boris Yeltsin and human rights campaigner Andrey Sakharov winning seats. In 1991, local elections brought nationalist candidates to power in the

### FIRST IN SPACE

It was under Krushchev that the Soviet Union achieved her greatest coup against the West, launching the first Sputnik into space in 1957. That same year the dog Laika was the first living creature in space, aboard Sputnik II. She never came down again, but four years later Yuriy Gagarin made spectacular history as the first man in space, returning to a hero's welcome. The Soviets lost the race to put a man on the moon, but their space programme worked as powerful propaganda, backing up the claims of politicians that Russia would soon catch up with and overtake the prosperity of the West.

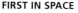

Sputnik II and the space dog Laika, 1957

## TIMELINE

| 1950 | 1960 | 1970 | 1980 |
|---|---|---|---|
| **1950–1954** Korean War  **1961** Stalin's body removed from its place alongside Lenin in Red Square. Yuriy Gagarin is first man in space | **1962** Cuban missile crisis  **1964** Brezhnev becomes General Secretary | **1982** Death of Brezhnev; replaced by Andropov  **1970** Solzhenitsyn wins Nobel Prize for Literature | |
| **1953** Stalin dies  **1955** Krushchev comes to power. Warsaw Pact is established | **1957** Sputnik I is launched  **1956** Stalin denounced by Krushchev at 20th Party Congress. Hungarian uprising is crushed | **1968** Soviet troops enter Czechoslovakia to suppress "Prague Spring"  **1969** Strategic Arms Limitation Talks (SALT) with USA  *Leonid Brezhnev (1906–82)* | **1979** USSR invades Afghanistan |

**Demonstrations on Palace Square during the 1991 coup**

Communism and the albeit limited social protection it offered.

The social problems are still being resolved. Major companies have, however, continued to invest, and by early 1999 relative stability had been achieved. The elections of December 1999 dramatically reduced the power of the Communists, bringing in young liberal reformers and confirming optimism about Russia's future. The religious revival continues, and churches of all denominations have been restored to their original purpose, having been used as warehouses in the Soviet era.

republics, and democrats in the major Russian local councils. Russia and the Baltic Republics seceded from the Soviet Union, while the people of Leningrad, always in the vanguard of progressive movement and led by the reformist lecturer in law, Anatoly Sobchak, voted to restore the city's original name, St Petersburg.

**The new Russian State Emblem**

With his great victory in the election for President of the Russian Republic, Yeltsin was able to deal the death blow to the Soviet Union. It came after the military coup against Gorbachev in August 1991, when Yeltsin's stand against tanks in Moscow made him a hero. In St Petersburg no tanks were on the street, but nonetheless Sobchak rallied supporters of democracy. By the end of the year, the Soviet Union no longer existed.

In March 2000, Vladimir Putin was elected President of the Russian Federation, and re-elected in 2004. Dmitry Medvedev became President in 2008, with Putin as Prime Minister. Both Putin and Medvedev are graduates of the St Petersburg State University and were also born in the city.

### ST PETERSBURG TODAY

The economic reforms which Russia has undergone since 1991 have widened the gap between rich and poor and, while some revel in the new opportunities for work and travel, others cry out for a return to

**A church wedding, popular again since religion has gained new importance among the young**

# ST PETERSBURG AT A GLANCE

A city built on water, St Petersburg offers beautiful scenery and a wide range of sights. The Peter and Paul Fortress *(see pp66–7)*, the city's first building, contrasts with Baroque monasteries and Neo-Classical palaces. The city's short but stormy history is reflected in many of its museums, which display everything from Catherine the Great's fine art collection in the Hermitage to

memorabilia of the Revolution in the Kshesinskaya Mansion *(see p72)*.

To help you make the most of your stay, the following 12 pages are a time-saving guide to the best museums and palaces and the most interesting of the many bridges and waterways. The cultural figures that made St Petersburg a city of importance are also featured. Below is a selection of sights that should not be missed by any visitor.

## ST PETERSBURG'S TOP TEN ATTRACTIONS

**Russian Museum**
*See pp104–7*

**Mariinskiy Theatre**
*See p119*

**Nevskiy Prospekt**
*See pp46–9*

**Church on Spilled Blood**
*See p100*

**The Hermitage**
*See pp84–93*

**Stieglitz Museum**
*See p127*

**Cathedral of Our Lady of Kazan**
*See p111*

**St Isaac's Cathedral**
*See pp80–81*

**Cathedral of SS Peter and Paul**
*See p68*

**Alexander Nevsky Monastery**
*See pp130–31*

◁ The Neo-Classical Kazan Cathedral with its impressive semi-circle of granite columns

# St Petersburg's Best: Bridges and Waterways

Like its waterbound sisters, Amsterdam and Venice, St Petersburg is built around a network of canals and rivers which are still the life-blood of the city. They contribute to its unique atmosphere by creating eerie mists which rise from the ice-laden waters in winter and, in summer, a glittering mirror of façades during the glowing sunsets and bright White Nights.

Bridges, necessary for communication between the islands, were also an excellent means to adorn the city with decorative sculptures, elaborate lampposts and wrought-iron work.

A walk or a boat trip *(see pp134–5, pp226–7)* is the best way to enjoy them.

**Winter Canal**
*Laid out in 1718–20, this narrow canal is crossed by three bridges and Yuriy Velten's Hermitage Theatre foyer (1783–7).*

**Blagoveshchenskiy Bridge**
*Rebuilt in 1936–8, this bridge still retains its original cast-iron seahorse railings, designed by Bryullov.*

**Lion Bridge**
*One of the earliest of its kind, this pedestrian suspension bridge dates from 1825–6. Its cables are anchored inside four cast-iron lions, by sculptor Pavel Sokolov.*

**Egyptian Bridge**
*This bridge spanning the Fontanka was decorated in the Egyptian style fashionable at the time of its construction, in 1826.*

Malaya Neva

Vasilevskiy Island

Bolshaya Neva

Palace Embankment

Moyka

Sennaya Ploshchad

Kanal Griboedova

Fontanka

| 0 metres | 500 |
| 0 yards | 500 |

### Trinity Bridge

*The ten-arched Trinity Bridge (1897–1903) is famous for its Style-Moderne lampposts and railing decorations, the work of the skilful French engineers Vincent Chabrol and René Patouillard.*

### Swan Canal

*This tree-lined canal (1711–19) leading out to the Neva is named after the swans which were once drawn to its peaceful waters.*

### Bridge Passage

*Cleverly designed to span the confluence of the Moyka and the Griboedov, the Theatre and Small Stable bridges were constructed by Traitteur and Adam in 1829–31.*

### Anichkov Bridge

*This three-span bridge, carrying Nevskiy prospekt across the Fontanka, was built in 1839–41. At each corner are Pyotr Klodt's impressive sculptures of men taming wild horses.*

**Petrogradskaya**

**Neva**

**Gostinyy Dvor**

### Lomonosov Bridge

*The distinctive domed granite towers, built in 1785–7, originally contained the bridge's opening mechanism. The bridge was rebuilt in 1912, but the towers were kept.*

### Bank Bridge

*Dating from the same time as the Lion Bridge, and designed by the same team, this bridge is adorned by four magnificent cast-iron griffons. Its name derives from the nearby former Assignment Bank.*

# Exploring St Petersburg's Bridges and Waterways

A boat trip on St Petersburg's canals and waterways is one of the highlights of any visit to the city. From the Anichkov Bridge the river boats *(see p226)* loop along the Neva, Fontanka and Moyka rivers, taking in many impressive bridges and landmarks. Alternatively, you can choose your route to explore the city's rich architectural heritage by taking a water taxi *(see p227)*. A pleasant wander along the embankments of the Griboedov Canal leads past imposing 19th-century apartment houses and fancifully decorated bridges. In winter it is possible (but not recommended) to walk on the frozen Neva.

The ice-laden Neva river in front of the Peter and Paul Fortress

## THE NEVA AND ITS BRANCHES

Greatest of St Petersburg's numerous waterways, the Neva flows from Lake Ladoga in the east through the city to the Gulf of Finland, a distance of only 74 km (46 miles) in total. Vasilevskiy Island, one of more than 100 islands in the Neva Delta, divides the river into two separate branches, Bolshaya (Great) Neva and Malaya (Small) Neva.

Icebound for at least four months of the year, the Neva usually shows the first signs of cracking in March. The official Opening of Navigation is announced by the port authority in mid-April. Until the Revolution the event was marked with great ceremony. The Commander of the Peter and Paul Fortress *(see pp66–7)*, at the head of a naval flotilla, would scoop some icy water into a silver goblet which he presented to the tsar in the Winter Palace *(see pp92–3).*

## RIVERS AND CANALS

Inspired by Amsterdam, Peter the Great kept the many streams of the delta as canals, which also helped to drain the swampy ground. As the city grew new ones were dug to improve the canal network.

The **Moyka** originally flowed from a swamp near the Field of Mars *(see p94)*. In the 19th century the aristocracy lined its quays with impressive Neo-Classical mansions which are still their main attraction. Canal boats and barges ply the 7-km (4-mile) long **Fontanka**, widest and busiest of the waterways, which was once the border of the city. These two rivers are linked by the **Kryukov Canal**, dug in the 18th century.

The **Griboedov Canal**, first known as the Catherine Canal in honour of Catherine the Great, was designed to move cargo from Sennaya Ploshchad. Today the atmosphere here is more tranquil. The stretch of water running south from the Lion Bridge is particularly picturesque. The narrowest

waterway is the **Winter Canal**, just to the east of the Winter Palace. Nearby is the delightful **Swan Canal** which runs along the Summer Garden *(p95)*.

Steady industrial growth in the 19th century prompted the construction of a new canal, the **Obvodnyy**, in 1834, to take the increasing number of heavy cargo barges and supply water to the city outskirts.

## NEVA BRIDGES

The most central of the Neva bridges is the **Palace Bridge** (Dvortsovyy most). The present structure, built early in the 20th century, replaced a seasonal pontoon bridge which linked the mainland to Vasilevskiy Island. The other

View of the Moyka and its south bank with a water taxi in foreground

Peter the Great Bridge, crossing the Neva near Smolnyy Institute

bridge to this island, **Blago-veshchenskiy Bridge** (Blago-veshchenskiy most, *see p63*) was the first permanent bridge over the Neva. Once known as Lieutenant Schmidt Bridge, it returned to its original name in 2007. The **Trinity Bridge** (Troitskiy most, *see p73*) was built in 1897–1903 by the French Batignolles company. At 582 m (1,910 ft), the Trinity Bridge was the Neva's longest, until the construction of the **Alexander Nevsky Bridge** (Most Aleksandra Nevskovo) in the 1960s, which is some 900 m (2,950 ft). Between these two is the **Liteynyy Bridge** (Liteynyy most) built in 1874–9. In 1917, the city authorities tried to prevent rebel workers crossing the Neva from the Vyborg Side by raising the central bridge span. The tactic failed since the revolutionaries decided to cross on foot over the frozen ice.

Near the Smolnyy Institute is the **Peter the Great Bridge** (Most PetraVelikovo), also known by its Soviet name Bolsheokhtinskiy most. It has a central drawbridge and distinctive steel twin arches, erected in 1909–11.

From April to November almost all Neva bridges are raised at night to give ships access to the Volga *(see p209)*.

## DECORATIVE BRIDGES

In the beginning, wooden bridges spanned the canals and rivers of St Petersburg. They were usually known by their colour – red, blue, green, and so on. The **Red Bridge** (Krasnyy most) which carries Gorokhovaya ulitsa over the Moyka, has preserved its original name. Built in 1808–14, this iron bridge is decorated with picturesque lamps on four granite obelisks. Lamps are also a feature of the **Lantern Bridge** (Fonarnyy most) which crosses the Moyka river near to the Yusupov Palace *(see p120)*. Here the gilded lampposts are shaped to look like treble clefs. **Singer's Bridge** (Pevcheskiy most) at the other end of the Moyka takes its name from the choir of the nearby Glinka Capella. Its engineer, Yegor Adam, also designed the lace-like patterning of the railings.

At the junction where the Griboedov meets the Moyka is an interesting ensemble, formed by the wide **Theatre Bridge** (Teatralnyy most) and

Lamppost, St Panteleymon's Bridge

**Small Stable Bridge** (Malo-Konyushennyy most). The latter is cunningly designed to look like two bridges.

Among the more attractive bridges is Georg von Traitteur's pedestrian **Bank Bridge** (Bankovskiy most), crossing the Griboedov. Its cables are held up by two pairs of gold-winged griffons. The **Lion Bridge** (Lvinyy most), also by Traitteur, uses a similar device; in this case the suspension cables emerge from the open jaws of four proud lions.

**St Panteleymon's Bridge** (Panteleymonovskiy most, *see p99*) spans the Fontanka near the Summer Gardens. It was Russia's first chain bridge (1823–4). The Empire-style decoration has survived and includes gilded fasces and double-headed eagles perched on laurel wreaths. Next to the Nevskiy prospekt, the **Anichkov Bridge** (Anich-kov most) is famous for its four vibrant bronze sculptures of wild horses and their powerful tamers, all of them in different poses. Further down the Fontanka, framed by a handsome Neo-Classical square by Carlo Rossi, is the **Lomonosov Bridge** (Most Lomonosova) with its unusual stone turrets.

The **Egyptian Bridge** (Egipetskiy most) spans the Fontanka close to the Kryukov Canal. It is ornamented with bronze sphinxes and bridgeheads resembling the entrance to an Egyptian temple. Originally constructed in 1826, the bridge collapsed under the weight of a passing cavalry squadron in 1905 but was rebuilt in 1955.

A 19th-century illustration of one of the many floods in St Petersburg

## A CITY UNDER WATER

Peter the Great should have known it was a bad idea to found a city here. The first flood, just three months after he started the fortress in 1703, swept away his building materials. The water rises dangerously high on average once a year, but four floods, in 1777, 1824, 1924 and 1955, wrought massive damage. In 1824 the whole city went under water and 462 buildings were totally destroyed. This inspired Pushkin's poem *The Bronze Horseman (see p78)*. Markers showing record waterheights can be found by the Winter Canal and the Peter and Paul Fortress. In 1989 construction of a dam was begun to prevent future destruction.

# St Petersburg's Best: Palaces and Museums

St Petersburg boasts more than 90 museums, many of them housed in palaces or other buildings of historical importance. Some are well known throughout the world, such as the Hermitage which began as Catherine the Great's private collection of European art. Others, including the Russian Museum and the Summer Palace, highlight local art, history and culture. Some of the most evocative museums are those commemorating the lives and work of famous artists, writers and musicians. This selection represents the most interesting in each category.

**The Hermitage**
*Incorporating the breathtaking state rooms of the Winter Palace, the world-famous Hermitage holds nearly three million exhibits which range from Fine Arts to archaeological finds.*

**Menshikov Palace**
*This grandiose Baroque palace on Vasilevskiy Island is testimony to the power of Peter the Great's friend and advisor, Prince Menshikov.*

*Petrograd*

*Malaya Neva*

*Vasilevskiy Island*

*Bolshaya Neva*

*Palace Embankment*

*Sennaya Ploshchad*

## IMPERIAL COUNTRY PALACES

To escape the pressures of the capital, successive Russian rulers built sumptuous retreats in the rural hinterland of St Petersburg. These offer a fascinating insight into the lifestyle of the Romanov dynasty.

**Tsarskoe Selo's** Catherine Palace was built by Rastrelli in a flamboyant Baroque style.

**Peterhof's** palace and pavilions are enhanced by the splendid cascades and fountains adorning the attractive grounds.

**Pavlovsk's** Great Palace is set in an extensive naturalistic landscaped park, embellished with ponds, pavilions and monuments.

| 0 km | 15 |
| 0 miles | 15 |

**Kshesinskaya Mansion**
*Built for a prima ballerina of the Mariinskiy Theatre, this attractive Style-Moderne mansion now houses the Museum of Russian Political History containing souvenirs from the Revolution.*

*Neva*

**Summer Palace**
*Interiors and furniture, such as Peter the Great's original four-poster bed, give an idea of the tsar's relatively modest lifestyle.*

**Stieglitz Museum**
*A rich collection of applied art is displayed in Messmacher's magnificent building which was inspired by palaces of the Italian Renaissance.*

*Gostinyy Dvor*

**Russian Museum**
*Carlo Rossi's Mikhaylovskiy Palace is the splendid setting for an outstanding collection of Russian art, ranging from medieval icons to contemporary paintings and sculptures. This semi-abstract work* Blue Crest *by Vasily Kandinsky dates from 1917.*

**Pushkin House-Museum**
*Period furnishings and personal belongings such as this inkstand recreate the atmosphere of Alexander Pushkin's last home.*

| 0 metres | 500 |
|---|---|
| 0 yards | 500 |

# Exploring St Petersburg's Palaces and Museums

The city's palaces range from imperial excess to the tasteful homes of the nobility, while art museums cover the fine and applied arts and folk crafts. The history of St Petersburg, from its foundation as Peter the Great's "window on the West" to its role as the "cradle of the Revolution", is covered by a variety of museums while its culture is documented in the apartments of writers, composers and artists. More specialist interests, from railway engines and military paraphernalia to insects and whales, also find reflection in the wealth of museums.

**Peter the Great's Summer Palace overlooking the Fontanka**

## PALACES

The fabulous wealth of imperial St Petersburg is reflected in the magnificence of its palaces. No trip to the city is complete without a visit to at least one of the spectacular out-of-town imperial summer residences, **Peterhof** *(see pp148–51)*, **Pavlovsk** *(see pp158–61)* or the Catherine Palace *(see pp152–3)* at **Tsarskoe Selo**. These palaces, built and added to in the last 200 years of Romanov rule, illustrate the extravagance of the imperial court and the wealth of the empire's natural resources. An abundance of gold, lapis lazuli, malachite, marble and other precious minerals decorates many of the rich palace interiors. The palace parks and grounds are landscaped and filled with follies and monuments.

At the centre of the city, the **Winter Palace** *(see pp92–3)* is home to the Hermitage art museum and epitomizes the opulence of the court. Peter the Great's more intimate

**Summer Palace** is nearby *(see p95)* and makes a pleasing contrast. Peter's friend and counsellor, Prince Alexander Menshikov, also built two sumptuous residences, the **Menshikov Palace** *(see p62)* on Vasilevskiy Island, and his summer palace at **Oranienbaum** *(see p146)*, Lomonosov.

Overlooking the Moyka river is the **Yusupov Palace** *(see p120)* which is famed as the murder scene of Rasputin, the extraordinary peasant who exerted his malign influence over the Russian court.

For those in search of a tranquil setting, a pleasant day can be spent exploring the **Yelagin Palace** *(see p126)* and the island of the same name.

## ART MUSEUMS

One of the world's greatest collections of Western art is housed in the **Hermitage** *(see pp84–93)* which owns over 3 million pieces of art. With collections ranging from Egyptian mummies to Scythian gold, Greek vases,

**Bedroom in the Chinese Palace (1760s), Oranienbaum**

Colombian emeralds and a vast and dazzling array of Old Master, Impressionist and Post-Impressionist paintings, it is essential to be selective.

The **Russian Museum** *(see pp104–107)* is a showcase for Russian art, including the 20th-century avant-garde and the folk crafts which influenced it. Exhibitions from its holdings are also in the **Mikhaylovskiy Castle** *(see p101)*, **Marble Palace** *(see p94)* and **Stroganov Palace** *(see p112)*.

The **Academy of Arts** *(see p63)* exhibits work by past students as well as models of the city's notable buildings.

There are fascinating displays of applied arts from around the world in the **Stieglitz Museum** *(see p127)* which includes ceramics, wood carving, ironwork and embroidery. Its interiors and the glass-roofed exhibition hall are equally impressive.

**The Cyclist (1913) by Natalya Goncharova, Russian Museum**

## HISTORY MUSEUMS

St Petersburg's dramatic 300-year history is proudly recorded in a number of the city's museums. The **Cabin of Peter the Great** *(see p73)* was the earliest building to be constructed in the city and it offers an intriguing insight into the surprisingly humble lifestyle of this tsar.

A group of historic sights lies within the Peter and Paul Fortress. The **Cathedral of SS Peter and Paul** *(see p68)* houses the tombs of all but two of Russia's tsars since Peter the Great. The preserved cells of the grim **Trubetskoy Bastion** *(see p69)* act as a reminder of the hundreds of political prisoners to be confined within the fortress walls. In the **Commandant's House** *(see p69)*, the courthouse where prisoners were once interrogated, an exhibition looks at medieval settlements in the area, while the **Engineer's House** *(see p68)* focuses on daily life in St Petersburg before the Revolution.

A wealth of revolutionary memorabilia, including Stalin era posters and a huge propaganda stained-glass panel, can be found in the **Museum of Russian Political History**. The museum is located within the Kshesinskaya Mansion *(see p72)* which, in 1917, housed the Bolshevik headquarters. The **Cruiser Aurora** *(see p73)* also played a part in the Revolution, having fired a warning shot before the storming of the Winter Palace in October 1917.

For an impression of the prestigious pre-revolutionary school where poet Alexander Pushkin was a student, some of the class rooms of the **Lycée** at Tsarskoe Selo *(see p155)* have been restored to their 19th-century appearance.

On the southern outskirts of the city, in Victory Square *(see p131)*, the **Monument to the Heroic Defenders of Leningrad** poignantly evokes the Siege of Leningrad (1941–4) and acts as an important reminder of the great hardships endured by St Petersburgers during World War II.

Office of Leningrad party secretary Sergey Kirov, Kirov Museum

## SPECIAL INTEREST MUSEUMS

Remnants of Peter the Great's legendary "cabinet of curiosities" can be found in the city's oldest museum, the **Kunstkammer** *(see p60)*. Housed under the same roof is a **Museum of Anthropology and Ethnography**, displaying a large collection of artifacts from all over the world. For natural history, the **Zoological Museum** *(see p60)* encompasses most known life forms, including a unique collection of molluscs and blue corals.

The **Naval Museum** *(see p60)* fascinates all ages with its model ships, small boats, figureheads and flags, while the **Artillery Museum** *(see p70)* covers military hardware, from pikes to ballistic missiles. Train enthusiasts will find plenty to enjoy in the **Railway Museum** *(see p123)*, including an 1835 engine built for the Tsarskoe Selo railway.

The **Museum of Musical Life** in the Sheremetev Palace *(see p129)* displays period

instruments and explains the role of the Sheremetev family as leading music patrons in 19th-century St Petersburg. A stunning array of beautiful stage costumes are on display alongside photos, set designs and other theatrical ephemera in the **Theatre Museum** which is situated on Ostrovskiy Square *(see p110)*.

## HOUSE-MUSEUMS

A handful of evocative museums commemorates some of the city's most famous residents. The **Pushkin House-Museum** *(see p113)*, the **Nabokov Museum** *(see p122)* and the **Dostoevsky House-Museum** *(see p130)* recapture something of the life and character of their former residents.

The **Anna Akhmatova Museum** in the former service quarters of the Sheremetev Palace *(see p129)* traces the dramatic life of the poetess who lived here for many years.

For an insight into the life of a powerful Communist official of the 1930s, visit the **Kirov Museum** *(see p72)*. The museum is devoted to the popular leader whose assassination on Stalin's orders initiated the Great Terror *(see p27)*.

Outside the city in **Repino** *(see p146)*, the house of the painter Ilya Repin is set in beautiful woodland on the Gulf of Finland.

**18th-century violin and score in Museum of Musical Life, Sheremetev Palace**

# Celebrated St Petersburgers

As the residence of the Russian imperial family and court from the early 18th century, St Petersburg was the focus of patronage and an almost boundless source of wealth. It was the perfect seed bed for creativity and the flowering of ideas. Institutions such as the Academy of Arts, the University, the Kunstkammer and the Imperial School of Ballet trained generations of cultural figures and scientists to the highest standards. So successful were they that, by the dawn of the 20th century, St Petersburg had become one of the most important cultural centres in Europe.

### Nikolai Gogol

*A merciless satirist of St Petersburg society, Gogol lived on Malaya Morskaya ulitsa (see p82) for three years.*

### Grigoriy Kozintsev

*Director Kozintsev confirmed his reputation in the West with his interpretation of Shakespeare's* Hamlet *(1964), made at Lenfilm (see p70).*

**Petrogradsk**

*Malaya Neva*

**Vasilevskiy Island**

### Ilya Repin

*This outstanding realist painter is seen here teaching life drawing at the Academy of Arts (see p63) where he was a professor.*

*Bolshaya Neva*

**Sennaya Ploshchad**

### Pyotr Tchaikovsky

*Tchaikovsky graduated from the Conservatory (see p120) in 1865 and went on to compose his world-famous operas and ballets.*

### Anna Pavlova

*A prima ballerina at the Mariinskiy Theatre (see p119), Pavlova took Paris by storm in 1909 when she toured in* Les Sylphides *with the Ballets Russes.*

### Alexander Pushkin
*The great poet, who sketched this self-portrait on a manuscript, died in the flat which is now a house-museum (see p113).*

### Sergey Diaghilev
*Driving force behind the Ballets Russes, Diaghilev also produced the influential* World of Art *magazine in his flat on 45 Liteynyy prospekt. He is shown here with Jean Cocteau (left).*

*Neva*

*Palace Embankment*

### Anna Akhmatova
*The poetess' most famous poem,* Requiem, *is a powerful and moving indictment of the Stalinist regime. Akhmatova, seen here in a portrait by Nathan Altman, lived in the service quarters of the Sheremetev Palace (see p129).*

*Gostinyy Dvor*

### Dmitriy Shostakovich
*Shostakovich's* Seventh Symphony *was broadcast live on the radio from the Great Hall of the Philharmonia (see p98) in August 1942, while the city was under siege. Many testified to its role in boosting the morale of the besieged citizens.*

### Fyodor Dostoevsky
*The novelist Dostoevsky lived for many years among the slums of Sennaya Ploshchad (see p122) which provided the setting for his greatest work,* Crime and Punishment.

| 0 metres | 500 |
| --- | --- |
| 0 yards | 500 |

# Remarkable St Petersburgers

The streets of St Petersburg are redolent with literary and artistic associations. Fascinating art collections, house-museums, theatres and concert halls evoke the memory of famous St Petersburgers. The world of the 18th-century genius Lomonosov and 19th-century writers Pushkin and Dostoevsky can be imagined. So too, can the spirit of Russian ballet when dancers such as Anna Pavlova and Vaslaw Nijinsky thrilled the Mariinskiy audiences. During these early years of the 20th century, writers, musicians, dancers and painters flocked to St Petersburg, bringing with them a wealth of creativity.

**Symbolist "Silver Age" poet, Andrei Bely (1880–1934)**

## WRITERS

Considered the father of modern Russian literature, **Alexander Pushkin** (1799–1837) was simultaneously intoxicated by St Petersburg's beauty and sensitive to the underlying climate of political suspicion and intolerance which constrained writers in the wake of the Decembrist rebellion of 1825 *(see p23)*. **Nikolai Gogol** (1809–52) responded to these constraints by satirising the status quo. In *The Nose*, he targeted the city's bureaucrats with their inflated sense of self worth and mind-numbing conformity.

Another aspect of the city altogether is revealed by **Fyodor Dostoevsky** (1821–81). His novel *Crime and Punishment*, one of more than 30 works set in the city, takes place against a backdrop of squalor in the notorious slums of Sennaya Ploshchad *(see p122)*. The story of the murder of an old moneylender was based on a real crime and the novel's publication in 1866 was blamed for a series of subsequent copy-cat killings.

Poetry, which flourished in the "Golden Age" of Pushkin, only regained its ascendancy over the novel in the "Silver Age" during the first decade of the 20th century. Some of the most exciting poets of the period, including **Aleksandr Blok** (1880–1921), **Andrei Bely** (1880–1934) and **Anna Akhmatova** (1889–1966), gathered at The Tower, a flat overlooking the Tauride Gardens *(see p128)*. Bely later wrote *Petersburg*, one of the earliest stream-of-consciousness novels. Akhmatova is honoured by a museum in the Sheremetev Palace *(see p129)* while one of her protégés, **Joseph Brodsky** (1940–96) went on to receive the Nobel Prize for literature in 1987. Brodsky became the bête-noire of the Leningrad literary establishment in the 1960s. The refusal of the authorities to publish his poetry, which they condemned as decadent, finally forced him to emigrate in 1972.

(see p120)
(see p128)
(see p129)

## MUSICIANS

The first important composer to emerge from the nationalist movement was **Mikhail Glinka** (1804–57), the earliest composer of Russian opera. In 1862, the Conservatory *(see p120)* was founded by **Anton Rubinstein** (1829–94) and this became the focus of musical life in St Petersburg. **Nikolai Rimsky-Korsakov** (1844–1908) taught here for 37 years and together with composers such as **Modest Mussorgsky** (1839–81), and **Aleksandr Borodin** (1834–87), he formed "the mighty handful". They were a largely self-taught group aiming to develop a musical language based on Russian folk music and Slav traditions. Many of them wrote operas premiered at the Mariinskiy *(see p119)*.

One of the musical geniuses of the 20th century was **Igor Stravinsky** (1882–1971). He spent much time abroad but, as works like *The Rite of Spring* testify, his cultural roots were firmly in his homeland.

The city's most important concert venue is the Great Hall of the Philharmonia *(see p202)* where **Pyotr Tchaikovsky**'s (1840–93) *Sixth Symphony* was premiered in 1893 and **Dmitriy Shostakovich**'s (1906–75) *Seventh Symphony*, his most famous work, was performed in 1942.

**Portrait of composer Mikhail Glinka painted by Ilya Repin in 1887**

*The Circus* (1919) by avant-garde artist Marc Chagall

## ARTISTS

From the 18th century, the Academy of Arts *(see p63)* was the centre of artistic life in St Petersburg. **Dmitriy Levitskiy** (1735–1822), **Orest Kiprenskiy** (1782–1836), **Silvestr Shchedrin** (1791–1830), and Russia's first internationally recognised artist, **Karl Bryullov** (1799–1852), were all trained here.

In 1863, a group of students rebelled against the Academy and went on to establish the Wanderers movement *(see p106)*. To some extent the Academy and the Wanderers became reconciled when the most versatile of these artists, **Ilya Repin** (1844–1930), was appointed professor of painting at the Academy in 1893.

Five years later **Sergey Diaghilev** (1872–1929) and painter **Alexandre Benois** (1870–1960) launched the *World of Art* magazine *(see p107)*, proclaiming "Art for art's sake". Another collaborator, **Leon Bakst** (1866–1924), designed the most famous of the Ballets Russes costumes. Bakst also taught **Marc Chagall** (1889–1985) who later settled in France and had a profound impact on art in the West as well as in Russia. Other members of the Russian avant-garde include **Kazimir Malevich** (1878–1935) and **Pavel Filonov** (1883–1941).

Works by all of these artists can be seen at the Russian Museum *(see pp104–107)*.

## DANCERS AND CHOREOGRAPHERS

The skills of Russian dancers are legendary and the performances of the Mariinskiy (Kirov) Ballet Company continue to enthral audiences all over the world. Since 1836 the dancers have been trained at the former Imperial Ballet School *(see p110)*. In 1869–1903 the outstanding choreographer at the Mariinskiy was **Marius Petipa**. He inspired a generation of dancers including **Matilda Kshesinskaya** *(see p72)*, **Vaslaw Nijinsky** (1890–1950) and the legendary **Anna Pavlova** (1885–1931). Petipa's successor, **Mikhail Fokin** (1880–1942), is famous as the principal choreographer of the Ballets Russes *(see p119)*. The Mariinskiy tradition was revived after the Revolution by another graduate of the Ballet School, **Agrippina Vaganova** (1879–1951). Her groundwork paved the way for the modern generation of dancers including **Rudolf Nureyev** (1938–93) and more recently, **Galina Mezentseva** and **Emil Faskhoutdinov**.

## FILM DIRECTORS

The Lenfilm Studios (see p70) were founded in 1918 on the site where the first Russian cine film had been shown in 1896. In its heyday Lenfilm produced 15 movies a year. Its two most remarkable

Poster for *The Youth of Maxim* (1935) directed by Kozintsev

directors, **Grigoriy Kozintsev** (1905–73) and **Leonid Trauberg** (1902–90), first joined forces in 1922 and began making short experimental films. The pair then went on to direct *The New Babylon* (1929), remarkable for its montage and lighting effects, and *The Maxim Trilogy* (1935–39). Kozintsev's versions of *Hamlet* (1964) and *King Lear* (1970), with music composed by Shostakovich for both films, mark the height of his success in the West.

## SCIENTISTS

The great polymath Mikhail Lomonosov

The foundations of modern Russian science were laid in the 18th century by **Mikhail Lomonosov** (1711–65) *(see p61)* who worked for over 20 years in the Kunstkammer *(see p60)*. His treatise, *Elementa Chymiae Mathematica*, published in 1741, anticipates Dalton's theory of the atomic structure of matter.

In 1869, **Dmitriy Mendeleev** (1834–1907), a professor of chemistry, compiled the Periodic Table of Elements. Many people believe that the world's first radio signal was sent by **Aleksandr Popov** (1859–1906) from the laboratories of St Petersburg University on 24 March 1896.

In 1904, the world-famous physiologist **Ivan Pavlov** (1849–1936) won the Nobel Prize for medicine for his theory of conditioned reflexes which he demonstrated by experimenting on dogs and their hearing responses.

# Nevskiy Prospekt
## From the Admiralty to the Griboedov Canal

A pleasant stroll along this first stretch of
St Petersburg's main artery reveals a wealth of
attractive buildings. A profusion of architectural
styles ranges from the Baroque Stroganov Palace
to the magnificent Neo-Classical Cathedral of Our
Lady of Kazan and the striking Style-Moderne
Singer House. The stately avenue was once
known as the "Street of Tolerance", referring to
the clutch of churches of different denominations
that were established here in the late 18th and
early 19th centuries. *(See also p108.)*

**Literary Café**
*Once called the Wolf and Beranger,
this café was known for its fashionable
clientele. Pushkin left from here
for his fatal duel in 1837 (see p83).*

**Admiralty
(p78)**

**Palace Square (p83) and the
Hermitage (pp84–93)**

**The 1760s apartment blocks** at Nos. 8
and 10 are an example of early
St Petersburg Neo-Classicism.

ADMIRALTEYSKIY PROSPEKT

N E V S K I Y   P R O S P E K T

BOLSHAYA MORSKAYA ULITSA

MALAYA MORSKAYA ULITSA

BOLSHAYA MORSKAYA ULITSA

**St Isaac's Cathedral
(pp80–81) and
Astoria Hotel (p79)**

**Admiralty Garden**
*This garden was laid out in
1872–4. Near the fountain
are busts of composer Mikhail
Glinka, writer Nikolai Gogol
and poet Mikhail Lermontov.*

| 0 metres | 100 |
|---|---|
| 0 yards | 100 |

**School No. 210**
*This school carries a sign,
dating from the Siege,
warning, "Citizens!
This side of the street is
more dangerous during
artillery bombardment".*

**Aeroflot Building**
*Marian Peretyatkovich's severe granite
building (1912) is uncharacteristic of the
city's architecture. The upper storeys were
inspired by the Palazzo Medici in Florence;
the arcades by the Doge's Palace, Venice.*

**STAR SIGHT**

★ Cathedral of Our Lady
of Kazan

**LOCATOR MAP**

NEVSKIY PROSPEKT

НЕВСКИЙ ПРОСПЕКТ

**Dutch Church Building**
*The Dutch church was housed behind the central Neo-Classical portico of Paul Jacot's seemingly secular building (1831–7). The elongated wings are still occupied by offices, flats and shops.*

**Stroganov Palace**
*The façade of this splendid Baroque palace, one of the oldest buildings on the street (1753), is embellished with sculptural ornaments and the Stroganov coat of arms (see p112).*

**The Fashion House**
*Marian Lyalevich designed this building for Mertens Furriers in 1911–12. The impact of the Neo-Classical arches is heightened by the beautiful plate glass.*

NAB REKI MOYKI

BOLSHAYA KONYUSHENNAYA UL

MALAYA KONYUSHENNAYA ULITSA

**N E V S K I Y    P R O S P E K T**

KAZANSKAYA ULITSA

KAZANSKIY MOST

KANAL GRIBOEDOVA

**Singer House** was built for the Singer Sewing Machine Company in 1902–4 by Pavel Syuzor. The building is distinguished by a glass globe on a conical tower.

→ Continued
(pp48–9)

**The Lutheran Church**
(1833) was an important centre for the evangelical community. Converted into a swimming pool during the Soviet era, it is once again open as a church *(see p112)*.

**The Griboedov Canal**,
originally known as the Catherine Canal, was renamed in 1923 after the 19th-century Russian playwright Aleksandr Griboedov.

★ **Cathedral of Our Lady of Kazan**
*Ninety-six Corinthian columns, arranged in four rows, form an arc facing Nevskiy prospekt. Andrey Voronikhin's design was inspired by Bernini's colonnade for St Peter's in Rome (see p111).*

# Nevskiy Prospekt
## From the Griboedov Canal to the Fontanka

Nevskiy Prospekt has been the main focus for St Petersburg's shopping and entertainment since the mid-18th century. As the prospekt continues towards the handsome Anichkov Bridge on the Fontanka river, there are growing numbers of cafés, bars and restaurants as well as three historic shopping arcades, the Silver Rows, Gostinyy Dvor and Passazh. Bustling with life, this stretch of the avenue also has many sights of historic and architectural interest, including the Anichkov Palace.

**Passazh Arcade**
*This popular shopping mall is covered by a glass canopy stretching 180 m (590 ft). The arcade opened in 1848 and was reconstructed in 1900.*

**Church on Spilled Blood** *(p100)*

**The Small Hall of the Philharmonia** was the city's main concert hall in the early 19th century.

**The Church of Saint Catherine** (1762–82), by Vallin de la Mothe, is a mixture of Baroque and Neo-Classical styles. It is the oldest Roman Catholic church in Russia.

**Grand Hotel Europe** *(p101)*

**Russian Museum** *(pp104–107)*

**The Armenian Church** (1771–80) is a fine example of Yuriy Velten's decorative Neo-Classical style *(see p108).*

KANAL GRIBOEDOVA

**Nevskiy Prospekt 2 (Griboedova Canal)**

MIKHAYLOVSKAYA ULITSA

NEVSKIY PROSPEKT

**Nevskiy Prospekt 1**

DUMSKAYA ULITSA

**Gostinyy Dvor**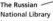

SADOVAYA ULITSA

**Silver Rows Arcade (1784–7)**

**The Duma Tower** was built in 1804 as a watchtower for fires. The Duma building was the centre of local government from 1786–1918.

**The Russian National Library** houses over 33 million items, including the earliest surviving handwritten Russian book (1057).

**Portik Rusca Perinnyie Ryadi**
*Now standing alone, the six-columned portico by Luigi Rusca was originally the entrance to a long arcade of shops. The portico was dismantled during the construction of the metro and rebuilt in 1972.*

★ **Gostinyy Dvor**
*This striking arcade has been St Petersburg's main bazaar since the mid-18th century (see p108). It houses more than 300 outlets which sell everything from clothes and cosmetics to souvenirs and chocolates.*

| 0 metres | 100 |
|---|---|
| 0 yards | 100 |

**★ Yeliseev's**
*Famous for its beautiful Style-Moderne decor, this building was once home to Yeliseev's delicatessen. It now houses the Akimov Comedy Theatre (see p109).*

### LOCATOR MAP

### STAR SIGHTS

★ Yeliseev's

★ Gostinyy Dvor

**Beloselskiy-Belozerskiy Palace**
*Now a cultural centre and Waxworks Museum, this sumptuous palace was designed in Neo-Baroque style by Andrey Stakenschneider in 1847–8. The red façade is decorated with Corinthian pilasters and atlantes upholding balconies.*

**Quarenghi's Stalls** were built in 1803–6 as trading rows. They were then handed over to the imperial chancellor and became known as the Cabinet.

**Number 66** was occupied by the music publishers Bessel and Co in the 19th century. Tchaikovsky was one of many composers who frequented their offices.

**The Central District Tax Office** has a Neo-Classical appearance, but was not built until the 1940s.

NEVSKIY PROSPEKT

OSTROVSKOVO

FONTANKA

ANICHKOV MOST

FONTANKA

**Aleksandrinskiy Theatre**

**A statue of Catherine the Great** stands in Ostrovskiy Square *(see p110).*

**The Anichkov Palace** was first built as a present from Tsarina Elizabeth to her lover, Aleksey Razumovskiy. It later became the winter residence of the heir to the throne *(see p109).*

**Moskovskiy railway station**

**Anichkov Bridge**
*Four dynamic bronze statues of rearing horses and their tamers adorn this well-known landmark. They were designed in the 1840s by Pyotr Klodt (see p35).*

# ST PETERSBURG THROUGH THE YEAR

Whatever the weather, Russians are always ready to celebrate and consequently take their public holidays very seriously. Flowers have great symbolic significance, from mimosa for International Women's Day, to lilac to mark the beginning of summer. Every official holiday, as well as some local festivals such as City Day, are celebrated both in the centre of town and in the many

**Lilac, a symbol of summer**

different districts, with regattas, balloon rides and fireworks at night, when the torches on the Rostral Columns (*see p60*) are lit. Classical music is the central theme of a large number of festivals each year, attracting talented performers from all over the world. But even without an official holiday, Russian people love to get out and about, whether to ski or ice-skate in the winter months or gather mushrooms in late summer and autumn.

## SPRING

Spring has set in for good when the first sunbathers gather on the beaches outside the Peter and Paul Fortress (*see pp66–7*) and when, in early April after the waterways have thawed, the city's bridges open to allow ships through.

To warm themselves up after the months of cold, locals celebrate "maslennitsa", the making of pancakes (*blini*) prior to Lent. They then gather bunches of willow as a symbol of the approaching Palm Sunday. On the eve of Lent, "Forgiveness Sunday", it is common practice to ask for forgiveness of those you might have offended during the year.

Once the snows have gone, the first trips to the *dacha*, or country house, are made to put the gardens in order.

**Early sunbathers on the banks of the Peter and Paul Fortress**

## MARCH

**International Women's Day** (*Mezhdunarodnyy zhenskiy den*), 8 Mar. Men rush around the city buying flowers for their womenfolk. It is a

**Candles lighting up Russian Ortho-dox church during Easter service**

tradition to say *s prazdnikom* (congratulations on the holiday) to everyone. There are even special performances and concerts and, however sexist it may seem to non-Russians, it is a very popular day.
**From the Avant Garde to the Present** (*Ot avangarda do nashih dney*), mid-Mar. A celebration of 20th-century art and music in a city-wide festival.
**Easter Sunday** (*Paskha*). The dates on which Lent and Easter fall change every year. On Easter Sunday, St Petersburg churches are filled with worshippers, the evocative sound of ethereal music and chanting and the smell of incense. Russians traditionally greet each other with *Khristos voskres* (Christ is risen), to which the reply is *Voistine voskres* (He is truly risen).

## APRIL

**Musical Spring in St Petersburg** (*Muzikalnaya Vesna v Sankt-Peterburge*),

**Proud war veteran on Victory Day**

mid-Apr. As warm clothing and heavy boots are laid aside after the cold winter months, the public flock to concert halls throughout the city.
**Cosmonauts' Day** (*Den Kosmonavtiki*), 12 Apr. Space exploration was one of the glories of the Soviet Union and this occasion is celebrated with fireworks at 10pm.

## MAY

**Labour Day** (International Workers' Solidarity Day (*Den Truda*), 1 May. Public holiday.
**Peterhof Fountains** (*Fontany v Petergofe*), first weekend in May. Bands and orchestras accompany the switching on of the famous fountains at Peterhof (*see p151*). **Victory Day** (*Den Pobedy*), 9 May. After a sombre ceremony at Piskarevskoe Cemetery (*see p126*), smartly dressed veterans fill Nevskiy prospekt (*see pp46–9*) and Palace Square (*see p83*) in commemoration of the Nazi surrender in 1945. **City Day** (*Den goroda*), last week of May. A great variety of events, mainly taking place around the Peter and Paul Fortress (*see pp66–7*), mark the founding of the city on 27 May 1703.
**Musical Olympus International Festival**, late May/early Jun. Young musicians from all over the world are accompanied by St Petersburg's most famous orchestra.

### AVERAGE DAILY HOURS OF SUNSHINE

Hours

Jan Feb Mar Apr May Jun Jul Aug Sep Oct Nov Dec

**Sunshine Hours**
*St Petersburg's climate can vary dramatically from hot, sunny days and occasional heavy downpours during the summer months, to winters with sub-zero temperatures and snow. From mid-June to mid-July, it never gets dark. During the winter months the days are extremely short, but there can be days of bright sunshine.*

## SUMMER

A lilac in flower is the real symbol that warm weather has set in and there is an air of excitement once the Field of Mars *(see p94)* comes into bloom. Throughout the warm months, the city is deserted at weekends when people go off to their *dacha,* which is usually a summer house outside the city.

St Petersburg's main festive season is during the acclaimed White Nights in June, when the sun hardly sets and it never quite gets dark. Concerts, ballets and other performances take place all over the city, which fills with thousands of visitors *(see p201)*. The most favoured place to be at night-time is on the embankments of the Neva, which are crowded with revellers watching the bridges being raised at 2am.

## JUNE

**International Protection of Children Day** *(Den Zatschity detey)*, 1 Jun.

Performances and events for children are held throughout the city.
**Russia Day** *(Den Rossii)*, 12 Jun. The day Russia became "independent" of the Soviet Union is marked with fireworks at 10pm.
**Trinity Sunday** *(Troytsa)*, 50 days after Easter. Believers and atheists alike go to tidy the graves of their loved ones and raise a glass of vodka for their souls.
**The White Nights Swing, Jazz Festival**, mid-June. A large jam session supported by local and visiting musicians for anyone with an interest in jazz.
**Stars of the White Nights, Classical Music Festival** *(Zvezdy Belykh nochey)*, late Jun. This is the original White Nights festival, with first-class opera, classical music and ballet concerts performed at all major venues.
**White Nights, Rock Music Festival** *(Belye nochi)*, late Jun. Numerous outdoor rock concerts are held at the Peter and Paul Fortress *(see pp66–7)*.

**Russian battleships moored on the Neva, Navy Day**

**Festival of Festivals** *(Festival-festivaley)*, last week in Jun. This is an international non-competitive film festival showing the best international films released over the past year. The festival attracts film stars from all over the world.
**Tsarskoe Selo Carnival** *(Tsarskoselskiy karnaval)*, last weekend in June. Funny costumes, music and mayhem fill the centre of Tsarskoe Selo *(see pp152–5)*.

## JULY

**Sporting Competitions**. St Petersburg has become an increasingly popular sporting venue in recent years, offering everything from tennis to yachting.
**Navy Day** *(Den Voenno-morskovo Flota)*, first Sun after 22 July. The Neva resembles a shipyard, with submarines and torpedo boats adorned with flags and bunting.

## AUGUST

With schools on holiday and temperatures at their highest, this is a quiet time, with most families escaping to their *dacha* outside the city.

**Bridge opening in front of the Peter and Paul Fortress on a White Night**

## AVERAGE MONTHLY RAIN AND SNOWFALL

MM
100
80
60
40
20
0

Inches
4
3
2
1
0

Jan Feb Mar Apr May Jun Jul Aug Sep Oct Nov Dec

### Rain and Snow-fall Chart

*St Petersburg summers are humid and wet, but the downpours are a welcome relief from the summer heat. In winter frequent snowfalls build up to create metre-high drifts, usually not thawing until late March.*

■ Rainfall (from axis)
■ Snowfall (from axis)

## AUTUMN

City life begins to gain pace as people return from their *dacha* and families begin to prepare for the start of school.

In September, when theatres re-open after the summer break, the city's cultural life resumes. The Mariinskiy (Kirov) returns from touring, and new plays and operas are premiered. October marks the start of the festival season, with guest musicians and theatre groups from all over the world taking part.

The crisp autumn weather is ideal for gathering mushrooms.

**Chanterelle mushrooms**

Popular hunting spots can be found to the northwest of the city around Zelenogorsk and Repino *(see p146)*. Enthusiastic mushroom-gatherers rise early to hunt for chanterelles, oyster mushrooms, *podberyozoviki* (brown mushrooms) and *podosinoviki* (orange-cap bolens). The locals are skilled in identifying edible mushrooms while amateur pickers should be aware of the dangers of poisonous ones.

An activity with fewer potential side-effects might be a trip on the hydrofoil to Peterhof *(see pp148–51)* to see the magnificent fountains before they are switched off for the winter.

**Autumn colours in the park at Tsarskoe Selo**

**Children dressed up for the first day of school**

### SEPTEMBER

**Knowledge Day**
*(Den znaniy)*, 1 Sep. The city is full of children heading for their first day back at school, laden with flowers.

### OCTOBER

**International Theatre Festival Baltic House** *(Baltiyskiy dom)*, Oct. Actors, clowns and pantomime artists gather from the Baltic countries to perform in theatres and on the streets with two weeks of mayhem.

### NOVEMBER

**Day of National Unity**,
4 Nov. A reminder that the Russian Federation is a multi-national country with various religions and political parties.
**Sound Ways, Modern Music Festival** *(Zvukovyye puti)*, mid-Nov. A chance to catch up with some of the most avant-garde trends in jazz and contemporary classical music from Russia and the rest of Europe. Musicians invited from abroad abound, and many of Russia's most renowned performers refuse international engagements in order to take part in this exciting home-grown festival.

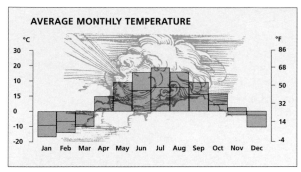

## AVERAGE MONTHLY TEMPERATURE

**Temperature Chart**
*St Petersburg's climate is maritime and milder than might be expected. Summers are warm and often punctuated with hot days as early as May, though during the winter months temperatures often fall below freezing. St Petersburg's average minimum and maximum temperatures throughout the year are shown in this chart.*

## WINTER

As the ice thickens on the waters and the snow deepens, people head for the outdoors once more. Children's sledges are not expensive to buy, and all other equipment can be hired. Cross-country skiing needs no lessons to make it fun. Tsarskoe Selo *(see pp152–5)* and Pavlovsk *(see pp158–61)* parks provide ski and sledge hire at the ski bases *(lyzhnaya baza)*. Skates can be hired for use in the rink at Moskovskiy Park Pobedy, by Park Pobedy metro station in the southern suburbs, and also at the Central Park of Culture and Rest (Krestovskiy Ostrov metro station).

The truly hardened members of the local "walruses" swimming club break the ice by the Peter and Paul Fortress *(see pp66–7)* every day to take an early morning dip.

In the midst of winter activities come New Year and Christmas. New Year is the big holiday, while Christmas itself is celebrated according to the Orthodox calendar, on 7 January. Many people also still

Sledging on the frozen Neva outside the Hermitage *(see pp84–93)*

celebrate Old New Year, which falls on 14 January. A seasonal delight is the Christmas ballet, *The Nutcracker*, at the Mariinskiy Theatre *(see p119)*.

### DECEMBER

**Constitution Day** *(Den konstitutsii)*, 12 Dec. When Yeltsin's new constitution replaced the Brezhnev version, a new constitution day replaced the old one. Fireworks are set off all over town at 10pm.
**Musical Encounters in the Northern Palmyra** *(Muzykalnyye vstrechi v Severnoy Palmire)*, Dec–Jan. This classical music festival is the last one of the year and is made even more magical by the outside backdrop of snowy streets and frozen waterways.
**New Year's Eve** *(Novyy god)*, 31 Dec. Still the biggest holiday of the year, New Year's Eve is best celebrated with the local "champagne", Shampanskoye *(see p183)*. This is considered to be a family celebration, with people dressed as Grandfather Frost (the Russian equivalent of Santa Claus) and the Snow Maiden, the traditional bearers of gifts.

Drilling a hole through the ice for winter-time fishing

### JANUARY

**Russian Orthodox Christmas** *(Rozhdestvo)*, 7 Jan. Christmas is celebrated in a quieter fashion than Easter, with a traditional visit to an evening service on Christmas Eve (6th), when the church bells ring out all over the city.

### FEBRUARY

**Defenders of the Motherland Day** *(Den zashchitnikov rodiny)*, 23 Feb. The male equivalent of Women's Day. Men are congratulated and given flowers and presents.

### PUBLIC HOLIDAYS

**New Year's Day** (1 Jan)
**Russian Orthodox Christmas** (7 Jan)
**International Women's Day** (8 Mar)
**Easter Sunday** (Mar/Apr)
**Labour Day** (1 May)
**Victory Day** (9 May)
**Independence Day** (12 Jun)
**Day of Reconciliation** (7 Nov)
**Constitution Day** (12 Dec)

Water taxis ferrying tourists past the grand Stroganov Palace on the Moyka river ▷

# ST PETERSBURG AREA BY AREA

# VASILEVSKIY ISLAND

It was Peter the Great's intention that Vasilevskiy Island *(Vasilevskiy ostrov)*, the largest island in the Neva delta, was to be the administrative heart of his new capital. However, lack of access (the first permanent bridge was not built until 1842) and the hazards of floods and stormy crossings led to the abandonment of Peter's project, and the centre grew up

**Allegorical sculpture of Neptune on the façade of the Naval Museum**

across the river around the Admiralty *(see p78)* instead. The island's original street plan, based on canals that were never dug *(see p20)*, survives in the numbered streets known as lines

*(linii)*, which run from north to south. The focal point of the island is at the east end with the fine ensemble of public buildings around the spit or Strelka. The rest of the island developed with the spread of industrialization in the 19th century and it became a middle-class haven. There was also a thriving German community here which is reflected in the several Lutheran churches. Today much of the island has a sedate air, with broad tree-lined avenues, a clutch of museums and some attractive 19th-century architecture.

## SIGHTS AT A GLANCE

**Museums**
Kunstkammer ❹
Menshikov Palace ❻
Naval Museum ❷
Zoological Museum ❸

**Historic Buildings and Monuments**
Academy of Arts ❾
Rostral Columns ❶
Twelve Colleges ❺

**Churches**
St Andrew's Cathedral ❽

**Streets and Bridges**
Blagoveshchenskiy Bridge ❿
Bolshoy Prospekt ❼

**KEY**

| | |
|---|---|
| ▨ | Street-by-Street map *See pp58–9* |
| Ⓜ | Metro |
| 🚋 | Tram stop |

0 metres   400
0 yards    400

◁ **One of the two imposing 14th-century BC sphinxes situated in front of the Academy of Arts**

# Street-by-Street: the Strelka

The eastern end of Vasilevskiy Island is known as the Strelka, or "spit". Once St Petersburg's main centre of commerce, it has become an area of learning. The Academy of Sciences and St Petersburg University are situated here, as are various museums, institutes and libraries, housed in the former warehouses and customs buildings. The nautical theme is preserved in the Naval Museum and the two Rostral Columns. In front of these lighthouses is a lawn, a popular spot for newly married couples to have their picture taken. From here there are views across the Neva towards the Peter and Paul Fortress *(see pp66–7)* and the Hermitage *(see pp84–93).*

The Naval Museum and Rostral Columns from across the Neva

**The Lomonosov Monument** honours Mikhail Lomonosov (1711–65), who taught at the Academy of Sciences.

**Twelve Colleges**
*Originally erected to house the 12 ministries of Peter the Great's government, they now form the main building of St Petersburg University* ⑤

**The Academy of Sciences** was founded in 1724. The present building was constructed by Giacomo Quarenghi in 1783–5.

**★ Kunstkammer**
*The Kunstkammer houses Peter the Great's collection of biological curiosities. Its tower, crowned by a sundial, is a St Petersburg landmark* ④

Palace Embankment

**Zoological Museum**
*With over 1.5 million specimens the museum is one of the finest of its kind in the world. The exhibits include a set of stuffed animals that belonged to Peter the Great and a world-famous collection of mammoths* ③

**STAR SIGHTS**

★ Naval Museum

★ Kunstkammer

**Academy of Sciences Library** was founded in 1714 with Peter the Great's personal book collection. It now has over 17 million volumes.

**Sakharov Monument**

**LOCATOR MAP**
*See Street Finder, map 1*

**The New Exchange Bazaar** was designed by Quarenghi in the early 19th century. At the time a busy market filled its Neo-Classical loggias. Today students have replaced the shoppers, as the building houses departments of the university.

**The Institute of Russian Literature** was built in 1832. Also known as Pushkin House, it includes a literary museum.

BIRZHEVOY MOST → Peter and Paul Fortress

NABEREZHNAYA MAKAROVA

BIRZHEVOY PROEZD

BIRZHEVAYA PLOSHCHAD

★ **Naval Museum**
*Among the museum's many fine model boats is the* botik, *also known as the "Grandfather of the Russian Navy", on which Peter the Great learnt to sail* ❷

**Rostral Columns**
*Originally lighthouses guiding ships through the busy port of St Petersburg, these imposing 32-m (105-ft) high columns are a distinctive feature of St Petersburg's skyline. They are still lit for Navy Day (see p51) and other festivals* ❶

**KEY**

- - - Suggested route

0 metres    4
0 yards     4

## Rostral Columns ❶
Ростральные колонны
*Rostralnye kolonny*

Birzhevaya ploshchad. **Map** 1 C5.
🚌 7, 10, 47, K-47, K-128, K-141,
K-147, K-187, K-209, K-228.
🚎 1, 7, 10.

Situated on the Strelka
before the Naval
Museum, the impressive
twin russet-coloured
Rostral Columns were
designed as lighthouses by
Thomas de Thomon in
1810. During the 19th
century the oil lamps were
replaced by gas torches
which are still lit on
ceremonial occa-
sions. Following a
Roman custom, the
columns are decorated
with protruding ships'
prows in celebration
of naval victories. The
monumental figures
around the base represent four
of Russia's rivers, the Neva,
Volga, Dnieper and Volkhov.

**Rostral Column
on the Strelka**

## Naval Museum ❷
Центральный
Военно-Морской музей
*Tsentralnyy Voenno-Morskoy
muzey*

Birzhevaya ploshchad 4. **Map** 1 C5.
**Tel** 328 2502. 🚌 7, 10, 47, K-47,
K-128, K-147, K-187, K-209, K-252.
🚎 1, 7, 10 ◯ 11am–
6pm Wed–Sun.
🎦 🖥 🚻 🛈 English.
**www**.museum.navy.ru

The former Stock
Exchange *(birzha)*
was built in 1805–
10 as the focal
point of the Strelka.
The building was
designed by the
Swiss architect
Thomas de Thomon
and was modelled
on one of the
famous Greek tem-
ples at Paestum in
Italy. Above the col-
umned east façade is
an allegorical sculpt-
ure featuring the
sea-god Neptune in
a chariot drawn by
sea horses; a remin
der that maritime

commerce was traditionally
the lifeblood of this sea-
oriented city.
 The exchange
became redundant
after the Revolution
and in 1940 it was
turned into a museum.
Beneath the magnifi-
cent coffered ceiling of
the spacious trading
hall is an exhibition
on the history of the
Russian and Soviet
navy from its origins
under Peter the Great
to the present day.
Pride of place belongs
to the *botik*, the small
masted wood-
en vessel on
which Peter
learned to sail.
There is plenty
of interest be
sides, from
model ships and
carved prow
figureheads to uniforms, flags
and guided missile submarines.
There is also a superb diorama
of the storming of the Winter
Palace *(see pp28–9)* on the
second-floor landing.
 The photographic displays
around the hall concentrate
on the revolutionary period.
These were redesigned only
in 1995 to present a more
balanced view of events, such
as the involvement of Western
powers in World War II.

**Neo-Classical façade of the Naval Museum,
overlooking the Strelka**

## Zoological Museum ❸
Зоологический музей
*Zoologicheskiy muzey*

Universitetskaya naberezhnaya 1/3.
**Map** 1 C5. **Tel** 328 0112. 🚌 7,
10, 47, K-47, K-128, K-147, K-187,
K-209. 🚎 1, 7, 10. ◯ 11am–6pm
Sat–Thu. 🎦 (free Thu). 🖥 🛈
🚻 English.

Housed in a former customs
warehouse designed by
Giovanni Lucchini in 1826,
this museum has one of the
world's largest natural history
collections containing more
than 1.5 million specimens.
Some of the stuffed animals
belonged to Peter the Great's
*Kunstkammer* collection,
including the horse he rode at
the Battle of Poltava *(see p18)*.
 Dioramas recreate natural
habitats for giant crabs,
weasels, polar bears and blue
whales. The museum is
renowned for its collection of
mammoths. One prized carcass
was exhumed from the frozen
wastes of Siberia in 1902 and
is almost 44,000 years old.

**Weasel in the Zoological Museum**

## Kunstkammer ❹
Кунсткамера
*Kunstkamera*

Universitetskaya naberezhnaya 3.
**Map** 1 C5. **Tel** 328 1412. 🚌 7, 10,
47, K-47, K-128, K-147, K-187,
K-209. 🚎 1, 7, 10. ◯ 11am–6pm
Tue–Sun. 🎦 🛈 English.
**www**.kunstkamera.ru

The delicate, sea green lantern tower of the Baroque
Kunstkammer ("art chamber")
is visible across this part of
Vasilevskiy Island. The building, by Georg Mattarnoviy, was
constructed in 1718–34 to ex-
hibit Peter the Great's infamous
*Kunstkammer* collection.
While touring Holland in 1697
Peter attended the lectures of

**The restrained Baroque façade of the Kunstkammer (1718–34), St Petersburg's first museum**

Frederik Ruysch (1638–1731), the most celebrated anatomist of his day. He was so impressed with Ruysch's collection of rarities that on a return visit in 1717, he purchased the entire collection of over 2,000 anatomical preparations. He transported it to St Petersburg and exhibited it to a wide-eyed public, who were enticed by free glasses of vodka. At the time, Peter's collection also included bizarre, live exhibits of deformed or unusual people, including an hermaphrodite. This, Russia's first museum, also included a library, an anatomical theatre and an observatory.

Today the Kunstkammer houses the Museum of Anthropology and Ethnography, with the remnants of Peter's bizarre collection on display in the central rotunda. Included are the heart and skeleton of Peter's personal servant, "Bourgeois", a giant at 2.27 m (7.5 ft), and a cabinet of teeth extracted by the tsar who was an enthusiastic amateur dentist. Most gruesome of all is the collection of pickled oddities which include Siamese twins and a two-headed sheep.

The halls surrounding the *Kunstkammer* collection contain exhibitions on the peoples of the world. Often neglected by visitors, these marvellously old-fashioned displays present an informative range of artifacts, from an Inuit kayak to Javanese shadow puppets.

# Twelve Colleges ❺
Двенадцать коллегий
*Dvenadtsat kollegiy*

Universitetskaya naberezhnaya 7. **Map** 1 C5. 🚌 7, 47, K-47, K-128, K-147, K-209. 🚎 1, 10. ⬤ to public.

This distinguished Baroque building of red-and-white stuccoed brick is almost 400 m (1,300 ft) in length. It was intended for Peter the Great's newly streamlined administration of 12 colleges or ministries. The single, uninterrupted façade was designed to symbolize the government's unity of purpose, while the curious alignment, at right angles to the embankment, is explained by Peter's unrealized plan for a large

**Mikhail Lomonosov (1711–65)**

**A section of the west façade of Trezzini's Twelve Colleges**

square with an unbroken view across the Strelka. Another popular theory is that Prince Menshikov changed the plan in Peter's absence so that the building would not encroach on his grounds. Domenico Trezzini won the competition for the design in 1723, but subsequent bureaucratic wrangling delayed its completion for 20 years. The building's function gradually changed and in 1819 part of it was acquired by St Petersburg University. A string of revolutionaries, including Lenin in 1891, were educated here. Among the famous Russian lecturers to teach here were the chemist Dmitriy Mendeleev (1834–1907) *(see p45)* and the physiologist Ivan Pavlov (1849–1936) *(see p45)*.

Overlooking the Neva, outside the Twelve Colleges, is an engaging bronze statue of the great 18th-century polymath Mikhail Lomonosov (unveiled in 1986). The son of a fisherman, Lomonosov was the first Russian-born member of the nearby Academy of Sciences. A "universal genius", he wrote poetry, systematized Russian grammar and was a pioneer in mathematics and the physical sciences. Thanks to his scientific discoveries, the art of porcelain, glass and mosaic production began in Russia.

**The southern façade of Prince Menshikov's 18th-century palace**

# Menshikov Palace ❻
Меншиковский дворец
*Menshikovskiy dvorets*

Universitetskaya naberezhnaya 15.
**Map** 5 B1. *Tel* 323 1112. 🚌 7, 47,
K-47, K-128, K-147, K-187, K-209.
🚊 1, 10. 🚋 1, 11. ◯ 10:30am–
6pm Tue–Sat; 10:30am–5pm Sun. 📷
🎫 compulsory (English, French,
German available).

The ochre-painted Baroque
Menshikov Palace, with
its beautifully carved pilasters,
was one of the earliest stone
buildings in St Petersburg.
Designed by Giovanni Fontana
and Gottfried Schädel for the
infamous Prince Menshikov,
the palace was completed in
1720. The palace estate originally extended as far as the
Malaya Neva river to the north.
Prince Menshikov entertained
here on a lavish scale, often
on behalf of Peter the Great,

who adopted the palace as a
pied-à-terre. Guests would
cross the Neva by boat and
arrive to the grand welcome
of a liveried orchestra.
The palace is now a branch
of the Hermitage *(see pp84–
93)* with exhibitions on early
18th-century Russian culture,
revealing the extent to which
Peter the Great's court was
influenced by Western tastes.
The conducted tour begins
on the ground floor; besides
the kitchen there are displays
of Peter's cabinet-making
tools, period costumes, sturdy
oak chests and ships' com-
passes. Adorning the beautiful
vaulted hallway are marble
statues imported from Italy
which include a Roman Apollo
dating to the 2nd century AD.
Upstairs, the secretary's
rooms are decorated with 17th-
century Dutch engravings of
Leyden, Utrecht and Kraków.
A series of breathtaking rooms
are lined with hand-painted
blue and white 18th-century
Dutch tiles. Tiles were not
only fashionable, but
also a very practical
means of deterring
flies and dust.
In the tiled bed-
room of Varvara
(Menshikov's
sister-in-law and
confidante) is a
German-made four-
poster bed, with a
Turkish coverlet
woven from cotton, silk
and silver thread. Hanging
behind it is an exquisite 17th-
century Flemish tapestry.
Menshikov and Peter often
received guests in the aptly
named Walnut Study which
has Persian walnut panelling
and commanding views of
the Neva. Paintings hang from
coloured ribbons, as was the

fashion, including a late 17th-
century portrait of Peter the
Great by the Dutch painter Jan
Weenix. The mirrors were a
novelty at that time and such
displays of vanity were ana-
thema to the Orthodox Church.
The Great Hall, decorated
in gold and stucco, is where
balls and banquets were held.
On one famous occasion, it
was the setting for a "dwarfs'
wedding" which Menshikov
arranged for the amusement
of his royal master.

**The fine, Style-Moderne *apteka*,
just off Bolshoy prospekt**

# Bolshoy Prospekt ❼
Большой проспект
*Bolshoy prospekt*

**Map** 1 A5. Ⓜ *Vasileostrovskaya.*
🚌 6, 7, 41, 42, 128, 151, 152,
K-346, K-350, K-690. 🚊 10.

This imposing avenue was
opened early in the 18th
century to connect Menshikov's
estate to the Gulf of Finland.
The mix of architectural
styles ranges from the elegant
Neo-Classicism of St Catherine's
Lutheran Church (1768–71) at
No. 1 to the simple Troyekurov
House (No. 13, 6-ya liniya) in
17th-century Petrine Baroque.
Other buildings of note include the arcaded St Andrew's
food market (1789–90) and
two Style-Moderne edifices.
One of these is the former
pharmacy or *apteka* (1907–10)
around the corner on 7-ya
liniya, and the other is
Adolph Gaveman's Lutheran
orphanage at No. 55 (1908).

---

## PRINCE MENSHIKOV

A leading advisor, com-
rade-in-arms and
friend of Peter the
Great, Aleksandr
Menshikov
(1673–1729)
rose from hum-
ble origins to
his position as
the first governor
of St Petersburg.
After Peter's death
in 1725, Menshikov
engineered the ascension
of Catherine I (Peter's wife,
and Menshikov's former
mistress) to the throne, thus
maintaining his power until
her demise. His notorious
extravagance and venality
eventually caught up with
him. Accused of treason,
he died in exile in 1729.

**The Academy of Arts (1764–88) on the Neva embankment, an example of early Russian Neo-Classicism**

# St Andrew's Cathedral ❽
Андреевский собор
*Andreevskiy sobor*

6-ya liniya 11. **Map** 5 B1. **Tel** *323 3418.* 7, 128, K-209. 10.

First built on the initiative of Peter the Great's second wife, Catherine I *(see p21)*, who donated 3,000 roubles towards its construction, the original wooden church on this site was destroyed by fire.

The present Baroque church with its distinctive steeple-like bell tower was constructed by Aleksandr Vist in 1764–80. The most stunning feature of the interior is the elaborately carved 18th-century icono-stasis which incorporates icons from the original church.

**The treasure of St Andrew's Cathedral, its beautiful Baroque iconostasis**

Situated next door is Giuseppe Trezzini's small Church of the Three Saints (1740–60) which is dedicated to SS Basil the Great, John Chrysostom and Gregory of Nazianzus.

# Academy of Arts ❾
Академия Художеств
*Akademiya Khudozhestv*

Universitetskaya naberezhnaya 17. **Map** 5 B1. **Tel** *323 3578.* 7, 47, K-147, K-209. 10. 11am–6pm Wed–Sun. www.rah.ru

Founded in 1757 to train home-grown artists in the preferred Western styles and techniques of art, the Academy spawned a galaxy of talent, including the great painter Ilya Repin *(see p42)* and architects Andrey Zakharov (1761–1811) and Andrey Voronikhin (1759–1814).

The innate con-servatism of the Academy tended to discourage innova-tion and experiment and in 1863 a band of 14 students walked out of their graduation exams in protest. They went on to found a realist art movement and became known as the Wanderers or *peredvizhniki (see pp106–7)*.

The imposing Academy, built be-tween 1764–1880 by Aleksandr Kokorinov and Vallin de la Mothe, is an exam-ple of the transition from Baroque to Neo-Classicism. Still

an art school, it exhibits the work of students past and present, including canvases, plaster casts of famous sculp-tures, architectural drawings and models of many of the city's notable buildings, such as the magnificent Smolnyy Convent *(see p128)*.

The splendid Neo-Classical halls and galleries, though faded, retain something of their original grandeur. Of note are the Conference Hall on the first floor, with its ceiling painting by Vasiliy Shebuev, and the adjoining Raphael and Titian galleries, adorned with copies of Vatican frescoes.

Flanking the river stairs outside the Academy are two sphinxes from the 14th century BC. Discovered among the ruins of Thebes in ancient Egypt, they were installed here in 1832. The faces are thought to bear a likeness of the pharaoh Amenhotep III.

# Blagoveshchenskiy Bridge ❿
Благовещенский Мост
*Blagoveshchenskiy Most*

**Map** 5 B2. 6, K-154, K-350.

Opened in 1842 with this name, this was the first per-manent crossing of the Neva. In 1855 the bridge was renamed Nicholas Bridge but in 1918, after the revolution, it was called Lieutenant Shmidt Bridge to commemorate a sailor who led an uprising of the Black Sea fleet in 1905. Reconstruction carried out in 1936–8 incorporated Aleksandr Bryullov's original railings, adorned with sea horses and tridents. In 2007 the bridge reverted to its original name.

# PETROGRADSKAYA

The city was founded on the northern banks of the Neva river in 1703, at the height of the Great Northern War (see p18). Building began with the construction of a wooden fortress and Petrogradskaya, or the Petrograd Side, soon became a marshy suburb of wooden cabins occupied by craftsmen working on Peter the Great's new city.

Nearby, the area around Trinity Square was originally a small merchants' quarter centred around a now demolished church and St Petersburg's first stock exchange.

**Detail on bridge to Peter and Paul Fortress**

Petrogradskaya was sparsely populated until the late 1890s when the construction of the Trinity Bridge made the area accessible from the city centre. The bridge caused a housing boom at the height of a fashion for Style-Moderne architecture which is still in evidence today. The population quadrupled and the area became very popular with artists and professionals.

The highlight of the area, which is still largely residential, is the Peter and Paul Fortress with its cathedral, museums and grim history.

## SIGHTS AT A GLANCE

**Museums**
Artillery Museum ⑦
Cabin of Peter the Great ⑬
Commandant's House ④
Cruiser Aurora ⑫
Engineer's House ②
Kirov Museum ⑩
Kshesinskaya Mansion ⑪
Trubetskoy Bastion ⑥

**Gates**
Neva Gate ⑤
St Peter's Gate ①

**Cathedrals**
Cathedral of SS Peter and Paul ③

**Streets, Squares and Parks**
Aleksandrovskiy Park ⑧
Kamennoostrovskiy Prospekt ⑨
Trinity Square ⑭

0 metres 400
0 yards 400

**KEY**

| | |
|---|---|
| ▨ | Street-by-Street map *See pp66–7* |
| Ⓜ | Metro |
| 🚊 | Tram stop |
| ⛴ | River boat stop |

◁ The Baroque Cathedral of SS Peter and Paul in the Peter and Paul Fortress

# Street-by-Street: Peter and Paul Fortress

The founding of the Peter and Paul Fortress on 27 May 1703, on the orders of Peter the Great, is considered to mark the founding of the city. It was first built in wood and was later replaced, section by section, in stone by Domenico Trezzini. Its history is a gruesome one, since hundreds of forced labourers died while building the fortress and its bastions were later used to guard and torture many political prisoners, including Peter's own son Aleksey.

The cells where prisoners were once kept are open to the public, alongside a couple of museums and the magnificent cathedral which houses the tombs of the Romanovs.

**The Archives of the War Ministry** occupy the site of the "Secret House", a prison for political criminals in the 18th and 19th centuries.

**Artillery Museum** *(see p70)*

**Kronverkskiy most**

**Zotov Bastion**

**Trubetskoy Bastion**
*From 1872–1921 the dark, damp, solitary-confinement cells in the bastion served as a grim prison for enemies of the state. Today, the bastion is open to visitors* **6**

**The Mint,** founded in 1724, still produces ceremonial coins, medals and badges.

**The Naryshkin Bastion** (1725) is where the noon cannon is fired. The tradition began in 1873, stopped after the revolution and was resumed in 1957.

**The beach** is popular in summer and in winter, when members of the "walruses" swimming club break the ice for an invigorating dip.

**Commandant's House**
*For 150 years this attractive Baroque house was the scene of interrogations and trials of political prisoners. It now houses a museum of local history* **4**

**Neva Gate**
*This riverside entrance, also known as "Death Gateway", leads to the Commandant's pier from which prisoners embarked on their journey to execution or exile. The Neva river's flood levels (see p37) are recorded under the arch* **10**

★ **Cathedral of SS Peter and Paul**
*Marbled columns, glittering chandeliers and painted decor combine with Ivan Zarudnyy's carved and gilded iconostasis to create a magnificent setting for the tombs of the Romanov monarchs* ❸

**The Boat House** is now a ticket office and souvenir shop.

**LOCATOR MAP**
*See Street Finder, map 2*

**Golovkin Bastion**

**The Grand Ducal burial vault** is the last resting place of several Grand Dukes shot by the Bolsheviks in 1919 and of Grand Duke Vladimir who died in exile in 1992.

**St Peter's Gate**
*The entrance to the fortress, by Domentco Trezzini, completed in 1718, features the Romanov double eagle with an emblem of St George and the dragon* ❶

**STAR SIGHT**

★ SS Peter and Paul Cathedral

| 0 metres | 100 |
|---|---|
| 0 yards | 100 |

**Ioannovskiy Ravelin** contains a ticket office.

**Ivan Gate**, in the outer wall, was constructed from 1731–40.

**Ioannovskiy most**

**Kamennoostrovskiy prospekt, Gorkovskaya Metro and Trinity Bridge**

This statue of **Peter the Great** is by Mikhail Chemiakin (1991).

**Peter I Bastion**

**Engineer's House**
*This building, dating from 1748–9, houses temporary exhibitions of artifacts used in everyday life in St Petersburg before the revolution* ❷

**KEY**

— — — Suggested route

## St Peter's Gate ❶
Петровские ворота
*Petrovskie vorota*

Petropavlovskaya krepost. **Map** 2
E3. Ⓜ *Gorkovskaya.* 🚌 *46, 49,
K-46, K-76, K-223.*

The main entrance to the
Peter and Paul Fortress is
through two contrasting arches.
The plain Neo-Renaissance
Ivan Gate (1730s) leads to the
more imposing St Peter's Gate
(1708–18), an ornate Baroque
structure with scrolled wings
and a rounded-gable pediment.
Domenico Trezzini redesigned
the Peter Gate, retaining Karl
Osner's expressively carved
bas-relief which allegorizes
Peter the Great's victory over
Charles XII of Sweden *(see
p18)*. It depicts St Peter
casting down the winged
sorcerer Simon Magus.

**Peter Gate, entrance to fortress**

## Engineer's House ❷
Инженерный дом
*Inzhenernyy dom*

Petropavlovskaya krepost. **Map** 2 D3.
**Tel** *232 9454, 230 0329.*
Ⓜ *Gorkovskaya.* ◯ *11am–5pm
Thu–Mon, 11am–4pm Tue.* 🈺
🎫 *English.* **www**.spbmuseum.ru

The Engineer's House, built
in 1748–9, has a changing
exhibition which gives a
fascinating glimpse of daily
life in St Petersburg before
the Revolution. Architectural
backdrops and historical paintings give way to an engaging
miscellany of artifacts, ranging
from model boats to duelling
pistols and court costumes.
    In 1915 there were more
than 100 outlets selling musical
instruments in the city and the

**An accordion and organ surrounded by Style-
Moderne furniture, Engineer's House**

museum displays an excellent
collection which includes
phonographs, gramophones,
symphoniums and piano
accordions of the period.
    A section on vintage tech-
nology features Singer sewing
machines, typewriters, Bakelite
telephones and box cameras.

## Cathedral of SS Peter and Paul ❸
Петропавловский собор
*Petropavlovskiy sobor*

Petropavlovskaya krepost. **Map** 2 D4.
**Tel** *232 9454.* Ⓜ *Gorkovskaya.*
◯ *10am–6pm Thu–Mon, 11am–
5pm Tue.* 🈺 🎫 *English.*
**www**.spbmuseum.ru

Domenico Trezzini designed
this magnificent church
within the fortress in 1712.
Employed by Peter the Great,
who wished to turn his back
on traditional Russian church

architecture, Trezzini
produced a Baroque
masterpiece of
singular elegance.
The bell tower was
completed first to
test the foundations
and this served as
an excellent view-
point from which
Peter could oversee
the construction
work of his new
city. The cathedral
was surrounded in
1733, but was badly
damaged by fire in
1756 when the soaring 122-m
(400-ft) spire was struck by
lightning. The gilded needle
spire, crowned by a weather-
vane angel, remained the
tallest structure in St Petersburg until the building of the
TV transmitter in the 1960s.
    The interior, with its glitter-
ing chandeliers, pink and
green Corinthian columns and
overarching vaults, is also a
far cry from the traditional
Russian Orthodox church.
Even the iconostasis is a
Baroque flight of fancy. This
masterpiece of gilded wood-
carving was designed by Ivan
Zarudnyy and executed in the
1720s by Moscow craftsmen.
    After Peter's death in 1725,
the cathedral became the last
resting place of the tsars. The
sarcophagi are all of a uniform
white Carrara marble, except
the tombs of Alexander II and
his wife Maria Alexandrovna,
which are carved from Altai

**Cathedral of SS Peter and Paul, with Dvortsovyy most in foreground**

PETROGRADSKAYA **6 9**

jasper and Ural rhodonite.
Peter the Great's tomb lies to
the right of the iconostasis.

The only tsars who are not
buried here are Peter II, Ivan
VI and, until recently,
Nicholas II. In 1998 a
controversial decision was
taken to rebury the remains
of the last Romanov tsar, his
wife and children, and the
servants that died together
with them, in a chapel by the
entrance to the cathedral.

The Grand Ducal Mauso-
leum, where relatives of the
tsars are buried, was added to
the northeast of the cathedral
at the end of the 19th century.

# Commandant's House ❹
Комендантский дом
*Komendantskiy dom*

Petropavlovskaya krepost. **Map** 2 D4.
***Tel*** 232 9454. Ⓜ *Gorkovskaya.*
◻ *10am–6pm Thu–Mon, 11am–*
*5pm Tue.* 🖼 🖪 *English.*

Dating from the 1740s, the
plain brick, two-storey
Commandant's House served
both as the residence of the
fortress commander and as a
courthouse. Over the years,
political prisoners, including
the Decembrist rebels *(see
p23)*, were brought here for
interrogation and sentencing.

The house is now a museum,
with a ground-floor exhibition
on medieval settlements in
the St Petersburg region, and
temporary exhibitions upstairs.

# Neva Gate ❺
Невскине ворота
*Nevskie vorota*

Petropavlovskaya krepost. **Map** 2 E4.
Ⓜ *Gorkovskaya.*

This austere river entrance
to the fortress was once
known as the "Death Gate".
Prisoners to be transported
to the even more notorious
Schlüsselburg Fortress (to
the east of St Petersburg) for
capital punishment, or to a
"living death" in penal servitude, were led down the
granite steps and taken away
by boat. The appropriately
dour, grey gateway dates from

**Neva Gate leading from the river into the Peter and Paul Fortress**

1730–40 (reconstructed in
1784–7) and is unornamented
apart from an anchor in the
pediment. In the archway,
brass plaques mark record
flood levels. The catastrophic
inundation of November 1824
is the one commemorated in
Pushkin's poem, *The Bronze
Horseman (see p78).*

# Trubetskoy Bastion ❻
Трубецкой бастион
*Trubetskoy bastion*

Petropavlovskaya krepost. **Map** 2 D4.
***Tel*** 232 9454. Ⓜ *Gorkovskaya.*
◻ *10am–6pm Thu–Mon, 11am–*
*5pm Tue.* 🖼 🖪 *English.*

Peter the Great's son, the
Tsarevich Aleksey, was the first
political prisoner to be
detained in the grim fortress
prison. Unjustly accused of
treason in 1718 by his over-
bearing father, Aleksey escaped
abroad only to be lured back
to Russia with the promise of a

pardon. Instead, he was
tortured and beaten to death,
almost certainly with Peter's
consent and participation.

For the next 100 years prisoners were incarcerated in the
much feared Secret House,
since demolished. In 1872 a
new prison block opened in
the Trubetskoy Bastion which
has existed as a museum since
1924. On the ground floor
there is a small exhibition of
period photographs, prison
uniforms and a model of the
guardroom. Upstairs are 69
isolation cells, restored to their
original appearance, while
downstairs there are two un-
heated, unlit punishment cells
where the recalcitrant were
locked up for 48 hours at a
time. Once every two weeks,
all detainees were taken to the
Bath House in the exercise
yard for de-lousing. Here
prisoners were also put in
irons before being carted off to
penal servitude in Siberia.

**POLITICAL PRISONERS**

The fortress' sinister role as a prison for political activists
continued until after the Revolution. Generations of rebels
and anarchists were interrogated and imprisoned here,
including Leon Trotsky in the
wake of the 1905 Revolution.
Other prominent detainees were
the leading Decembrists in 1825
*(see p23)*, Dostoevsky in 1849
*(see p123)* and, in 1874–6, the
anarchist Prince Pyotr Kropotkin.
In 1917 it was the turn first of
the tsar's ministers, then of
members of the Provisional
Government. Then, in the Civil
War *(see p27)*, the Bolsheviks
held hostage four Romanov
Grand Dukes who were subsequently executed in 1919.

**Leon Trotsky (1879–1940) in
the Trubetskoy Bastion**

**Rocket launcher in the courtyard of the Artillery Museum**

## Artillery Museum ❼
Музей Артиллерии
*Muzey Artillerii*

Alexandrovskiy Park 7, Kronverk-
skaya Embankment. **Map** 2 D3.
***Tel*** *232 0296.* Ⓜ *Gorkovskaya.*
◯ *11am–5pm Wed–Sun.* ◉ *last
Thu each month.* 🖼

This vast, horseshoe-shaped
building in red brick stands on
the site of the Kronverk, the
outer fortifications of the
Peter and Paul Fortress *(see
pp66–7)*. Designed by Pyotr
Tamanskiy and constructed in
1849–60, the building was
originally used as the arsenal.
   More than 600 pieces of artillery and military vehicles
include tanks and the armoured
car in which Lenin rode in
triumph from Finland Station
*(see p126)* to Kshesinskaya
Mansion *(see p72)* on 3 April
1917. There are uniforms,
regimental flags, muskets and
small arms dating to medieval
times, as well as several rooms
devoted to World War II.

## Aleksandrovskiy Park ❽
Александровский парк
*Aleksandrovskiy park*

Kronverkskiy prospekt. **Map** 2 D3.
Ⓜ *Gorkovskaya.* ♿

The park's unique character
as a centre of popular culture
and entertainment was
established in the year 1900
with the inauguration of the
Nicholas II People's House.
This was where pantomime
artists, wild animal trainers,
magicians and circus acts

entertained the crowds, while
the more serious-minded were
drawn to the lecture halls,
reading galleries and tea
rooms. The *pièce de résistance*
was the magnificent domed
Opera House (1911), where
the legendary bass singer,
Fyodor Chaliapin, sometimes
gave performances.
   Today the Opera
House offers less
highbrow entertain-
ment, as its change
of name to Music Hall
suggests. The adjoin-
ing 1930s buildings
include the innovative
Baltic House Theatre,
the Planetarium and a
waxworks museum.
   The park still draws crowds
on summer weekends and
public holidays, although some
of the attractions, especially
the zoo, are now rather tawdry.

## Kamennoostrovskiy Prospekt ❾
Каменноостровский проспект
*Kamennoostrovskiy prospekt*

**Map** 2 D2. Ⓜ *Gorkovskaya or Petrogradskaya.* 🚌 *46, K-30, K-76, K-223.*

Developed during the con-
struction boom of the late
1890s, this eye-catching avenue
is noted for its Style-Moderne
architecture. The first house,
at No. 1–3 (1899–1904) was
designed by Fyodor Lidval.
The multi-textured façade,
windows of contrasting shapes
and sizes, ornate iron balconies and fanciful carvings
are the most typical features
of this Russian version of Art
Nouveau. The neighbouring

house (No. 5) was once occupied by Count Sergey Witte,
a leading industrialist who
negotiated the peace treaty
with Japan in 1905 *(see p26)*.
   Situated just off the start of
the avenue is the city's only
mosque (1910–14). Designed
by Russian architects, its minarets, majolica tiling and the
rough granite surfaces of the
walls are fully in keeping with
the surrounding Style-Moderne
architecture. The mosque was,
in fact, modelled on the
Mausoleum of Tamerlane in
Samarkand and involved
Central Asian craftsmen.
   At No. 10 is the tall portico
of the Leningrad Film Studios
(Lenfilm). It was on this site,
in May 1896, that the Lumière
brothers showed the first moving picture in Russia. Since its
founding in 1918, some of the
most innovative Soviet film
directors such as Leonid Trauberg and Grigoriy
Kozintsev *(see p45)*
have worked there.
   At the intersection
with ulitsa Mira, each
house has indivi-
dually designed
turrets, spires, reliefs
and iron balconies,
forming a handsome
Style-Moderne
ensemble. Other buildings of
interest include No. 24
(1896–1912), with its red
brick majolica and terracotta
façade; No. 26–28 where
Sergey Kirov lived *(see p72)*;
and on the corner of Bolshoy
prospekt, the "Turreted House"
with its Neo-Gothic portal.

**Griffon, No. 1–3
Kamennoostrovskiy**

**Turreted House (1913–15),
Kamennoostrovskiy prospekt**

# Style Moderne in St Petersburg

**Kshesinskaya
Mansion railing detail**

In vogue throughout Europe from the 1890s to the 1900s, Art Nouveau marked a break with imitation of the past. The movement, known as Style Moderne in Russia, began in the decorative arts and was then reflected in architecture, where it led to an abundance of ornamental elements. Inspired by new industrial techniques, artists and architects made lavish use of natural stone and brick, wrought iron, stucco, coloured glass and ceramic tiles.

Dominated by sinuous and undulating lines, with a predominance of floral and vegetal elements, even traditional forms such as doors and windows are broken up, distorted or given unexpected curves.

In fin-de-siècle St Petersburg, the Style Moderne flourished as the city underwent a building boom, particularly on Petrogradskaya. The city became a showcase for the talents of leading architects such as Fyodor Lidval and Aleksandr von Gogen.

**Kshesinskaya Mansion** *reveals von Gogen's relatively severe version of Style Moderne. Asymmetrical in composition, it is enlivened with wrought iron and glazed tiles* (see p72).

**Yeliseev's** *is evidence of the skill of Gavriil Baranovsky, who made excellent use of industrial techniques in the creation of large window spaces. The rich exterior detailing is matched by elegant shop-fittings and chandeliers inside* (see p109).

**28 Bolshaya Zelenina ulitsa** *is one of the most outstanding examples of the use of stylized animal and fish motifs and a variety of surface decoration techniques. Fyodor von Postel's 1904–5 apartment block is reminiscent of the work of his contemporary, the Catalan architect Gaudí.*

**1–3 Kamennoostrovskiy pr** *is the work of St Petersburg's master of Style Moderne, Fyodor Lidval. Delicate details such as floral and animal reliefs stand out against a background of discreetly elongated proportions and unusual window shapes.*

**Singer House** *(1910–14) reveals Pavel Syuzor's use of an unusually eclectic mix of architectural styles. Ornate Style-Moderne wrought-iron balconies and decorative wooden window frames combine with elements of Renaissance and Baroque revivals.*

**Portrait of Sergey Kirov (1930s), in the Kirov Museum**

# Kirov Museum ⑩

Музей С. М. Кирова
*Muzey S M Kirova*

Kamennoostrovskiy prospekt 26–28, 4th floor. **Map** 2 D1. *Tel* 346 0217, 346 0289. Ⓜ *Petrogradskaya.* ⬤ *11am–6pm Thu–Mon (5pm Tue).* 🈂 🅴 English. **www**.spbmuseum.ru

From 1926–36 this flat was home to one of Stalin's closest political associates, Sergey Kirov. As the charismatic first Secretary of the Leningrad Communist Party, Kirov soon gained national importance. His increasing popularity led Stalin to see in him a potential rival. On 1 December 1934, Kirov was gunned down at his office at the Smolnyy Institute *(see p128)* by Leonid Nikolaev, a party malcontent. Stalin used the assassination as an excuse to launch the Great Purges *(see p27)*, although most historians believe Stalin himself was behind Kirov's murder.

Kirov acquired the status of a martyr after his death, with countless buildings named in his honour. His apartment, preserved as it was in his lifetime, is an example of the near cult status awarded Party leaders, with documents and photographs chronicling his political career, and a touching array of memorabilia including his shooting attire and favourite books.

# Kshesinskaya Mansion ⑪

Особняк М. Кшесинской
*Osobnyak M Kshesinskoy*

Ulitsa Kuybysheva 4. **Map** 2 E3. *Tel* 233 7052. Ⓜ *Gorkovskaya.* ⬤ *10am–6pm Fri–Wed.* ⬤ *last Mon of month.* 🈂 🅴 *English.* **www**.polithistory.ru

This remarkable example of Style-Moderne architecture was commissioned for prima ballerina Matilda Kshesinskaya. Designed in 1904 by the court architect, A von Gogen, the building is almost playfully asymmetric with a single, octagonal tower. Most eye-catching of all are the many contrasting building materials with bands of pink and grey granite, cream-coloured bricks, delicately ornamented iron railings and majolica tiles.

The most impressive interior is the splendid recital hall with its pillared archway and palms. Nearby, the Kshesinskaya memorial room has some of the dancer's possessions, including sketches of Nicholas II.

In March 1917 the mansion was commandeered by the Bolsheviks and became their headquarters and, on Lenin's return to Russia *(see p126)*, he addressed the crowds from the balcony facing the square. The mansion, previously home to a museum glorifying the October Revolution, now houses a Museum of Russian Political History. On the first floor the Bolshevik Party secretariat and Lenin's office have been faithfully restored. Upstairs is a fascinating collection of memorabilia from the revolutionary era, including Communist posters, Nicholas II coronation mugs and even a police file on Rasputin's murder *(see p121)*.

The museum has temporary exhibitions covering recent political history, taking in the theory and consequences of perestroika and the policies of contemporary parties.

## MATILDA KSHESINSKAYA

One of the finest prima ballerinas ever to grace the stage of the Mariinskiy Theatre *(see p119)*, Matilda Kshesinskaya (1872–1971) graduated from the Imperial Ballet School *(see p118)* in 1890. She was equally famous for her celebrated affair with the tsarevich, later Tsar Nicholas II, which began soon after she graduated. Kshesinskaya emigrated to Paris in 1920 where she married the Grand Duke Andrey Vladimirovich, another member of the imperial family and the father of her 11-year old son. It was in Paris that she wrote her controversial memoirs, *Dancing in St Petersburg*, which tells the tale of her affair with the last Russian tsar.

**A von Gogen's elegant recital hall in the Kshesinskaya Mansion**

The historic cruiser Aurora (1900), moored in front of the Neo-Baroque Nakhimov Naval Academy (1912)

## Cruiser Aurora ⑫
Крейсер Аврора
*Kreyser Avrora*

---

Petrogradskaya naberezhnaya 3.
**Map** 2 F3. **Tel** 230 8440. 🚌 14.
🚊 3, 6, 40. ⬜ 10:30am–4pm Tue–
Thu, Sat & Sun. 🗣 English, German
or French, for a fee. Phone to book.

According to the annals of the Revolution, at 9:40pm on 25 October 1917, the cruiser *Aurora* signalled the storming of the Winter Palace *(see p28)*, by firing a single blank round from its bow gun.

The ship entered active service in 1903. It was later converted into a training ship and at the start of the Siege of Leningrad *(see p27)* it was sunk to protect it from German forces. The ship was raised in 1944, 950 days later, and has been a museum since 1956. The famous gun, bell and the crew's quarters can be viewed, along with an exhibition on the history of the *Aurora*.

## Cabin of Peter the Great ⑬
Музей-домик Петра I
*Muzey-domik Petra I*

---

Petrovskaya naberezhnaya 6. **Map**
2 F3. **Tel** 232 4576, 314 0374.
Ⓜ Gorkovskaya. ⬜ 10am–5:30pm
Wed–Sun. 🖼 ♿

This pine-log cabin was built for Peter the Great by his soldier-carpenters in just three days in 1703. Peter lived here for six years while overseeing the construction of his new

city *(see pp20–21)*. Catherine the Great, ever keen to glorify Peter, had a protective brick shell erected around the cabin.

There are only two rooms, both with period furnishings, and a hallway which doubled as a bedroom. Among Peter's personal possessions are a compass, a frock coat and his rowing boat.

Adorning the steps outside are two statues of the Shih Tze frog-lions, brought from Manchuria during the Russo-Japanese War (1904–5).

## Trinity Square ⑭
Тройцкая площадь
*Troitskaya ploshchad*

---

**Map** 2 E3. Ⓜ Gorkovskaya. 🚌 46.
🚊 6, 40.

Throughout the early 18th century, the whole of Petrogradskaya was known as Trinity Island. The name was derived from the Church of the Trinity (built in 1710; demolished 1930s) in Trinity Square, which formed the nucleus of the city's merchant quarter. In 2002–3 the Trinity Chapel was built here to honour the 300th anniversary of St Petersburg. Despite having no direct links to the mainland until the early 20th century, the area flourished with shops, a printing house and the city's first stock exchange.

In the 1905 Revolution *(see p26)* the square witnessed the massacre of 48 workers, killed by government troops. During the Communist era, the square became known as ploshchad Revolyutsii.

From the square, across the widest point of the Neva, the Style-Moderne Trinity Bridge *(see p35)* stretches nearly 600 m (1,970 ft). Its construction led to a building boom on Petrogradskaya *(see p65)* and its completion in 1903 coincided with the city's bicentenary.

The ornate Trinity Bridge, crossing the Neva from Trinity Square

# PALACE EMBANKMENT

In terms of sheer scale and grandeur, St Petersburg's magnificent south waterfront has few equals. Its formidable granite quays, stretching over 2 km (1 mile) from the Senate building in the west to Peter the Great's Summer Palace in the east, and the surrounding area of stately aristocratic palaces and ornamental canal bridges are justly famous worldwide.

Every aspect of the city's history is juxtaposed in this rich area. Falconet's statue of Peter the Great, the Bronze Horseman, is an eloquent testimony to imperial ambition while the square in which it stands is named in honour of the Decembrist rebels who rose up against the tsarist regime in 1825. In Palace Square, Rastrelli's Winter Palace (part of the Hermitage) evokes the opulence of Imperial Russia while the Eternal Flame, flickering in the Field of Mars, is a more sombre reminder of revolutionary sacrifice.

Dominating St Petersburg's skyline are the magnificent dome of St Isaac's Cathedral and the gilded spire of the Admiralty. Some of the best views can be appreciated by making a boat trip along the waterways (see pp226–7), or by strolling through the Summer Garden.

**Alexander Column, Palace Square**

## SIGHTS AT A GLANCE

**Palaces and Gardens**
Marble Palace ⑭
Summer Garden ⑯
Summer Palace ⑰

**Museums**
The Hermitage pp84–93 ⑫

**Historical Buildings and Monuments**
The Admiralty ①
The Bronze Horseman ③
Horseguards' Manège ④
House of Fabergé ⑨

**Churches**
St Isaac's Cathedral pp80–81 ⑤

**Streets and Squares**
Decembrists' Square ②
Field of Mars ⑮
Malaya Morskaya Ulitsa ⑧
Millionaires' Street ⑬
Palace Square ⑪
St Isaac's Square ⑥

**Hotels and Cafés**
Astoria Hotel ⑦
Literary Café ⑩

| 0 metres | 400 |
| 0 yards | 400 |

## KEY

Street-by-Street map
See pp76–7

River boat stop

◁ **The golden dome of St Isaac's Cathedral above elegant façades along the Neva**

# Street-by-Street: St Isaac's Square

**Detail from the frieze on the Admiralty gate tower**

The highlight of St Isaac's Square is the imposing cathedral at its centre, which opened in 1858 and is the fourth church to stand on this site. The cathedral, and subsequently the square, were named after St Isaac of Dalmatia, because Peter the Great's birthday fell on this saint's day. The busy square, used as a market place in the first half of the 19th century, is now at the heart of an area teeming with buildings and statues of historical and architectural interest. Among them are the Admiralty, the Mariinskiy Palace and the Bronze Horseman.

**Horseguards' Manège**
*Built in 1804–7 by Giacomo Quarenghi, this building housed the Life Guards' Mounted Regiment* ❹

**The Bronze Horseman**
*Etienne Falconet's magnificent statue of Peter the Great, his horse trampling the serpent of treason, captures the spirit of the city's uncompromising and wilful founder* ❸

**Decembrists' Square**
*Dominating the western side of the square are Carlo Rossi's monumental Senate and Synod buildings, linked by a triumphal arch* ❷

**The Glory Columns**, topped by bronze angels, were erected in 1845–6.

**Myatlev House**

★ **St Isaac's Cathedral**
*The magnificent golden dome of the cathedral is visible all across the city. 100kg (220lb) of gold leaf were needed to cover the dome's surface* ❺

**The Former German Embassy** was designed by Peter Behrens in 1911–12.

| 0 metres | 100 |
|---|---|
| 0 yards | 100 |

The Hermitage and Winter Palace

LOCATOR MAP
See Street Finder maps 2, 5 & 6

### The Admiralty
*Sculptures and reliefs, celebrating the power of Russia's navy, decorate the Admiralty's façade. The archway of the main entrance is framed by nymphs carrying globes on their shoulders* ❶

**Former Prince Lobanov-Rostovskiy Mansion** is now a design institute. The lions in front of the arcade are by Italian sculptor Paolo Triscorni.

ADMIRALTEYSKIY PROSPEKT

GOROKHOVAYA UL

VOZNESENSKIY PROSPEKT

Nevskiy prospekt

MAL MORSKAYA UL

**The Former Ministry of State Property,** designed by Nikolay Yefimov in 1844, is a fine example of Neo-Renaissance architecture.

MORSKAYA UL

REKI MOYKI

Siniy most *(see p79)*

**The Mariinskiy Palace,** named in honour of Maria, daughter of Nicholas I, now houses the St Petersburg city hall.

**KEY**

– – – Suggested route

**STAR SIGHT**

★ St Isaac's Cathedral

### Angleterre Hotel
*The elegant ground floor hallway of the Angleterre Hotel (see p174) reflects the major refurbishment undertaken in the early 1990s. Now under new management, the hotel enjoys an enviable location in the heart of the city* ❼

### St Isaac's Square
*Overlooking the square is Pyotr Klodt's statue of Tsar Nicholas I. The reliefs on the pedestal depict episodes from his reign. Tellingly, two of them show the suppression of rebellions* ❻

# The Admiralty ❶
Адмиралтейство
*Admiralteystvo*

Admiralteyskaya naberezhnaya 2.
**Map** 5 C1 🚌 *7, 10, K-187, K-209, K-228.* 🚊 *1, 7, 10, 17, 22.*

Having founded a city and built a fortress, Peter the Great's next priority was to create a Russian navy to guarantee access to the sea and dominance over Sweden.

The Admiralty began life as a fortified shipyard built on this site between 1704–11. Two years later, some 10,000 men were employed in building the first battleships of the embryonic Russian navy.

One of Russia's most inspired architects, Andrey Zakharov, began to rebuild the Admiralty in 1806. The remarkable façade is 407 m (1,335 ft) in length and is adorned with an abundance of sculptures and reliefs which document the glory of the Russian fleet. Zakharov retained some of the original features, including the central gate tower and spire which he recast in Neo-Classical style with columned porticos and pavilions. The heightened spire was gilded and topped with a model frigate. This has become a symbol of the city, just like the trumpet-blowing pair of angels on the portals of the façade overlooking the Neva.

In the 1840s, shipbuilding was moved downstream and the Admiralty was handed over to the Russian navy. It has been occupied by the Naval Engineering School since 1925.

Tower and spire of the Admiralty (1806–23)

# Decembrists' Square ❷
Площадь Декабристов
*Ploshchad Dekabristov*

**Map** 5 C1. 🚌 *3, 10, 22, 27.* 🚊 *5, 22.*

The name of this square alludes to the momentous event which took place here on 14 December 1825 *(see p23)*. During the inauguration of Nicholas I, Guards officers intent on imposing a constitutional monarchy attempted to stage a coup d'état in the square. After a confused stand-off which lasted several hours, the rebel forces were routed with grapeshot by the new tsar and loyalist troops. Five of the ringleaders were later executed and 121 others

exiled to Siberia, thus effectively ending Russia's first revolution.

The imposing Neo-Classical buildings that command the western side of Decembrists' Square were intended to harmonize with the Admiralty. Designed by Carlo Rossi between 1829–34, they were the headquarters of two important institutions which were originally created by Peter the Great: the Supreme Court, or Senate, and the Holy Synod which was responsible for the administration of the Orthodox Church. The two buildings, which now house historical archives, are linked to each other by a triumphal arch supported by Corinthian columns and decorated with a Neo-Classical frieze and a plethora of statuary.

The Bronze Horseman (1766–78)

# The Bronze Horseman ❸
Медный Всадник
*Mednyy Vsadnik*

*Ploshchad Dekabristov.* **Map** 5 C1. 🚌 *3, 10, 22, 27.* 🚊 *5, 22.*

The magnificent equestrian statue of Peter the Great was unveiled in Decembrists' Square in 1782, as a tribute from Catherine the Great. The statue is known as the Bronze Horseman after Pushkin's famous poem. A French sculptor, Etienne Falconet, spent more than 12 years overseeing this ambitious project. The pedestal alone weighs

---

## THE BRONZE HORSEMAN BY PUSHKIN

1956 stamp of Pushkin and the statue that inspired his poem

The famous statue of Peter the Great is brought to life in Alexander Pushkin's epic poem *The Bronze Horseman* (1833). In this haunting vision of the Great Flood of 1824 *(see p37)*, the hero is pursued through the mist-shrouded streets by the terrifying bronze statue. Pushkin's words evoke the domineering and implacable will for which the tsar was renowned: *"How terrible he was in the surrounding gloom! … what strength was in him! And in that steed, what fire!"*

1,625 tonnes and was hewn from a single block of granite, which was hauled from the Gulf of Finland. It bears the simple inscription "To Peter I from Catherine II" in Latin and Russian. A serpent, symbolizing treason, is crushed beneath the horse's hooves.

Newlyweds often pose for photographs under the statue which is meant to bring luck.

## Horseguards' Manège ❹

Конногвардейский манеж
*Konnogvardeyskiy manezh*

Isaakievskaya ploshchad 1. **Map** 5 C2. *Tel* 312 2243, 571 4157 *(ticket office).* ⬤ *variable.* 🚌 3, 22, 27. 🚋 5, 22. 📷 ▢

The enormous indoor riding school of the Life Guards' Mounted Regiment was built by Giacomo Quarenghi in 1804–7 to resemble a Roman basilica. Two clues to the building's original function are the dynamic frieze of a horse race beneath the pediment and the statues on either side of the portico. The statues of the unclad twin sons of Zeus reining in wild horses are copies from the Quirinale Palace in Rome. The Holy Synod, scandalized by this display of nakedness so near to St Isaac's Cathedral, ordered their removal. The statues were re-erected in 1954.

Next to the manège, which is now used as an exhibition hall, are two marble pillars surmounted by bronze angels cast in Berlin, which were sent over as a gift in 1840.

## St Isaac's Cathedral ❺

*See pp80–81.*

## St Isaac's Square ❻

Исаакиевская площадь
*Issakievskaya ploshchad*

**Map** 5 C2. 🚌 3, 10, 22, 27. 🚋 5, 22.

Dominated by Auguste de Montferrand's majestic St Isaac's Cathedral, this impressive square was created during the reign of Nicholas I,

St Isaac's Cathedral, statue of St Nicholas I and the Astoria, St Isaac's Square

although a few of its earlier buildings date from the 18th century. The monument to Nicholas I at its centre was also designed by Montferrand. Erected in 1859 and sculpted by Pyotr Klodt, it depicts the tsar in the uniform of one of Russia's most prestigious regiments, the Kavalergardskiy guards. The pedestal is embellished with allegorical sculptures of his daughters and his wife who represent Faith, Wisdom, Justice and Might.

On the western side of the square at No. 9, the Myatlev House is a Neo-Classical mansion, dating from the 1760s, which belonged to one of Russia's most illustrious families. The French encyclopedist, Denis Diderot, stayed here in 1773–4 following an invitation from Catherine the Great. In the 1920s it became the premises of the State Institute of Artistic Culture where some of Russia's most influential avant-garde artists, including Kazimir Malevich and Vladimir Tatlin *(see p107)*, worked.

The forbidding granite-faced building alongside is the former German embassy, designed in 1911–12 by the German architect, Peter Behrens.

Across the 100-m (330-ft) wide Siniy most (Blue Bridge), which was the site of a serf market until 1861, the Mariinskiy Palace *(see p77)* dominates the southern end of the square.

## Astoria Hotel ❼

Гостиница Астория
*Gostinitsa Astoriya*

Bolshaya Morskaya ulitsa 39. **Map** 6 D2. *Tel* 494 5757. 🚌 3, 10, 22, 27, K-169, K-190, K-289. 🚋 5, 22. *See Where to Stay p180.*

Now one of St Petersburg's leading hotels, the sevenstorey Astoria was designed by Fyodor Lidval in the Style Moderne *(see p71)* in 1910–12.

American writer, John Reed, author of the famous eyewitness account of the Revolution *Ten Days that Shook the World*, was staying here when the Bolsheviks seized power.

In 1925, the poet Sergey Yesenin, husband of Isadora Duncan, hanged himself in the annexe, after daubing the walls of his room with a farewell verse in his blood "To die is not new – but neither is it new to be alive".

The hotel's banqueting hall was to be the venue for Hitler's prematurely planned victory celebration, so sure was he that he would conquer the city.

Restored Style-Moderne foyer in the Astoria Hotel, on the eastern edge of St Isaac's Square

# St Isaac's Cathedral ❺

Исаакиевский собор
*Isaakievskiy sobor*

St Isaac's, one of the world's largest cathedrals, was designed in 1818 by the then unknown architect Auguste de Montferrand. The construction of the colossal building was a major engineering feat. Thousands of wooden piles were sunk into the marshy ground to support its weight of 300,000 tonnes and 48 huge columns were hauled into place. The cathedral opened in 1858 but was designated a museum of atheism during the Soviet era. Officially still a museum today, the church is filled with hundreds of impressive 19th-century works of art.

**The Dome**
*From the dome there are panoramic views over the city which include the Admiralty (see p78) and the Hermitage (see pp84–93). Adorning the gilded dome are angels sculpted by Josef Hermann.*

**The mosaic icons** on the iconostasis are by Bryullov, Neff and Zhivago.

**Angels with Torch**
*Ivan Vitali created many of the cathedral's sculptures, including the pairs of angels supporting gas torches which crown the four attic corners.*

**This chapel** honours Alexander Nevsky who defeated the Swedes in 1240 *(see p17)*.

★ **Iconostasis**
*Three rows of icons surround the royal doors through which a stained-glass window (1843) is visible. Above the doors is Pyotr Klodt's gilded sculpture,* Christ in Majesty *(1859).*

**The north pediment** is ornamented with a bronze relief (1842–4) of the Resurrection designed by François Lemaire.

**Malachite** and lapis lazuli columns frame the iconostasis. About 16,000 kg (35,280 lbs) of malachite decorate the cathedral.

**Exit**

**St Catherine's Chapel** has an exquisite white marble iconostasis, crowned by a sculpted Resurrection (1850–4) by Nikolay Pimenov.

The silver dove (1850) hanging in the cupola is a symbol of the Holy Spirit.

**★ Ceiling Painting**
*The celestial* Virgin in Majesty *by Karl Bryullov (see p105), dating to 1847, covers an area of 816 sq m (8,780 sq ft). It is ringed by exuberant gilded stucco mouldings and white marble.*

**Portraits of apostles and evangelists**

**Statue of St Matthew**

**The entrance** is through the side doors on St Isaac's Square.

**South Doors**
*Three great doors of oak and bronze (1841–6), weighing 20 tonnes, are decorated with carved reliefs by Ivan Vitali. The exteriors of the doors show scenes from the life of Christ and saints, including Alexander Nevsky (see p130).*

**The relief** of St Isaac blessing the Emperor Theodosius and his wife Flaccilla is by Ivan Vitali. On the extreme left, Montferrand is depicted clutching a model of his cathedral.

**The walls** are adorned with 14 coloured marbles and 43 other types of semi-precious stones and minerals.

**The vast interior** covers 4,000 sq m (43,000 sq ft).

**Red granite columns**, each weighing 114 tonnes, were transported from Finland by specially constructed ships.

## STAR SIGHTS

★ Iconostasis

★ Ceiling Painting

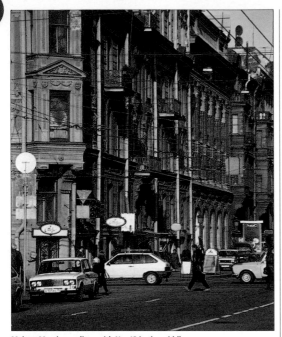

**Malaya Morskaya ulitsa with No. 13 in the middle**

## Malaya Morskaya Ulitsa ❽
Малая Морская у лица
*Malaya Morskaya ulitsa*

**Map** 6 D1. 🚌 *3, 10, 22, 27.* 🚎 *5, 22.*

Malaya Morskaya Ulitsa used to be referred to as ulitsa Gogolya after the great prose-writer, Nikolai Gogol (1809–52) who lived at No. 17 from 1833–6. It was here that Gogol wrote *The Diary of a Madman* and *The Nose*, two biting satires on the archetypal Petersburg bureau-crat "drowned by the trivial, meaningless labours at which he spends his useless life". Gogol's bitingly humorous, fantastical and grotesque tales reveal a nightmarish and deeply pessimistic view of modern urban life.

The composer, Pyotr Tchaikovsky *(see p42)*, died in the top floor apartment of No. 13 shortly after the completion of his *Pathétique* symphony in November 1893. Officially he was supposed to have died of cholera, but it is commonly believed that he

committed suicide, due to pressure from Conservatory colleagues wishing to avoid a scandal after Tchaikovsky's alleged homosexual affair.

The house at No. 23 was occupied by the novelist Fyodor Dostoevsky *(see p123)* from 1848–9. It was here that he was arrested and charged with political conspiracy for his participation in the socialist Petrashevsky circle *(see p123)*. Today, the street manages to exude a 19th-century feel despite the many busy shops and businesses.

## House of Fabergé ❾
Дом Фаберже
*Dom Faberzhe*

Bolshaya Morskaya ulitsa 24.
**Map** 6 D1. 🔵 *to public.* 🚌 *3, 22, 27.* 🚎 *5, 22.*

The world-famous Fabergé jeweller's was established in Bolshaya Morskaya ulitsa in 1842 by Gustav Fabergé, of French Huguenot origin. It was not until the 1880s that his sons Carl and Agathon abandoned conventional jewellery-making for intricate and exquisitely crafted *objets d'art* of a highly innovative design. Most fam-ous of all their works are the imaginatively designed Easter eggs made for the tsars.

In 1900 Carl moved the business from No. 16–18 into purpose-built premises at No. 24, where it remained until the Revolution. The exterior, designed by his relative, Karl Schmidt, has striking triangular roof gables and multi-textured stonework. The original show-room, with its squat red granite pillars, was on the ground floor. It is still a jeweller's, but with no connection to Fabergé. In the workshops above, boy apprentices were trained by master craftsmen in the arts of enamelling, engraving, stone cutting and jewelling.

In 1996, the 150th anniver-sary of Carl Fabergé's birth was marked by the unveiling of a memorial plaque at No. 24 and of a monument, designed by the sculptor Leonid Aristov and others, on the corner of Zanevskiy prospekt and prospekt Energetikov.

### FABERGE EGGS

In 1885 Alexander III commissioned the Fabergé brothers to create an Easter egg for Tsarina Maria Fyodorovna. Inside the shell of gold and white enamel was a beautifully sculpted golden hen. A tradition was established and, by the Revolution, there were 54 Fabergé Easter eggs, no two of which were alike. The *pièce de résistance* is the Siberian Railway Egg, commissioned by Nicholas II in 1900. The Bonbonnière Egg was commissioned by Kelch, a wealthy industrialist, for his wife Varvara in 1903. Regrettably, the only eggs on public display in Russia today are in the State Armoury of the Kremlin in Moscow.

**The Kelch Bon-bonnière Egg**

## DEATH OF A POET

In November 1836 Pushkin received an anonymous letter which awarded him the title of "Grand Master of the Most Serene Order of Cuckolds". It had been sent by Georges d'Anthès, a ne'er-do-well cavalry officer who for some time had been making overtures towards Pushkin's wife, the beauty and socialite Natalya Goncharova. Pushkin challenged d'Anthès to a duel and, on the afternoon of 27

**A Naumov's painting of Pushkin, fatally wounded after his duel**

January 1837, he met his opponent in snow-bound woodland to the north of the city. D'Anthès fired first and Pushkin was mortally wounded. He died two days later, aged 38. D'Anthès was later reduced to the ranks and banished from Russia.

**Sign outside the Literary Café**

# Literary Café ⓾
Литературное кафе
*Literaturnoe kafe*

Nevskiy prospekt 18. **Map** 6 E1.
***Tel*** 312 6057. ◯ *11am–1am.*
Ⓜ *Nevskiy Prospekt.* ♿
*See* Restaurants and Cafés *p187.*

Also known as the Café Wulf et Beranger after its original owners, this café is famous for its association with Alexander Pushkin, Russia's greatest poet *(see p43)*. It was here that Pushkin met his second, Konstantin Danzas, before setting out for his ill-fated duel with Baron d'Anthès. The café was a popular haunt for St Petersburg writers from its beginning, frequented by Fyodor Dostoevsky and the poet Mikhail Lermontov (1814–41), among others.

Despite its hallowed literary importance and elegant setting, in Vasiliy Stasov's handsome building of 1815, the café itself does not merit the high prices.

# Palace Square ⓫
Дворцовая площадь
*Dvortsovaya ploshchad*

**Map** 6 D1 🚌 *7, 10, K-169, K-187, K-190, K-209, K-228.* 🚎 *1, 7, 10.*

Palace Square has played a unique role in Russian history. Before the Revolution the square was the setting for colourful military parades, often led by the tsar on horse-back. In January 1905, it was the scene of the massacre of "Bloody Sunday" *(see p26)* when gathered troops fired on thousands of unarmed demonstrators. Then, on 7 November 1917, Lenin's Bolshevik supporters secured the Revolution by attacking the Winter Palace *(see pp28–9)* from the square, as well as its west side. It is still a favourite venue for political meetings and events such as rock concerts *(see p51).*

The resplendant square is the work of the inspired architect Carlo Rossi *(see p110).* Facing the Winter Palace on its southern side is Rossi's magnificent General Staff Building (1819–29), the headquarters for the Russian army. Rossi demolished an entire row of houses to make room for it.

The two graceful, curving wings (the eastern one now a branch of the Hermitage) are connected by a double arch leading to Bolshaya Morskaya ulitsa. The arch is crowned by a sculpture of Victory in her chariot (1829), by Stepan Pimenov and Vasiliy Demut-Malinovskiy. Forming the eastern side of this striking architectural ensemble is the Guards Headquarters, designed by Aleksandr Bryullov in 1837–43. To the west lies the Admiralty *(see p78).*

The Alexander Column in the centre of the square is dedicated to Tsar Alexander I for his role in the triumph over Napoleon *(see pp22–3).* On the pedestal are inscribed the words "To Alexander I, from a grateful Russia". The red granite pillar is balanced by its 600-tonne weight, making it the largest free-standing monument in the world. The column was designed by Auguste de Montferrand in 1829 and it took 2,400 soldiers and workmen two years to hew and transport the granite. It was erected in 1830–34. The column is topped by a bronze angel, and together they stand 47 m (154 ft) high.

**The Alexander Column and General Staff Building in Palace Square**

# The Hermitage ⑫
Эрмитаж
*Ermitazh*

One of the most famous museums in the world, the Hermitage occupies a grand ensemble of buildings. The most impressive is the Winter Palace *(see pp92–3)*, to which Catherine the Great added the more intimate Small Hermitage. In 1771–87, she built the Large Hermitage to house her growing collection of art. The Theatre was built in 1785–7, the New Hermitage in 1839–51. The New and Large Hermitages were opened by Nicholas I in 1852 as a public museum. From 1918 to 1939 the Winter Palace was slowly incorporated into the museum ensemble. In the late 1990s the majestic, Neo-Classical General Staff Building was added. Mid and late 19th-century collections are gradually moving there.

**The New Hermitage** (1839–51) was designed by Leo von Klenze to form a coherent part of the Large Hermitage. It is the only purpose-built museum within the whole complex.

**Court ministries** were located here until the 1880s.

**Atlantes**
*Ten 5-m (16-ft) tall granite Atlantes hold up what was the public entrance to the Hermitage museum from 1852 until after the Revolution.*

**The Winter Canal** *(see p36)*

**A gallery** spanning the canal connects the Theatre to the Large Hermitage and forms the theatre foyer.

**The Large Hermitage** was designed by Yuriy Velten to house Catherine's paintings.

**Theatre**
*During Catherine's reign, there were regular performances held in Quarenghi's theatre. Today it hosts exhibitions and concerts (see p202).*

★ **Raphael Loggias**
*Catherine was so impressed by engravings of Raphael's frescoes in the Vatican that in 1787 she commissioned copies to be made on canvas. Small alterations were made, such as replacing the Pope's coat of arms with the Romanov two-headed eagle.*

### Hanging Gardens
*This unusual raised garden is decorated with statues and fountains. During the Siege of Leningrad (see p27) Hermitage curators grew vegetables here.*

**The Small Hermitage** (1764–75), by Vallin de la Mothe and Yuriy Velten, served as Catherine's retreat from the bustle of the court.

### Winter Palace Façade
*Rastrelli embellished the palace façades with 400 columns and 16 different window designs.*

## STAR SIGHTS

★ Winter Palace State Rooms

★ Pavilion Hall

★ Raphael Loggias

Palace Square

Main entrance via courtyard

General Staff Building

River Neva

**The Winter Palace** (1754–62) was the official residence of the Imperial family until the Revolution.

### ★ Pavilion Hall (1850–58)
*Andrey Stakenschneider's striking white marble and gold hall replaced Catherine's original interior. It houses Englishman James Cox's famous Peacock Clock (1772), which was once owned by Catherine's secret husband, Prince Grigory Potemkin.*

### ★ Winter Palace State Rooms
*The tsars spared no expense in decorating rooms such as the Hall of St George. These rooms were not intended for private life, but were used for state ceremonies.*

# The Hermitage Collections

Catherine the Great purchased some of Western Europe's best collections between 1764 and 1774, acquiring over 2,500 paintings, 10,000 carved gems, 10,000 drawings and a vast amount of silver and porcelain with which to adorn her palaces. None of her successors matched the quantity of her remarkable purchases. After the Revolution, the nationalization of both royal and private property brought more paintings and works of applied art, making the Hermitage one of the world's leading museums.

**The Knights' Hall** (1842–51) is used for displays of armour and weapons from the former Imperial arsenal.

**Stairs to ground floor**

**Skylight Rooms**

**Raphael Loggias** (see p84)

**First Floor**

**The Gallery of Ancient Painting** (1842–51) is decorated with scenes from ancient literature. It houses a superb display of 19th-century European sculpture.

★ **Litta Madonna** (c.1491)
*One of two works by Leonardo da Vinci in the museum, this masterpiece was admired by his contemporaries and was frequently copied.*

**Ground Floor**

**European Gold Collection**

**The Hall of Twenty Columns** (1842–51) is painted in Etruscan style.

**Main entrance**

**Entrance for tours and guided groups**

## STAR EXHIBITS

- ★ Abraham's Sacrifice by Rembrandt
- ★ Ea Haere la Oe by Gauguin
- ★ La Danse by Matisse
- ★ Litta Madonna by Leonardo da Vinci

## GALLERY GUIDE

*Enter via Palace Square, then cross the main courtyard; group tours use other entrances. Start with the interiors of the Winter Palace state rooms on the first floor to get an overview of the museum. For 19th- and 20th-century European Art use either of the staircases on the Palace Square side of the Winter Palace. Note collections may move.*

★ **Abraham's Sacrifice** (1635)
*In the 1630s Rembrandt was painting religious scenes in a High Baroque style, using dramatic and striking gestures rather than detail to convey his message.*

**Second Floor**

**Stairs to first floor**

**The Numismatic Collection** consists of over 1 million objects. Only part of it is on display in temporary exhibitions.

**Stairs to first floor**

**Stairs to Numismatic collection**

**Stairs to second floor**

**Stairs to second floor, Numismatic Collection only**

**Greek and Oriental Gold collection**

**The Winter Palace** state rooms *(see pp92–3)* contain magnificent Russian and European *objets d'art*.

★ **Ea Haere Ia Oe** (1893)
*This is one of the first paintings by Paul Gauguin after he had left France for Tahiti. His desire to escape convention and artificiality found expression in his innovative use of primitive art as inspiration.*

★ **La Danse** (1910)
*Henri Matisse used strong tones of three colours – blue, green and red – to heighten the drama and concentration of the figures, totally lost in their dance.*

**Statue of Voltaire** (1781)
*Catherine the Great corres-ponded with Voltaire for over 15 years. She commissioned Jean-Antoine Houdon's marble statue, in which the French writer is dressed as a Greek philosopher.*

## KEY TO FLOORPLAN

- **Prehistoric:** Rooms 11–24, 26, 33
- **Classical:** 102, 107–117, 121, 127–131
- **Oriental:** 34–47, 55–66, 69, 100, 351–371, 381–397
- **Russian:** 147–153, 155–189, 190–198, 204, 260, 269–271, 282, 304–307
- **Italian and Spanish:** 207–223, 226–242
- **Flemish, Dutch and German:** 243, 245–254, 258–259, 261–268
- **French and English:** 272–281, 283–287, 290–302
- **19th- and 20th-century European:** 314–325, 328–350
- **Temporary exhibition space**
- **Non-exhibition space**
- **No access**

# Exploring the Hermitage Collections

It is impossible to absorb the Hermitage's vast, encyclopedic collection in one or even two visits. Whether it be Scythian gold, antique vases and cameos, or Iranian silver, every room has something to capture the eye. The furniture, applied art, portraits and rich clothing of the imperial family went to make up the Russian section, which also includes the superb state rooms. The collection of European paintings was put together largely according to the personal taste of the imperial family while most of the 19th- and 20th-century European art, notably the Impressionists, Matisse and Picasso, came from private collections after the Revolution.

**Scythian gold stag dating from 7th–6th century BC**

## PREHISTORIC ART

Prehistoric artifacts found all over the former Russian Empire include pots, arrow heads and sculptures from Palaeolithic sites, which date back nearly 24,000 years, and rich gold items from the time of the Scythian nomads living in the 7th–3rd centuries BC.

Peter the Great's famous Siberian collection of delicate gold work includes Scythian animal-style brooches, sword handles and buckles. Objects continued to be discovered in Siberia and in 1897 a large stylized stag, which once decorated an iron shield, was found at Kostromskaya. This and other gold pieces are held in the European Gold Collection (for which a separate ticket is required). Copies are on display in the Scythian rooms.

Greek masters also worked for the Scythians, and from the Dnepr region came a late 5th-century comb decorated with amazingly naturalistic figures of Scythians fighting, as well as the late 4th-century Chertomlyk Vase with scenes depicting animal taming.

Excavations in the Altai, notably at Pazyryk in 1927–49, uncovered burials nearly 2,500 years old. Many perishable materials were preserved by the frozen land, including textiles, a burial cart and even a man's heavily tattooed skin.

**Gonzaga Cameo (285–246 BC), made in Alexandria**

## CLASSICAL ART

The large number of Graeco-Roman marble sculptures range from the famous Tauride Venus of the 3rd century BC, acquired by Peter the Great in 1720, to Roman portrait busts. The smaller objects, however, are the real pride and joy of the Classical department.

The collection of red-figured Attic vases of the 6th–4th centuries BC is unequalled anywhere in the world. Exquisitely proportioned and with a lustrous shine, they are decorated with scenes of libation, episodes from the Trojan War, and in one case a famous image of the sighting of the first swallow (c.510 BC).

In the 4th and 3rd centuries BC, Tanagra was the centre for the production of small, elegant terracotta figurines. They were discovered in the 19th century and became so popular that fakes were produced on a grand scale. The Russian ambassador in Athens, Pyotr Saburov, put his collection together in the 1880s before the copies appeared, making it unusually valuable.

Catherine the Great's true passion was for carved gems, which she bought en masse. In just ten years, she purchased some 10,000 pieces. The largest and most stunning gem in the Classical collection, however, is the Gonzaga Cameo, which was presented by Napoleon's ex-wife Josephine Beauharnais to Tsar Alexander I in 1814.

The Greek and Oriental Gold Collection contains some items of 5th-century gold jewellery made by Athenian craftsmen. They used a filigree technique for working gold so finely that the detail can only be seen through a magnifying glass.

## ORIENTAL ART

This selection of artifacts covers a wide range of cultures; from ancient Egypt and Assyria, through Byzantium, India, Iran, China, Japan and the marvels of Uzbekistan and Tajikistan. The most complete sections are those where excavations were conducted by the Hermitage, mainly in China and Mongolia before the Revolution, and in Central Asia during the Soviet period.

Dating back to the 19th century BC, at the time of the Middle Kingdom, is a seated porphyry portrait of Pharaoh

**8th-century fresco of a wounded warrior from Tajikistan**

Excavations and expeditions to Central Asia have produced carpets, bronzes and wonderful glazed tiles. Uzbekistan and Tajikistan revealed marvellous frescoes in complexes of 8th-century buildings at Varaksha, Adjina-Tepe and Pendzhikent. Rare Mughal jewelled vessels, Iranian weapons and Chinese gold objects are displayed in the Greek and Oriental Gold Collection.

## RUSSIAN ART

Although major Russian works of art were transferred to the Russian Museum (*see pp104–107*) in 1898, everything else that belonged to the imperial family was nationalized after the Revolution. This included anything from official portraits and thrones to looking glasses and petticoats. Over 300 items of apparel belonging to Peter the Great alone survive. Later, the department also began acquiring medieval Russian art, including icons and church utensils.

The tsars from Peter the Great onwards invited foreign

**Universal sundial (1714–19) from Peter the Great's collection**

Amenemhet III. The star of the Egyptian collection is an extremely rare, small, wooden statue of a standing man from the 15th century BC.

From the Far East – Japan, India, Indonesia, China and Mongolia – comes an array of objects ranging from Buddhist sculptures and fabrics to a display of tiny netsukes (ivory toggles). Excavations at the cave temple of the Thousand Buddhas near Dun Huan in western China revealed 6th–10th-century icons, wall paintings and plaster sculptures, including the lions that once guarded the cave. During the 13th-century Mongol invasion, the town of Khara-Khoto was destroyed and taken over by the surrounding desert. The sand preserved many usually perishable objects, from 12th-century silks to woodcuts.

From Byzantium come early secular items, such as icons, religious utensils and a 5th-century ivory diptych with scenes from a Roman circus.

Iran produced a large number of silver and bronze vessels, many of which were taken by medieval traders to Siberia and the Urals where they were rediscovered by specialists in the 19th century. There is also a large collection of traditional Persian miniatures and a rich display of 19th-century Persian court portraits, which combine traditional elements with western oil painting, as in the *Portrait of Fatkh-Ali Shah* (1813–14).

craftsmen and artists to train locals. Peter studied with them and his fascination for practical things is reflected in his large collection of sundials, instruments and wood-turning lathes which includes the universal sundial by Master John Rowley. A bust by Bartolomeo Carlo Rastrelli (1723–30), however, portrays Peter as the mighty and cruel emperor.

Russian artists were soon combining traditional art forms with European skills to create such intricate marvels as the openwork walrus ivory vase by Nikolay Vereshchagin (1798), and the large silver sarcophagus and memorial to Alexander Nevsky, truly Russian in scale (1747–52).

The gunsmiths of Tula (south of Moscow) perfected their technique to such an extent that they began producing unique furniture in steel inlaid with gilded bronze, such as the decorative, Empire-style dressing table set (1801).

The state interiors (*see pp92–3*) are the pride of the Russian department, revealing the work of Russian and foreign craftsmen from the mid-18th to the early 20th century. The discovery of large deposits of coloured stones in the Urals inspired Russian artists to decorate whole rooms with malachite and to fill every corner of the Winter Palace with marble vases. It was through these rooms that the imperial family paraded on state occasions, greeting courtiers and ambassadors en route in the Field Marshals' Hall.

**Steel dressing table set from Tula dating from 1801**

## ITALIAN AND SPANISH ART

The display of Italian art contains some fine pieces. A few early works reveal the rise of the Renaissance in the 14th and 15th centuries and the styles then in vogue. Simone Martini's stiff *Madonna* (1340–44) contrasts with Fra Angelico's more humane fresco of the Virgin and Child (1424–30).

In the late 15th and early 16th century, artists disputed the merits of line, as practised by the Florentine school, and the merits of colour, virtue of the Venetians. The former can be seen in the *Litta Madonna* (c.1491) and the *Madonna Benois* (1478) by Leonardo da Vinci, a marble *Crouching Boy* by Michelangelo (c.1530) and two early portraits of the Virgin by Raphael (1502 and 1506). Venice is represented by *Judith* by Giorgione (1478–1510) and an array of works by Titian (c.1490–1576). The Skylight Rooms are packed with vast Baroque canvases, including works by Luca Giordano (1634–1704) and Guido Reni (1575–1642), and even larger 18th-century masterpieces by Tiepolo. The works of the Italian sculptor Antonio Canova (1757–1822) (*Cupid and Psyche, The Three Graces*) stand in the Gallery of Ancient Painting.

The Spanish collection is more modest, but Spain's greatest painters can all be seen, from El Greco with *The Apostles Peter and Paul* (1587–92), through to Ribera, Murillo, and Zurbarán with *St Lawrence* (1636). The portrait of a courtier, *Count Olivares*, painted c.1640 by Velázquez, contrasts with a much earlier genre scene of a peasant's breakfast (1617–18).

*Venus and Cupid* (1509) by Lucas Cranach the Elder

## FLEMISH, DUTCH AND GERMAN ART

The small collection of early paintings from the Netherlands includes a marvellous, jewel-like *Madonna and Child* (1430s) by the Master of Flemalle. He is thought to have been the teacher of Rogier van der Weyden, who is represented by *St Luke Painting the Madonna* (c.1435).

Over 40 works by Rubens include religious subjects (*The Descent from the Cross*, 1617–18) and scenes from Classical mythology (*Perseus and Andromeda*, 1620–21), as well as landscapes and an immensely obese *Bacchus* (1636–40). His portraits, such as the *Infanta's Maid* (1625), reveal the link with his famous pupil Van Dyck, whose paintings include a series of formal, full-length portraits and a dashing and romantic self-portrait from the late 1620s.

The Dutch section is rich in Rembrandts. Within a short period of time he produced the dramatic *Abraham's Sacrifice* (1636), the gentle *Flora* (1634) and the brilliant effects of *The Descent from the Cross* (1634). One of his last works was the *Return of the Prodigal Son* (1668–9), with an emotional depth unseen before.

Among the many small-genre paintings is Gerard Terborch's *Glass of Lemonade* from the mid-17th century. All the usual elements of a genre scene are imbued with psychological tension and heavy symbolism.

In the German collection, it is the works of Lucas Cranach the Elder which captivate the viewer. His *Venus and Cupid* (1509), the stylish *Portrait of a Woman in a Hat* (1526) and the tender *Virgin and Child Beneath an Apple Tree* reveal the varied aspects of his talent.

## FRENCH AND ENGLISH ART

French art was *de rigueur* for collectors in the 18th century. Major artists of the 17th century, including Louis Le Nain and the two brilliant and contrasting painters Claude Lorrain and Nicolas Poussin, are well represented. Antoine Watteau's elegant *Embarrassing Proposal* (c.1716), *Stolen Kiss* (1780s) by Jean Honoré Fragonard and François Boucher's fleshy and certainly far-from-virtuous

*A Young Man Playing a Lute*, by Michelangelo Caravaggio (1573–1610)

*Still Life with the Attributes of the Arts* (1766), by Jean-Baptiste Chardin

heroines represent the more wicked side of 18th-century taste, but Catherine the Great preferred didactic or instructional works. She bought *Still Life with Attributes of the Arts* (1766) by Chardin and, on the advice of Denis Diderot, Jean-Baptiste Greuze's moralizing *The Fruits of a Good Education* (1763). She also patronized sculptors, purchasing works by Etienne-Maurice Falconet (*Winter,* carved 1771) and Jean-Antoine Houdon (Voltaire, 1781).

**The Green Frog Service, Wedgwood (1773–4)**

Catherine also acquired English works, including a portrait of the philosopher John Locke (1697) by Sir Godfrey Kneller, who was also author of a portrait of Pyotr Potemkin (1682) in Russian 17th-century court dress. From Sir Joshua Reynolds Catherine commissioned *The Infant Hercules Strangling the Serpents* (1788). Her most daring purchase was of works by the still largely unknown Joseph Wright of Derby. *The Iron Forge* (1773) is a masterpiece of artificial lighting, but *Firework Display at the Castel Sant'Angelo* (1774–5) is a truly romantic fiery spectacle. She provided much work for English cabinet-makers and carvers of cameos. She became one of Josiah Wedgwood's most prestigious clients, ordering the famous Green Frog Service for her Chesma Palace *(see p130)*.

## 19TH- & 20TH-CENTURY EUROPEAN ART

Although the royal family did not patronize the new movements in art in the 19th century, there were far-sighted private individuals whose collections were nationalized and entered the Hermitage after the 1917 Revolution. Thanks to them, the Barbizon school is represented by works such as Camille Corot's charming silvery *Landscape with a Lake,* French Romanticism by two richly-coloured Moroccan scenes of the 1850s by Delacroix. But Nicholas I himself did acquire works by the German Romantic painter Caspar David Friedrich, among them *On the Prow of the Ship* (1818–20).

Two collectors, Ivan Morozov and Sergey Shchukin, brought the Hermitage its superb array of Impressionist and Post-Impressionist paintings. Monet's art can be admired both in his early *Woman in a Garden* (1860s) and in the later, more exploratory *Waterloo Bridge, Effect of Mist* (1903). Renoir and Degas perpetually returned to women as subjects, as in Renoir's charming *Portrait of the Actress Jeanne Samary* (1878) and Degas' pastels of women washing (1880s–90s). Pissarro's *Boulevard Montmartre in Paris* (1897) is typical of his urban scenes.

A change in colour and technique appeared as artists investigated new possibilities. Van Gogh used deeper tones in his *Women of Arles* (1888) and stronger brushstrokes in *Cottages* (1890). Gauguin turned to a different culture for inspiration, and his Tahitian period is represented by enigmatic works, such as *Ea Haere Ia Oe* (1893). In *The Smoker* (c.1890–2) and *Mont Ste-Victoire* (1896–8), Cézanne introduced experiments with plane and surface which were to have a strong influence on the next generation.

Matisse played both with colour and surface, in the carpet-like effect of *The Red Room* (1908–9) and the flatness of the panels *La Musique* and *La Danse* (1909–10). His visit to Morocco introduced new light effects, as in *Arab Coffeehouse* (1913), but it was Picasso who took Cézanne's experiments one stage further. In early works such as *Visit* (1902) from his Blue Period, Picasso concentrates on mood, but the surface destruction of the Cubist period of 1907–12, including *L'Homme aux Bras Croisés,* fills a whole room.

*L'Homme aux Bras Croisés,* painted by Pablo Picasso in 1909

# The Winter Palace

Preceded by three earlier versions on this site, the existing Winter Palace (1754–62) is a superb example of Russian Baroque. Built for Tsarina Elizabeth, this opulent winter residence was the finest achievement of Bartolomeo Rastrelli. Though the exterior has changed little, the interiors were altered by a number of architects and then largely restored after a fire gutted the palace in 1837. After the assassination of Alexander II in 1881, the imperial family rarely lived here. During World War I a field hospital was set up in the Nicholas Hall and other state rooms. Then, in July 1917, the Provisional Government took the palace as its headquarters, which led to its storming by the Bolsheviks *(see pp28–9)*.

**The 1812 Gallery** (1826) has portraits of Russian military heroes of the Napoleonic War, most by English artist George Dawe.

**The Armorial Hall** (1839), with its vast gilded columns, covers over 800 sq m (8,600 sq ft). Hospital beds were set up here during the First World War.

★ **Small Throne Room**
*Dedicated in 1833 to the memory of Peter the Great, this room houses a silver-gilt English throne, made in 1731.*

**The Field Marshals' Hall** (1833) was the reception room where the devastating fire of 1837 broke out.

**The Hall of St George** (1795) has monolithic columns and wall facings of Italian Carrara marble.

**The Nicholas Hall**, the largest room in the palace, was always used for the first ball of the season.

**North façade overlooking the Neva**

★ **Main Staircase**
*This vast, sweeping staircase (1762) was Rastrelli's masterpiece. It was from here that the imperial family watched the Epiphany ceremony of baptism in the Neva, which celebrated Christ's baptism in the Jordan.*

★ **Malachite Room**
*Over two tonnes of ornamental stone were used in this sumptuous room (1839) which is decorated with malachite columns and vases, gilded doors and ceiling, and rich parquet flooring.*

**Alexander Hall**
*Architect Aleksandr Bryullov employed a mixture of Gothic vaulting and Neo-Classical stucco bas-reliefs of military themes in this reception room of 1837.*

## BARTOLOMEO RASTRELLI

The Italian architect Rastrelli (1700–71) came to Russia with his father in 1716 to work for Peter the Great. His rich Baroque style became highly fashionable and he was appointed Chief Court Architect in 1738. During Elizabeth's reign, Rastrelli designed several buildings, including the Winter Palace, the Palace of Tsarkoe Selo *(see pp152–7)* and Smolnyy Convent *(see p128)*. Unlike Elizabeth, Catherine the Great preferred Classical simplicity and Rastrelli retired in 1763, after she came to power.

**The French Rooms**, designed by Bryullov in 1839, house a collection of 18th-century French art.

**The White Hall** was decorated for the wedding of the future Alexander II in 1841.

**South façade on Palace Square**

**Dark Corridor**
*The French and Flemish tapestries here include* The Marriage of Emperor Constantine, *made in Paris in the 17th century to designs by Rubens.*

**The Rotunda**
(1830) connected the private apartments in the west with the state apartments on the palace's north side.

**West wing**

**The Gothic Library** and other rooms in the northwest part of the palace were adapted to suit Nicholas II's bourgeois lifestyle. This wood-panelled library was created by Meltzer in 1894.

### STAR FEATURES

★ Small Throne Room

★ Malachite Room

★ Main Staircase

**The Gold Drawing Room**
*Created in the 1850s, this room was extravagantly decorated in the 1870s with all-over gilding of walls and ceiling. It houses a display of Western European carved gems.*

## Millionaires' Street ⓭

Миллионная у лица
*Millionnaya ulitsa*

**Map** 2 E5.

Millionaires' Street takes its name from the aristocrats and members of the imperial family who once inhabited its opulent residences. Since the main façades and entrances overlook the river, some house numbers correspond to the embankment side.

On the eve of the Revolution, No. 26 (on the embankment) was the home of Grand Duke Vladimir Aleksandrovich who was responsible for firing on peaceful demonstrators on Bloody Sunday *(see p26)*. His consort, Maria Pavlovna, was one of Russia's leading society hostesses who gave soirées and balls that eclipsed even those of the imperial court. The building (1867–72), which was designed by Aleksandr Rezanov in the style of the Florentine Renaissance, is now the House of Scholars.

Putyatin's house, at No. 12 Millionaires' Street, witnessed the end of the Romanov dynasty. It was here that Grand Duke Mikhail Aleksandrovich, Nicholas II's brother, signed the decree of abdication in March 1917. Next door, No. 10, was where French novelist Honoré de Balzac stayed in 1843, while courting his future wife, Countess Eveline Hanska. The mid-19th-century house was designed by Andrey Stakenschneider for his own use.

**The delicately sculpted façade of No. 10 Millionaires' Street**

**Gala staircase of the Marble Palace**

## Marble Palace ⓮

Мраморный дворец
*Mramornyy dvorets*

Millionnaya ulitsa 5 (entrance from the Field of Mars). **Map** 2 E4. **Tel** *312 9054.* 46, 49, K-76. 10am–6pm Wed–Sun, 10am–5pm Mon. *English.* **www**.rusmuseum.ru

The Marble Palace was built as a present from Catherine the Great to her lover Grigoriy Orlov who had been instrumental in bringing her to power in 1762 *(see p22)*. An early example of Neo-Classical architecture, dating from 1768–85, the building is considered to be Antonio Rinaldi's masterpiece.

The palace takes its name from the varied marbles used in its construction. Most of the interiors were reconstructed in the 1840s by Aleksandr Bryullov, although the gala staircase and the Marble Hall are Rinaldi's originals. The latter has marbled walls of grey, green, white, yellow, pink and lapis lazuli, and a ceiling painting, the *Triumph of Venus* (1780s) by Stefano Torelli.

The palace, which housed a Lenin museum for 55 years, is now a branch of the Russian Museum *(see pp104–107)*. On display are works by foreign artists working in Russia and modern art bequeathed by the

**Eternal Flame, Field of Mars**

German collectors Peter and Irene Ludwig. Their collection includes a Picasso, *Large Heads* (1969), and work by post-war artists Jean-Michel Basquiat, Andy Warhol, Ilya Kabakov and Roy Lichtenstein.

In front of the palace stands a curious equestrian statue of Alexander III by Prince Pavel Trubetskoy. Unveiled on ploshchad Vosstaniya in 1911, the ridiculed statue was removed from its original site in 1937 and its vast pedestal was cut up to create statues of new heroes, such as Lenin.

## Field of Mars ⓯

Марсово Поле
*Marsovo Pole*

**Map** 2 F5. 46, 49, K-76.

Once a vast marshy expanse, this area was drained during the 19th century and utilized for military manoeuvres and parades, fairs and other festivities. It was appropriately named after Mars, the Roman god of war. Between 1917 and 1923 the area, by then a sandy expanse, was nicknamed the "Petersburg Sahara". It was landscaped and transformed into a war memorial. The granite *Monument to Revolutionary Fighters* (1917–19), by Lev Rudnev, and the Eternal Flame (1957) commemorate the victims of the Revolutions of 1917 and the Civil War *(see p27)*.

The west of the square is dominated by an imposing Neo-Classical building erected by Vasiliy Stasov in 1817–19. This was formerly the barracks of the Pavlovskiy Guards which were founded by Tsar Paul I in 1796. The military-obsessed tsar is said to have only recruited guardsmen with snub noses like his own. The Pavlovskiy officers were among the first to turn against the tsarist government in the 1917 Revolution *(see pp28–9)*.

Today the huge square is a popular spot for locals in the bright spring evenings, when it is alive with lilac blossom.

# Summer Garden ⑯

Летний сад
*Letniy sad*

Letniy Sad. **Map** 2 F4. 🚌 *46, 49.*
◯ *May–Sep: 10am–10pm daily;
Oct–Mar: 10am–6pm daily.* 🚻 ▢

In 1704 Peter the Great commissioned this beautiful garden which was among the first in the city. Designed by a Frenchman in the style of Versailles, the allées were planted with imported elms and oaks and adorned with fountains, pavilions and some 250 Italian statues dating from the 17th and 18th centuries. A flood in 1777 destroyed most of the Summer Garden and the English-style garden which exists today is largely the result of Catherine the Great's more sober tastes. A splendid feature is the fine filigree iron grille (1771–84) along the Neva embankment, created by Yuriy Velten and Pyotr Yegorov.

For a century the Summer Garden was an exclusive preserve of the nobility. When the garden was opened to "respectably dressed members of the public" by Nicholas I, two Neo-Classical pavilions, the Tea House and the Coffee House, were erected overlooking the Fontanka. These are now used for temporary exhibitions of art by modern St Petersburg artists.

Nearby, the bronze statue of Ivan Krylov, Russia's most famous writer of fables, is a favourite with Russian children. It was sculpted by Pyotr Klodt in 1854 with charming bas-reliefs on the pedestal depicting animals from his fables.

Ivan Krylov's statue amidst autumn foliage in the Summer Garden

# Summer Palace ⑰

Летний дворец
*Letniy dvorets*

Naberezhnaya Kutuzova. **Map** 2 F4.
**Tel** *314 0374.* ◯ *May–Nov:
11am–5:30pm Wed–Mon.* ◐ *last
Mon of each month.* 🚌 *46, 49.*
🖼 🎫

Built for Peter the Great, the modest two-storey Summer Palace is the oldest stone building in the city. It was designed in the Dutch style by Domenico Trezzini and was completed in 1714. The Prussian sculptor Andreas Schlüter created the delightful maritime bas-reliefs (1713) as an allegorical commentary on Russia's naval triumphs under Peter the Great's stewardship.

Grander than his wooden cabin (*see p73*), Peter's second St Petersburg residence is still by no means comparable to the magnificent palaces built by his successors.

On the ground floor, the reception room is hung with portraits of the tsar and his ministers and contains Peter's oak Admiralty Chair. The tsar's bedroom has its original four-poster bed with a coverlet of Chinese silk, and an 18th-century ceiling painting showing the triumph of Morpheus, the god of sleep. Next door is the turnery which contains some original Russian lathes as well as an elaborately carved wooden meteorological instrument, designed in Dresden in 1714.

The palace boasted the city's first plumbing system with water piped directly into the kitchen. The original black marble sink can still be seen, along with the beautifully tiled kitchen stove and an array of early 18th-century cooking utensils. The kitchen opens onto the exquisite dining room, imaginatively refurbished to convey an atmosphere of domesticity. It was used only for small family gatherings since major banquets were held at the Menshikov Palace (*see p62*).

An original staircase leads up to the first floor and the more lavish suite of Peter's second wife, Catherine. The throne in the aptly named Throne Room is ornamented with Nereides and other sea deities. The glass cupboards in the Green Room once displayed Peter's fascinating collection of curiosa before it was transferred to the Kunstkammer (*see p60*).

The remarkable stove in the Summer Palace's tiled kitchen

# GOSTINYY DVOR

The Great Bazaar, Gostinyy Dvor, was the commercial heart of St Petersburg at the beginning of the 18th century and today it still hums with activity. A profusion of smaller retail outlets soon appeared on and around Nevskiy prospekt. Thriving communities of foreign merchants and businessmen also took up residence in the neighbourhood.

Until the mid-19th century, shops in this area catered almost exclusively for the luxury end of the market, fulfilling the limitless demand, created by the royal and aristocratic households, for gold and silverware, jewellery and

**Statues on façade of the Russian Museum**

haute couture. Increasing commercial and financial activity created a new middle class of business entrepreneurs. By the Revolution, banks proliferated around Nevskiy prospekt, their imposing new offices introducing diverse architectural styles to a largely Neo-Classical setting. Today the wheels of capitalism are turning again and Nevskiy prospekt still attracts a wealthy clientele. In contrast to the bustling commercial atmosphere of much of the area is the calm oasis of Arts Square, with the Russian Museum and other institutions which act as a reminder of the city's rich cultural life.

## SIGHTS AT A GLANCE

**Churches**
Armenian Church **7**
Cathedral of Our Lady of Kazan **15**
*Church on Spilled Blood p100* **1**
Lutheran Church **17**

**Museums**
Mikhaylovskiy Castle **2**
Pushkin House-Museum **19**
*Russian Museum pp104–107* **3**

**Streets and Squares**
Arts Square **4**
Nevskiy Prospekt **6**
Ostrovskiy Square **11**
Ulitsa Zodchego Rossi **12**

**Markets and Shops**
Apraksin Market **14**
Gostinyy Dvor **8**
Yeliseev's **9**

**Palaces**
Anichkov Palace **10**
Stroganov Palace **16**
Vorontsov Palace **13**

**Hotels**
Grand Hotel Europe **5**

**Historic Buildings**
Glinka Capella **18**
Imperial Stables **20**

## KEY

Street-by-Street map
*See pp98–9*

**M** Metro

0 metres 300
0 yards 300

◁ Side view of the imposing Mikhaylovskiy Castle *(see p101)*, a branch of the Russian Museum

# Street-by-Street: Around Arts Square

**Peter the Great statue**

The aptly named Arts Square, one of Carlo Rossi's finest creations, is surrounded by buildings revealing the city's impressive cultural heritage. The grand palace housing the Russian Museum is flanked by theatres and the Philharmonia concert hall. Behind it is the leafy Mikhaylovskiy Garden, a haunt of St Petersburg's intellectuals. The gardens stretch down to the beautiful Moyka river which together with two other waterways, the Griboedov and Fontanka, create a shimmering frame for this picturesque area.

★ **Church on Spilled Blood**
*Colourful mosaics and elaborate stone carving are the main features the church's exterior, which emulates traditional 17th-century Russian style* ❶

**Mikhaylovskiy Garden**

★ **Russian Museum**
*Located in Rossi's Mikhaylovskiy Palace, this famous gallery boasts a fabulous collection of Russian painting, sculpture and applied art. The grand staircase and White Hall are original features* ❸

**Statue of Pushkin (1957)**

**Nevskiy prospekt**

**Arts Square**
*The square's present name derives from the number of cultural institutions situated here. On the western side, the Mikhailovskiy Theatre opened in 1833 for opera performances* ❹

**The Great Hall of the Philharmonia** is one of the major concert venues in St Petersburg (*see p202*).

**Grand Hotel Europe**
*This famous St Petersburg hotel was constructed by Ludwig Fontana in 1873–5. Mighty atlantes adorn its eclectic façade which stretches all the way down to Nevskiy prospekt* ❺

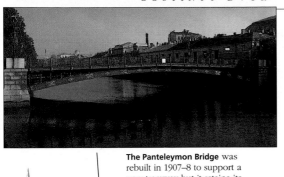

**The Panteleymon Bridge** was rebuilt in 1907–8 to support a new tramway but it retains its original Empire-style decor by Lev Ilyin *(see p37).*

**The bird statue**, cast in 1995 by Rezo Gabriadze, refers to a popular rhyme about vodka drinking.

**Statue of Peter the Great (1747)**

**LOCATOR MAP**
*See Street Finder map 6*

**Mikhaylovskiy Castle**
*Originally built for Paul I in 1797–1801, this castle was acquired by the Guards Corps of Engineers in 1823. Today it forms part of the Russian Museum and displays historical portraits* ❷

**STAR SIGHTS**

★ Russian Museum

★ Church on Spilled Blood

**KEY**

– – – Suggested route

0 metres 100
0 yards 100

PLOSCHAD BELINSKOVO

ZAMKOVAYA ULITSA
NAB REKI FONTANKA
FONTANKA
SADOVAYA ULITSA
INZHENERNAYA I ULITSA
KLENOVAYA ALLEYA
KARAVANNAYA ULITSA
MANEZHNAYA PLOSCHAD

Nevskiy prospekt

**Museum of Hygiene**, with macabre displays of preserved human organs, was established in 1919 to teach the public about health and hygiene.

**The Circus** or *"tsirk"* began performing in the 19th century when it was known as the Ciniselli Circus. It still offers traditional performances *(see p201)* in its historic venue by the Fontanka. Its original façade was reinstated in 2003.

# Church on Spilled Blood ❶

Храм Спаса-на-Крови
*Khram Spasa-na-Krovi*

**VISITORS' CHECKLIST**

Kanala Griboedova 2b. **Map** 2
E5. **Tel** *315 1636.* Ⓜ *Gostinyy
Dvor, Nevskiy Prospekt.* ⬜ *May-
Sep: 10am–11pm (Oct–Apr:
11am–7pm) Thu-Tue.* 🖼️ 🚫 ♿

The Church on Spilled Blood, also known as the
Resurrection Church of Our Saviour, was built on the
spot where on 1 March 1881 Tsar Alexander II was
assassinated *(see p26).* In 1883 his successor, Alexander
III, launched a competition for a permanent memorial.
The winning design, in the Russian Revival style
favoured by the tsar himself, was by Alfred
Parland and Ignatiy Malyshev. The foundation
stone was laid in October 1883.

A riot of colour, the overall effect of the
church is created by the imaginative juxtaposition of materials. Inside, more than 20 types of
minerals, including jasper, rhodonite, porphyry
and Italian marble are lavished on the mosaics
of the iconostasis, icon cases, canopy and
floor. The interior reopened in 1998 after
more than 20 years of restoration.

**Mosaic Tympanum**
*Mosaic panels showing scenes from the
New Testament adorn the exterior. They
were based on designs by artists such as
Viktor Vasnetsov and Mikhail Nesterov.*

**Coat of Arms**
*The 144 mosaic coats
of arms on the bell
tower represent the
regions, towns and
provinces of the
Russian empire.
They were intended
to reflect the grief
shared by all
Russians
in the wake of
Alexander's
assassination.*

**Jewellers' enamel** was
used to cover the
1,000 sq m
(10,760 sq ft) surface
of the five domes.

**Glazed** ceramic
tiles enliven
the façade.

**Twenty** dark red
plaques of Norwegian
granite are engraved in
gilt letters with the most
outstanding events of
Alexander II's reign
(1855–81). Among the
historic events recorded
are the emancipation of
the serfs in 1861 and
the conquest of Central
Asia (1860–81).

The tent-roofed
**steeple** is 81 m
(265 ft) high.

**Intricate Detailing**
*The flamboyant
Russian Revival style
of the exterior
provides a dra-
matic contrast to
the Neo-Classical
and Baroque
architecture
which dominates
the centre of
St Petersburg.*

**Mosaic** portraits
of the saints are
set in tiers of
*kokoshniki* gables.
Almost 7,000 sq m
(75,300 sq ft) of
mosaics embellish
the church's extra-
vagant exterior.

**Window Frames**
*The windows are
flanked by carved
columns of ornate
Estonian marble. The
casings are in the form
of double and triple
kokoshniki (tiered
decorative arches).*

**South façade of Mikhaylovskiy Castle and statue of Peter the Great**

# Mikhaylovskiy Castle ❷

Михайловский замок
*Mikhaylovskiy zamok*

Sadovaya ulitsa 2. **Map** 2 F5. **Tel** 570 5112. 46, K-46, K-76. 10am–6pm Wed–Sun, 10am–5pm Mon. book by phone.

The imposing red brick castle overlooking the Moyka and Fontanka rivers is also known as the Engineers' Castle. It was erected in 1797–1801 by Vasiliy Bazhenov and Vincenzo Brenna for Tsar Paul I. The tsar's obsessive fear of being assassinated led him to surround his new residence with moats and drawbridges, and to build a secret underground passage to the barracks on the Field of Mars *(see p94)*. Unfortunately, all these precautions proved futile and, after living in his fortified castle for just 40 days, Paul fell victim to a military conspiracy which resulted in his murder *(see p22)*.

In 1823 the fortress was acquired by the Guards Corps of Engineers and was renamed. The school's most famous graduate was the writer Fyodor Dostoevsky *(see p123)*. Today the castle serves as a branch of the nearby Russian Museum. It is used for temporary exhibitions.

The Church of the Archangel Michael is accessed via the exhibition and is a good example of Brenna's Neo-Classical style.

In front of the castle stands a bronze statue of Peter the Great on horseback, designed by Bartolomeo Carlo Rastrelli and cast in 1747.

# Russian Museum ❸

See pp104–107.

# Arts Square ❹

Площадь Искусств
*Ploshchad Iskusstv*

**Map** 6 F1. Ⓜ Nevskiy Prospekt, Gostinyy Dvor.

Several of the city's leading cultural institutions are located on this imposing Neo-Classical square, hence its name. The attractive square was designed by Carlo Rossi in the early 19th century to harmonize with the magnificent Mikhaylovskiy Palace (now the Russian Museum) which stands on its northern side.

On the opposite side of the square is the Great Hall of the St Petersburg Philharmonia, also known as the Shostakovich Hall *(see p43)*. This is where the Philharmonic Orchestra has been based since the 1920s *(see p202)*. Constructed by Paul Jacot in 1834–9, it started as a Nobles' Club where concerts were held. Among the works premiered here were Beethoven's *Missa Solemnis* in 1824 and Tchaikovsky's *(see p42) Pathétique* in 1893.

On the square's western side is the Mikhailovsky Theatre *(see p202)*, rebuilt by Albert Kavos in the mid-19th century. In the centre of the square is a sculpture of one of Russia's greatest literary figures, Alexander Pushkin *(see p43)*. The statue was executed by leading post-war sculptor, Mikhail Anikushin.

**Grand Hotel Europe's elegant Style-Moderne restaurant *(see p188)***

# Grand Hotel Europe ❺

Гранд Отель Европа
*Grand Otel Evropa*

Mikhaylovskaya ulitsa 1/7.
**Map** 6 F1. **Tel** 329 6000. Ⓜ Nevskiy Prospekt, Gostinyy Dvor. See Where to Stay p175.

One of Russia's most famous hotels, the ornate Grand Hotel Europe (1873–5) was designed by Ludwig Fontana. The building owes much of its character to alterations made in the 1910s by Style-Moderne architect Fyodor Lidval.

Before the Revolution, the hotel's magnificent restaurant was a favourite rendezvous for members of the diplomatic corps and secret police. In the 1970s, the hotel café became a popular meeting place for young intellectuals and artists.

**Pushkin's statue in front of the Russian Museum, Arts Square**

**The Church on Spilled Blood, a magical reminder of old Russia** ▷

# Russian Museum ❸

Русский Музей

*Russkiy Muzey*

The museum is housed in the Mikhaylovskiy Palace, one of Carlo Rossi's finest Neo-Classical creations which was built in 1819–25 for Grand Duke Mikhail Pavlovich. Alexander III's plans to create a public museum were realized by his son, Nicholas II, when the Russian Museum opened here in 1898. Today, the museum holds one of the world's greatest collections of Russian art.

**The Benois Wing,** named after its main architect Leontiy Benois, was added in 1913–19.

**Stairs to ground floor**

★ **Princess Olga Konstantinovna Orlova** (1911)
*By the turn of the 20th century, Valentin Serov was the most successful portrait painter in Russia.*

**Entrance**

**Temporary exhibitions** of 20th-century art are often displayed.

**Stairs to first floor of Benois Wing**

**A Meal in the Monastery** (1865–76)
*Vasiliy Perov's canvas exposes the hypocrisy of the Orthodox clergy, with the juxtaposition of good and evil, rich and poor, false piety and true faith.*

## GALLERY GUIDE

*The main entrance on Arts Square leads to the ticket office in the basement. The exhibition starts on the first floor. It is arranged chronologically, starting with icons in Room 1. It continues on the ground floor of the main building and Rossi Wing, then the first floor of the Benois Wing. Exhibitions are changed regularly.*

## STAR EXHIBITS

★ Princess Olga Konstantinovna Orlova by Serov

★ The Last Day of Pompeii by Bryullov

★ Barge-Haulers on the Volga by Repin

**Folk Art Toy** (1930s)
*This clay toy from Dykomovo is part of the colourful selection of folk art which also includes lacquer boxes, painted ceramics and textiles.*

★ **The Last Day of Pompeii** (1833)
*Karl Bryullov's Classical subject embodies the aesthetic principles of the Academy of Arts. This vivid depiction of the eruption of Vesuvius won him the Grand Prix at the Paris Salon.*

★ **Barge-Haulers on
the Volga** (1870–73)
*Ilya Repin was the most famous member
of the Wanderers, a group of artists
dedicated to social realism and Russian
themes. His powerful indictment of
forced labour imbues the oppressed
victims with sullen dignity.*

**Stairs to
ground floor**

14
15
12
13
16
17
11
10
9
8
7
6
5
4
1
2
3

**The White
Hall** contains
original Empire-
style furniture
by Carlo Rossi.

**Rossi Wing**

**Start of
exhibition**

44 43 42 41 40 39
52 53 54 35
55 36
57 56
33
34 32
31
30 29 28 27 26
25 24
18 19 20 23
22
21
38

**Entrance points
from basement
ticket office**

**Phryne at the Festival of Poseidon
in Eleusin** (1889)
*Henryk Siemiradzki's paintings are fine
examples of late European Neo-Classicism.
He is renowned for his academic scenes
of life in ancient Greece and Rome.*

**KEY**

| | |
|---|---|
| ☐ | Old Russian art |
| ☐ | 18th-century art |
| ☐ | Early 19th-century art |
| ☐ | Late 19th-century art |
| ☐ | Late 19th–early 20th-century art |
| ☐ | 20th-century art |
| ☐ | 18th–20th-century sculpture |
| ☐ | Folk art |
| ☐ | Temporary exhibitions |
| ☐ | Non-exhibition space |

**The portico** of
eight Corinthian
columns is the
central feature of
Rossi's façade.
Behind is a frieze
of Classical figures,
designed by Rossi
and executed by
Demut-Malinovskiy.

**Stairs to
first floor**

**The main
entrance** is
through a small door
which leads to the
basement with a ticket
office, a cloakroom,
toilets and a café.

# Exploring the Russian Museum

Housing one of the world's greatest collections of Russian art, the museum originally comprised officially approved works from the Academy of Arts *(see p63)*. When the museum was nationalized after the Revolution, art was transferred from palaces, churches and private collections. By the 1930s, Socialist Realism had become state policy and avant-garde works were stored away, to re-emerge with the advent of *perestroika* in the 1980s.

**The Angel with the Golden Hair**, an icon from the early 12th century

## OLD RUSSIAN ART

The museum's fine collection begins with icons dating from the 12th–17th centuries. Russian icons derive from the Orthodox tradition and thus, just like Byzantine icons, tend to be sombre, marked by an absence of movement and a remote, mystic characterization of the saints. A superb example is one of the earliest icons, *The Angel with the Golden Hair,* in which the large, expressive eyes and delicate modelling of the Archangel Gabriel's face convey a sense of ethereal grace.

The Novgorod School *(see p165)* encouraged a much bolder and brighter style with a greater sense of drama and movement. And yet it is the poetically expressive and technically refined work of Andrey Rublev (c.1340–c.1430) that is considered by many to mark the pinnacle of Russian icon painting.

## 18TH–19TH-CENTURY ART

The first secular portraits (which owed much to the static quality of the icons) appeared in the second half of the 17th century. It was, however, under Peter the Great that Russian painting fully cast off from its Byzantine moorings. Peter the Great himself was the first patron to send young artists, often serfs, to study abroad. Secular art began to gain momentum in 1757 with the establishment of the Academy of Arts *(see p63)* which placed a heavy emphasis on Classical and mythological subjects.

European influence permeates the work of Russia's first important portrait painters, Ivan Nikitin (1688–1741) and Andrey Matveev (1701–39). The art of portraiture matured with Dmitriy Levitskiy (1735–1822), amongst whose best known works is a series of portraits of noble girls from the Smolnyy Institute.

Russian landscape painting was stimulated by the Romantic movement and in particular artists who sought inspiration abroad, including Silvestr Shchedrin (1791–1830) and

**Portrait of E I Nelidova (1773), by Dmitriy Levitskiy**

Fyodor Matveev (1758–1826). Ivan Aivazovskiy's (1817–1900) vast marine paintings, however, have something purely Russian in their scale and mood. Romanticism also influenced history painters such as Karl Bryullov (1799–1852), as in his depiction of *The Last Day of Pompeii.*

In 1863 a group of students, led by Ivan Kramskoy (1837–87), rebelled against the conservatism of the Academy of Arts. Seven years later they went on to set up the Association of Travelling Art Exhibitions, and came to be better known as the Wanderers *(Peredvizhniki),* or the Itinerants. They demanded that painting should be more socially relevant, and were fundamentally committed to Russian subject matter.

The most versatile of the Wanderers was Ilya Repin *(see p43)* whose bold canvas *Barge-Haulers on the Volga*

**Knight at the Crossroads (1882), by Viktor Vasnetsov**

*The Six-Winged Seraph* (1904), by Mikhail Vrubel

combines a visually powerful attack on forced labour with a romantic view of the Russian people. Meanwhile, *A Meal in the Monastery* by Vasiliy Perov (1833–82) is a satirical and equally effective attack on social injustice.

The nationalist element led history painters such as Nikolay Ge (1831–94) and Vasiliy Surikov (1848–1916) to turn to Russian history for inspiration, treating their subjects with a new psychological acuity, as in Ge's canvas of 1871–2, in which Peter the Great interrogates his sullenly resistant son.

The general Slavic revival also breathed new life into landscape painting, concentrating on the beauties of the Russian countryside. The master of the genre was Isaak Levitan (1860–1900), whose *Golden Autumn Village,* dated 1889, is almost Impressionist in style, a sign perhaps that the ascendancy of the Wanderers was coming to an end.

Viktor Vasnetsov (1848–1926) turned to Russia's heroic, and often legendary, pre-European past, in realistically painted canvases such as the *Knight at the Crossroads*. A haunting metaphor for Russia's uncertain future, the painting reveals that Vasnetsov was unable to avoid the fin-de-siècle melancholy and mysticism which was so potently expressed in the work of the next up-and-coming generation of artists, notably the Symbolists.

## 20TH-CENTURY ART

The dark, brooding canvases of Symbolist Mikhail Vrubel (1856–1910) combine Russian and religious themes with a more international outlook. Vrubel used colour and form to depict emotion and in *The Six-Winged Seraph* he employs a broken, vibrant, surface to express tension.

Another major contribution to 20th-century art was the "World of Art" movement, founded by Alexandre Benois and Sergey Diaghilev in the 1890s *(see p26)*. It rejected the notion of "socially useful art" in favour of a new tenet, "art pure and unfettered", and also opened up Russian painting to Western influences. Many members of the group,

*Portrait of the Director Vsevolod Meyerhold* (1916), Boris Grigorev

including Benois and Leon Bakst, designed stage sets and costumes for Diaghilev's Ballets Russes *(see p119)*.

The Russian avant-garde grew out of these local influences, plus the art of Cézanne, Picasso and Matisse. Mikhail Larionov (1881–1964) and Natalya Goncharova (1881–1962) both made brilliant use of Russian folk art as inspiration for primitivist works such as Goncharova's *Bleaching Canvas* (1908). They often altered their style in response to changing stimuli and later turned to Futurism's cult of the machine, as in Goncharova's *Cyclist* (1913) *(see p40)*.

The link between innovation in painting and the arts in general at this time is strikingly depicted in Boris Grigorev's angular portrait of Meyerhold, himself renowned for his radical approach to theatre.

Kazimir Malevich's (1878–1935) fascination with the juxtaposition of simple geometric shapes inspired the Suprematist movement. Vasily Kandinsky (1866–1944), a leading member of Munich's Blaue Reiter group, was also a key figure in the growth of Russian abstract art. Marc Chagall (1887–1985), El Lissitskiy (1890–1941) and Alexander Rodchenko (1891–1956) are also represented.

Due to the high demand for the loan of avant-garde works abroad, a changing selection by the major artists is on show.

## FOLK ART

Folk art became a strong influence on the development of modern Russian art in the 1860s when the wealthy industrialist and patron Savva Mamontov established an artists' colony at Abramtsevo, near Moscow. Vasiliy Polenov (1844–1927), Ilya Repin and Viktor Vasnetsov were among the painters encouraged to work alongside, and learn from, the serf craftsmen on the estate. The museum's collection of folk art is wonderfully diverse and includes exquisitely embroidered tapestries, traditional headdresses, painted tiles, porcelain toys, and lacquered spoons and dishes.

## Nevskiy Prospekt ❻
Невский проспект
*Nevskiy prospekt*

**Map** 6 D1–8 D3. Ⓜ *Nevskiy Prospekt, Gostinyy Dvor. See also pp46–9.*

Russia's most famous street, Nevskiy prospekt, is also St Petersburg's main thoroughfare and artery. In the 1830s, the novelist Nikolai Gogol *(see p42)* declared with great pride: "There is nothing finer than Nevskiy Avenue…in St Petersburg it is everything…is there anything more gay, more brilliant, more resplendent than this beautiful street of our capital?". In this respect very little has actually changed, for Nevskiy prospekt's intrinsic "all-powerful" value still prevails today.

Laid out in the early days of the city, it was first known as the Great Perspective Road, running 4.5 km (3 miles) from the Admiralty *(see p78)* to the Alexander Nevsky Monastery *(see pp130–31).* In spite of roaming wolves and uncontrollable flooding from the Neva *(see p37)* which made the avenue navigable in 1721, fine mansions, such as the Stroganov Palace *(see p112)* soon started to appear. Shops and bazaars, catering for the nobility, and inns for travelling merchants followed. A magnet pulling rich and poor alike, by the mid-18th century the avenue had become the place to see and be seen, to meet for gossip, business and pleasure.

Today, the street still teems with people until late into the night throughout the year. Many of the city's sights are close to the stretch between the Admiralty and Anichkov Bridge *(see pp46–7).* Some of the best shops *(see pp194–5)* can be found around Gostinyy dvor and Passazh arcade. Nevskiy prospekt also offers a wealth of cultural interest: the Small Philharmonia concert hall *(see p202),* the Russian national library, Beloselskiy-Belozerskiy Palace *(see p49)* and a wide variety of museums, theatres, churches, including the Church of St Catherine *(see p48),* shops, cinemas and eateries.

Armenian Church portico (1771–9)

## Armenian Church ❼
Армянская церковь
*Armyanskaya tserkov*

Nevskiy prospekt 40–42. **Map** 6 F1. **Tel** 318 4108. Ⓜ *Gostinyy Dvor.* ⏰ 9am–9pm.

Yuriy Velten designed the beautiful blue and white Armenian Church of St Catherine, with its Neo-Classical portico and single cupola. The church, which opened in 1780, was financed by a wealthy Armenian businessman called Ioakim Lazarev, who acquired the money from the sale of a Persian diamond which Count Grigoriy Orlov purchased for Catherine the Great *(see p22).*

Closed in 1930, the building has now been returned to the Armenian community and visitors are welcome to attend a service.

## Gostinyy Dvor ❽
Гостиный двор
*Gostinyy dvor*

Nevskiy pr 35. **Map** 6 F2. **Tel** 710 5408. Ⓜ *Gostinyy Dvor.* ⏰ 10am–10pm daily.

The term *gostinyy dvor* originally meant a coaching inn, but as trade developed around the inns, with travelling merchants setting up their stalls, it later came to mean "trading rows". The original wooden structure of this *gostinyy dvor* was destroyed by fire in 1736. Twenty years later, Bartolomeo Rastrelli

View along the bustle of Nevskiy prospekt, the hub of St Petersburg

designed a new building but the project proved too costly and ambitious. Building recommenced in 1761 and continued until 1785. Vallin de la Mothe created the striking sequence of columned arcades and massive porticos. The prominent yellow building forms an irregular quadrangle which is bounded on one side by Nevskiy prospekt. The combined length of its façades is nearly 1 km (3,300 ft).

In the 19th century the gallery became a fashionable promenade where more than 5,000 people were employed. Serious damage during the Siege of Leningrad *(see p27)* led to major reconstruction, making it more like a modern department store. Even now, with all the changes, it has retained its layout of "stalls" of individual trading units. Today it includes branches of foreign shops and a wide range of goods, making it the city's most important store *(see p195).*

Style-Moderne stained-glass windows in Yeliseev's

building, designed by Gavriil Baranovskiy in 1901–3, it is adorned with bronzes, heroic sculptures and huge windows. A plaque by the main door honours the grandsons.

Today the second floor of the building is home to the Akimov Comedy Theatre, while the ground floor is likely to be snapped up by another business.

## Anichkov Palace 🔟
Аничков дворец
*Anichkov dvorets*

Nevskiy prospekt 39.
**Map** 7 A2. Ⓜ *Gostinyy Dvor.*
🚌 *3, 7, 22, 24, 27.* 🚊 *1, 5, 7, 10, 11, 22.* ◐ *to public except for special events.*

In the early days, the broad Fontanka river was lined by palaces accessible mainly by boat. One of them was the Anichkov Palace (1741–50), remodelled in Baroque style in 1754. The palace was a gift from Tsarina Elizabeth to her lover Aleksey Razumovskiy. It was named after Lieutenant Colonel Mikhail Anichkov who set up camp on this site at the time of the founding of the city. Over the years the palace was rebuilt and altered many

times, according to the tastes of each successive owner. After Razumovskiy's death, Catherine the Great in turn gave the building to her lover, Prince Potemkin *(see p25).* In the early 19th century, Neo-Classical details were added by Carlo Rossi.

The palace then became the traditional winter residence of the heir to the throne. When Alexander III became tsar in 1881, he continued to live here, however, rather than move to the Winter Palace as was customary. After his death, his widow Maria Fyodorovna stayed on until the Revolution.

The palace originally had large gardens to the west but these were curtailed in 1816 when Ostrovskiy Square *(see p110)* was created and two Neo-Classical pavilions were added. The elegant colonnaded building overlooking the Fontanka to the east was commissioned by Giacomo Quarenghi in 1803–5. It was initially built as an arcade where goods from the imperial factories were stored before being allocated to the palaces. Later it was converted into government offices and now also houses the Cultural Centre of Children's Creative Work.

Columned arcades, Gostinyy dvor

## Yeliseev's 🟨
Елисеевский гастроном
*Yeliseevskiy gastronom*

Nevskiy prospekt 56. **Map** 6 F1.
Ⓜ *Gostinyy Dvor.*

The successful Yeliseev dynasty was founded by Pyotr Yeliseev, an ambitious peasant who, in 1813, opened a wine shop on Nevskiy prospekt. By the turn of the century his grandsons owned a chocolate factory, numerous houses, inns and this famous former food store. The city's most opulent Style-Moderne

Quarenghi's addition to the Anichkov Palace from Nevskiy prospekt

**Porticoed façade of Alexandrinskiy Theatre (1828–32), Ostrovskiy Square**

# Ostrovskiy Square ⓫
Площадь Островского
*Ploshchad Ostrovskovo*

**Map** 6 F2. Ⓜ *Gostinyy Dvor.* 🚎 *3, 7, 22, 27.* 🚊 *1, 5, 7, 10, 22.* **Russian National Library Tel** *310 2856.* ⏰ *9am–9pm.* **Theatre Museum Tel** *571 2195.* ⏰ *11am–6pm Thu–Mon, 1–7pm Wed.* ⚫ *last Fri of each month and public hols.* 📷 📷 **www**.theatremuseum.ru

One of Russia's most brilliant architects, Carlo Rossi, created this early 19th-century square, which is now named in honour of the dramatist Aleksandr Ostrovskiy (1823–86).

The focal point of the square is the elegant Alexandrinskiy Theatre *(see p202)*, designed in the Neo-Classical style which Rossi favoured. The portico of six Corinthian columns is crowned by a chariot of Apollo, sculpted by Stepan Pimenov.

The building was the new home to Russia's oldest theatre company, set up in 1756. Plays premiered here include Nikolai Gogol's *The Inspector General* (1836) and Anton Chekhov's *The Seagull* (1901). In Soviet times the theatre was renamed the Pushkin Theatre.

In the garden just in front of the theatre is a monument to Catherine the Great, the only one in the city. It was designed principally by Mikhail Mikeshin and unveiled in 1873. The statue depicts Catherine surrounded by states-men and other worthies, and includes the female president (1783–96) of the Academy of Sciences, Princess Yekaterina Dashkova.

The benches behind the monument are packed during the summer months with chess players and spectators. On the west side of the square, opposite the Anichkov Palace *(see p109)* is an elegant colonnade decorated with Classical sculptures. This is the extension of the Russian Library, made by Rossi in 1828–34. Founded in 1795, the library currently holds more than 28 million items. A prized possession is the personal library of the French philosopher Voltaire, which Catherine the Great purchased to show her appreciation of her sometime mentor and correspondent.

In the southeast corner of the square, at No. 6, is the Theatre Museum which traces the evolution of the Russian stage from its origins in mid-18th-century serf and imperial theatres. Amid the eclectic array of playbills, photographs, costumes, set designs and other artifacts, there are also some set designs by one of the great innovators of modern theatre, the director Vsevolod Meyerhold (1874–1940).

# Ulitsa Zodchego Rossi ⓬
Улица Зодчего Росси
*Ulitsa Zodchevo Rossi*

**Map** 6 F2. Ⓜ *Gostinyy Dvor.*

There could be no better memorial to Carlo Rossi than the near perfect architectural ensemble of identical arcades and colonnades forming "Architect Rossi Street". The 22-m (72-ft) high buildings stand precisely 22 m (72 ft) apart and stretch for 220 m (720 ft). In 2008 the street had its 180-year anniversary. Seen from ploshchad Lomonosova, the perspective hypnotically coaxes the eye towards the Alexandriinskiy Theatre.

At No. 2 is the home of the former Imperial School of Ballet, now named after the teacher Agrippina Vaganova (1879–1951), one of the few dancers not to emigrate after the Revolution. The school began in 1738 when Jean-Baptiste Landé began training orphans and palace servants' children to take part in court entertainment. It has produced many of Russia's most celebrated dancers *(see p118)*, including Anna Pavlova and Rudolf Nureyev.

**19th-century photograph of ulitsa Zodchego Rossi (1828–34)**

---

### ARCHITECT CARLO ROSSI

Carlo Rossi (1775–1849) was one of the last great exponents of Neo-Classicism in St Petersburg. He found an ideal client in Alexander I, who shared his belief in the use of architecture to express the power of the ruling autocracy. By the time of his death, Rossi had created no fewer than 12 of St Petersburg's impressive streets and 13 of its squares, including Palace Square *(see p83)*. Rossi's status as Alexander I's favourite architect encouraged rumours that Rossi was the offspring of an affair between Tsar Paul I and Rossi's Italian ballerina mother.

**Central corpus of Vorontsov Palace**

# Vorontsov Palace ⑬
Воронцовский дворец
*Vorontsovskiy dvorets*

Sadovaya ulitsa 26. **Map** 6 F2.
🌑 *to public.* M *Gostinyy Dvor,
Sennaya Ploshchad.*

The most exclusive military school in the Russian empire, the Corps des Pages, occupied the Vorontsov Palace from 1810–1918. Among those privileged enough to study here were a number of the Decembrists *(see pp22–3)* and Prince Felix Yusupov *(see p121).* Today the palace houses the Suvorov Military Academy.

Designed by Bartolomeo Rastrelli *(see p93),* the handsome palace, which once stood in its own extensive grounds, was built in 1749–57 for Prince Mikhail Vorontsov, one of Tsarina Elizabeth's leading ministers. Rastrelli's graceful wrought-iron railings are among the earliest examples of their kind in Russia.

# Apraksin Market ⑭
Апраксин двор
*Apraksin dvor*

Sadovaya ulitsa. **Map** 6 E2.
M *Gostinyy Dvor, Sennaya
Ploshchad.*

Founded in the late 18th century, the market takes its name from the Apraksin family who owned the land it was built on. When fire destroyed the original wooden stalls in 1862, the arcade was erected. By 1900 there were more than 600 outlets selling everything from food, wine and spices to furs, furniture and haberdashery. In 2009 the large street market here moved to Rustavelli Street, far from the city centre. The historic Apraksin Market is to be reconstructed; in the meantime arcade shops continue to open.

# Cathedral of Our Lady of Kazan ⑮
Собор Казанской
Богоматери
*Sobor Kazanskoy Bogomateri*

Kazanskaya pl 2. **Map** 6 E1. *Tel 318
4528.* M *Nevskiy Prospekt.* 🚌 *3, 7,
22, 27.* 🚊 *1, 5, 7, 10, 22.*
⏰ *9am–7:30pm daily.* 📷 ♿

One of St Petersburg's most majestic churches, the Cathedral of Our Lady of Kazan was commissioned by Paul I and took over a decade to build (1801–11). The impressive design by serf architect Andrey Voronikhin was inspired by St Peter's in Rome. Its 111-m (364-ft) long, curved colonnade disguises the orientation of the building which runs parallel to Nevskiy prospekt, conforming to a religious stipulation that the main altar face east. In Voronikhin's original design he intended to duplicate the colonnade on the south side. The cathedral is named after the miracle-working icon of Our Lady of Kazan. The icon is now kept in the cathedral.

The interior decoration is generally subdued. Its most impressive features are the great 80-m (262-ft) high dome and the massive pink Finnish granite columns with bronze capitals and bases. Occupied in the Communist era by a Museum of Atheism, the building was returned to exclusive religious use in 1999.

Completed in 1811, the cathedral is intimately linked with the wars against Napoleon *(see p22)* fought during the same period. In 1813 Field Marshal Mikhail Kutuzov (1745–1813), mastermind of a successful retreat from Moscow following the invasion of Napoleon's Grand Army in 1812, was buried here with full military honours. Kutuzov has been immortalized in Tolstoy's great novel *War and Peace* (1865–9). His statue and that of his comrade-in-arms, Mikhail Barclay de Tolly (1761–1818), both by Boris Orlovskiy, have stood outside the cathedral since 1837.

**Pink granite columns and mosaic floor in main nave, Kazan Cathedral**

## Stroganov Palace ⑯

Строгановский дворец
*Stroganovskiy dvorets*

Nevskiy prospekt 17. **Map** 6 E1.
***Tel** 571 8238.* Ⓜ *Nevskiy Prospekt.*
🚌 *3, 7, 22, 24, 27.* 🚎 *1, 5, 7, 10,
17.* ◻ *10am–6pm Wed–Sun
(10am–5pm Mon).* 🖼

This Baroque masterpiece
was designed in 1752–4 by
Bartolomeo Rastrelli *(see
p93)*. Commissioned by the
enormously wealthy Count
Sergey Stroganov, the palace
was occupied by his descendants until the 1917 Revolution.
The vast Stroganov fortune
was amassed mainly through
the monopoly the family held
on salt, which they mined
from their territories in the
north of the Russian empire.

The pink and white palace,
which overlooks both Nevskiy
prospekt and the Moyka river,
was one of the city's most
impressive private residences.
The magnificent river façade is
decorated with Doric columns,
cornices, pediments and inven-
tive window surrounds.

The Stroganovs were noted
collectors of everything from
Egyptian antiquities and Roman
coins to icons and Old Masters.
The palace was nationalized
after the Revolution and then
preserved for ten years as a
museum of the life of the
decadent aristocracy. When it

**Neo-Romanesque portal of the
Lutheran Church (1832–8)**

was closed, some of the objects
were auctioned in the West,
and the rest were transferred
to the Hermitage *(see pp84–
93)*. The building now belongs
to the Russian Museum *(see
pp104–107)* and has temporary exhibitions and a collection
of waxwork figures.

## Lutheran Church ⑰

Лютеранская церковь
*Lyuteranskaya tserkov*

Nevskiy prospekt 22–24. **Map** 6 E1.
Ⓜ *Nevskiy Prospekt.*

Set back a little from Nevskiy
prospekt, the attractive, twin-
towered Lutheran church is
dedicated to St Peter. Built in
its present form during the

1830s, the church served
St Petersburg's ever-growing
German community *(see p57)*.
The prize-winning design by
Aleksandr Bryullov is in an un-
usual, Neo-Romanesque style.

From 1936 the church was
used as a vegetable store until,
in the late 1950s, it was converted into a swimming pool.
The basin was carved out of
the nave floor, the gallery
lined with spectator benches
and there was a high diving
board under the apse. The
building has now been handed
back to the German-Lutheran
Church of Russia. The church
has been fully restored and
now offers regular services.

**The Academic Capella concert hall**

## Academic Capella ⑱

Академическая капелла
*Akademicheskaya kapella*

Naberezhnaya reki Moyki 20. **Map** 2
E5. ***Tel** 314 1058.* Ⓜ *Nevskiy
Prospekt.* ◻ *for concerts only.* 🖼
🎟 *See* Entertainment *p194.*

Enclosed within a courtyard
off the Moyka river is this
ochre-coloured concert hall
with a façade in the French
Classical style of Louis XV.
The Academic Capella was
designed by Leontiy Benois in
1887–9 as the residence of the
Imperial Court choir. Founded
during the reign of Peter the
Great, the choir is as old as
the city itself. Its former
directors have included the
distinguished Russian composers Mikhail Glinka
(1804–57) and Nikolai
Rimsky-Korsakov (1844–1908).

With its excellent acoustics,
the Academic Capella can
claim to be one of the best
concert halls in the world.
Outside is the aptly named
Singers' Bridge (Pevcheskiy
most), which was designed by
Yegor Adam in 1837–40.

**Elaborate west façade of the Stroganov Palace overlooking the Moyka river**

**Personal effects in Pushkin's study, Pushkin House-Museum**

# Pushkin House-Museum ⑲
Музей-квартира
А. С. Пушкина
*Muzey-kvartira AS Pushkina*

Naberezhnaya reki Moyki 12. **Map** 2 E5. **Tel** *571 3531.* ⏲ *10am–6pm Wed–Mon.* ⬤ *last Fri of each month and public hols.* 📷 ✂

Every year on the anniversary of Alexander Pushkin's death (29 January 1837), loyal devotees of Russia's greatest poet come to lay floral tributes outside his apartment. Pushkin was born in Moscow in 1799, but spent many years of his life in St Petersburg and the museum is one of several places in the city with which the poet is associated.

From the autumn of 1836 until his death, Pushkin lived in this fairly opulent apartment overlooking the Moyka, with his wife Natalya, their four children and Natalya's two sisters. It was here on the couchette in the study that he bled to death after his fateful duel with d'Anthès *(see p83)*.

Some half dozen rooms on the first floor have been refurbished in the Empire style of the period. By far the most evocative is Pushkin's study, which is arranged exactly as it was when he died. On the writing table is an ivory paper knife given to the poet by his sister, a bronze handbell and a treasured inkstand *(see p39)*. Embellished with the figure of an Ethiopian boy, the inkstand is a reminder of Pushkin's great grandfather, Abram Hannibal. Bought by the Russian ambassador in Constantinople as a

slave in 1706, Hannibal served as a general under Peter the Great. He was the inspiration for the unfinished novel *The Negro of Peter the Great* on which Pushkin was working at the time of his death.

On the wall in front of his desk is a Turkish sabre presented to Pushkin in the Caucasus, where he had been exiled in 1820 for his radical views. Ironically it was there that he spent some of his happiest years. It was there too that he began his most famous work, *Eugene Onegin*, a novel in verse written in 1823–30.

The most impressive feature of the apartment is the poet's library which contains more

than 4,500 volumes in a staggering 14 European and Oriental languages. Among these are works by the authors whom Pushkin most admired, including Shakespeare, Byron, Heine, Dante and Voltaire.

# Imperial Stables ⑳
Конюшенное Ведомство
*Konyushennoe Vedomstvo*

Konyushennaya ploshchad 1. **Map** 2 E5. **Church** ⏲ *10am–7pm daily.* ✚ ✂

The long, salmon-coloured building running parallel to the Moyka embankment is the former Imperial stables. Originally built in the first part of the 18th century, the stables were reconstructed by Vasiliy Stasov in 1817–23.

The only part of the building open to the public lies behind the central section of the long south façade, crowned by a silver dome and cross. This is the church where Alexander Pushkin's funeral took place on 1 February 1837. Its Neo-Classical interior is in the form of a basilica and is decorated with yellow marble pillars. It is now a fully functional Orthodox church.

**North façade of Imperial Stables (left) and Little Stable Bridge on the Moyka**

# SENNAYA PLOSHCHAD

The western part of St Petersburg is an area of contrasts, home to some of the city's wealthiest residences and most poverty-stricken dwellings. The palatial architecture along the English Quay is a world away from the decrepit living quarters around bustling Sennaya ploshchad, which have changed little since Dostoevsky *(see p123)* described them. In between lies the old maritime quarter, once inhabited by Peter the Great's shipwrights, many of whom were English. This area extended all the way from the New Holland warehouses to

**Coat of arms on Yusupov Palace**

St Nicholas' Cathedral, which stands on the site of the naval parade ground. Theatre Square has been a hub of entertainment since the mid-18th century. It is dominated by the prestigious Mariinskiy Theatre and the Rimsky-Korsakov Conservatory, where many of Russia's greatest artists began their careers. Before 1917, the streets leading off the square were home to theatre directors, actors, ballerinas, artists and musicians. Today, performing artists are once more returning to live in this shady backwater, attracted by the peace of the tree-lined canals.

## SIGHTS AT A GLANCE

### Cathedrals
St Nicholas' Cathedral ❷

### Historic Buildings and Areas
Choral Synagogue ❺
Main Post Office ❽
New Holland ❻
Rimsky-Korsakov
  Conservatory ❸

### Theatres
Mariinskiy Theatre ❶

### Palaces
Yusupov Palace ❹

### Streets and Squares
Bolshaya Morskaya Ulitsa ❾
The English Quay ❼
Sennaya Ploshchad ❿

### Museums
Railway Museum ⓫

### KEY

▢ Street-by-Street map
  *See pp116–17*

Ⓜ Metro

0 metres    600
0 yards     600

◁ **Gilded Baroque interior of the upper church of St Nicholas' Cathedral**

# Street-by-Street: Theatre Square

Theatre Square was once known as Carousel Square and was frequently used as the site for fairs and festivals. During the 19th century when St Petersburg became the cultural capital of Russia, the Mariinskiy Theatre and Rimsky-Korsakov Conservatory were established, and the neighbourhood became home to many artists. Today, the tradition of entertainment is still thriving and Theatre Square remains a focal point for theatrical and musical life *(see p202)*. Nearby, the tree-lined canal embankments and the gardens surrounding the beautiful St Nicholas' Cathedral are enchanting places to stroll.

**Atlas on prospekt Rimskovo-Korsakova**

**The Monument to Rimsky-Korsakov**, who taught at the Conservatory for 37 years, was designed by Veniamin Bogolyubov and Vladimir Ingal and erected in 1952.

**Yusupov Palace**
*Historic site of the gruesome murder of Rasputin* (see p121), *this grand palace belonged to the wealthy Yusupov family. Its opulent interiors include this Italian marble staircase and a tiny Rococo theatre* ❹

**Rimsky-Korsakov Conservatory**
*Tchaikovsky, Prokofiev and Shostakovich (see p43) were among the talents nurtured by Russia's first conservatory, founded in 1862 by pianist and composer Anton Rubinstein* ❸

Monument to
Mikhail Glinka
*(see p44)*

★ **Mariinskiy Theatre**
*This theatre has been home to the world-famous Mariinskiy (Kirov) Opera and Ballet Company since 1860. Hidden behind its imposing façade is the sumptuous auditorium where many of Russia's greatest dancers* (see p118) *have performed* ❶

**The Lion Bridge** *(Lvinyy Most)* is one of a number of quaint and curious suspension bridges on the narrow, tree-lined Griboedov canal *(see p36)*. These bridges are well-known meeting places, notably for romantic trysts.

**LOCATOR MAP**
*See Street Finder, map 5*

**The House of Mikhail Fokin** at No. 109 is where the renowned ballet-master and choreographer lived before the Revolution.

**STAR SIGHT**

★ Mariinskiy Theatre

**The Benois House** belonged to an artistic dynasty which included the co-founder of the World of Art movement, Alexandre Benois *(see p107)*.

**The Belfry**, an elegant four-tiered structure with a gilded spire, was built to mark the main entrance to St Nicholas' Cathedral.

**St Nicholas' Cathedral**
*A fine example of 18th-century Russian Baroque, the lofty upper church is richly decorated with icons, gilding and this carved iconostasis. The lower church, beautifully lit with candles, is also open for worship* ❷

**KEY**

━ ━ ━ Suggested route

NAB KANALA GRIBOEDOVA

SKOVO-KORSAKOVA

NIKOLSKIY PEREULOK

KANAL GRIBOEDOVA

SADOVAYA ULITSA

| 0 metres | 100 |
| 0 yards | 100 |

**The former Nicholas market**, characterized by its long arcade and steep roof, was constructed in 1788–9. In the 19th century it became an unofficial labour exchange as many unemployed workers gathered here.

# Ballet in St Petersburg

Admired throughout the world, Russian ballet traces its origins back to 1738 when a French dancing master, Jean-Baptiste Landé, established a school in St Petersburg to train the children of palace employees. The Imperial Ballet School, as it soon became known, flourished under a string of distinguished foreign teachers, culminating in Marius Petipa (1818–1910). Petipa first joined the school in 1847 as a principal dancer and later choreographed over 60 ballets, inspiring such famous dancers as Matilda Kshesinskaya *(see p72)*.

**Matilda Kshesinskaya's ballet shoes**

Following the 1905 Revolution, a reaction against Classicism led to an increasing number of defections from the Imperial theatres to the new private companies like Sergey Diaghilev's Ballets Russes. The dispersion of talent increased after the Bolsheviks seized power in 1917 and many artists went into exile abroad. Fortunately for Soviet Russia, the distinguished prima ballerina Agrippina Vaganova remained to train the next generation of dancers. St Petersburg's Russian Ballet Academy now bears her name *(see p110)*.

**Anna Pavlova's** *(1885–1931) most famous role, The Dying Swan, was created especially for her by Mikhail Fokin. In 1912 Pavlova left Russia to form her own touring company, spreading her enthusiasm for ballet throughout Europe.*

**Vaslaw Nijinsky** *(1890–1950) had one of his greatest roles as the golden slave in Schéhérazade which took Paris by storm in 1910. A principal of the Ballets Russes before World War I, he revolutionized male roles. His incomparable technical skills and expressive qualities influenced future generations of dancers.*

**Rudolf Nureyev** *(1938–93), seen here in Sleeping Beauty at the Mariinskiy, defected to the West in 1961. As both choreographer and dancer, Nureyev continued to enthral audiences for over 30 years until his death in 1993.*

**The Mariinskiy Ballet,** *usually known abroad as the Kirov, is now reviving some of the original productions of the Ballets Russes, including their version of Giselle, previously not shown in Russia.*

## THE BALLETS RUSSES

The legendary touring company which revolutionized ballet between 1909 and 1929 was the brainchild of the impresario and art critic Sergey Diaghilev (*see p43*). Diaghilev found a kindred spirit in the choreographer Mikhail Fokin, who shared his vision of a spectacle that would fuse music, ballet and decor in a seamless artistic whole.

Diaghilev had the pick of dancers from the Mariinskiy and, in 1909, he brought his Ballets Russes to Paris. The company went from strength to strength with successful tours worldwide.

Diaghilev's new company had a remarkable impact on the contemporary art world. The ballets of Fokine, in particular, prepared audiences for greater innovation and experiment. Exciting contributions from costume and set designers Léon Bakst and Alexandre Benois, the composer Igor Stravinsky and the dancers Vaslaw Nijinsky, Anna Pavlova and Tamara Karsavina all played a part in expanding back the artistic frontiers. After Diaghilev's death in 1929, the Ballets Russes fragmented but its ethos and traditions have been preserved in many of today's leading companies.

**Early 20th-century programme for the Ballets Russes**

One of Russia's most important cultural institutions, the Mariinskiy Theatre

# Mariinskiy Theatre ❶
Мариинский театр
*Mariinskiy teatr*

Teatralnaya ploshchad 1 & Dekabristov ulitsa 37. **Map** 5 B3.
**Tel** 346 4141. 🚌 3, 22, 27.
🚊 5, 22. ⬭ For information on performances see p202. 📷 ⬜
📷 ⬜ www.mariinsky.ru

Named in honour of Tsarina Maria Alexandrovna, wife of Alexander II, the theatre is known abroad by its Soviet title, the Kirov, while at home it has reverted to its original name, the Mariinskiy Theatre. A new concert hall opened here in 2007; there are also plans to build a new stage for the theatre itself.

The building was erected in 1860 by the architect Albert Kavos, who designed the Bolshoy Theatre in Moscow. It stands on the site of an earlier theatre which was destroyed by fire. In 1883–96, the Neo-Renaissance façade was remodelled by Viktor Schröter, who added most of the ornamental detail. The pale blue and gold auditorium, where so many illustrious dancers have made their debut, creates a dazzling impression. Its architectural decoration of twisted columns,

**Imperial eagle on the royal box**

atlantes, cherubs and cameo medallions has remained unchanged since the theatre's completion, and the imperial eagles have been restored to the royal box. The ceiling painting of dancing girls and cupids by Italian artist Enrico Franchioli dates from c.1856, while the superb stage curtain was added during Russian ballet's golden age in 1914. Equally remarkable is the glittering festive foyer, decorated with fluted pilasters, bas-reliefs of Russian composers and mirrored doors.

Although the Mariinskiy is better known abroad for its ballet company, it is also one of the country's leading opera houses. Most of the great 19th-century Russian operas were premiered here, including Mussorgsky's *Boris Godunov* (1874), Tchaikovsky's *Queen of Spades* (1890), and Shostakovich's controversial opera *Lady Macbeth of Mtsensk* (1934).

**The Mariinskiy's luxuriant stage curtain, designed by Aleksandr Golovin in 1914**

# St Nicholas' Cathedral ❷

Никольский собор

*Nikolskiy sobor*

Nikolskaya ploshchad 1/3. **Map** 5 C4. **Tel** 714 0862. 🚌 3, 22. ☐ 7am–7pm daily.

This stunning Baroque cathedral by Savva Chevakinskiy, one of Russia's great 18th-century architects, was built in 1753–62. Founded for sailors and Admiralty employees housed in the neighbourhood, and named after St Nicholas, the patron saint of sailors, the cathedral became known as the "Sailors' Church".

The beautiful exterior is decorated with white Corinthian pilasters and surmounted by five gilded cupolas. Nearby, within the cathedral's leafy grounds and overlooking the intersection of the Kryukov and Griboedov canals, is a slender four-tiered bell tower crowned by a spire.

Following the Russian tradition, there are two churches within the cathedral. The lower church, intended for daily use, is lit by icon lamps, candles and chandeliers, creating a magical effect. The icons (1755–7) are the work of the brothers Fedot and Menas Kolokolnikov. In total contrast, the upper church, used mainly on Sundays and for weddings, has a brighter, airy feel and a typically Baroque exuberance, with gilt and stucco ornamentation and Italianate paintings.

**The pale blue and white Baroque façade of St Nicholas' Cathedral**

**Islamic arches and coffered ceiling in the Moorish Room, Yusupov Palace**

The most impressive feature is the magnificent gilded iconostasis dating from 1755–60.

# Rimsky-Korsakov Conservatory ❸

Консерватория имени Римского-Корсакова

*Konservatoriya imeni Rimskovo-Korsakova*

Teatralnaya ploshchad 3. **Map** 5 B3. **Tel** 571 8574. 🚌 3, 22, 27. 🚊 5, 22. ☐ for performances only. 🎦 🎦 by appt (**Tel** 312 2507).

Russia's oldest music school, the conservatory was founded in 1862 by the piano virtuoso Anton Rubinstein (1829–94). The present building was designed in 1896 by Vladimir Nicolas.

Among those to graduate from the school before the Revolution were Tchaikovsky (*see p42*) and Sergey Prokofiev. In the Soviet years, the school continued to flourish, and the greatest musical figure to emerge from this era was composer Dmitriy Shostakovich (1906–75) (*see p43*).

In the forecourt outside the school are two statues. On the left, a 1952 memorial honours the school's influential teacher, Nikolai Rimsky-Korsakov, after whom the conservatory is now named. On the right, the statue of Mikhail Glinka (1906) by Robert Bach is a reminder that the conservatory stands on the original site where Russia's first opera, Glinka's *A Life for the Tsar*, was premiered in 1836 in the old Kamennyy (Stone) Theatre.

# Yusupov Palace ❹

Юсуповскис дворец

*Yusupovskiy dvorets*

Naberezhnaya reki Moyki 94. **Map** 5 B3. **Tel** 314 9883. 🚌 3, 22, 27. ☐ 11am–5pm daily. 🎦 English (audio tours only).

Overlooking the Moyka, this yellow, colonnaded building (1760s) was designed by Vallin de la Mothe. The palace was acquired in 1830 by the aristocratic Yusupov family to house their superb collection of paintings. Major work was then carried out on the interior by Andrey Mikhaylov and Ippolito Monighetti.

The interiors, notable among them the exotic Moorish Room, with its fountain, mosaics and arches, can be viewed by guided or audio tour only. Separate tickets are needed for the tour of the cellars, which house an exhibition on Grigoriy Rasputin, the infamous "holy man" who was murdered here by Prince Felix Yusupov.

The elegant, Rococo-style family theatre seats just 180, and attending a concert (*see p202*) is an experience in itself.

## THE GRIM DEATH OF RASPUTIN

The Russian peasant and mystic Grigoriy Rasputin (1869–1916) exercised an extraordinarily powerful influence over the court and government of Russia *(see p26)*. The mysterious circumstances of his dramatic death on 17 December 1916 are legendary. Lured to Yusupov's palace on the pretext of a party, Rasputin was poisoned, then shot by Prince Felix Yusupov and left for dead. Returning to the scene the prince found Rasputin still alive and a struggle ensued before Rasputin disappeared into the courtyard. Pursued by the conspirators he was shot another three times and brutally battered before being dumped in the river. When his corpse was found three days later, clinging to the supports of a bridge, water in his lungs indicated death by drowning.

## Choral Synagogue ❺
Хоральная Синагога
*Khoralnaya Sinagoga*

Lermontovskiy prospekt 2.
**Map** 5 B3. 🚇 *3, 6, 22, 27, K-27.*

In 1826 Tsar Nicholas I decreed that all Jews, save 29 employed on behalf of the Court, be exiled from St Petersburg. Further "purifications" took place in the 1830s. However, after Nicholas' death in 1855 the Jewish population grew rapidly and in 1879 a site was approved for a permanent house of prayer.

Designed in Moorish style by architects Ivan Shaposhnikov and Viktor Shreter, the Synagogue opened in 1893, by which time the Jewish community had reached 16,500, nearly 2 per cent of the city's population. Accommodating 1,200 or more, the Synagogue was the only Jewish place of

**Vallin de la Mothe's impressive arch on the Moyka, leading into New Holland**

prayer to survive the repressions of the 1930s. It continued to function even during the Siege of 1941; the community remaining largely intact whilst other Jewish communities in Eastern Europe were decimated. Today, the Synagogue still has an active community.

## New Holland ❻
Новая Голландия
*Novaya Gollandiya*

Naberezhnaya reki Moyki.
**Map** 5 B3. 🚇 *3, 22.* ⬤ for restoration.

Created when the Kryukov canal was constructed between the Moyka and Neva rivers in 1719, this triangular island was originally used for storing ship timber. The name is in honour of the Dutch shipbuilders who inspired Peter the Great's naval ambitions.

In 1765, the original wooden warehouses were rebuilt in red brick by Savva Chevakinskiy. At the same time Vallin de la Mothe designed the austere but romantic arch facing onto the

Moyka which creates an atmospheric entrance to the timber yard. Barges would pass through the arch and into a turning basin beyond, then return loaded with timber along the canals towards the Admiralty ship-yards. A cultural complex is now being constructed here, and is due to be completed in 2012.

## The English Quay ❼
Английская набережная
*Angliyskaya naberezhnaya*

**Map** 5 A2. 🚇 *11, K-154, K-350.*

English merchants settled here in the 1730s, and were soon followed by craftsmen, architects, artists, innkeepers and factory owners. By 1800 the area was one of the city's most fashionable addresses.

It still boasts impressive buildings. The Neo-Classical mansion at No. 10 was the fictional setting for the debutante ball of Natasha Rostova in Tolstoy's novel *War and Peace*. No. 28 was occupied by the lover of ballet dancer Matilda Kshesinskaya *(see p72)*, and is the former headquarters of the Socialist-Revolutionary Party. On ploshchad Truda, the former palace of Grand Duke Nikolai Nikolaevich (son of Nicholas I) was given in 1917 to the trades unions. No. 44, Rumyantsev Palace, is part of the State Museum of the History of St Petersburg.

**Quarenghi's grand porticoed façade, at No. 32 on the English Quay**

# Main Post Office ❽
Главпочтамт
*Glavpochtamt*

Pochtamtskaya ulitsa 9. **Map** 5 C2.
**Tel** 315 8022. 🚌 3, 22. 🞏 to the
public.

The building's main exterior
feature is the arched gallery
spanning Pochtamtskaya
ulitsa. Built as an extension to
Nikolay Lvov's main building,
the gallery was added by
Albert Kavos in 1859. Under
the Pochtamt (Post Office)
sign on the arch is a clock
showing the time in major
cities around the world.

Inside the post office, behind
Lvov's porticoed Neo-Classical
façade of 1782–9, is a splendid
Style-Moderne hall characterized by decorative ironwork
and a glass ceiling over the
vast, tiled floor space. The
hall was created in the early
20th century when a roof
was constructed over what
had originally been the
courtyard stables.

**Porticoed façade, Main Post Office**

# Bolshaya Morskaya Ulitsa ❾
Большая Морская улица
*Bolshaya Morskaya ulitsa*

**Map** 5 C2. 🚌 3, 22, 27.

Always one of St Petersburg's
most fashionable streets,
shady Bolshaya Morskaya ulitsa
is the choice of the artistic
elite to this day. It has some
exceedingly handsome 19th-
century mansions hidden away
between St Isaac's Square *(see
p79)* and Pochtamtskiy most.

**Stone atlas at No. 43 Bolshaya
Morskaya ulitsa (1840)**

The mansion at No. 61 was
built by Albert Kavos in the
1840s for the St Petersburg
Stage Coach Company. No. 52,
nearby, was acquired by the
Russian Union of Architects in
1932. Built by Aleksandr Pel
in 1835–6, it was formerly the
residence of the celebrated
patron of the arts Aleksandr
Polovtsov, who built up the
impressive collection of the
Stieglitz Museum *(see p127)*.
The striking late 19th-century
interiors with mahogany panelling, tapestries and carved
ceilings were designed by
Maximilian Messmacher and
Nikolay Brullov and can be
admired from the Osobnyak
Polovtseva restaurant within.

Just across the street, No. 47
is a particularly fine example
of Style-Moderne architecture
with sculpted stone rosettes,

delicate iron tracery and a
beautiful mosaic frieze of
pink flowers. This is the work
of Mikhail Geisler and Boris
Guslistiy, dating from 1901–2.
It was in this mansion that the
celebrated émigré novelist
Vladimir Nabokov (1899–1977)
grew up, and there is a small
museum to him on the first
floor. Admired for his linguis-
tic ingenuity in both English
and Russian, Nabokov hit the
headlines across the world
with the publication of *Lolita*,
his *succès de scandale* of 1959.

Next door at No. 45 is the
Union of Composers, the former home of socialite Princess
Gagarina who lived here in
the 1870s. The mansion was
reconstructed in the 1840s by
Auguste-Ricard de Montferrand,
and it retains elements of the
original 18th-century building.

Montferrand also built the
former residence of millionaire
industrialist Pyotr Demidov at
No. 43. A mass of Renaissance
and Baroque elements, with
atlantes, vases, winged glories
and rustication, the façade also
has Demidov's coat of arms.

# Sennaya Ploshchad ❿
Сенная площадь
*Sennaya ploshchad*

**Map** 6 D3. Ⓜ *Sennaya Ploshchad,
Sadovaya.*

This is one of the oldest
squares in St Petersburg. The
square's name, meaning
Haymarket, derives from the
original market where livestock, fodder and firewood
were sold which opened in
the 1730s. Although fairly close
to the city centre, the area
around the square was inhabited by the poor and the
market was the cheapest and
liveliest in the city (the so-called
"belly of St Petersburg"). The

**Style-Moderne mosaic frieze at No. 47 Bolshaya Morskaya ulitsa (1901–2)**

## FYODOR DOSTOEVSKY

One of Russia's greatest writers, Fyodor Dostoevsky *(see pp43–4)* was born in 1821 in Moscow but spent most of his adult life in St Petersburg, where many of his novels and short stories are set. A defining moment in his life occurred in 1849 when he was arrested and charged with revolutionary conspiracy. After eight months of solitary confinement in the Peter and Paul Fortress *(see pp66–7)*, Dostoevsky and 21 other "conspirators" from the socialist Petrashevsky Circle were subjected to a macabre mock execution before being exiled to hard labour in Siberia until 1859. The sinister experience is recalled in his novel *The Idiot* (1868). He died in 1881.

oldest building, at the centre of the square, is the former guardhouse, a single-storey Neo-Classical building with a columned portico, which dates to 1818–20. The guardsmen's duties ranged from supervising the traders to flogging serfs, mostly for minor misdemeanours. By that time the neighbourhood had become synonymous with dirt, squalor, crime and vice. At No. 3 is the site of "Vyazemskiy's Monastery", the nickname for a notorious tenement overrun with pubs, gambling dens and brothels in the 1850s and '60s.

This was the squalid world so vividly evoked in Fyodor Dostoevsky's masterpiece *Crime and Punishment.* As the

The guardhouse on bustling Sennaya ploshchad

contemptuous hero of the novel, Raskolnikov, wanders around the market, he absorbs the "heat in the street.... the airlessness, the bustle and the plaster, scaffolding, bricks and dust.... that special St Petersburg stench.... and the numerous drunken men" which "completed the revolting misery of the picture". The novel was finished in 1866 while Dostoevsky was living at Alonkin's House, (No. 7 Przhevalskovo ulitsa), to the west of the square.

During the Soviet era the square was given a new image, stallholders were banished, trees were planted and it was optimistically renamed Peace Square (ploshchad Mira). The five-storey, yellow and white apartment blocks that surround the square today were also built then, in Stalin's version of Neo-Classicism. Sadly, in 1961, the square's most attractive monument, the Baroque Church of the Assumption, built in 1765, was pulled down to make way for one of the city's earliest metro stations.

## Railway Museum ⑪
Музей железнодорожного транспорта
*Muzey zheleznodorozhnovo transporta*

Sadovaya ulitsa 50. **Map** 6 D4.
***Tel*** 315 1476. Ⓜ *Sennaya ploshchad, Sadovaya.* ⃝ *11am–5pm Sun–Thu.* ⬤ *last Thu of month.* ✂ *English.*

More than 6,000 fascinating exhibits illustrate the history of the Russian railway system since 1813. The most interesting sections of the museum deal with the earliest railways, including Russia's first from Tsarskoe Selo to St Petersburg which began running in 1837, and the 650-km (404-mile) line from Moscow to St Petersburg (1851).

Exhibits include models of the first Russian steam engine, built by the Cherepanovs in 1834, and of an armoured train used by Trotsky in the defence of the city during the Civil War *(see p27)*. An insight into luxury travel in the late tsarist period can be gained from the walk-through section of a first-class sleeping compartment with velvet upholstery and Style-Moderne decoration.

Model of 1830s engine for the Tsarskoe Selo railway, Railway Museum

# FURTHER AFIELD

While the majority of St Petersburg's sights are centrally located, the outlying areas of the city have a number of places of architectural, cultural and historical importance.

To the east is the Smolnyy district, taking its name from the tar yard which supplied the city's embryonic shipbuilding industry in the 18th century. The highlight of this area is Rastrelli's dazzling Baroque Smolnyy Convent. Nearby, the Smolnyy Institute is famed for its historic role as the Bolshevik headquarters during the October Revolution *(see pp28–9)*.

Ceramic tile from 1770s stove, Stieglitz Museum

Southeast of the centre lies the Alexander Nevsky Monastery where many of Russia's celebrated artists, architects and composers are buried.

The southern suburbs offer a strikingly different perspective of the city, with rows of pompous 1930s–50s houses, a reminder that Stalin sought to destroy the city's historical heart by relocating the centre from the old imperial district to the area around Moskovskaya ploshchad. The south also has the Chesma Church and the 1970s Victory Monument, a memorial to the suffering of St Petersburgers during the Siege of Leningrad.

## SIGHTS AT A GLANCE

**Palaces**
Sheremetev Palace ⑨
Tauride Palace ⑥
Yelagin Palace ①

**Museums**
Dostoevsky House-Museum ⑩
Stieglitz Museum ④

**Churches**
Alexander Nevsky Monastery ⑪
Cathedral of the
   Transfiguration ⑤
Chesma Church ⑫
Smolnyy Convent ⑦

**Historic Buildings and Monuments**
Finland Station ③
Piskarevskoe Memorial
   Cemetery ②
Smolnyy Institute ⑧
Victory Monument ⑬

**KEY**

| | |
|---|---|
| ▮ | Central St Petersburg |
| ▮ | Greater St Petersburg |
| ✈ | Airport |
| 🚉 | Railway station |
| ⛴ | Ferry port |
| ▬ | Major road |
| ═ | Minor road |

0 kilometres   3

0 miles        3

◁ **The Baroque Sheremetev Palace on the east bank of the Fontanka river**

East façade of Yelagin Palace with Srednaya Nevka river in foreground

## Yelagin Palace ❶
Елагин дворец
*Yelagin dvorets*

Yelagin ostrov 1. **Tel** *430 1131.*
M *Krestovskiy ostrov.*
◯ *10am–5pm Wed–Sun.* 🈺
🔩 *to ground floor.* 🔲

One of the northernmost islands of St Petersburg, Yelagin Island is named after a court official who built a palace here at the end of the 18th century. Alexander I then bought the island in 1817 for his mother, Maria Fyodorovna, and commissioned Carlo Rossi to rebuild the palace. The magnificent Neo-Classical palace (1818–22), enlivened on the east façade by a half rotunda flanked by Corinthian porticoes, is part of an ensemble which includes an orangery, a horseshoe-shaped stable block and porticoed kitchens.

The palace interior was destroyed by fire during World War II but is now undergoing restoration. The Oval Hall is resplendent with statuary and trompe l'oeils while the rooms leading from it are exquisitely decorated with stucco, *faux marbre* and painted friezes, executed by a collective of gifted artists and craftsmen.

**Statue of Mother Russia (1956–60), Piskarevskoe Memorial Cemetery**

In the Soviet period, the whole of the wooded island became the Central Park of Culture and Rest (*see pp136–7*). Festivals and public entertainments are held here, and there is an exhibition of decorative art in the palace's former stables.

## Piskarevskoe Memorial Cemetery ❷
Пискаревское мемориальное кладбище
*Piskarevskoe memorialnoe kladbishche*

Prospekt Nepokorennykh 72–74.
**Tel** *247 5716.* M *Akademicheskaya.*
🚌 *123, 178.* ◯ *24 hours daily.*
*Memorial halls 10am–5pm daily.* 🔲

This vast, bleak cemetery is a memorial to the two million people who died during the Siege of Leningrad, 1941–4 (*see p27*). With little food and no electricity, water or heating, the citizens of Leningrad perished in vast numbers from starvation, cold and disease. Thousands of corpses were dragged on sledges to collection points from where they were taken for burial to mass cemeteries on the outskirts of town. Piskarevskoe was the largest, with 490,000 burials.

Today the cemetery is a place of pilgrimage for those who lost relatives and friends during those desperate times. The memorial complex, designed by Yevgeniy Levinson and Aleksandr Vasiliev, opened in 1960, on the 15th anniversary of the end of the war. Two memorial halls, one of which contains an exhibition on the Siege, flank the stairs down to a 300-m (984-ft) long avenue, which culminates in a towering, heroic bronze statue of Mother Russia by Vera

Isayeva and Robert Taurit. On the wall behind are verses composed by Olga Bergholts, herself a survivor of the Siege. The funereal music broadcast over the whole cemetery adds to the sombre atmosphere.

On either side of the avenue are 186 grassy mounds, each with a granite slab marking the year and indicating, with a red star or hammer and sickle, whether those interred were soldiers or civilians.

**Locomotive 293, Finland Station**

## Finland Station ❸
Финляндский вокзал
*Finlyandskiy vokzal*

Ploshchad Lenina 6. **Map** 3 B3.
M *Ploshchad Lenina.*
*See also p221.*

On the night of 3 April 1917, the exiled Vladimir Lenin and his Bolshevik companions arrived at Finland Station after travelling from Switzerland on a sealed train. A triumphant reception awaited their return to Russia and, on leaving the station, Lenin spoke to cheering crowds of soldiers, sailors and workers. A statue erected outside the station in 1926 depicts Lenin delivering his speech.

The modern terminal was opened in the 1960s. On platform 5 there is a huge glass case containing Locomotive 293 which Lenin rode when fleeing the capital for a second time in July 1917. After spending the summer as a fugitive in Russian Finland, Lenin returned on the same train and spurred on the October Revolution (*see pp28–9*).

# Stieglitz Museum ❹
Музей Штиглица
*Muzey Shtiglitsa*

Solyanoy pereulok 13–15. **Map** 3
A5. *Tel* 273 3258. 📺 46, K-100, K-217. ☐ Sep–Jul: 11am–5pm
Tue–Sat. ⬤ last Fri of month. 📷 📁

The millionaire industrialist Baron Aleksandr Stieglitz founded the Central School of Industrial Design in 1876. His aim was to provide a top quality collection of original works for the use of Russian students of applied arts and design.

With a large budget and the good taste of Stieglitz's son-in-law, Aleksandr Polovtsov *(see p122)*, the collection, unusual in covering both Western European and Oriental art, soon outgrew the school and in 1896 a Museum of Applied Arts opened next door. This magnificent building, designed by Maximilian Messmacher, was inspired by Italian Renaissance palaces. Inside, the halls and galleries were decorated in an impressive variety of national and period styles, echoing French and German Baroque and, above all, Italian Renaissance

**19th-century crystal vase, Stieglitz Museum**

monuments, such as St Mark's Library in Venice, the Raphael Loggias of the Vatican and the Villa Madama, also in Rome.

After the Revolution the school was closed and the museum became a branch of the Hermitage *(see pp84–93)*. Serious damage to the building was inflicted during the Siege of Leningrad *(see p27)* and restoration continues. At the end of the war the school was revived to train gilders and carvers for the huge restoration programme needed to repair the damaged city.

Situated on the ground floor, the exhibition features opulent displays of glassware, ceramics and majolica, as well as porcelain from all the great European manufacturers. One room, decorated in the style of the medieval Terem Palace in the Kremlin, provides a superb backdrop for a collection of colourfully embroidered dresses and headgear made by Russian peasant women.

Some pieces of decorative metalwork including locks, keys and craft tools date back to the Middle Ages. The workmanship seen on the wooden furniture is breathtaking. The

Neo-Gothic cabinet is a beautiful example. Its finely inlaid doors, depicting church naves in skilful perspective, open to reveal sculpted biblical scenes.

One way to end your visit is with a look at the stunning Grand Exhibition Hall with its curving staircase of Italian marble and magnificent glass roof.

# Cathedral of the Transfiguration ❺
Спасо-Преображенский собор
*Spaso-Preobrazhenskiy sobor*

Preobrazhenskaya ploshchad 1. **Map** 3 B5. *Tel* 272 3672. Ⓜ Chernyshevskaya. 📺 46. 🚋 3, 8, 15. ☐ 8am–8pm daily.

Despite its monumental Neo-Classicism, and the surrounding fence made of guns captured during the Russo-Turkish wars *(see p22)*, Vasiliy Stasov's church has an intimate air as it nestles in its leafy square. The original church on this site was built by Tsarina Elizabeth to honour the Preobrazhenskiy Guards, but it was rebuilt after a fire in 1825. Today, the church is famous for its excellent choir, which is second only to that in the Alexander Nevsky Monastery *(see pp130–31)*.

**Dolls in 17th–19th century Russian folk costumes, in front of the Terem Room, Stieglitz Museum**

## Tauride Palace ❻
Таврический дворец
*Tavricheskiy dvorets*

Shpalernaya ulitsa 47. **Map** 4 D4.
Ⓜ *Chernyshevskaya.* 🚌 *46, 136.*
⬤ *to public.*

This finely proportioned
palace by Ivan Starov was
built in 1783–9 as a present
from Catherine the Great to
her influential lover Prince
Grigoriy Potemkin *(see p25).*
Potemkin had successfully
annexed the Crimea (Tauris) to
Russia in 1783 and was given
the title of Prince of Tauris,
hence the palace's name.

Uncompromising in its lack
of external ornamentation, the
long, yellow building with its
distinctive six-columned portico was one of Russia's first
Neo-Classical designs. Sadly,
the magnificent interiors have
been badly damaged both
by Catherine's son, Paul I,
who turned the palace into a
barracks, and by the many
reconstructions undertaken.

The palace has played a vital
role in 20th-century cultural
and political life. In 1905, the
impresario Sergey Diaghilev
*(see p43)* organized the first
ever exhibition of Russian 18th-
century portraiture here. The
following year the palace host-
ed Russia's first parliament, the
State Duma. After the February
Revolution of 1917 it became
the seat of the Provisional
Government, then the Petrograd Soviet of Workers' and
Soldiers' Deputies. Today it is
still a government building.

The lovely gardens, with
winding streams, bridges and
an artificial lake, are among
the city's most popular parks.

**Façade of the Smolnyy Cathedral with adjacent convent buildings**

## Smolnyy Convent ❼
Смольный монастырь
*Smolnyy monastyr*

Ploshchad Rastrelli 3/1. **Map** 4 F4.
**Tel** 577 1422. 🚌 *46, 136.*
⭕ *10am–5pm Tue–Thu.* 📷 ♿
📷 *English.*

The crowning glory of this
architectural ensemble is the
stunning cathedral with its
dome and four supporting cupolas topped by golden orbs.

As a symbol of her majesty,
Tsarina Elizabeth founded the
convent where many young
noblewomen were to be
educated. It was designed in
1748 by Bartolomeo Rastrelli
*(see p93),* who conceived a
brilliant fusion of Russian and
Western Baroque styles. Work
advanced extremely slowly;
50,000 wooden piles were
used to secure the foundations
in the marshy soil and the
architect's model alone, now in
the Academy of Arts *(see p63),*
took seven years to build.

Catherine the Great disliked
Rastrelli's work and had little
sympathy for the late Elizabeth.
When she came to power in
1762, funding for the project

stopped. It was only in 1835
that Nicholas I commissioned
the Neo-Classical architect
Vasiliy Stasov to complete the
cathedral. His austere white
interior contrasts dramatically
with the luxuriant exterior.

Exhibitions are now held
here, as well as regular weekly
concerts of church music *(see
p202).* There are spectacular
views of the city from the
cathedral tower.

## Smolnyy Institute ❽
Смольный Институт
*Smolnyy Institut*

Smolnyy proezd 1. **Map** 4 F4.
**Tel** 710 3159, 710 3143. 🚌 *54, 74,
136, K-15, K-76, K-136.* 🚊 *5, 7, 15,
16.* **Smolnyy Museum** ⭕ *11am–
4pm Mon–Fri by appt only.* 📷 ♿
📷 *English.*

Built in 1806–8 to house a
school for young noblewomen
which had outgrown its premises at the Smolnyy Convent,
Giacomo Quarenghi
considered this Neo-Classical
building to be his masterpiece.

It was from here, on 25
October 1917, that Lenin directed the Bolshevik *coup d'état*
while the second All-Russian
Congress of Soviets was con-
vening in the Assembly Hall.
The Congress confirmed Lenin
in power and this was his seat
of government until March
1918. With the Germans
advancing and the outbreak
of civil war *(see p27),* the government left for Moscow. The
Institute was taken over by the
Leningrad Communist Party.
On 1 December 1934, the First
Secretary of the party, Sergey
Kirov *(see p72),* was murdered
here, an event that was to

**View of Tauride Gardens and the Tauride Palace beyond the lake**

**Isaak Brodskiy's 1927 painting of Lenin, Smolnyy Institute Assembly Hall**

provide cover for the purges of the late 1930s (see p27).

The rooms where Lenin lived and worked can be viewed by appointment. The rest of the institute is now the Mayor's Office. The imperial eagle has replaced the hammer and sickle, but the statue of Lenin has survived.

## Sheremetev Palace ⓑ
Шереметевский дворец
*Sheremetevskiy dvorets*

Naberezhnaya reki Fontanki 34. **Map 7 A1.** Ⓜ *Mayakovskaya, Gostinyy Dvor.* 🚌 *15, 22, 27, K-15, K-90, K-187, K-258.* 🚎 *3, 8, 15.* **Anna Akhmatova Museum** *Tel 571 7239.* ◻ *10:30am–6:30pm Tue–Sun.* 🎫 📷 *English.* **Museum of Musical Life** *Tel 272 4441.* ◻ *noon–6pm Wed–Sun.* 🌑 *last Wed of each month.* 🎫 📷

The Sheremetev family lived here from 1712, when the palace was built by Field Marshal Boris Sheremetev, until the Revolution. The palace is also known as the Fountain House, or *Fontannyy dom*, because of the many fountains that once adorned its grounds. The Baroque building dates from the 1750s when it was designed by Savva Chevakinskiy and Fyodor Argunov, although numerous later alterations were made.

Field Marshal Sheremetev's descendants were fabulously wealthy, at one time owning some 200,000 serfs. They were among Russia's leading artistic patrons and the palace is now home to the Museum of Musical Life, which charts the family's contribution to the music of the city. In the 18th and 19th centuries, serf composers, musicians and actors from rural estates owned by the family performed in concerts and plays at the palace. Among those to praise the fine Sheremetev choir was the composer Franz Liszt.

The museum's exhibits include a variety of period instruments and a number of scores, some of which are compositions by the Sheremetevs themselves.

One of Russia's greatest 20th-century poets, Anna Akhmatova, lived in one of the service blocks of the palace from 1933 to 1941 and then between 1944 and 1954. Her flat is open to the public as the Anna Akhmatova Museum *(Muzey Anny Akhmatovoy)* and is reached through the courtyard of No. 53 Liteynyy prospekt. By the time she moved into the palace, it had been divided into dingy communal apartments. The rooms where she lived and worked display some of her personal possessions, tracing her intriguing life. Recordings of the poetess reading her own poems can also be heard.

### ANNA AKHMATOVA

By 1914 Anna Akhmatova (1889–1966) was a leading light of Russia's "Silver Age" of poetry *(see p44)*. Tragedy gave her work a new dimension when first her husband was shot by the Bolsheviks, and then, in the 1930s, her son and her lover were arrested in Stalin's purges. Anna herself was placed under police surveillance and officially silenced for more than 15 years. Her most famous poem, *Requiem* (1935–61), inspired by her son's arrest, was written in fragments and distributed amongst friends to memorize. Anna was partially rehabilitated late in her life and received honorary awards abroad in 1965.

**Pilastered façade of Sheremetev Palace on the Fontanka embankment**

# Dostoevsky House-Museum ⑩
Музей Достоевского
*Muzey Dostoevskovo*

Kuznechnyy pereulok 5/2. **Map** 7 B3.
**Tel** 571 4031. Ⓜ *Vladimirskaya.*
🚃 3, 8, 15. 🚋 49. ⚪ *11am–6pm
Tue–Sun.* 🏛️ 🎫 *English.*

This evocative museum
was the final home of the
famous Russian writer, Fyodor
Dostoevsky *(see p44),* who
lived here from 1878 until his
death in 1881. Dostoevsky
was then at the height of his
fame, and it was here that he
completed his last great novel,
*The Brothers Karamazov,* in
1880. Gambling and debts,
however, confined him to a
fairly modest lifestyle in this
five-roomed apartment.

Although Dostoevsky's
public persona was dour and
humourless, he was a devoted and affectionate husband
and father. The delightful nurs-
ery contains a rocking horse,
silhouettes of his children and
the book of fairy tales which
he read aloud to them. In
Dostoevsky's study are his
writing desk and a reproduction of his favourite painting,
Raphael's *Sistine Madonna.*

Chesma Church (1777–80), a very early
example of Neo-Gothic in Russia

# Chesma Church ⑫
Чесменская церковь
*Chesmenskaya tserkov*

Ulitsa Lensoveta 12. Ⓜ *Moskovskaya.*
🚃 16. 🚋 29, 45. ⚪ *10am–7pm
daily.*

There is little Russian about
the highly unusual Chesma
Church, which was designed
by Yuriy Velten in 1777–80.
Its fanciful terracotta-coloured

façade is decorated with
thin vertical stripes of
white moulding which
direct the eye upwards to
its zig-zagged crown and
Neo-Gothic cupolas.

The name commemo-
rates the great Russian
naval victory over the
Turks at Chesma in the
Aegean in 1770. During
the Communist era the
church became a museum
to the battle, but today
the building is once
again used as a church.

On the opposite side
of ulitsa Lensoveta is
the Neo-Gothic Chesma
Palace (1774–77), formerly
*Kekerekeksinen,* or Frog
Marsh Palace. Also de-
signed by Velten, it served
as a staging post for
Catherine the Great en route to
Tsarskoe Selo *(see pp152–5).*
Wedgwood's famous dinner
service with its frog emblem,
now in the Hermitage *(see
p91),* was designed specially
for the Chesma Palace.

The palace achieved noto-
riety when Rasputin's body
lay in state here after his murder in 1916 *(see p121).* Now
substantially altered, it serves
as a home for the elderly.

# Alexander Nevsky Monastery ⑪
Александро-Невская лавра
*Aleksandro-Nevskaya lavra*

Ploshchad Aleksandra Nevskovo.
**Map** 8 E4. **Tel** 274 2635.
Ⓜ *Ploshchad Aleksandra Nevskovo.*
🚃 8, 27, 46. 🚋 1, 14, 16, 22. 🚋 7,
65. **Holy Trinity Cathedral** ⚪ *6am–
8pm daily.* **Church of the Annunciation Tel** 274 2635. ⚪ *9:30am–
5pm; closes 6pm in summer.*
⚫ *Mon & Thu.* 🏛️ *cemeteries &
Church of the Annunciation.* 🎫

Founded by Peter the
Great in 1710, this
monastery is named
after Alexander
Nevsky, the prince of
Novgorod, who
defeated the Swedes
in 1240. Peter himself
defeated them again in
1709 *(see p18).*

From the entrance, a path
runs between two large,
walled cemeteries, then across

a stream and into the main
monastic complex. The oldest
building is the Church of the
Annunciation (1717–22), designed by Domenico Trezzini.
The church, its ground floor
recently opened to the public,
was the burial place for non-
ruling members of the Russian
royal family. A series of red
and white, mid-18th-century
monastic buildings, including
the Metropolitan's House
(1755–8), surround the
courtyard. Among the
trees in the courtyard
lie the graves of atheist
Soviet scholars and
leading Communists.
Dominating the
essentially Baroque
complex is the twin-
towered and domed
Neo-Classical Holy
Trinity Cathedral, con-
structed by architect
Ivan Starov in 1776–90. The
wide nave inside is flanked
by Corinthian columns with

**Dostoevsky's
tombstone**

statues by Fedot Shubin. This
leads to the impressive red
agate and white marble iconostasis, which features copies
of works by Van Dyck, Rubens
and others. To the right of the
iconostasis is a silver reliquary
that contains the remains of
Alexander Nevsky, transferred

**Reliquary with Alexander Nevsky's
remains, Trinity Cathedral**

# Victory Monument ⓭

Монумент Защитникам
Ленинграда
*Monument Zashchitnikam
Leningrada*

Ploshchad Pobedy. **Tel** 371 2951,
373 6563. Ⓜ *Moskovskaya.* ▦ 3, 11,
39, 55. ▦ 27, 29, 45. **Memorial
Hall** ◯ 10am–6pm Thu & Sat–Mon,
10am–5pm Tue & Fri. ● *last Tue of
each month.* 📷 *book by phone.*

Erected in 1975 to coincide
with the 30th anniversary of
the end of World War II, this is
on the site of a temporary
triumphal arch built to greet
the returning troops. Named
the Monument to the Heroic
Defenders of Leningrad, it

commemorates the victims of
the Siege *(see p27)*, and its
survivors. It was designed by
Sergey Speranskiy and Valentin
Kamenskiy and sculpted by
Mikhail Anikushin. A 48-m
(157-ft) high obelisk of red
granite is near a vast, circular
enclosure which symbolizes
the vice-like grip of the siege.
Sculptures of soldiers, sailors
and grieving mothers
surround the monument.

An underpass on Moskovskiy
prospekt leads to the gloomy,
subterranean Memorial Hall.
Here solemn music gives way
to the persistent beat of a
metronome, the wartime radio
signal, intended to represent
the city's defiant heartbeat.

The subdued lighting com-
prises 900 dim, orange lamps,
one for each day of the Siege.
Tablets are inscribed with the
names of the 650 Heroes of
the Soviet Union awarded the
title after the war; and a
mosaic depicts the women of
the city greeting their menfolk
at the end of the conflict.

Around the hall a small
display of artifacts, including
Shostakovich's violin *(see p43)*,
records the contribution of
different sections of the community to the war effort, while
an illuminated relief map
illustrates the battle lines.
Most disturbing is the tiny
piece of bread, which was
many people's daily ration.

Heroic partisans facing south towards the enemy during the Siege of Leningrad, detail of Victory Monument

to the previous church on
this site in 1724. Behind the
reliquary hangs a painting of
Nevsky, who has been venerated as a saint in Russia since
the mid-16th century.

Many of the nation's leading
cultural figures are buried in
the two monastic cemeteries
near the main entrance. The
city's oldest graveyard, the
Lazarus Cemetery, to the east,
contains the graves of the
polymath Mikhail Lomonosov
*(see p45)* and a number of
prominent architects, including
Andrey Zakharov, Thomas de
Thomon, Giacomo Quarenghi,
Carlo Rossi *(see p110)* and
Andrey Voronikhin. Clustered
together along the northern
wall of the Tikhvin Cemetery
(to the west) are the tombs of
some of Russia's most famous
composers. Many of their
tombs are inscribed with musical motifs. Fyodor Dostoevsky
*(see p44)* is also buried here,
to the right of the entrance.

## TOMBS OF INTEREST AT TIKHVIN CEMETERY

**1** Mikhail Glinka
(Composer, 1804–57)
**2** Ivan Krylov
(Poet, 1769–1844)
**3** Marius Petipa
(Choreographer,
1818–1910)
**4** Pyotr Klodt
(Sculptor, 1805–67)
**5** Ivan Kramskoy
(Painter, 1837–87)
**6** Pyotr Tchaikovsky
(Composer, 1840–93)

**7** Modest Mussorgsky
(Composer, 1839–81)
**8** Nikolai Rimsky-
Korsakov
(Composer, 1844–1908)
**9** Fyodor Dostoevsky
(Writer, 1821–81)

Main
entrance

**KEY**

✚ Gate church

0 metres       50

0 yards       50

# THREE GUIDED WALKS

Many of St Petersburg's sights are best appreciated on foot. The three walks chosen present different aspects of the city's character, though water plays a central part in each.

The first walk follows the Moyka river and the Griboedov canal, which criss-cross the heart of the city, and reveals the manificent scale of the buildings erected in the 18th and 19th centuries. It highlights the contrasts between rich palaces and overcrowded apartment blocks, gilded bridges and the dilapidation of the area around Sennaya ploshchad. An alternative way to appreciate the glorious old buildings set on the canals is to take a boat trip *(see pp226–7)*.

19th-century urn on the steps of Yelagin Palace

The second walk explores Yelagin and Kamennyy islands, where Petersburgers traditionally spend much of their free time. The islands to the north of the centre were once the preserve of the rich, who spent the hot summers in the cool of their *dachas*. Now locals come to walk and row boats in summer, to ski and skate in winter, and simply to breathe the fresh spring air.

The third walk follows the river Neva on the Petrograd side, from where there are awe-inspiring views of the city's grand south waterfront and of the river itself. The walk encompasses some significant historic sites including Trinity Square, the Cabin of Peter the Great and the cruiser *Aurora*.

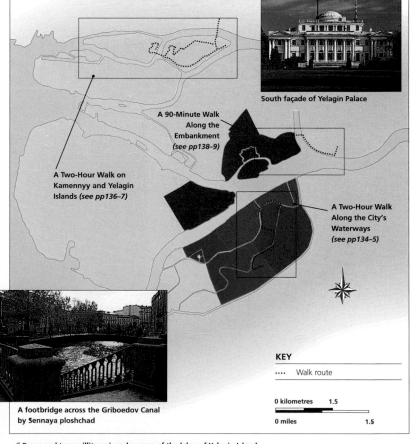

South façade of Yelagin Palace

A 90-Minute Walk Along the Embankment *(see pp138–9)*

A Two-Hour Walk on Kamennyy and Yelagin Islands *(see pp136–7)*

A Two-Hour Walk Along the City's Waterways *(see pp134–5)*

A footbridge across the Griboedov Canal by Sennaya ploshchad

**KEY**

···· Walk route

0 kilometres 1.5

0 miles 1.5

◁ Peace and tranquillity enjoyed on one of the lakes of Yelagin Island

# A Two-Hour Walk Along the City's Waterways

A stroll along the embankments of the Moyka river and the Griboedov canal is a chance to appreciate the history and splendid architecture of this beautiful city. The two waterways present interesting contrasts. The Moyka winds past the Imperial Summer and Winter Palaces and the lavish mansions of the aristocracy, while the Griboedov is lined with 19th-century apartments, once home to merchants, civil servants and, towards Sennaya Ploshchad *(see p122)*, the working class. The walk also includes a short stretch of the majestic Nevskiy prospekt.

## TIPS FOR WALKERS

*Starting point:* Church on Spilled Blood.
*Length:* 5.8 km (3 miles).
*Getting there:* Nevskiy Prospekt metro. *Stopping-off points:* Bistro Layma, nab kanala Griboedova 16.

**View of the Church on Spilled Blood ① and the Griboedov canal**

## The Moyka River

Begin the walk at the recently restored Church on Spilled Blood ① *(see p100)*, built over the spot where Alexander II was assassinated in 1881 *(see p26)*. From here, walk around the church beside the park, crossing the canal bridge to Konyushennaya ploshchad. The square is embraced by the elongated façade of the former Imperial Stables ② *(see p113)*. Straddling the junction of the Griboedov canal and the Moyka river are two ingeniously linked bridges, the Malo-Konyushennyy most (Small Stable Bridge) and Teatralnyy most (Theatre Bridge) *(see p37)*. Cross over these bridges to the north bank of the Moyka and the expansive façade of the Adamini House ③, designed by Domenico Adamini in 1823–7. Between 1916 and 1919 the basement was used

by an artists' and writers' club known as "The Bivouac of the Comedians". Visitors included the avant-garde theatre director Vsevolod Meyerhold and the poets Aleksandr Blok and Anna Akhmatova *(see p44)*.

Turn left onto naberezhnaya reki Moyki and walk past the Round Market ④ built in 1790 by Giacomo Quarenghi, who had shopping arcades as one of his specialities. Continue along the embankment, passing Adam's Bolshoy Konyushennyy most (Great Stables Bridge) to Prince Abamelek-Lazarev's former mansion ⑤ built in 1913–15. The handsome façade, with Corinthian pilasters and graceful reliefs of dancing figures, is by Ivan Fomin. On the opposite bank is the 17th-century apartment block where Pushkin spent the last few months of his life. His flat is now a museum ⑥ *(see p113)*.

At the intersection of Millionaya ulitsa and the beautiful Winter Canal (Zimnaya Kanavka) are the former barracks of the elite First Regiment of the Preobrazhenskiy Life-Guards. This prestigious corps was formed by Peter the Great in the 1690s.

**Quarenghi's arcaded Round Market (1790) ④, overlooking the Moyka river**

## KEY

••• Tour route

M Metro station

**View of the tree-lined Griboedov canal**

Across the Winter Canal is the New Hermitage ⑦ *(see p84)*. Ten granite atlantes bear the weight of the elaborate porch. Returning to the Moyka, the route passes a green, three-storey house ⑧, built by F Demertsov for Alexander I's military advisor and sometime chief minister, Count Aleksey Arakcheev. The Moyka now makes a curve behind the majestic buildings of Palace Square *(see p83)* which includes the Staff of the Guards Corps ⑨ and the huge crescent of Carlo Rossi's imposing yellow General Staff Building ⑩. Cross the Pevcheskiy most (Singers' Bridge) *(see p37)* ⑪ and follow the Moyka down to the Zelenyy most (Green Bridge). The yellow building on the other side of the Moyka is the Literary Café ⑫, renowned as a meeting-place for writers in Pushkin's day *(see p83)*.

### Nevskiy Prospekt

Turn left onto St Petersburg's main street, where a range of architectural styles can be seen. On the left, the elegant façade of Paul Jacot's Dutch Church building ⑬ *(see p47)* hides a series of shops. Across

the road, the superb façade of the Baroque Stroganov Palace ⑭ *(see p112)* contrasts starkly with the triple-arched glass frontage of the Style-Moderne Fashion House ⑮ *(see p47)*. The colonnaded forecourt of the Cathedral of Our Lady of Kazan ⑯ *(see p111)* can be seen further along.

### The Griboedov Canal

Cross Nevskiy prospekt by the attractive Singer Sewing Machine Building *(see p47)* and follow the Griboedov south. When you reach Georg von Traitteur's Bankovskiy most *(see p35)* ⑰, decorated with golden griffons, cross the canal and continue past the wrought-iron railings to the rear of the former Assignment Bank ⑱ (now occupied by a finance and economics university). Further south the humped Kamennyy most (Stone Bridge) has survived since 1776 despite an attempt by the revolutionary group, Peoples' Will, to blow it up as Tsar Alexander II passed in his carriage. Across the Demidov most, on the corner of Kaznacheyskaya ulitsa ⑲ (No.1),

**Griffons on Bank Bridge (1826), Griboedov canal**

is the apartment where Dostoevsky wrote *Notes from the House of the Dead* (1861). Also with literary associations, the former Zverkov House ⑳ was where the novelist and dramatist Nikolai Gogol *(see p44)* lived in the 1830s.

The walk ends in Sennaya ploshchad *(see p122)*, where there are two metro stations.

**Apartment block where Dostoevsky lived ⑲, on the Griboedov canal**

# A Two-Hour Walk on Kamennyy and Yelagin Islands

An area of rolling parkland, birch and lime groves and fine river views, the northern islands of the Neva delta offer a retreat from city life. The imperial family built palaces on Kamennyy and Yelagin islands at the end of the 18th century and were soon joined by wealthy aristocratic families. Before the Revolution, many government ministers, industrial magnates and celebrities built themselves a *dacha* here. Today these neglected houses, some intimate, some palatial, in styles ranging from Neo-Gothic to Neo-Classical and Style Moderne, are being returned to their former glory by the new business elite.

Continue west, and cross the canal bridge to reach the wooden Kamennoostrovskiy Theatre ⑤ which took only 40 days to erect in 1827. Its Neo-Classical portico, rebuilt by Albert Kavos in 1844, is still impressive. The banks of the Krestovka river, with views across to the boatyards of Krestovskiy Island, offer many ideal spots for a picnic (but bear in mind that admission is charged at weekends). To rejoin the walk, return to the path and cross 1-y Yelagin most to Yelagin Island.

### Yelagin Island

This island is an oasis of calm, popular with those wishing to escape the city. A tollgate marks the entrance to the grounds of Carlo Rossi's graceful Yelagin Palace ⑥

**Wooden façade of Dolgorukov Mansion ③**

### South Kamennyy Island

Begin at Chernaya Rechka metro station and head south to Bolshaya Nevka river, then cross Ushakovskiy most to Kamennyy Island, an area of recreation and relaxation. Just across the main road is the small red-brick Church of St John the Baptist ①, designed in Neo-Gothic style by Yuriy Velten in 1776–8. Nearby a yellow gateway leads to the grounds of Kamennoostrovskiy Palace ② (which is now a retirement home) from where Alexander I led the 1812 Russian campaign against Napoleon *(see p26)*.

Follow Kamennoostrovskiy prospekt to the Malaya Nevka river, then turn right on to naberezhnaya Maloy Nevki where there is an imposing wooden mansion ③ at No. 11 with a white-columned portico. The Dolgorukov Mansion was built in 1831–2 by Smaragd

Shustov for the Dolgorukovs, one of Russia's oldest aristocratic families.

From this point you can see across to Aptekarskiy or Apothecary's Island, named after the medicinal herb gardens founded by Peter the Great in 1714. St Petersburg's Botanical Gardens are still located there. Continue along the path, which turns into naberezhnaya reki Krestovki. The house on the left, towards the Malo-krestovskiy most, is the former home of Sergey Chaev ④, who was the chief engineer of the Trans-Siberian railway. Chaev commissioned the fashionable architect, Vladimir Apyshkov, to build this rather splendid Style-Moderne mansion in 1913–14.

**The tower of the Church of St John the Baptist (1776–8) ①**

**Kamennoostrovskiy Theatre's impressive façade (1827)** ⑤

*(see p126)*. The western spit of the island is ideal for viewing the spectacular sunsets over the Gulf of Finland, especially during the White Nights *(see p51)*. If you want to venture further, head south across 2-y Yelagin most to Krestovskiy Island and the Kirov Stadium, Maritime Victory Park and Primorskiy Park Pobedy. Or, to the north, 3-y Yelagin most leads to Primorskiy prospekt and the Tibetan-inspired Buddhist Temple, erected by Gavriil Baranovskiy in 1909–15.

### North Kamennyy Island

Return to Kamennyy Island across 1-y Yelagin most, taking the left fork on to Teatralnaya alleya from where you can see the former mansion of Aleksandr Polovtsov ⑦, minister of foreign affairs under Nicholas II. This splendid Neo-Classical mansion with Style-Moderne touches was built by Ivan Fomin in 1911–13. Leave Teatralnaya alleya and cut through the quiet and restful park, passing between the ponds and the canal. Near the junction with Bolshaya alleya are two more early 20th-century mansions. Follenveider's mansion ⑧ on the left, with its distinctive

**Early 20th-century Polovtsov Mansion** ⑦

tented tower, was designed by Roman Meltzer in 1904 and now belongs to the Danish consulate. Yevgeniya Gausvald's dacha ⑨ dates from 1898 and stands as one of the earliest Style-Moderne buildings in St Petersburg. It was designed by Vasiliy Schöne and Vladimir Chagin.

Finally, the last stage of the walk leads along the 2-ya Berezovaya alleya, back to the starting point at Ushakovskiy most and Chernaya Rechka metro.

### KEY

• • • Walk route

Ⓜ Metro station

### TIPS FOR WALKERS

**Starting point:** Chernaya Rechka metro station (see p215).
**Length:** 6 km (3.5 miles).
**Stopping-off points:** Café in former stables of Yelagin Palace (summer only) and plenty of places to picnic.

**The tree-shrouded grassy banks of the Krestovka river**

# A 90-Minute Walk Along the Embankment

Muscovites envy St Petersburgers their dramatic and open skyline, and this stroll along the northern banks of the Neva offers grand views, not only of the magnificent south waterfront, but also of the Petrogradskaya Side, as seen from Trinity Bridge where it crosses the river at its widest point. In winter the Neva lies frozen, an expanse of whiteness. In warmer months the water pulses hypnotically through the city. The walk encompasses the best of the city's Style-Moderne architecture, the Cabin of Peter the Great, the cruiser *Aurora*, whose guns began the 1917 Revolution, and the train that brought Lenin to Russia.

**Manchurian Lion** ⑦

needle-sharp steeple of the Baroque Cathedral of SS Peter and Paul ⑤. The bridge was completed in time for the city's bicentenary in 1903 by the French firm Batignol, which also constructed the Eiffel Tower.

Return to the shore, and stroll east along Petrovskaya Embankment, passing the Cabin of Peter the Great ⑥ *(see p73)*. The tiny cabin was built from pine logs in 3 days

### Kamennoostrovskiy Prospekt
From Gorkovskaya metro station, cross the road via the underpass and walk south along Konverskiy prospekt, an avenue noted for its Style-Moderne architecture. Almost immediately, the minarets of the city's only mosque jut up ahead. Sobornaya Mosque ① *(see p70)*, one of Europe's

### Trinity Square
Until the fall of the USSR, the square was known as Revolution Square in memory of the 48 workers who were mown down here by government troops. Walk onto Style-Moderne Trinity Bridge ④ *(see p35)*, which spans the Neva at its widest point and affords fine views of the river and the Peter and Paul Fortress *(see pp66–7)*. Look out for the

**Interior of the tiny Cabin of Peter the Great** ⑥

**View of Peter and Paul Fortress with the Cathedral of SS Peter and Paul** ⑤

largest, was built in 1913. Slightly further on, at the junction with ulitsa Kuybysheva is the Kshesinskaya Mansion ② *(see p72)*, a delicate, asymmetrical Style-Moderne building commissioned in 1906 for the ballerina Matilda Kshesinskaya (Nicholas II's former lover). Once the Bolshevik Party HQ, from whose balcony Lenin addressed the crowds, it now houses the Museum of Russian Political History with exhibits from the Revolutionary era.

Take a right down ulitsa Kuybysheva then bear left onto Kamennoostrovskiy prospekt *(see p70)*. To your left is Trinity Square ③ *(see p72)*, the heart of the old city's merchant quarter, and site of the "Bloody Sunday" massacre during the 1905 Revolution, and of the relatively new Trinity Chapel.

**The cruiser *Aurora* (1900) moored in front of the Nakhimov Naval Academy** ⑨

MAL POSADSKAYA ULITSA

MICHURINSKAYA

PETROGRADSKAYA

Бол

Gorkovskaya

KAMENNOOSTROVSKIY PROSPEKT

KONNYY PER

UL KUYBYSHEVA ULITSA

PENKOVAYA ULITSA

НАБ

⑨

ALEKSANDROVSKIY PARK

①

②

⑥

PETROVSKAYA NAB

③ TRINITY SQUARE

PETROVSKAYA NAB

⑦

⑤

④

TROITSKIY MOST

SAMPS

0 metres    300
0 yards    300

View across the frozen River Neva featuring the golden dome of St Isaac's Cathedral on the south embankment

in May 1703, and Peter lived here for 6 years, supervising the building of his city. The brick shell was added later by Catherine the Great. On the steps outside the cabin are the Manchurian Lions ⑦, two odd statues brought from Manchuria during the disastrous (for Russia) Russo-Japanese War of 1904–5.

shots that signalled the storming of the Winter Palace. This event brought the Bolsheviks to power in 1917. The battleship is now partly open and contains a museum.

Further along the embankment, the Neo-Baroque building on the left is the Nakhimov Naval Academy ⑨, built in 1910–11.

Now cross Sampsonievskiy most onto Pirogovskaya nab. From here it is possible to catch tram No. 6 to the end of the

**TIPS FOR WALKERS**

**Starting point:** Sobornaya Mosque.
**Getting there:** Gorkovskaya metro station (see p223).
**Length:** 3.5 km (2 miles).
**Stopping off points:** There are places selling snacks along the north embankment, especially around the cruiser Aurora and the Cabin of Peter the Great.

**Ploshchad Lenina**

The majority of statues of Lenin were torn down after the collapse of the USSR. This one was erected in 1926. Note the famous "'taxi-hailing" pose that was so popular among architects of monuments to "Grandfather Lenin", as Soviet children were taught to refer to him. Directly opposite the square, on the other side of the river, looms the "Bolshoy Dom", the gloomy former headquarters of the KGB. Here, death sentences were passed on an estimated 47,000 citizens of St Petersburg, who were then executed by firing squad. It is now the FSB's (the KGB's successors) HQ and a prison. Finally, walk across Ploshchad Lenina to Finland Station ⑫ (see p126), home to the train that brought Lenin to Russia to lead the 1917 October Revolution – and to alter the destiny of the largest country on earth. From here, it is a short walk to Ploshchad Lenina metro station.

**KEY**

••• Walk route

Ⓜ Metro station

🚊 Tram stop

🚆 Train station

**The Cruiser Aurora**

Follow the embankment to Petrogradskaya nab and the historic old cruiser Aurora ⑧ (see p73), famous for firing the

walk if you wish.

Continuing on foot, the embankment leads down to Arsenalnaya nab, past the Military Medical Academy ⑩ – built in the time of Tsar Paul I in a High-Classical style. Turn left onto Ploshchad Lenina ⑪. In the centre of the square stands one of the city's few remaining statues of Lenin.

Statue of Lenin in Ploshchad Lenina ⑪, near Finland Station

# BEYOND ST PETERSBURG

# BEYOND ST PETERSBURG

T*he countryside around St Petersburg is typical of northwest Russia. Among its flat sweeps of land, pine forests and lakes there are sights of cultural interest, including the imperial palaces and the walled medieval city of Novgorod. Venturing away from St Petersburg allows a richer and deeper insight into this splendid land.*

Before St Petersburg was founded in 1703, the surrounding landscape was a marshy and inhospitable wilderness, inhabited by wolves. Nevertheless, the area from the Gulf of Finland to Lake Ladoga was of strategic importance for trading and thus one of the reasons for continuous wars between Sweden and Russia. At the time the only city of importance here was Novgorod, an independent and quite wealthy principality *(see p17)*. It has retained its medieval atmosphere, so different from the imperial palaces adorning the countryside south of St Petersburg. They each reflect the tastes of their owners. Peter the Great's fine residence, Peterhof, is dominated by water; the Gulf and the fountains mirror his maritime interest. Elizabeth wanted vibrant colour and excess to

**Muse of love and poetry, Pavlovsk**

accommodate her extravagant balls, hence the grand Baroque palace at Tsarskoe Selo. Catherine the Great's love of intimacy led her to add private apartments to Tsarskoe Selo, and the exquisite Chinese Palace at Oranienbaum. Paul I's military mania made him turn Gatchina into a castle, while his wife Maria Fyodorovna created a feminine, elegant residence at Pavlovsk. All the palaces except Oranienbaum suffered devastating damage during World War II *(see p27)*. A great deal of effort has been made to restore them painstakingly over the last 50 years.

While the aristocracy indulged in their extravagances, the middle classes had more modest country houses. The comfortable *dacha* of the artist Repin, northwest of the city, gives visitors a feel of his more bohemian lifestyle.

**The Novgorod Kremlin with the Cathedral of St Sophia and its belfry**

◁ **The gilded maze of the main staircase at Peterhof's Grand Palace**

# Exploring St Petersburg's Surroundings

Most St Petersburgers leave the city to spend time at their *dacha* or country house for weekends and holidays. But there are several ways of experiencing the countryside around St Petersburg. There are many stunning imperial palaces, spread out like pearls in a necklace south of the city. Each one of them offers splendid interiors as well as beautifully laid out parks and gardens with lakes. Around the artist's studio at Repino is a more typical Baltic landscape, with pine and fir trees stretching down to the pebbly beaches of the Gulf of Finland.

Further away to the south, the medieval town of Novgorod is a great representative of an old Russian city, complete with a walled kremlin and onion-domed churches.

Façade of the Chinese Palace at Oranienbaum

## GETTING AROUND

It is relatively easy to get to all of the imperial palaces, and to Repino, by suburban train or by taking a guided tour by coach *(see p208)*. Driving is less convenient, often taking longer than the train, and driving standards are variable. In the summer, the hydrofoil service is an alternative way to get to Peterhof *(see p229)*. Each of these sights can easily be visited in a day. Novgorod is situated further away, however, and so it makes sense to spend longer there. Mainline trains depart from Moscow railway station *(see p229)* for Novgorod.

Coastal landscape along the Gulf of Finland

## SIGHTS AT A GLANCE

Gatchina ❹
Novgorod ❼
Oranienbaum ❷
Pavlovsk ❻
Peterhof ❸
Repino ❶
Tsarskoe Selo ❺

**KEY**

Area of main map

**KEY**

— Major road

═══ Minor road

— Scenic route

─── Main railway

─── Minor railway

Gilded cupolas of the
chapel of Catherine
Palace at Tsarskoe Selo

# Repino ●
Репино
*Repino*

47 km (29 miles) NW of St Petersburg.
⊟ *from Finland Station.* 🚃 *211 from Chernaya Rechka metro.* **Penaty**
Primorskoe shosse 411. *Tel 432 0834.*
◯ *10:30am–4pm Wed–Sun.* 🖼
🎟 *English.* ♿ *ground floor.*

Only about an hour's drive from St Petersburg on Primorskoe shosse, the northern coastal road, is a region of lakes, pine-scented forests and sandy beaches. Among the green-painted *dachas* and sanatoria is Repino, a resort named after one of Russia's greatest artists, Ilya Repin *(see p106–7),* who lived here for over 30 years until his death in 1930 at the age of 86. His extraordinary *dacha,* with its steeply pitched glass roof and angled windows, was restored after damage in World War II and is now open as a museum.

Named Penaty in honor of the Roman household gods, *penates,* the house was re-designed by Repin himself to accommodate all that an artist might need, including a glass-panelled veranda downstairs, which was used as a winter studio. On display in the first floor studio are the artist's brushes and a number of his works, including an unfinished portrait of Pushkin *(see p44)* and Repin's last self-portrait.

Works by the artist adorn the dining room, including portraits of the singer Fyodor Chalyapin and writer Maxim Gorky who were among Repin's many visitors. A revolving dining table enabled guests to serve themselves and to store away their

**Studio of the eminent artist Ilya Repin at his home in Repino**

used dishes, since there were no servants. Anyone failing to obey this household rule had to give an impromptu speech from the lectern in the corner.

In the garden, two small wooden follies are hidden among the trees, and Repin's grave is marked by a simple cross on the top of a hillock.

# Oranienbaum ●
Ораниенбаум
*Oranienbaum*

Oranienbaum, 40 km (25 miles) W of St Petersburg. *Tel 422 3753, 423 1627 or 422 8016 (excursions).*
⊟ *from Baltic station.* **Grounds**
◯ *10am–7pm.* **Chinese Palace**
◉ *temporarily.* **Palace of St Peter III** ◯ *May–Sep: 10:30am–5pm daily (Oct–Apr: Sat & Sun only).* **Sliding Hill Pavilion** ◯ *temporarily.* 🖼 🎟

As the extravagant project of Peter the Great's closest friend and main political advisor, Aleksandr Menshikov *(see p62),* Oranienbaum was far more ambitious in conception than Peter's palace at Peterhof *(see pp148–51),* which lies just 12 km (7 miles) to the west.

The grandiose plan bankrupted Menshikov and, when he fell from grace in 1727, the estate entered the state treasury.

The Baroque appearance of Oranienbaum's Great Palace has changed little since it was constructed in 1710–25. Built by Gottfried Schädel and Giovanni-Maria Fontana, its sweeping wings culminate in two remarkable pavilions. Parts of the palace and the east (Japanese) pavilion are now open to the public.

From 1743 to 1761 the estate became the residence of the heir to the throne, the future Peter III, who built himself a miniature fortress with a small lake for his "navy" and a parade ground where he was fond of playing war games with soldiers. Peter also commissioned Antonio Rinaldi to build him a modest palace.

Peter's wife, Catherine (later Catherine the Great), abhorred her isolated existence here, but after Peter's murder *(see p22)* she recovered her spirits and created what she described as her "personal *dacha*". Built by Rinaldi in the 1760s and known as the Chinese Palace, it is famous for its Rococo interiors and chinoiserie.

The most unusual building at Oranienbaum is Rinaldi's Sliding Hill Pavilion, built in 1762 on Catherine's initiative. Wooden sledging hills were a common source of amusement among the Russian nobility. Catherine's visitors would climb the blue and white pavilion before descending at top speed by sledge or toboggan along a roller coaster run. The track, 500 m (1,640 ft) long, was originally flanked by a

**Façade of Menshikov's Great Palace (1710–25), Oranienbaum**

colonnade. Sadly, this structure collapsed in 1813 but there is a model in the pavilion.

A pleasant few hours can be spent in the grounds with their secluded paths, pine woods, ponds and bridges.

Oranienbaum was the only local palace to escape German occupation during World War II *(see p27)*. In 1948, the estate was renamed Lomonosov after the famous 18th-century physicist *(see p45)* who laid many of the foundations of modern Russian science. The complex has now reverted to its original name, an allusion to the exotic orange trees planted here by Menshikov.

Austere central section of Gatchina palace

Orlov died, two years later, Catherine transferred the estate to her son and heir Paul (later Paul I). Paul asked his favourite architect Vincenzo Brenna to re-fashion the palace to match his pronounced martial tastes. Brenna's large-scale alterations included the construction of an additional storey and a moat with a drawbridge.

The next Romanov to spend any time here was Alexander III who made it his permanent family residence in the late 19th century. The estate pro-vided a safe and remote haven from the sporadic social unrest which was threatening the capital *(see p26)*. The imperial family led a simple and secluded existence here. In keeping with the increasingly bourgeois tastes of the nobility in the whole of Europe, they scorned the state rooms, confining themselves instead to the cosy and more intimate servants' quarters. In 1917, immediately after the

Bolshevik party had seized power, the proclaimed leader of the Provisional Government, Aleksandr Kerensky, fled to Gatchina where he made a last ditch attempt to rally his supporters. After a week, he deserted his troops and slipped away into exile.

After World War II, in which the palace was badly damaged, Gatchina was used for many years as a military academy. The lengthy and thorough restoration process is still under way. Of the restored rooms, the three most impressive are the Marble Dining Room, Paul I's gloomy bedroom at the top of one of Brenna's towers and the magnificent White Ballroom. There is also a display of weaponry on the ground floor.

The delightful grounds are the wildest of all the palace parks. Among the attractions are the circular Temple of Venus (1792–3) on the secluded Island of Love and the Birch House (1790s). The latter appears to be a pile of logs, but it actually conceals a suite of exquisite rooms.

The lake has boats for hire and its clean water makes it an ideal spot for swimming.

Chinoiserie decorations in Catherine the Great's Chinese Palace, Oranienbaum

# Peterhof ❸

*See pp148–51.*

# Gatchina ❹
Гатчина
*Gatchina*

45 km (28 miles) SW of St Petersburg. *from Baltic Station.* K-18, K-100 *from Moskovskaya metro station,* 431 *from pl Pobedy.* **Tel** *8 81371 93492.* 10am–6pm Tue–Sun. *English (phone to book).* **www**.gorod.gatchina.biz

In 1765, Catherine the Great presented the village of Gatchina to her lover, Prince Grigoriy Orlov. He commis-sioned Antonio Rinaldi to build a Neo-Classical palace which was completed in 1781. When

# Tsarskoe Selo ❺

*See pp152–5.*

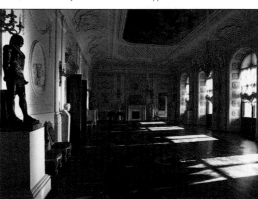
Gatchina's sumptuous White Ballroom with its pseudo-Egyptian statues

# Peterhof ❸

Петергоф

*Petergof*

With its commanding views of the Baltic, Peterhof is a perfect expression of triumphalism. Originally designed by Jean Baptiste Le Blond, the Great Palace (1714–21) was transformed during the reign of Tsarina Elizabeth when Bartolomeo Rastrelli added a third storey and wings with pavilions at either end. He tried to preserve Le Blond's early Baroque exterior, but redesigned the interiors, indulging his love for gilded Baroque decoration. Peterhof stands at the centre of a magnificent landscaped park, with both French and English gardens.

**View from palace of Grand Cascade leading down to the Gulf of Finland**

Neptune Fountain

Oak Fountain

Mezheumnyy Fountain

**The Upper Gardens** are framed by borders and hedges and punctuated with ornamental ponds.

**The Imperial Suite**

*The imperial suite lies in the palace's east wing. Peter's Oak Study is one of the few rooms to have survived unaltered from Le Blond's design. Some of the oak panel designs are originals (1718–21) by Nicholas Pineau.*

Cottage Palace

Orangery

Roman Fountain

★ **The Grand Cascade**

*The dazzling cascade (1715–24) is a sequence of 37 gilded bronze sculptures, 64 fountains and 142 water jets (see p151), descending from the terraces of the Great Palace to the Marine Canal and the sea.*

Pyramid Fountain

Monplais

Adam Fountain

| 0 metres | 25 |
| 0 yards | 25 |

## PETER THE GREAT'S PALACE

After his victory over the Swedes at Poltava in 1709, Peter the Great decided to build a palace "befitting to the very highest of monarchs". A visit to Versailles in 1717 furthered Peter's ambitions and he employed more than 5,000 labourers, serfs and soldiers, supported by architects, water-engineers, landscape gardeners and sculptors. Work proceeded at a frenetic pace from 1714 until Peterhof was officially opened in 1723.

Le Blond's Great Palace was completed in 1721 and has changed considerably over the decades. Catherine the Great commissioned Yuriy Velten to redecorate some of Rastrelli's interiors in the 1770s, including the Throne Room and the Chesma Room.

**Jean Baptiste Le Blond's original two-storey Great Palace**

### VISITORS' CHECKLIST

Petrodvorets, 30 km (19 miles) W of St Petersburg. **Tel** 420 0073.
🚆 from Baltic station (see p220) to Novyy Petergof. 🚌 Hermitage (May–Oct) (see p220). **Great Palace** ◻ 10:30am–6pm Tue–Sun. ⬤ last Tue of each month. **Other pavilions** ◻ May–Sep: 11am–5pm Tue–Sun; Oct–Apr: 11am–5pm Sat & Sun. **Fountains** ◻ May–early Oct; 10:30am–5pm. 🏛 ♿ 🅿 🍴 🛍

★ **Main Staircase**
*Caryatids and gilded carvings adorn Rastrelli's glittering staircase. The ceiling fresco depicts Aurora and Genius chasing away the night.*

**Golden Hill Cascade**

**Marly and Hermitage**

**Eve Fountain**

**Samson Fountain**

### STAR FEATURES

★ Grand Cascade

★ Main Staircase

★ The State Rooms

**Hydrofoil and Gulf of Finland**

**The Marine Canal** enabled the tsars to sail from the Gulf of Finland up to the Great Palace.

★ **The State Rooms**
*The highlight of the State Rooms is the opulent Throne Room, redesigned by Yuriy Velten in 1770. The relatively restrained stucco ornamentation, red velvet hangings and parquet floor provide an exquisite setting for portraits of Russia's imperial family.*

# Exploring Peterhof Park

The grounds at Peterhof include the Upper, Lower and Alexandria parks, covering an area of around 607 hectares (1,500 acres). As well as the numerous palaces and fountains, there are tree-lined avenues, wooded paths and the Baltic shore. Le Blond designed the grounds next to the Great Palace to be laid out in the formal French style with geometrically arranged flower beds, sculptures, summerhouses and pergolas. The trees and shrubs, including limes, elms, maples and roses, were imported from all over Russia and abroad.

**Cottage Palace in Alexandria Park**

**Monplaisir palace (1714–22), overlooking the Gulf of Finland**

### Monplaisir
This delightfully unpretentious palace was designed in 1714 by Johann Braunstein. Even after the Great Palace was built, Peter continued to live and entertain at Monplaisir where his guests were usually subjected to a punishing regime of heavy drinking. At breakfast the coffee cups were filled with brandy and by nightfall guests were often discovered wandering drunk in the park.

While not as lavish as those of the Great Palace the interiors are still impressive, in particular the wood-panelled Ceremonial Hall. A painting on its vaulted ceiling depicts Apollo surrounded by characters from a masque. Russian icon painters skilfully carried out the decoration of the exquisite Lacquered Study in the Chinese style then in vogue. Peter's collection of canvases by Dutch and Flemish artists hang in the rooms and there are wonderful views of the gulf from the tsar's Naval Study.

Adjoining Monplaisir is the Catherine Wing, which was built for Tsarina Elizabeth by Rastrelli in 1747–54. Catherine the Great was staying here in 1762 when her lover, Count Orlov, arrived with news of the coup which was to bring her to the throne (see p24).

### Marly Palace
Named after Marly-le-Rois, the king of France's hunting lodge which Peter the Great visited on a tour of Europe in 1717, this beautifully proportioned country residence was built for the tsar's guests. The rooms open to the public

**Elaborate tiled kitchen in the Marly Palace (1720–3)**

include the Oak and Plane Tree studies, Peter's bedroom and the Dining Room. It is set in its own formal garden with sculptures, fountains, a large pond and Niccolò Michetti's Golden Hill Cascade, which was added in 1731–7.

### The Hermitage
Standing in splendid isolation on the shores of the gulf, this elegant pavilion (1721–5), by Braunstein, was conceived as a private dining venue for the tsar and his friends. To highlight the need for solitude, the building was raised on a plinth and surrounded by a moat that was crossed by a small drawbridge. The stuccoed façade is decorated with Corinthian pilasters, elaborate wrought-iron balconies and enlarged windows. All the servants were confined to the ground floor and a mechanical device took meals up from the kitchen.

### Cottage Palace
The romantic landscaped grounds of Alexandria Park, named after Alexandra, wife of Nicholas I, provide a perfect setting for the Cottage Palace. The Neo-Gothic house is more imposing than the term cottage suggests. The Scottish architect, Adam Menelaws, designed it in 1826–9 for Nicholas I and his wife, who wanted a domestic environment in keeping with their bourgeois tastes.

The Gothic theme is pursued throughout, most effectively in the Great Drawing Room with the rose window motif in the carpet and the lace-like tracery of the stuccoed ceiling. The exquisite 5,200-piece crystal and porcelain dinner service in the Dining Room was made for the royal couple at the Imperial Porcelain factory.

# The Fountains at Peterhof

Jean-Baptiste Le Blond submitted his "water plan" to Peter the Great in 1717, by which time the tsar had begun sketching his own ideas. The centrepiece is the Grand Cascade, fed by the underground springs of the Ropsha Hills about 22 km (14 miles) away. The cascade is a celebration of the triumph of Russia over Sweden *(see p19)*, symbolized by Mikhail Kozlovskiy's glorious

**Detail of the Mezheumnyy Fountain**

sculpture of Samson rending the jaws of a lion. An imaginative variety of fountains, mostly concentrated in the Lower Park, includes triton and lion fountains, dragon fountains with checker-board steps, and smaller fountains with fish-tailed boys blowing sprays of water through conches. Most playful are trick fountains such as the Umbrella which "rains" on those who come too close.

**The Roman Fountains** *were designed by Ivan Blank and Ivan Davydov in 1738–9. The two-tiered marble fountains were inspired by one in St Peter's Square in Rome.*

**The Adam Fountain,** *sculpted by Giovanni Bonazza, was commissioned by Peter in 1718, along with a similar statue of Eve. The two fountains suggest the earthly paradise the tsar had recreated at Peterhof.*

**The Neptune Fountain** *predates Peterhof by more than 50 years. The Baroque sculpture was erected in 1658 in Nuremberg to mark the end of the Thirty Years War and was sold to Tsar Paul I in 1782 because there was not enough water to make it work.*

**The Grand Cascade** *was originally adorned with lead statues which weathered badly and were recast in bronze and gilded after 1799. Shubin, Martos and other noted sculptors worked to create this stunning cascade.*

**The Pyramid Fountain** *(1720s) is one of a number of fountains whose jets create a special shape. Over 500 jets of water rise in seven tiers to create an "obelisk" commemorating the Russian victory over Sweden.*

# Tsarskoe Selo ❺

Царское Село
*Tsarskoe Selo*

The lavish imperial palace at Tsarskoe Selo was designed by Rastrelli *(see p93)* in 1752 for Tsarina Elizabeth. She named it the Catherine Palace in honour of her mother, Catherine I, who originally owned the estate. The next ruler to leave her mark on the palace was Catherine the Great, and during her reign she commissioned the Scotsman Charles Cameron to redesign the Baroque interiors according to her more Neo-Classical taste. Cameron also built the ensemble for taking traditional Russian cold and warm baths, containing the Agate Rooms, and the Cameron Gallery. Post-war restoration of the palace continues and 20 state rooms are now open, as well as the beautiful park.

★ **The Great Hall**
*Light streams into Rastrelli's glittering hall illuminating the mirrors, gilded carvings and the vast ceiling painting,* The Triumph of Russia *(c.1755), by Giuseppe Valeriani.*

**The Great Staircase** (1860), by Ippolito Monighetti, ascends to the state rooms on the first floor.

**Entrance**

**Atlantes**
*The stunning 300-m (980-ft) long Baroque façade is adorned with a profusion of atlantes, columns, pilasters and ornamented window framings.*

| 0 metres | 25 |
|---|---|
| 0 yards | 25 |

**The Agate Rooms** *(see p154)* are part of the imperial baths and faced with semi-precious stones from the Urals. (Temporarily closed.)

**The Cameron Gallery** *(see p154)*

**The Cavaliers' Dining Room**
*The table is laid for Tsarina Elizabeth's gentlemen-in-waiting, in the refined gold and white room created by Rastrelli.*

**The Royal Chapel** is richly decorated in dark blue and gold. Built by Chevakinskiy in the 1740s, it contains an elaborate six-tiered iconostasis.

## VISITORS' CHECKLIST

Tsarskoe Selo, 25 km (16 miles) S of St Petersburg. 🚉 from Vitebsk station to Detskoe Selo, then 🚌 371 or 382. **Palace Tel** 465 2024. ⬜ 10am–5pm Wed–Mon; open to individuals only noon–2pm & 4–5pm. ⬤ last Mon of month. 📷 🎫 🔔 🛍 **Agate Rooms** ⬤ temporarily. **Cameron Gallery** ⬜ 10am–5pm Wed–Mon. **Park** ⬜ daily. 🎫 mid-May–Sep. **www**.tzar.ru

★ **Amber Room**
*The original amber panels (1709) by Andreas Schlüter were a gift from Friedrich Wilhelm I of Prussia to Peter the Great. The room has been recreated from photos, complete with carved reliefs and panels in Florentine mosaic.*

**The Blue Drawing Room** is characterized by blue floral motifs painted on silk. Among the royal portraits hanging here is a painting of Peter the Great by Ivan Nikitin, dating from around 1720.

To the Lycée and the Church of the Sign *(see p155)*

**The Picture Gallery** displays canvases by Italian, French, Dutch and Flemish masters of the 17th and 18th centuries.

**The French-style formal gardens** were laid out in the 1740s. Their formality and symmetry contrasts with the naturalistic English-style landscaping of the park *(see p154)*, created in 1768.

★ **Green Dining Room**
*Cameron's restrained Neo-Classical style contrasts with the Baroque flamboyance of Rastrelli's work. The exquisite stucco bas-reliefs, sculpted by Ivan Martos, were based on motifs from frescoes discovered in Pompeii.*

**Small Enfilade**
*A varied selection of furniture and objets d'art make up the exhibition in these unrestored rooms. Chinese lacquer furniture and Oriental rugs are among the treasures used to furnish the palace in the 19th century.*

## STAR FEATURES

★ The Great Hall

★ Amber Room

★ Green Dining Room

# Exploring Tsarskoe Selo

The magnificent parks and gardens of Tsarskoe Selo (the Tsar's Village) were created out of dense forest by thousands of soldiers and labourers. Work began on the formal gardens in 1744 but later, in 1768, Catherine the Great commissioned one of Russia's first landscaped parks. The 567 hectares (1,400 acres) of grounds are dotted with captivating pavilions set around the central lake. The grounds and the town of Tsarskoe Selo, to the northeast of the palace, are also a delight to explore.

Formal gardens in front of Catherine Palace, Catherine Park

## Catherine Park

The formal gardens to the southeast of the palace are laid out geometrically with radiating avenues, parterres and terraces, decorous ponds, hedges, elegant pavilions and Classical statuary. Nearest to the palace are Cameron's **Agate Rooms** (1780–87), which are currently closed. Their heavily rusticated lower storey contrasts with the upper tier, modelled on a Renaissance villa. The building takes its name from the agate, jasper and malachite covering the interior.

The impressive **Cameron Gallery**, built in 1783–7, has a rusticated stone ground floor, surmounted by a Neo-Classical peristyle of 44 Ionic columns. Ranged along the colonnade are bronze busts of ancient philosophers, poets and rulers. In 1792–4 Cameron added a long stone ramp to facilitate access to the gardens for the ageing Catherine the Great.

Girl with a Pitcher by Pavel Sokolov (1816)

The Neo-Classical **Lower and Upper Baths** were built by Ilya Neyelov in 1777–80. The domed Lower Baths were for the use of courtiers while the exquisite Upper Baths were reserved for members of the imperial family.

Construction work on Rastrelli's **Grotto** began in 1749, but the original decoration of the interior with more than 250,000 shells continued well into the 1770s.

The gardens' main avenue leads to the **Hermitage** (1756), a Baroque pavilion built by Rastrelli, where Elizabeth would entertain small groups of guests for dinner.

The romantic landscaped area of the lower park was begun in 1768 by master gardeners such as John Bush, who worked under the overall supervision of the architect, Vasiliy Neyelov. A 16-km (10-mile) waterway was built to feed the numerous canals, cascades and man-made lakes,

including the *pièce de résistance,* the **Great Pond**. From Giacomo Quarenghi's pavilion (1786) on the island, musicians would serenade Catherine and her courtiers as they floated by in gilded gondolas.

A naval theme links Vasiliy Neyelov's Dutch, Neo-Gothic **Admiralty** (1773–7) with the 25-m (82-ft) high **Chesma Column** which is decorated with ships' prows. The column, designed by Antonio Rinaldi in 1771, commemorates the Russian victory over the Turks in the Aegean.

The reflection of the pink dome and minaret of the **Turkish Bath** shimmers in the placid waters on the far side of the lake. Nearby is Neyelov's colonnaded **Marble Bridge** (1770–76). Perched on a rock overlooking the pond is the **Girl with a Pitcher**, a statue by Pavel Sokolov. The figure inspired Pushkin to write his memorable poem, *Fountain at Tsarskoe Selo,* in which he muses on the girl who has broken her urn and now "sits timelessly sad over the timeless stream".

Evidence of the 18th-century craze for chinoiserie can be found on the border with the wilder Alexander Park where Cameron built his **Chinese Village** in 1782–96. Other examples are Yuriy Velten's **Creaking Pavilion**, so-called because it was designed to creak when visitors entered, and Neyelov's **Great Caprice** (1770s), a hump-backed bridge surmounted by a pagoda-like columned structure.

The Moorish-style Turkish Baths (1852) by Ippolito Monighetti

**Creaking Pavilion (1778–86)**

## The Town of Tsarskoe Selo

This town of 80,000 inhabitants was developed in the 19th century as a summer resort for the aristocracy. In 1937, it was renamed after the poet Alexander (*see p43*) who was educated at the local **Lycée** in 1811–17. One of Russia's most prestigious schools, it was founded by Alexander I in 1811 to educate members of the nobility. In 1998 the town took back its original name.

The attractive **Church of the Sign** (1734) is one of the town's oldest buildings. In a garden next door a statue by Roman Bach depicts Pushkin dressed in the Lycée uniform.

Pushkin and his new bride, Natalya, spent the summer of 1831 in the delightful wooden house, now named **Pushkin's Dacha**. The writer, Nikolai Gogol, was amongst the many friends they entertained here.

On the town's western edge is the **Alexander Palace**, commissioned by Catherine for her grandson, the future Alexander I. Designed in 1792 by Giacomo Quarenghi, the austere, Neo-Classical building has a colonnaded façade and protruding wings. It was the residence of Russia's last tsar, Nicholas II and his family from 1904 until their arrest in 1917 (*see p28*). There is an exhibition inside.

**Lycée** Sadovaya 2. *Tel* 476 6411. ◯ 10:30am–5:30pm Wed–Mon. ● last Fri of month.

**Pushkin's Dacha** Pushkinskaya 2/19. *Tel* 476 6990. ◯ 10:30am–5:30pm Wed–Sun. ● last Fri of month. **Alexander Palace** Dvortsovaya 2. *Tel* 466 6669. ◯ 10am–6pm Wed–Mon. ● last Mon of month. **www.**alexanderpalace.org

**Alexander Pushkin's statue (1900), by Roman Bach**

## TSARSKOE SELO PARK

0 metres 500
0 yards 500

Key to **Symbols** *see back flap*

**Imperial standard of the Romanovs flying at the Catherine Palace** ▷

# Pavlovsk ⑥

Павловск
*Pavlovsk*

To celebrate the birth of his heir, Catherine the Great presented her son, the Grand Duke Paul, with these lands in 1777. She also "gave" him her favourite architect, Charles Cameron, to design both palace and park. Work at Pavlovsk (from "Pavel" or Paul) began in 1780 and was continued by Paul's grieving widow, Maria Fyodorovna, long after his death. "English gardens" were at the height of fashion and inspired Cameron's design of a seemingly natural landscape dotted with pavilions (used for informal parties), romantic ruins and attractive vistas around the Slavyanka river.

**Cold Baths**
*This austere pavilion was built by Cameron in 1799 as a summer swimming pool, complete with elegant vestibule, paintings, furniture and rich wall upholstery.*

**The Apollo Colonnade**
*Cameron's colonnade (1782–83) encircles a copy of the Apollo Belvedere, above a romantically dilapidated cascade.*

**Three Graces Pavilion**

**The Centaur Bridge** by Voronikhin (1805) nestles on a bend of the Slavyanka river.

**Aviary**

**Cameron's Dairy** (1782) housed both a milking shed and a stylish salon.

**★ Pavlovsk Palace**
*Cameron's elegant Palladian mansion (1782–6) forms the central block of today's palace (see pp160–1), with wings added in 1789 by Paul's favoured architect, Vincenzo Brenna.*

**★ Temple of Friendship**
*This Doric temple (1780) was the first use of Greek forms in Russia.*

**Green Woman Alley**

**Pavlovsk Railway Station**

**Visconti Bridge**
*One of the most famous bridges which cross the winding Slavyanka, it was designed by Andrey Voronikhin in 1807.*

**The Étoile**
*The Étoile, the earliest landscaped area in the park, was laid out by Cameron in 1780. The circle of statues represents the nine Muses, protectresses of the arts and sciences.*

**The Beautiful Valley** was the favourite spot of Elizabeth, wife of Alexander I.

| 0 metres | 200 |
|---|---|
| 0 yards | 200 |

**Paul's Mausoleum** (1808–9) bears the inscription "To my beneficent consort".

**The Rose Pavilion** was the favourite haunt of Maria Fyodorovna from 1812. She held many concerts and literary evenings in this cottage.

### STAR FEATURES

★ Temple of Friendship

★ Great Palace

**Pil Tower and Bridge**
*Brenna's tower (1795–7) contained a spiral staircase, lounge and library. The bridge was a later addition made in 1808.*

# Exploring Pavlovsk Palace

Catherine commissioned Charles Cameron to build the Great Palace (1782–6) whilst Paul and his wife Maria Fyodorovna travelled around Europe incognito as the Comte and Comtesse du Nord. They, meanwhile, bought up everything they saw including French clocks, Sèvres porcelain, tapestries and furniture, to fill their new home.

**Late 18th-century clock, Grecian Hall**

**West façade of the Palladian mansion**

Once back in Russia, they brought in Brenna to add taller, more elaborate wings to Cameron's elegant Palladian mansion, turning it into a true palace.

## PLAN OF PAVLOVSK PALACE, FIRST FLOOR

**KEY**

☐ State rooms

☐ Southern wing

**Stairs to private apartments and Egyptian Vestibule on the ground floor**

1 Italian Hall
2 Paul's Study
3 Tapestry Room
4 Hall of War
5 Grecian Hall
6 Hall of Peace
7 Maria Fyodorovna's Library
8 Boudoir
9 State Bedroom
10 Dressing Room
11 Picture Gallery
12 Throne Room
13 Hall of Knights
14 Chapel

## STATE ROOMS

**The Italian Hall, originally by Cameron and Brenna, 1789**

Nearly all of the palace apartments at Pavlovsk, including the official ones, are relatively modest in scale. They reflect Maria Fyodorovna's intensely feminine tastes which have given Pavlovsk a distinct charm rather than grandeur.

A fire in 1803 necessitated some remodelling of the palace interiors by Andrey Voronikhin. The entrance hall, or Egyptian Vestibule, gained its present appearance after he added the painted bronze figures and zodiac medallions. At the top of the stairs is Brenna's State Vestibule, where the bas-reliefs reflected Paul's passion for all things military. It leads onto the Italian Hall, situated beneath the central cupola, with lantern windows and heavy doors of rosewood and mahogany.

The northern row of rooms on this floor were for Paul, the southern ones for Maria. Paul's Study is dominated by Johann Lampi's fine portrait of Maria (1794), who holds a drawing of six of their children. Beneath it is a model temple of amber, ivory and gilded bronze, made by Maria herself. Next door, the Tapestry Room is named after the Don Quixote tapestries made by Gobelin and presented to Paul by Louis XVI. The mahogany writing table was actually made for the new Engineers' Castle (see p101) but, after Paul's murder there in 1801 (see p22), Maria moved much of the specially designed furniture to Pavlovsk Palace.

The corner rooms are a Hall of War for Paul and Maria's contrasting Hall of Peace, both richly adorned with bas-reliefs and heavy gilding. Between the two lies the magnificent Grecian Hall, Cameron's Neo-Classical masterpiece.

Maria Fyodorovna's rooms commence with a small, comfortable library. The chair at the desk was designed for her by Voronikhin; note the pots built into the spine for flowers. Her Boudoir has pilasters painted with motifs copied from the Raphael Loggias in the Vatican, and a porphyry fireplace. The State Bedroom was reputedly never slept in, but was part of court ceremony. Opposite the

**Maria Fyodorovna's Boudoir, designed by Brenna, 1789**

**Brenna's Picture Gallery (1789), with chandeliers by Johann Zeck**

bed is a 64-piece Sèvres toilet set, complete with a coffee cup and an eye bath, which was a gift from Marie Antoinette.

Another present dominates the Dressing Room, a superb set of steel furniture including dressing table, chair, vases and ink stand made by the renowned gun-makers of Tula (1789). This was presented to Maria by Catherine the Great.

## SOUTHERN WING

From the elegantly curved picture gallery, built in 1798, there are excellent views. Only a few of the paintings, mostly purchased during the young couple's trip to France, are worthy of special notice, as their taste was for applied art.

The largest room in the palace is the Throne Room, designed by Brenna (1797) after Paul became tsar. Despite its name it was generally used for balls and state dinners. The tables are now laid with part of a 606-piece gilded dinner service. Vast blue Sèvres vases

stand on plinths, bought directly from the factory (Paul and Maria spent huge sums on porcelain there alone). The ceiling was painted during restoration after World War II *(see p26)*, and is taken from an original design which was never used.

The Knights of St John chose Paul as Grand Master when they fled Napoleon's occupation of Malta in 1798. This suited Paul's military taste and he commissioned lamps, thrones and decorative items (now in the Hermitage), as well as the Hall of Knights, for ceremonies of the Order. The pale green room is adorned with Classical statues, saved from the Germans in World War II by being buried in the grounds.

The suite of rooms ends with the Imperial Chapel of SS Peter and Paul, a very un-Orthodox church by Brenna (1797–8), decorated with copies of European paintings.

## PRIVATE APARTMENTS

Located on the ground floor are the private apartments. The Pilaster Room (1800), with its golden pilasters, is furnished with a dark mahogany suite. The Lantern Study, designed a few years later by Voronikhin, is named after its apsed bay window forming the "lantern".

Maria Fyodorovna's Dressing Room leads into the Bedroom (1805) she actually used (as opposed to the State Bedroom upstairs). Pieces of the original silk were saved in the war and used to edge the new curtains.

The small pink and blue Ballroom was for private parties and hung with paintings by the most fashionable artist of the day, Hubert Robert. The General Study, used as a family sitting room, is decorated with portraits of the family. The Raspberry Room, Paul's private study, contains paintings with views of Gatchina Palace, made for the Engineers' Castle.

**The Lantern Study, one of Voronikhin's most successfully designed interiors, 1804**

## MARIA FYODOROVNA (1759–1828)

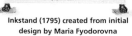

Paul's wife, Maria Fyodorovna, bore 10 children, and Pavlovsk was considered her 11th child. Paul himself preferred Gatchina *(see p147)* and in 1788 Maria was given Pavlovsk entirely. She devoted all her energy to adorning both palace and park, giving precise directions to designers and architects, who bemoaned their lack of independence. Born Sophia of Württemberg-Stuttgart, Maria had a practical German upbringing which she put to good use. Pieces of her own work, from furniture to family portraits, are throughout the palace.

**Inkstand (1795) created from initial design by Maria Fyodorovna**

# Novgorod ❼

Detail of bronze door on Cathedral of St Sophia

The ancient town of Novgorod (New Town) was founded in 859 by the Varangian (Viking) Prince Rurik *(see p17)*. The city's proud tradition of self-government began in the 11th century and lasted until 1478, when Ivan III subjugated the city. Favourably sited on the River Volkhov with convenient connections from Scandinavia to the Aegean, the city of Novgorod became a powerful trading community during this period. In 1570, Ivan the Terrible put Novgorod to the sword, torturing and massacring thousands of its inhabitants when the city plotted against him. It was, however, the rise of St Petersburg which finally set the seal on Novgorod's decline. Much of the city's splendid cultural heritage, damaged in World War II, is now being restored and can be appreciated in the many medieval churches and picturesque streets of the old town.

## The Kremlin

Situated on the left bank, or Sofiskaya Storona (Sophia side), of the River Volkhov, the formidable red-brick walls and cone-topped towers of the oval-shaped Detinets, or Kremlin, date from the 11th to the 17th centuries. According to the prevailing practice at the time, the first stone of the original walls was laid on the body of a living child.

Of the many towers, the 17th-century Kukui is the most remarkable, and also the tallest at 32m (105ft). The lower floors once contained a wine cellar and treasury chamber, while the octagonal room beneath the cupola was used, according to chronicles, "for surveying the whole town".

Kremlin walls, with the silver dome of St Sophia's Belfry (15th century)

At the heart of the fortress is Novgorod's oldest and largest church, the strongly Byzantine **Cathedral of St Sophia** (1045–62). It was modelled on the cathedral of the same name in Kiev, but the tendencies of the Novgorod school already appear in the lack of ornament and the scarcity of windows,

Bejewelled metal icon cover on display in the Chamber of Facets

necessary because of the cold. On the north wall a section of whitewash has been removed to reveal the original mosaic effect of the grey-yellow stone and brick façade.

The exquisitely sculpted and extremely rare bronze doors adorning the west side were seized as booty in 1187 from the Swedish town of Sigtuna. In the lower left hand corner there are portraits of the craftsmen, named in the Latin inscription as Riquin and Weissmut. The interior is divided by piers into five aisles, three ending in altar apses. Fragments of early frescoes survive, but the iconostasis is one of the oldest in Russia and contains icons from the 11th–17th centuries.

East of the cathedral is **St Sophia's Belfry**, much altered since it was first built in 1439. The bells, now displayed below, were cast in the late 16th and early 17th centuries.

The northwest corner of the Kremlin is occupied by the **Archbishops' Court**, in its heyday a powerful body with its own treasury, police force and military guard. Beneath the 15th-century clock tower an attractive staircase leads to the **Library**, housing magnificent medieval religious manuscripts. Backing onto the cathedral, the **Chamber of Facets** is the most famous part of this ensemble. A superb star-vaulted reception hall dates from 1433 and displays treasures from the cathedral, including goblets, jewelled mitres and icon covers in precious metals.

The 11th-century Cathedral of St Sophia, the landmark of Novgorod

Within the Kremlin is the **Museum of History, Architecture and Art**, which houses a magnificent collection of 12th–17th-century icons of the Novgorod school. One of the most remarkable is the 12th-century portable icon of the Virgin of the Sign, whose miraculous image is said to have saved Novgorod from the armies of Prince Andrey Bogolyubskiy of Suzdal in 1169. Scenes from the battle are depicted on a vibrant 15th-century icon *(see p165)*. There are also works by leading 18th- and 19th-century artists, including Dmitriy Levitskiy, Karl Bryullov and Vasiliy Serov *(see p106)*. The museum has a number of precious public documents and private letters written on birch bark, some of which date from the 11th century. These give details of ordinary, everyday life and are evidence of the unusually widespread literacy among the city's inhabitants.

In the Kremlin's central square, the huge, bell-shaped **Millennium Monument** was sculpted by Mikhail Mikeshin. The monument was unveiled in 1862, a thousand years after Rurik's arrival in Novgorod. The figure kneeling before the Orthodox cross personifies Mother Russia while, below, the decorative frieze depicts Rurik, Ivan III, Mikhail (the first Romanov tsar), Peter the Great and many others. The frieze around the base shows over 100 figures: heroes, statesmen, artists, composers, princes and chroniclers.

The carved Royal Gates of an iconostasis in the Museum of History, Architecture and Art

**Cathedral of St Sophia**
*Tel (8162) 773556.*
10am–6pm daily.
**Chamber of Facets**
*Tel (8162) 773608.* 10am–6pm Thu–Tue. English by appt.
**Museum of History, Architecture and Art**
*Tel (8162) 773770.* 10am–6pm Wed–Mon. English by appt.

**VISITORS' CHECKLIST**
190 km (118 miles) S of St Petersburg. 240,000. from Moscow Station. from Coach Station (see p221). Intourist Hotel, ul Velikaya 16, (8162) 774236.

**Yaroslav's Court**
Across the River Volkhov was the official seat of the princes, known as Yaroslav's Court. The palace of Yaroslav the Wise (1019–54) has since disappeared but several churches have survived. The area adjacent to the Court is Novgorod's commercial centre, once the site of the medieval market, part of whose wall still stands.

The oldest church on this side of the river, **St Nicholas' Cathedral** (1113–36), was built by Prince Mstislav. It dominates the area and once symbolized the prince's power.

Novgorod's merchants were keen to show their recognition of God's hand in their prosperity, and so funded many of the city's churches. **St Paraskeva Pyatnitsa**, erected in 1207 and then rebuilt in 1345, was dedicated to the patron saint of commerce. The more decorative **Church of the Holy Women** and **Church of St Procopius**, both 16th century, were financed by wealthy Moscow merchants. The fanciful tastes of the Muscovite patrons mark a departure from Novgorod's austere style.

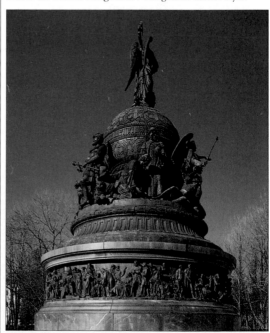
Millennium Monument, celebrating Novgorod's 1,000 years of history

Yuriev Monastery walls and bell tower with the silvery domes of the Cathedral of St George in the background

## Beyond Yaroslav's Court

In the 12th century, Novgorod boasted over 200 churches, while there are only 30 today. Many of these are hidden away in the quiet hinterland of 19th-century streets to the east of Yaroslav's Court. On Ilyina ulitsa, the arrangement of windows, niches and inset crosses on the **Church of the Saviour of the Transfiguration** façade (1374) is almost whimsical. Inside, there are original frescoes by one of Russia's greatest medieval artists, Theophanes the Greek (1335–c.1410), who came from Constantinople and decorated 40 Russian churches. Andrey Rublev (1360–1430), Russia's most famous icon painter, worked under Theophanes at the beginning of his career.

On the same street, the five-domed **Znamenskiy Cathedral**, or Cathedral of the Sign (1682–8), has an attractive gateway and faded frescoes on the outer walls. The beautiful interior was decorated in 1702 by Ivan Bakhmatov.

The **Church of Theodore Stratilates** on Mstinskaya ulitsa to the north was built in 1360–61 by the widow of a wealthy Novgorod merchant. The delicate purple and pink

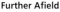

Fresco inside
Znamenskiy Cathedral

frescoes contrast with the harsher colours found in most 14th-century Novgorod frescoes. *The Annunciation*, for example, combines sensitivity and charm with religious intensity.

### Further Afield

A pleasant stroll 3 km (2 miles) south along the river bank leads to the **Yuriev Monastery**. This is the largest and most important monastery in the area, founded in 1030 and built on the orders of Prince Vsevolod. Its imposing Cathedral of St George was built in 1119–30 by "Master Peter", the first named architect in Russian chronicles. This beautifully proportioned church with its three asymmetrical cupolas was restored in the 19th century, and unfortunately most of the interior murals were lost. There were once 20 monastic buildings in the complex, dating mainly from the 19th century.

In the woods across the road lies the fascinating open-air **Museum of Wooden Architecture**, which displays churches and peasant huts moved from local villages. Of particular interest are the 17th-century two-tiered Kuritsko Church of the Dormition and the tiny wooden church of St Nicholas from Tukhel village.

✠ **Yuriev Monastery**
Yurevskaya nab. *Tel* (8162) 773020. ⬚ 10am–6pm daily.

🏛 **Museum of Wooden Architecture (*Vitoslavlitsi*)**
Yurevo. *Tel* (8162) 773770. ⬚ 24 hrs. Exhibitions: 10am–6pm (mid-Oct–mid-Apr: 10am–4pm) daily. 📷 📷

Rebuilt 19th-century peasant hut *(izba)*, Museum of Wooden Architecture

# Russian Icon Painting

The Russian Orthodox Church uses icons for both worship and teaching, but never for mere ornament, and there are strict rules for the creation of each image. Icons were believed to be imbued with the force of the saint depicted, and were therefore invoked for protection during wars. Because the content was considered more important than the style, old, revered icons were often repainted again and again.

**Early stone icon found in Novgorod**

The first icons were brought to Russia from Byzantium. Greek masters came too, to train local painters. The northern schools which developed during the 13th–15th centuries were less restricted by Byzantine canons and have an earthy style linked to Russian peasant life. Novgorod, never under the Mongol yoke and with a thriving economy, was the source of many of the finest icons made for the northern monasteries.

**Virgin of Vladimir**
*The most venerated icon in Russia, this 12th-century work was made in Constantinople. Its huge influence on Russian icon painting cannot be overstated.*

**Battle of Novgorod and Suzdal**
*This mid-15th-century work of the Novgorod School is thought to be Russia's earliest historical painting. Icons could have a political purpose – in this case to use Novgorod's great past as a justification for its independence from Moscow. Note the multiple touches of red – a colour central to everyday Russian life and typical for icons of the Novgorod School.*

## THE ICONOSTASIS

The iconostasis screens off the sanctuary from the main part of the church, as if it were a boundary between heaven and earth. In Russian practice it is covered with icons strictly arranged in up to six tiers, each with its own dogmatic purpose.

**The Festival Tier** shows the 12 major church festivals, such as the Entry into Jerusalem and the Crucifixion. Such pictorial representation aided the faith of the illiterate.

**Christ Enthroned**

**The Deesis Tier**, above the Royal Gates, contains Christ Enthroned, flanked by the Virgin and St John interceding on behalf of mortal sinners.

**The Royal Gates** represent the entrance from the temporal world to the spiritual, between which the priests pass during the service.

**The Local Tier** is for local saints, those the church is dedicated to and patron saints of major donors.

**Old Testament Trinity by Rublev**
*Andrey Rublev was one of the greatest artists of the Moscow School. He was strongly influenced by recent developments in Byzantine painting, brought to Russia by Greek masters in the late 14th century. His Trinity icon dates from the early 15th century.*

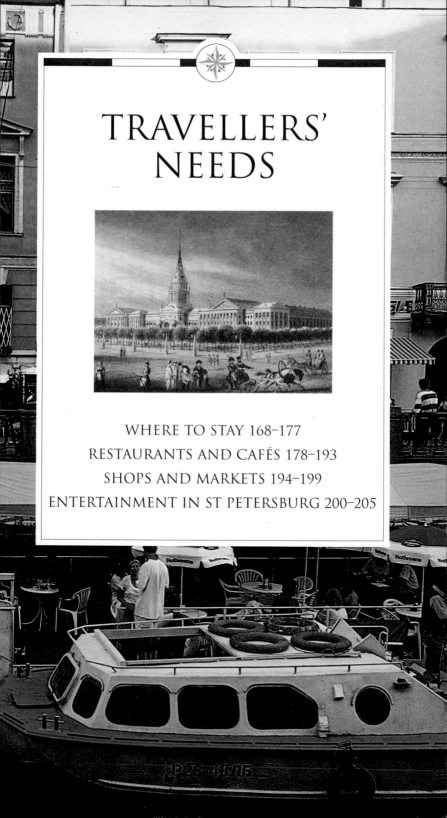

# TRAVELLERS'
# NEEDS

# WHERE TO STAY

Celebrations in 2003 of the 300th anniversary of the founding of St Petersburg did wonders for the range of hotel accommodation available. The city has sprouted many "mini-hotels" (privately run establishments in or near the centre with anything from 4 to 15 rooms), and investors have opened large, luxury hotels in outstanding locations. The quality of service has also risen dramatically. Many tourists visiting in the summer with a package tour, however, are still housed in large, somewhat anonymous modern hotels outside the centre. These provide reasonable service and full amenities such as restaurants, bars and fitness facilities. Travelling outside the White Nights period cuts costs and opens up the opportunity for booking one of the many excellent deals available at more central hotels. Bookings can be made independently or via an agency. For the summer months, particularly during the White Nights, reservations should be made well in advance for accommodation at all price levels. There is a selection of hotels on *pp174–7*.

**Doorman at Hotel Europe**

**Park Inn Pribaltiyskaya, a popular hotel for package tours** *(see p176)*

## WHERE TO LOOK

There are few large, inexpensive hotels in central St Petersburg. Many of those listed in this chapter are scattered around the city. Visitors on a package tour usually find themselves staying in a former Intourist hotel such as the Park Inn Pribaliyskaya or Pulkovskaya, situated in modern high-rise areas on the city's outskirts. Mini hotels and bed-and-breakfast establishments, by contrast, are frequently found in quiet streets near the centre. Independent travellers should consider their priorities from the start: is it location, price or facilities?

## HOW TO BOOK

Hotel reservations for the White Nights *(see p51)* should be made several months in advance, and as early as possible for the more popular establishments. Nearly all hotels can now be booked online or by fax. The larger hotels will require travellers to supply a credit card number, and money will be debited if a cancellation is made less than 72 hours in advance. Some of the smaller hotels can be booked through one of the agencies listed on page 171. All hotels and agencies recommended can provide visa support *(see p210)*, unless stated otherwise.

## FACILITIES

Rooms in all the hotels listed include at least a shower, a television and a telephone. Most have air conditioning. Large hotels have a luggage room for storing baggage after the midday check-out time. Bars frequently work at night, and extensive fitness and sauna facilities are more or less standard features in bigger establishments.

## PRICE

The most important thing to remember in St Petersburg is that prices in big hotels more than double for the six weeks or so of the White Nights and for the Economic Forum in early June. These higher prices are quoted throughout the hotel listings *(see pp174–7)*. Normal prices return during the "mid-season", usually April–May and late July–late September. Outside that period, particularly during the "White Days" of winter, there are frequently excellent deals to be had.

Large central hotels, it should be noted, nearly all fall into the luxury category, and offer everything from exclusive single rooms to imperial suites costing several thousand dollars a day. By opting for a smaller hotel

**Fitness centre at the Grand Hotel Europe** *(see p175)*

◁ **Floating bars on the Moyka river**

with fewer facilities or a bed and breakfast (usually a small, basic hotel rather than a family home), you can be just as central for much less money. Many smaller hotels have only shower cabins, not full baths.

Note that prices are not displayed in hotels, and that only some small hotels and hostels take credit cards. To avoid upset, it is important to be prepared to pay in cash.

Entrance to the luxurious, modern Corinthia Nevskij Palace *(see p176)*

## HIDDEN EXTRAS

Large hotels, which provide visa support and obligatory passport registration *(see p210)* for free, often do not include local taxes or breakfast in the prices they quote. Both of these can be a significant addition to the final bill. (The price categories used in the hotel listings on pages 174–7 include both breakfast and taxes.) Be warned that the cost of making international or even local phone calls from your room in the large hotels is likely to be prohibitive. On the other hand, phones which use the local network are relatively cheap and phone-cards can be purchased to make international calls from street booths or fixed phones *(see p216)*. In smaller hotels, breakfast tends to be included in the price, but you should expect to pay extra for the initial visa support. Calls from phones in small hotels and hostels may be free or very cheap if they use the local telephone system. Phonecards can be used to make interna-tional calls from such phones.

## SECURITY

Some top-range establishments have metal detectors and selec-tive bag searches at entrances. Smaller hotels have a door-man, who may ask to see a visitor's card or identification. Since this is simply a precau-tion for guests' protection, there is no reason to object.

Most hotels have safes in the rooms and/or security deposit boxes at the front desk. Large sums of money and valuables should always be left in one of these places.

## DISABLED TRAVELLERS

Due to the thick snow in winter, most buildings in St Petersburg have steps up to their entrances, making access extremely difficult for disabled visitors. Only a few of the élite hotels are fully wheelchair accessible, with staff trained to be of assistance, although other hotels are increasingly adding ramps, widening doors and trying to adapt to meet the needs of disabled travellers.

Room in the Grand Hotel Europe *(see p175)*

Those with special require-ments should contact their preferred hotel before booking.

## CHILDREN

St Petersburg has never been vaunted as a great children's destination, and few hotels cater specifically for families. It is, however, possible to arrange babysitters in all the large hotels, and increasingly in some of the smaller hotels. It is worth checking the situation before you book.

The elegant Winter Garden restaurant in the Astoria Hotel *(see p174)*

## MINI-HOTELS

St Petersburg has a very good range of mini-hotels available; far too many to list in full. The best, however, are included in this guide's hotel listings *(see pp174–7)*.

Not necessarily a truly budget option – because some are extremely luxurious – the city's extensive range of mini-hotels, with anything from 4 to 15 or 20 rooms, offer some of the most comfortable and pleasant accommodation available. And the personalized service on offer is often hard to beat.

Many mini-hotels can be booked through agencies, notably **Optima Tours**, **City Realty** and **Eridan Travel Company**, which include a selection on their websites.

**Interior of the renovated Petro Palace hotel** *(see p174)*

## BUDGET ACCOMMODATION

Truly cheap accommodation is hard to find in St Petersburg. If hostels are not for you but your budget is tight, choose one of the more modest mini-hotels, which usually describe themselves as "bed and breakfast". This usually means they offer a small number of rooms in a converted flat in an ordinary building, with a housekeeper who makes breakfast in the tiny kitchen. There may be a shared toilet rather than separate facilities.

Accommodation agencies such as Optima Tours and City Realty also offer short-term apartment rental, which can be very cheap for a group of friends who are sharing. The apartments are refurbished and central, with anything from one to five rooms, usually with satellite TV.

**Efficient and helpful Sindbad travel agency at the St Petersburg International Youth Hostel**

In some cases, although the apartment has been refurbished, the communal staircase to the building may be a little on the grubby side. This grittiness can be off-putting at first, but it does offer the feel of living in the true St Petersburg.

The best way to cut costs is, of course, to give up hopes of seeing the White Nights, and travel in the off season. Mini-hotels and short-let apartments can be extremely cheap at this time of year, and even the big hotels offer excellent deals. April can be dry and sunny, if still cold, and October can be beautiful, particularly if you catch the brief northern autumn. Travelling in February more or less guarantees the vision of a Russia covered in snow.

## HOSTELS

For the budget traveller seeking comfortable accommodation in a reasonably central location, there are now several centrally located hostels to choose from. All offer visa support and registration and are extremely friendly. **St Petersburg International**

**Youth Hostel**, with its attached budget travel company, **Sindbad**, is best known and is often booked up well in advance. The inexpensive but clean and comfortable **Nord Hostel**, on the other hand, is unmatched for location. You could also try **CubaHostel Backpackers**, which offers a wide selection of cheap accommodation.

Be aware that none of these are "youth" hostels as such, although young people do tend to dominate in the summer months. In the off season, however, 50 per cent of hostel guests tend to be in the over-forty age range.

## STAYING WITH FAMILIES

For a really good insight into Russian life, staying with a family can be an interesting and cheap option. The system works very much like any bed and breakfast in Europe, with prices including breakfast but no other meals. Extra meals can usually be provided at a small cost.

**HOFA** (Host Families Association) and **Ost-West** have a wide range of families on their books and a particularly good reputation in this area. Your hosts are likely to be extremely hospitable and will tend to overfeed you rather than otherwise. Many of HOFA's hosts are academics, well educated and speak several languages. As a general rule,

**Impressive façade of the Oktyabrskaya Hotel, dating from 1847** *(see p176)*

hosts will be keen to talk to you about their life in Russia and Western perceptions of their country.

Many Russian apartments are reached through scruffy entrance halls or courtyards, but do not let this put you off, as it gives little indication of the quality of the accommodation inside.

## CAMPING AND OUTDOOR LIVING

Russians love getting out of town for walks, swimming and mushroom gathering. All are possible on day trips from the city, but staying out of town is more complicated.

St Petersburg's cold winter weather does not make it ideal for camping, though the forests along the north side of the Gulf of Finland are excellent in milder seasons.

Those thinking of renting a *dacha* or small house in the country will find this difficult. Most people with modest

*dachas* let them to people they know. None of the firms specializing in lets to foreigners deal in *dachas,* and demand within 100 km (62 miles) of the city far outstrips properties available. As a result, rental costs can be exorbitant (about US$5,000 per week). In order to find anything at all, book as early as February. The best range of *dachas* (from around US$500 per week) is available through **Alexander**, but you will need to speak Russian or use a

**Dacha** in pine forest near Repino on the Gulf of Finland *(see p146)*

travel company that does to make a booking. The best option for cheaper living with modern facilities is to rent a chalet attached to a motel. **Retur Camping** offers chalets, camp sites, a swimming pool, sauna, tennis courts and riding.

## EXTENDED STAYS

Those intending to stay in St Petersburg for a month or more will find the cost of renting apartments much cheaper. While hostels do not offer long-term reductions, companies such as City Realty have plenty of flats that are available at more modest rates than those advertised for short lets. Be aware, however, that tourist visas cannot usually be registered *(see p210)* for more than three months, and that a longer stay will require a non-tourist visa arranged through a company that can legally register you for the period you will be in the country.

# DIRECTORY

## ACCOMMODATION AGENCIES

**Alexander**
Potemkinskaya ul 13.
**Map** 3 C4.
*Tel 327 1616.*
**www**.anspb.ru

**City Realty**
Muchnoi per 2.
**Map** 6 E2.
*Tel 570 6342.*
*Fax 315 9151.*
**www**.cityrealtyrussia.com

**Eridan Travel Company**
Ul Artilleriyskaya 1,
Business Centre Europa
House, Office 619.
**Map** 3 B5.
*Tel 324 23 05.*
*Fax 322 57 38.*
**www**.rus-tours.com

**HOFA Host Families Association**
Tavricheskaya ul 5,
Apartment 25.
**Map** 4 D5.
*Tel 7911 7665464.*
*Fax 275 1992.*
**www**.hofa.ru

**MIR Travel Company**
Nevskiy pr 11/2.
**Map** 6 D1. *Tel 325 7122.*
*Fax 315 3001.*
**www**.mir-travel.com

**Optima Tours Ltd**
Michurinskaya ul 19.
**Map** 2 E2.
*Tel 325 4044.*
**www**.saint-petersburg-
hotels.com

**Ost-West**
Nevskiy pr 105.
*Tel 327 3416.*
*Fax 327 3417.*
**www**.ostwest.com

**Sindbad**
2-ya Sovetskaya ulitsa 12.
**Map** 7 C2. *Tel 332 2020.*

## MINI-HOTEL NETWORKS

**Anabel**
*Tel 717 0800.*
*Fax 717 0255.*
**www**.mini-hotel.com

**Filippov Hotels**
*Tel 274 5363.*
*Fax 274 9084.*
**www**.filippovhotel.ru

**Hotels on Nevsky**
*Tel 703 3860.*
*Fax 703 3861.*
**www**.hon.ru

**Rinaldi Bed & Breakfast**
*Tel 325 4188.*
*Fax 325 4189.*
**www**.rinaldi.ru

## HOSTELS

**CubaHostel Backpackers**
Kazanskaya ul 5. **Map** 6
E2. *Tel 921 7115.*
**www**.cubahostel.ru

**Hostel All Seasons**
Yakovlevskiy per 11.
*Tel 327 1070.*
*Fax 327 1033.*
**www**.hostel.ru

**Na Muchnom**
Sadovaya ul 25.
**Map** 6 E2.
*Tel/Fax 310 0412.*
**www**.namuchnom.ru

**Nord Hostel**
Bolshaya Morskaya ul 10.
**Map** 6 D1.
*Tel/Fax 571 0342.*
**www**.nordhostel.com

**Prima Sport Hotel**
Nevskiy prospekt 5.
**Map** 6 D1.
*Tel/Fax 346 5049.*
**www**.prima-nomerov.net

**St Petersburg International Youth Hostel**
3-ya Sovetskaya ul 28.
**Map** 7 C2.
*Tel 329 8018.*
*Fax 329 8019.*
**www**.ryh.ru

**Useful Website**
**www**.russia-hostelling.ru

## CAMPING

**Retur Camping**
Bolshaya Kupalnaya str.
28, Sestroretsk.
*26 km (16 miles)
NW of St Petersburg.*
*Tel 434 5022.*
*Fax 437 7533.*
**www**.retur-motel.ru

# Popular Hotels in St Petersburg

Accommodation in St Petersburg has improved in recent years, but there is still really only a handful of hotels from which to choose. Unfortunately few of these are conveniently situated for the city centre and it is important to decide on your priorities, be it location, price, character, service or amenities. This selection represents the city's most popular hotels.

**Prestige Hotel**
*This hotel (see p174) is tucked away on a small residential street. Stay here and feel like a local, but with all modern comforts.*

**Rennaisance St Petersburg Baltic**
*Central and prestigious, yet set apart from the hurly-burly of Nevskiy prospekt, the Baltic feels like a small hotel while offering "big" hotel service (see p175).*

**Azimut Hotel St Petersburg**
*This 1970s hotel (see p176) offers wonderful views of the city centre from its bar. At sunset or during White Nights the vista is particularly magical.*

**Astoria Hotel**
*One of the city's most luxurious and centrally located hotels, the Astoria (see p174) is perfect for exploring St Petersburg on foot. The attractive building overlooks St Isaac's Square and Cathedral.*

### St Petersburg
*The package-holiday tourists who usually stay here get a wonderful, sweeping view across the broad expanse of the River Neva, towards Palace Embankment, from the bel-étage (see p177).*

### Grand Hotel Europe
*Situated in the heart of the city, this historic hotel (see p175) is one of the finest in St Petersburg. Elegant decor and refined service are complemented by many facilities.*

### Hotel Dostoevsky
*Located just a stone's throw from the tourist heart of St Petersburg, the Dostoevsky (see p176) combines old and new, historical and modern, in both its design and its service.*

### Park Inn Pulkovskaya
*Comfortable and clean, this vast modern hotel (see p176) has many business facilities, including an auditorium. The hotel's main advantage is its proximity to the airport.*

| 0 kilometres | 2 |
| 0 miles | 2 |

# Choosing a Hotel

Hotels have been selected across a wide price range for facilities, good value and location. All rooms have a shower, TV and telephone. The chart lists the hotels by area. Within each area, entries are organized alphabetically within each price category, from the least to the most expensive. For map references, *see pp238–45*.

**PRICE CATEGORIES**
The following price ranges are for a double room per night, including taxes and breakfast, during the high season. In the low season, prices can halve.
$ Under $100
$$ $100–$175
$$$ $175–$250
$$$$ $250–$325
$$$$$ over $325

## CITY CENTRE

### VASILEVSKIY ISLAND Prestige Hotel Престиж отель    $$

*3-ya liniya 52, Vasilevskiy ostrov* **Tel** *328 5011* **Fax** *328 4228* **Rooms** *10*    *Map 1 A4*

This is a modern hotel, set in a restored 19th-century building on a residential street on Vasilevskiy Island, just a short walk away from the Strelka and the sights, and the shops and bustling atmosphere around Vasileostrovskaya metro station. There is no lift, but there are few floors. Visa support is included in the price. **www.prestige-hotels.com**

### VASILEVSKIY ISLAND Shelfort Шелфорт    $$

*3-ya liniya 26, Vasilevskiy ostrov* **Tel** *328 0555* **Fax** *323 5154* **Rooms** *15*    *Map 1 A5*

Set on a quiet residential street a short walk from the Strelka, the Shelfort has good, plain interiors with beautifully restored tiled stoves. Two luxury suites have fireplaces; one also has a balcony. The hotel does not have a lift, but consists of ground and first floors only (wheelchair users can request a room on the ground floor). **www.shelfort.ru**

### PALACE EMBANKMENT Comfort Комфорт    $$

*Bolshaya Morskaya ulitsa 25* **Tel** *570 6700* **Fax** *570 6700* **Rooms** *18*    *Map 6 D2*

Despite limited facilities, the Comfort offers excellent value for money by virtue of its helpful staff and unbeatable location at the heart of the historic centre, which is packed with restaurants. Rooms are unfussy and airy. Cots are available. One suite is adapted for use as an office by those visiting on business. **www.comfort-hotel.org**

### PALACE EMBANKMENT Prestige Hotel Centre Престиж отель центр    $$

*Gorokhovaya ulitsa 5* **Tel** *312 0405* **Fax** *315 9357* **Rooms** *12*    *Map 6 D1*

A modest hotel in a plain building, tucked away by the Admiralty Gardens. Rooms are furnished with simple, inexpensive metal and plastic furniture; most have a shower but not a bath. The friendly concierge can book cars or guided tours. **www.prestige-hotels.com**

### PALACE EMBANKMENT Casa Leto    $$$$

*Bolshaya Morskaya ulitsa 34* **Tel** *600 1069* **Fax** *3146639* **Rooms** *5*    *Map 6 D2*

Run by an Italian-Russian couple, this tiny establishment is arguably the best of the "mini hotels". It boasts light-filled rooms, many complimentary extras and a superb central location. Personal service includes business support, and tour and ticket booking. The cheapest suite, Trezzini, has a shower only; others also have a bath. **www.casaleto.com**

### PALACE EMBANKMENT Angleterre Отель Англетер    $$$$$

*Bolshyaya Morskaya ulitsa 39* **Tel** *494 5666* **Fax** *494 5125* **Rooms** *193*    *Map 6 D2*

The Angleterre is the stylishly refurbished, Western-run sister hotel to the slightly superior Astoria next door, whose facilities it shares. There is a nightclub and a casino, and a rather good lunchtime brasserie. The superb central location on St Isaac's Square is within easy walking distance of the Hermitage and Nevskiy prospekt. **www.angleterrehotel.com**

### PALACE EMBANKMENT Astoria Отель Астория    $$$$$

*Isaakievskaya ploschad, Bolshaya Morskaya ulitsa 39* **Tel** *494 5750* **Fax** *494 5059* **Rooms** *211*    *Map 6 D2*

Fully renovated in 2002, the Astoria's historic interior none-the-less has the calm and grace of a hotel with a history. Rooms at the front offer outstanding views over St Isaac's Cathedral and Square, and along the river Moyka. You don't have to be staying here to visit for tea in the downstairs lounge. **www.thehotelastoria.com**

### PALACE EMBANKMENT Petro Palace Отель Петро палас    $$$$$

*Malaya Morskaya ulitsa 14* **Tel** *571 2880* **Fax** *571 2704* **Rooms** *193*    *Map 6 D1*

An elegant hotel, opened in 2005, that attracts many wealthy Russians as well as tourists. Its extensive facilities are unmatched at this price, particularly in the centre, and include a fitness suite, pool and massage services. The renovated and extended 19th-century building offers good views from the seventh floor. **www.petropalacehotel.com**

### PALACE EMBANKMENT Renaissance St Petersburg Baltic    $$$$$

*Pochtamtskaya ulitsa 4a* **Tel** *380 4000* **Fax** *380 4001* **Rooms** *102*    *Map 5 C2*

An elegant establishment, decorated on the theme of "historic St Petersburg", using old-fashioned materials and modern design. Some rooms offer views over St Isaac's Square, and the area is very quiet. Despite its luxury status, with one of the best fitness suites in the city, the hotel feels cosy. **www.marriot.com/ledbr**

**Key to Symbols** *see back cover flap*

### PALACE EMBANKMENT Taleon Imperial Hotel Тапион империал отель 🔲 🍴 🎿 🍽 🖥 🛗 $$$$$

*Naberezhnaya reki Moyki 59* **Tel** *324 9911* **Fax** *324 9957* **Rooms** *29*      *Map 6 D1*

Part of the Taleon Club, this is a luxury hotel, restaurant and casino complex with benefits for members. There is a wide range of inclusive services, a library, and a personal valet for every guest. Events for children are held. Rooms overlook the river Moyka. **www.eliseevpalacehotel.com**

### GOSTINYY DVOR Polikoff 📋 $$

*Karavannaya 11/64, apt 24–26* **Tel** *995 3488* **Fax** *995 3488* **Rooms** *15*      *Map 7 A2*

The interior is clean and unadorned – all blond wood and metal – and very light, even though most rooms overlook a courtyard. Some rooms have air-conditioning. The main drawback is the absence of a lift, as all rooms are on the second or third floors (known as the third and fourth in Russia). Service is efficient and friendly. **www.polikoff.ru**

### GOSTINYY DVOR Pushka Inn 📺 🍴 🖥 $$$$

*Naberezhnaya reki Moyki 14* **Tel** *312 0913* **Fax** *314 1055* **Rooms** *31*      *Map 2 E5*

This historic building, right on the river Moyka and next door to the Pushkin Museum, has been transformed into a comfortable, modern hotel. Simple furniture and interiors make no false allusions to wealth or grandeur. It is almost impossible to stay closer to the Hermitage! There are four "apartments" or family suites. **www.pushkainn.ru**

### GOSTINYY DVOR Grand Hotel Europe Гранд отель Европа 📺 🍴 🎿 🍽 🖥 🛗 $$$$$

*Mikhaylovskaya ulitsa 1/7* **Tel** *329 6000* **Fax** *329 6002* **Rooms** *301*      *Map 6 F1*

The Europe's facilities may no longer be unique in St Petersburg, but its location just off Nevskiy prospekt is close both to the main sights and to daily city life. There are historic interiors, and a wonderful, airy mezzanine café for coffee and cakes after an exhausting day's sightseeing. **www.grandhoteleurope.com**

### GOSTINYY DVOR Kempinski Hotel Moika 22 📺 🍴 🎿 🍽 🖥 🛗 $$$$$

*Naberezhnaya reki Moyki 22* **Tel** *335 9111* **Fax** *3359190* **Rooms** *197*      *Map 2 E5*

Pamper yourself here: take a room with a view over the Hermitage, take lunch in the restaurant with views right across the city, then, maybe, take a Turkish bath to relax after sightseeing, before attending a concert at the Capella next door. Moika 22 opened in 2005 and just gets better every day. **www.kempinski.com**

### SENNAYA PLOSHCHAD Alexander House Club 🍴 🖥 🛗 $$$$

*Naberezhnaya Kryukova kanala 27* **Tel** *575 3877* **Fax** *575 3879* **Rooms** *19*      *Map 5 C4*

In this family guest house, run as a boutique hotel, each room is named after and decorated in the style of a capital city. Most have views, and two luxury suites have working fireplaces. Breakfast can be taken in the rooms. Although there is no lift, rooms on the ground floor are accessible by wheelchair. **www.a-house.ru**

### SENNAYA PLOSHCHAD Ambassador Hotel 📺 🍴 🎿 🍽 🖥 🛗 $$$$$

*Rimskovo-Korsakova prospekt 5–7* **Tel** *331 8844* **Fax** *331 9300* **Rooms** *255*      *Map 6 D3*

The luxurious rooms at the Ambassador are decorated in tranquil pastel shades and all have good views of the city. The hotel is close to several historic sights, including St Nicholas' Cathedral, the Mariinskiy Theatre and the Yusupov Palace. Some rooms are accessible by wheelchair. **www.ambassador-hotel.ru**

## FURTHER AFIELD

### EAST OF THE FONTANKA Arbat Nord Арбат Норд 📺 🍴 🖥 🛗 $$$

*Artilleriyskaya ulitsa 4* **Tel** *703 1899* **Fax** *703 1898* **Rooms** *33*      *Map 3 B5*

The Arbat Nord is located close to the Summer Gardens and Field of Mars, in the residential and business district, and was built originally, in 2003, for business guests. Today it also caters for tourist groups and individual travellers. Rooms are modern with dark wood and pale walls; some are reserved for non-smokers. Free parking. **www.arbat-nord.ru**

### EAST OF THE FONTANKA Brothers Karamazov Братья Карамазовы 📺 🍴 🖥 🛗 $$$

*Sotsialisticheskaya ulitsa 11a* **Tel** *335 1185* **Fax** *335 1186* **Rooms** *28*      *Map 7 A4*

At the heart of Dostoyevsky country, close by the apartment (now a museum, *see p130*) where he wrote *The Brothers Karamazov*. Each room is named after a heroine of one of the author's works. Opened in 2004, the hotel is airy, decorated mainly in white and cream – no Dostoyevskian tragedy here! **www.karamazovhotel.ru**

### EAST OF THE FONTANKA Fifth Corner Business Hotel Пятый угол 🍴 🖥 🛗 $$$

*Zagorodnyy pr 13* **Tel** *380 8181* **Fax** *380 8181* **Rooms** *34*      *Map 7 A3*

Specifically marketed as a business hotel, with many Russian clients, Fifth Corner emphasizes business-related services. The hotel none the less provides visa and all other support for tourists, including excursions. All rooms are uncluttered and overlook the street, although some only have showers rather than a full bathroom suite. **www.5ugol.ru**

### EAST OF THE FONTANKA Moskva Москва 📺 🍴 🍽 🖥 🛗 $$$

*Aleksandra Nevskogo ploschad 2* **Tel** *274 0022* **Fax** *274 2130* **Rooms** *825*      *Map 8 E3*

The Moskva is the most centrally located of the package-tour establishments, next door to the metro station and bus stops, and opposite the Alexander Nevsky Monastery. It was completely renovated in 2007 and also has several bars and restaurants. **www.hotel-moscow.ru**

### EAST OF THE FONTANKA Oktiabrskaya Октябрьская

$$$

*Ligovskiy prospekt 10* **Tel** *578 1144* **Fax** *3157501* **Rooms** *484* ·     **Map** *7 C2*

An expensive hotel, if judged on its facilities, but the location is grand. The extension opposite Moscow Station has been renovated, so all rooms are now of a decent standard. In the main block, there is a glorious rabbit-warren of corridors, and a sense of faded grandeur. **www.oktober-hotel.spb.ru**

### EAST OF THE FONTANKA Hotel Dostoevsky Отель Достоевский

$$$$

*Vladimirskiy prospekt 19* **Tel** *331 3203* **Fax** *331 3203* **Rooms** *207*     **Map** *7 A3*

Part of the 24-hour Vladimirskiy Passazh shopping mall, but an élite, very modern hotel with its own entrance. Most rooms overlook courtyards, some offer views over the Vladimir Cathedral. The location is good for sightseeing, being near Nevskiy prospekt, and for shopping at and around Kuznechnyy Market. **www.dostoevsky-hotel.ru**

### EAST OF THE FONTANKA Novotel Новотель

$$$$

*Mayakovskovo ulitsa 3a* **Tel** *335 1188* **Fax** *335 1180* **Rooms** *233*     **Map** *7 B2*

Ultra-modern block tucked away a stone's throw from Nevskiy prospekt. Executive suites on the ninth floor offer superb views, and the Côte Jardin restaurant offers a Russian take on Mediterranean cooking. Business facilities are excellent and, unusually for this city, three rooms have been specially adapted for disabled visitors. **www.novotel.spb.ru**

### EAST OF THE FONTANKA Radisson SAS Royal Hotel

$$$$

*Nevskiy prospekt 49/2* **Tel** *322 5000* **Fax** *322 5001* **Rooms** *164*     **Map** *7 A2*

Opened in 2001, the Radisson is a modern hotel set inside a historic building right on the busy Nevskiy prospekt. A little removed from the central tourist area, its rooms and ground-floor Cannelle Bar and Café offer views of the main street, bustling with shoppers and promenaders throughout the year. **www.radissonsas.com**

### EAST OF THE FONTANKA Corinthia Nevskij Palace

$$$$$

*Nevskiy prospekt 57* **Tel** *380 2001* **Fax** *380 1937* **Rooms** *285*     **Map** *7 B2*

This was one of the first new, post-Soviet hotels, built in the early 1990s. Bright and modern, it has numerous non-smoking rooms and five bars and restaurants including the élite Landskrona, the Beerstube and, for tea and cakes, the Café Vienna. Check out Sunday brunch in the Imperial. **www.corinthia.ru**

### EAST OF THE FONTANKA Grand Hotel Emerald

$$$$$

*Suvorovskiy prospekt 18* **Tel** *740 5000* **Fax** *740 5001* **Rooms** *90*     **Map** *8 D2*

A post-modern exterior hides a pseudo-historic interior filled with soft piano music and pot plants. There is a superb fitness centre with a large sauna and Turkish bath. Afternoon tea is served in the atrium café in a glass-roofed courtyard. The location is not absolutely central, but public transport links are excellent. **www.grandhotelemerald.com**

### SOUTH OF THE CENTRE German Club Немецкий клуб

$

*Gastello ulitsa 20* **Tel** *371 5104* **Fax** *371 5690* **Rooms** *16*

One of the city's first "mini-hotels", the German Club is modest but cosy, and set in a quiet location a short walk from Moskovskaya metro station. Staff are very friendly and offer numerous extra, personalized services, from arranging guided tours and tickets, to simple advice on where to go and what to do. **www.hotelgermanclub.com**

### SOUTH OF THE CENTRE Mir Мир

$

*Gastello ulitsa 17* **Tel** *708 5166* **Fax** *708 5165* **Rooms** *200*

Mir is an unassuming 1970s hotel, popular with budget travellers. It is a short walk from Moskovskaya metro station (providing direct access to the centre) and next to the beautiful Chesme Church. Rooms with shared facilities start at $48, those with showers and phones at $78. Lots of Russians stay here. No visa support. **www.hotelmir.spb.ru**

### SOUTH OF THE CENTRE Azimut Hotel St Petersburg

$$

*Lermontovskiy prospekt 43/1* **Tel** *740 2604* **Fax** *251 8890* **Rooms** *897*     **Map** *5 B5*

Formerly Sovetskaya hotel, Azimut Hotel St Petersburg offers plenty of facilities with low rates and stunning views along the river. It is popular with tourists looking for standard accommodation. Despite rebranding, service remains quite "Soviet" and can leave much to be desired. **www.azimuthotels.com**

### SOUTH OF THE CENTRE Rossiya Россия

$$

*Chernyshevskovo ploschad 11* **Tel** *329 3932* **Fax** *329 3902* **Rooms** *413*

Set somewhat apart amidst the Stalinist buildings of Moskovskiy prospekt, and refurbished to European standards, the Rossiya remains unpretentious. It has 10 storeys, and rooms offer sweeping views of the southern part of town. Guests comprise both Russians and tourists, and there is a lively atmosphere in the restaurant. **www.rossiya-hotel.ru**

### SOUTH OF THE CENTRE Neptun Нептун

$$$

*Naberezhnaya Obvodnovo kanala 93a* **Tel** *324 4610* **Fax** *324 4611* **Rooms** *150*     **Map** *7 A5*

A reliable, no-frills Best Western hotel attached to St Petersburg's first business centre, opened in 1993. Set in a modern building in a business district, Neptun offers rooms that are smart but without pretension, and efficient service. It is a 15-minute walk from the nearest metro, and has a superb sports and leisure complex. **www.neptun.spb.ru**

### SOUTH OF THE CENTRE Park Inn Pulkovskaya Парк Инн Пулковская

$$$

*Pobedy ploschad 1* **Tel** *740 3900* **Fax** *740 3913* **Rooms** *840*

This hotel is close to the airport and conveniently located for trips to the palaces of Tsarskoe Selo, Pavlovsk and Gatchina. It is popular therefore with package tourists and business guests. In 2004 it was completely transformed from a Soviet Intourist hotel to an up-to-date and efficient establishment. **www.rezidorparkinn.com**

**Key to Price Guide** *see p174* **Key to Symbols** *see back cover flap*

## WEST OF THE CENTRE Park Inn Pribaltiyskaya Парк Инн Прибалтийская 📶🍽🔒 ⓢⓢⓢ
*Korablestroiteley ulitsa 14* **Tel** *329 2626* **Fax** *356 6094* **Rooms** *1200*

The Park Inn Pribaltiyskaya is a huge, 1980s package-tour hotel, set right on the Gulf of Finland. It boasts superb views across the water, and a new water-park with pool and sports facilities. It is a long walk to the metro from here – and in the winter it can be very windy – but buses and taxis are available. **www.rezidorparkinn.com**

## NORTH OF THE NEVA St Petersburg Санкт-Петербург 📶🔒 ⓢ
*Pirogovskaya naberezhnaya 5/2* **Tel** *380 1919* **Fax** *380 1920* **Rooms** *410*     *Map 3 A2*

A modern package-tour hotel, in a central location, but a little cut off from public transport. Its main attraction lies in the stunning views that can be had from rooms along the south side and the breakfast room on the bel-étage. In summer, however, when the sun hardly sets, guests may wish to trade the views for the restful dark. **www.hotel-spb.ru**

## NORTH OF THE NEVA Andersen Hotel 📶🍽🔒 ⓢⓢ
*Chapygina ulitsa 4A* **Tel** *740 5140* **Rooms** *140*

With pleasantly furnished rooms, the Andersen hotel opened in 2004 and offers well-priced accommodation which is favourably set on the Petrogradskaya Side, allowing good access to all St Petersburg's sights. The hotel also organizes tours of the city centre and suburbs. **www.andersenhotel.ru**

## NORTH OF THE NEVA Kronverk Кронверк 📶🍽🔒 ⓢⓢ
*Blokhina ulitsa 9* **Tel** *703 3663* **Fax** *449 6701* **Rooms** *26*     *Map 1 C3*

This hotel is in an unusual and extremely attractive location on Petrogradskaya, right by the Peter and Paul Fortress, a scenic walk across two bridges from the Hermitage. It is located in a high-tech business centre, and popular therefore with business people as well as tourists. Apartments are available for longer stays. No visa support. **www.kronverk.com**

## NORTH OF THE NEVA Stony Island Hotel 📶🍽 ⓢⓢ
*Kamennoostrovskiy prospekt 45* **Tel** *337 2434* **Fax** *346 1920* **Rooms** *50*     *Map 2 D1*

The historical building that houses the Stony Island Hotel was reconstructed in 2005 to a minimalist design, with straight lines and plain colours. It is located on the elegant main street of the Petrograd Side, near Petrogradskaya metro, and is aimed at regular visitors and those who dislike the busy city centre, rather than tourists. **www.stonyisland.ru**

## EAST OF THE NEVA Okhtinskaya Охтинская 📶🔒 ⓢⓢ
*Bolsheokhtinskiy prospekt 4* **Tel** *222 8638* **Fax** *227 2514* **Rooms** *294*     *Map 4 F3*

Rooms in this hotel overlook the river near the Smolny Cathedral, somewhat compensating for its out-of-town location. Public transport is widely available, but in summer the bridges are raised at 2am, so guests need to allow plenty of time to get back after a night out. The building is modern, with airy rooms and public spaces. **www.okhtinskaya.com**

# BEYOND ST PETERSBURG

## NOVGOROD Volkhov Волхов 📶🔒 ⓢ
*Predtechenskaya ulitsa 24* **Tel** *(8162) 335548* **Fax** *(8162) 339067* **Rooms** *127*

Volkhov has by far the best location of all the Novgorod hotels, in the historical centre by the Detinets or Kremlin. The building is five storeys tall, with plain interiors. Rooms have showers rather than baths, and facilities are only modest, though there is a sauna. There is also rather a lot of nylon in the decor. **www.novtour.ru**

## NOVGOROD Beresta Palace Береста палас отель 📶🍽🔒 ⓢⓢ
*Studencheskaya ulitsa 2a* **Tel** *(8162) 940910* **Fax** *(8162) 940925* **Rooms** *223*

The best equipped hotel in Novgorod, the Beresta Palace comprises a large, modern complex with huge conference halls, tennis courts and a rather smart pool. Many rooms have views over the river Volkhov, and even the semi-luxurious apartments are not very expensive. **www.beresta-hotel.ru**

## PUSHKIN Natali Натали 🔒ⓅⓎ ⓢ
*Malaya ulitsa 56a* **Tel** *466 2768* **Fax** *466 0277* **Rooms** *24*

A privately run hotel on a quiet residential street in the leafy town of Pushkin, not far from Tsarskoe Selo palace. The building is modern, opened in 2003. Although there is no lift, the Natali only has three storeys and some rooms are on the ground floor. There are "romantic" rooms under the eaves. Visa support is not offered. **www.hotelnatali.ru**

## STRELNA Baltic Star Hotel Отель Балтийская звезда 📶🍽🔒 ⓢⓢⓢ
*Berezovaya alleya 3* **Tel** *438 5700* **Fax** *438 5888* **Rooms** *106 and 20 cottages*

Set in the country between St Petersburg and Peterhof, beside the "re-created" presidential Constantine Palace, which is used for state events and receptions, the Baltic Star is popular with official delegations. The modern building has historic-style interiors, and 20 "cottages" for guests who prefer greater privacy. **www.balticstar-hotel.ru**

## ZELENOGORSK Gelios Гелиос отель 📶🍽🔒 ⓢ
*Primorskoe shosse 593* **Tel** *702 2626* **Fax** *702 2622* **Rooms** *195 and 3 cottages*

About 50km north of the city on the shore of the Gulf of Finland, this modern hotel surrounded by trees offers healthy walks, skiing in winter and a spa centre with mud and mineral water treatments, hydromassage and a gym. Cottages in the grounds must be booked well in advance. Visa support can be provided, but not registration. **www.gelios-otel.ru**

# RESTAURANTS AND CAFÉS

Huge changes have taken place on St Petersburg's restaurant scene in the past few years. The big, established places have been joined by numerous eateries large and small. In addition, the concept of the "business lunch", with an inexpensive fixed-price menu, has taken a firm hold – a boon to travellers who like to eat well despite a limited budget.

**Sign for Noble Nest**

Ethnic food from the former Soviet republics and abroad provides a wide selection of vegetarian dishes. Small cafés offer a chance to escape the more garish tourist traps found near some sights. And, though getting a plain green salad may still pose a problem, other fresh salads are offered by most restaurants and good-quality cafés. For a list of recommended restaurants and cafés, *see pp184–91*.

Podvorie restaurant, a re-creation of a 17th-century wooden house *(see p191)*

## WHERE TO EAT

Restaurants on Nevskiy prospekt tend to be more expensive than those in other streets. A few steps off Nevskiy, however, a variety of eateries line the streets – Bolshaya Konyushennaya, Karavannaya, Vladimirskiy prospekt and ulitsa Vosstaniya – offering something to suit most pockets and tastes. Venture out a little further, and the short ulitsa Belinskovo, for instance, offers at least five highly recommended options.

## TYPES OF RESTAURANT

All large hotels offer good eating opportunities, but hotel restaurants are included in the guide only if they are out-standing or found in places that are short on places to eat.
Style and fashion now dominate in some restaurants, so the food often suffers and prices can be unjustifiably high. Other establishments, however, manage to combine food, decor and service in fine

Russian style. Dining trends include "imperial Russian", in a historic interior (The Noble Nest, *see p188*); minimalism (Aquarel, *see p185*); and themed (Lenin's Mating Call, *see p188*). Top-range restaurants serve a mix of European and Russian dishes, with some Asian elements.
The former Soviet republics Georgia and Armenia have left their mark on Russian cuisine.

Outdoor café in the arcade of Gostinyy dvor *(see p108)*

Try Salkhino *(see p185)* or Lagidze Waters *(see p189)* for Georgian food, Erivan *(see p188)* for Armenian cuisine, and Apsheron *(see p188)* for an Azeri experience. Oriental restaurants are numerous if generally uninspiring; the Indonesian Sukawati *(see p187)* is a rare exception.

## READING THE MENU

Large restaurants and some cafés have menus in English. Any restaurant that accepts credit cards will have English-speaking waiters, and, in those places that do not, most waiters try to overcome language difficulties.

## PAYMENT AND TIPPING

Most venues give prices in roubles; however, some restaurants maintain the practice of pricing in "y.e." or "conditional units", a euphemism for dollars or euros. In such cases, it is wise to check the exact rouble value of one "y.e.". This information may appear on the menu or on a sign at the cash desk.
Major restaurants accept most credit cards, but it is advisable to check before-hand. The listings in the guide give an indication of price ranges in dollars, but restaurants cannot by law accept foreign currency *(see p215)*. Guests must pay with cash roubles or a credit card.
Tips are 10–15 per cent unless service is already inclu-ded in the bill. To ensure the waiter receives the tip, it is best to give it in cash, rather than as a credit card payment.

## OPENING TIMES

Most restaurants in St Petersburg open at noon and stay open until around 11pm or midnight. Increasingly, the more expensive restaurants, and particularly those that are attached to a casino or nightclub *(see pp204–5)*, may stay open well into the early morning hours. Cafés close early, usually around 10pm.

For those who wish to eat after an evening event, the Magrib café *(see p193)* serves a range of food all night long. A number of bars, for example Jili-bili *(see p193)*, offer food into the small hours. In addition, if all else fails, the lights of many fast-food outlets, such as Layma *(see p193)*, are often to be found burning after midnight.

The beautifully decorated interior of the Russian Room in the Demidoff *(see p190)*

Street sign for Pirosmani *(see p191)*

## MAKING A RESERVATION

It is always advisable to book ahead, especially during the White Nights *(see p51)* when upmarket restaurants may take bookings weeks in advance. Your hotel concierge can help. Smaller restaurants and cafés do not require reservations, but as they rely on special events such as weddings and birthdays they sometimes close unexpectedly.

## CHILDREN

Russians are acquiring the habit of taking their children out to dine with them. On the whole Russians love children, few restaurants will refuse them entry, and staff will often adjust dishes to meet their needs. A number of city eateries, such as La Strada *(see p187)* and Tres Amigos *(see p190)* have parties and even nannies at weekends. Fashionable bars such as Che *(see p204)* also arrange Sunday morning entertainments for the kids. Some places advertised to foreigners – but none in this guide – have "entertainment" that is not suitable for children.

## LIVE MUSIC

Most restaurants and cafés have some kind of music on Fridays or Saturdays – DJs spinning disks or live acts. The listings that follow on pages 184 to 191 note only those which have live music on other days as well.

## VEGETARIANS

Traditional Russian food is meat oriented, but the increasing number of eateries aimed at a more Westernized crowd, such as Krokodil *(see p186)*, include vegetarian options, and Georgian and Armenian cuisines offer a wide range of vegetable and bean dishes. At the time of writing, there are just a few vegetarian restaurants in St Petersburg, and a small number of vegetarian cafés.

For those who eat fish, however, there is always plenty of choice.

## SMOKING

Most restaurants still allow smoking, but ever more places either have non-smoking areas or – albeit more rarely – ban smoking altogether. A few have a small, separate room that can be booked in advance for any occasion and declared a "no smoking" zone. The disadvantage is that such rooms are cut off from the atmosphere of the main restaurant.

## DRESS CODE

Formal dress is *de rigueur* only in large and very fashionable restaurants, but guests should always be neatly and cleanly dressed. Trainers and tracksuits are acceptable in the less expensive cafés.

## DISABLED ACCESS

Only a few restaurants have ramps or no stairs at all, but waiters and doormen are used to intrepid Europeans in wheelchairs (Russians in wheelchairs rarely venture outside the home) and are usually very helpful.

Cafés and bars prove more problematic, with stairs and narrow doors, and certainly no disabled toilets. People with disabilities may find themselves confined to hotel dining or the more expensive eateries and bars.

### WEBSITES

Most restaurant websites are in Russian only, or are poorly maintained. Many places do not run independent websites, but appear on the St Petersburg restaurant site, which has an English-language version at: **www**.restoran.ru
For Russian speakers, there are now many listings and reviews online. Try: **www**.allcafe.info, which has many listings; **www**.menu.ru; or the excellent archive of reviews at the Time Out site, **www**.spb.timeout.ru

# The Flavours of St Petersburg

Russia's culinary reputation centres on warming stews, full of wintery vegetables such as cabbage, beetroot and potatoes. Yet St Petersburg was once the capital of a vast empire stretching from Poland to the Pacific and this is reflected in the variety of food on offer there. Aubergine (eggplant) and tomatoes, from the Caucasus in the south, bring in the flavours of the Mediterranean, while spices from Central Asia lend an exotic touch. On the stalls of the city's Kuznechniy Market, caviar and crayfish sit alongside honey from Siberia and melons and peaches from Georgia.

**Wild Mushrooms**

**Caviar, the roe of sturgeon from Russia's warm southern waters**

## RUSSIAN COUNTRYSIDE

Many St Petersburgers have small country houses within easy reach of the city, and spend weekends from spring to early winter tending their immaculate vegetable gardens, or combing the countryside for wild berries and mushrooms. Much of this bountiful harvest is made into preserves and pickles. There is a refreshing soup, *solianka*, in which pickled cucumbers impart a delicious salty taste. Pickled mushrooms in sour cream make a regular appearance on restaurant menus, as do a variety of fresh berry juices.

In a country where food shortages are a fairly recent memory, very little is wasted. *Kvas*, a popular, mildly alcoholic drink is frequently made at home by fermenting stale bread with sugar and a scattering of fruit. Summer visitors should make a point of trying the delicious cold soup *okroshka*, which is based on *kvas*.

Russia is also a land with hundreds of rivers and lakes, and has a long tradition of fish cookery. Dishes range from simple soups, such as *ukha*, to caviar and sturgeon, and salmon cooked in a bewildering variety of ways.

Blinis | Pickled mushrooms | Spiced feta | Rye bread | Gherkins | Pickled herring | Salted fish | Soured cream

**A typical spread of *zakuski* (cold appertizers)**

## LOCAL DISHES AND SPECIALITIES

*Borsch* (beetroot soup) and *blinis* (buttery pancakes) with caviar are perhaps two of the most famous Russian dishes – one a peasant dish which varies with the availability of ingredients and the other a staple for the week leading up to Lent, when rich food would be eaten to fatten up before the fast. Much of **Beetroot** Russia's cuisine is designed to make use of what is readily to hand or is warming and filling. A popular main course is *kulebiaka*, a hearty fish pie, larded with eggs, rice, dill and onion and encased in a buttery crust. Another is beef stroganoff with its creamy mushroom sauce, created in 18th-century St Petersburg by the chef of the wealthy Stroganoff family.

**Borsch** *Made with meat or vegetable stock, this beetroot soup is usually served with dill and soured cream.*

**Market vegetable stall in St Petersburg**

## THE CAUCASUS

The former Soviet states of the Caucasus – Georgia, Azerbaijan and Armenia – are renowned for their legendary banquets, where the tables are laden with an enormous quantity and variety of food and drink. They still supply Russia's cities with a tempting range of fine subtropical produce. Limes, lemons, oranges, walnuts, figs, pomegranates, peaches, beans, salty cheeses and herbs are all shipped in season to St Petersburg's markets and its many Georgian restaurants. The cuisine of Georgia, with its focus on freshly grilled meats, pulses, vegetables, yogurt, herbs and nut sauces – including the hallmark walnut sauce, *satsivi* – is famously healthy and Georgians are particularly known for their longevity.

## CENTRAL ASIA

From the Central Asian republics of the old Soviet Union come a range of

**Freshly picked lingonberries from Russia's bumper autumn harvest**

culinary traditions based on the nomadic lifestyles of Russia's one-time overlords, the Mongol or Tartar Hordes. The meat of fat-tailed sheep, which thrive in the dry desert air, is used to make communal piles of *plov* (pilaf) around which guests sit, eating in the traditional manner with their hands.

Served in St Petersburg's Uzbek restaurants, it shares the menu with delicious flat breads, spicy noodle soups, *manti* (tasty dumplings reminiscent of Chinese cuisine) and a variety of melons and grapes, which proliferate in the desert oases, and apricots and nuts, grown in the mountains.

### ZAKUSKI

A traditional Russian meal generally begins with *zakuski,* a selection of cold appetizers. These may include pickled mushrooms (*gribi*), gherkins (*ogurtsi*), salted herrings (*seliodka*), an assortment of smoked fish, blinis topped with caviar, various vegetable pâtés (sometimes known as vegetable caviars), stuffed eggs (*yaitsa farshirovanniye*), spiced feta cheese (*brinza*), beetroot salad (*salat iz svyokly*) and small meat pies (*pirozhki*), accompanied by rye bread and washed down with shots of vodka. A bowl of steaming soup often follows, before the main course reaches the table.

**Kulebiaka** *Rich, buttery puff pastry is wrapped around a mix of fish, hard-boiled eggs, rice, onion and chopped dill.*

**Pelmeni** *These meat-stuffed dumplings may be served in a clear broth, or with tomato sauce or soured cream.*

**Kissel** *A mix of red berries is used to make this soft, fruity jelly, which is served topped with a swirl of fresh cream.*

# What to Drink in St Petersburg

**Flavoured vodka**

Russian vodka is famous throughout the world and the Liviz distillery in St Petersburg is Russia's second largest distillery, the largest being in Moscow. Vodka first appeared in Russia sometime in the 14th or 15th century. Peter the Great *(see p18)* was particularly fond of anise- or pepper-flavoured vodkas and devised modifications to the distillation process which greatly improved the quality of the finished drink.

Tea is Russia's other national drink. Traditionally made using a samovar and served black, tea has been popular in Russia since the end of the 18th century, when it was first imported from China.

A 19th-century Russian peasant family drinking vodka and tea

## CLEAR VODKA

**Diplomat    Russian Standard    Five Star**

Vodka is produced from grain, usually wheat, although some rye is also used in Russia. Local Liviz vodkas dominate in St Petersburg, the best of which are Diplomat, Five Star and Russian Standard. Moscow's Kristall company, which produces Kristall and Gzhelka vodka, is increasingly popular, while Flagman distillery proudly proclaims that it is the official purveyor of vodka to the Kremlin. The range of vodkas available these days is over-whelming. There is one golden rule: if it is under $3 or $4 for half a litre, do not drink it.

**Kubanskaya**

Vodka is always served with food, often with a range of richly flavoured accompaniments called *zakuski (see p181)*, particularly black bread, pickled cucumbers and herring. Vodka is not always served ice cold, but it should be chilled.

## FLAVOURED VODKA

The practice of flavouring vodka has entirely practical origins. When vodka was first produced commercially in the Middle Ages, the techniques and equipment were so primitive that it was impossible to remove all the impurities. This left unpleasant aromas and flavours, which were disguised by adding honey together with aromatic oils and spices. As distillation techniques improved, flavoured vodkas became a speciality in their own right. Limonnaya, its taste deriving from lemon zest, is one of the most traditional, as is Pertsovka, flavoured with red chilli pepper pods. Klukvennaya (cranberry) and Oblepikha (sea buckthorn, an orange Siberian berry) are also favourites. Some of the best flavoured vodkas are made at home by soaking peach stones or whole berries in alcohol for months.

**Pepper vodka**

**Limonnaya          Klukvennaya          Oblepikha**

## MAJOR WINE REGIONS

- ■ Wine growing region
- ■ Moldova
- ■ Ukraine
- ■ Russia
- ■ Georgia
- ■ Armenia
- ■ Azerbaijan
- — International boundaries

## WINE

The Soviet Union was one of the world's largest producers of wine (*vino*), but many of the major wine regions are now republics in their own right. Several indigenous types of grape are cultivated in the different regions, along with many of the more familiar international varieties.

Georgia is considered the best wine-making area. Its wines include those made from the Rkatsiteli grape, characterized by a floral aroma and subtle, fruity flavour, and the Gurdzhaani which gives a unique, slightly bitter touch. Among its best red wines is the smooth Mukuzani. Moldova produces white, sparkling wines in the south and central regions, while the south is also known for its red wines. Since 1799, Moldova also produces a sweet, champagne-like wine called Shampanskoe.

**White and red Georgian wine**     **Shampanskoe**

## OTHER ALCOHOLIC DRINKS

Brandy (konyak) was originally a by-product of wine-making and commercial production only began in Russia in the 19th century. Armenian brandy is one of the finest with a distinctive vanilla fragrance, resulting from its ageing in 70–100-year-old oak barrels. Georgia and Daghestan also produce good brandies. St Petersburg beer (*pivo*) is amongst the best in Russia. Baltika, Vena and Stepan Razin make a full range of beers in bottles and on draught. In addition, Tver beers such as Afanasy are well worth trying. Various imported beers are also available.

**Baltika Beer**     **Armenian brandy**

## OTHER DRINKS

Kvas is a lightly fermented drink made from rye and barley, consumed by adults and children alike. Russia's vast range of mineral waters (*mineralnaya voda*) includes many with unusually high mineral contents. Mineral waters from the Caucasus are particularly prized. Also widely available are fruit juices (*sok, mors* or *kompot*), including cranberry (*klyukva*). Look out for traditional Russian *shiten*, made from honey and herbs.

**Mineral water**     **Kvas**     **Cranberry juice**

## TEA

Russian tea is served black with a slice of lemon and may be drunk from tall glasses or cups. Sweetened with jam instead of sugar, tea (*chay*) is an ideal accompaniment to rich cakes and pastries. The boiling water for tea traditionally comes from a samovar. The water is used to brew a pot of tea, from which a little is poured into a cup and is then diluted with more hot water.

**A glass of tea, with jam (*varenye*) to sweeten it**

### THE SAMOVAR

Made from brass or copper and heated by coals in the central chimney, samovars traditionally provided boiling water for a wide variety of domestic purposes and were an essential wedding gift. Modern electric ones are made of stainless steel and are used mainly for boiling water to make tea. The word samovar comes from *samo* meaning "itself" and *varit* meaning "to boil".

# Choosing a Restaurant

The restaurants in this section have been selected across a wide price range for their good value and exceptional food. Within each area, entries are listed alphabetically within each price category, from the least to the most expensive. For details of *Light Meals and Snacks*, see pages 192–3. For map references, *see pp238–45*.

**PRICE CATEGORIES**
The following price ranges are for a three-course meal for one including a glass of house wine, all unavoidable charges and a modest service charge (tip).
$ Under $25
$$ $25–$40
$$$ $40–$60
$$$$ $60–$80
$$$$$ over $80

## VASILEVSKIY ISLAND

### Troitskiy Most Троицкий мост                                                                $
*6-ya liniya 15, Vasilevskiy ostrov* **Tel** *325 2214*                                        **Map** *1 A5*

A no-smoking, vegetarian café-restaurant that does not serve coffee. The emphasis is on fresh vegetables in this rare establishment; one of the few non-fusion restaurants in the city that serves asparagus and spinach – and knows what to do with them. Try cheese and spinach salad or *tagliatelli* with mushroom sauce.

### Casa del Мясо                                                                              $$
*Birzhevoy proezd 6* **Tel** *320 9746*                                                         **Map** *1 C5*

This is in a very convenient location, just a short walk from the Rostral Columns and the Strelka in the historic part of the city. The restaurant is unusual in offering a wide variety of different meat dishes on the menu. The Naval Museum, Kunstkammer and Zoological Museum are also close by.

### Imperator Император                                                                        $$
*Tamozhennyy pereulok 2* **Tel** *323 3031*                                                     **Map** *1 C5*

The Strelka has a number of restaurants but none of them can match Imperator for price. Tucked away in the basement of the Academy of Sciences, next to the Kunstkammer, it serves the usual mix of European and Caucasian cuisine, with the slightly odd addition of Mexican dishes. The small non-smoking room should be booked ahead.

### Ketino Кэтино                                                                              $$$
*9-ya liniya 23, Vasilevskiy ostrov* **Tel** *326 0196*                                         **Map** *1 A5*

Ketino is the sister Georgian restaurant to Salkhino on Petrogradskaya, with a larger, slightly less intimate though none the less friendly setting. Take their advice on what to order, but not in great quantities: once you have tried one dish, you may want everything else on the menu. (*Llobio* with green beans and spices, for example.) Wine can be expensive.

### Russian Kitsch Русский китч                                                                $$$
*Universitetskaya naberezhnaya 25* **Tel** *325 1122*                                           **Map** *5 B1*

A slightly ironic, grand venue with luxurious, if not always tasteful, trappings from the period of *Perestroika* – painted ceilings, green marble and gilt. The menu consists of a mix of fusion and sushi rather than *pelmeni* and cabbage, but the popular dance floor is very Russian. Glass galleries give views across the Neva. **www.concord-catering.ru**

### New Island                                                                                 $$$$$
*Rumyantsevskiy spusk, Universitetskaya naberezhnaya* **Tel** *320 2100*                        **Map** *5 B1*

This floating restaurant, much loved by the powerful, has played host to Bush, Putin and Chirac. In winter the boat is reserved for banquets, but from late spring to autumn it sails four times daily (at 2pm, 4pm, 8pm and 10:30pm). Eat caviar and *blini* as the boat sails past the Winter Palace towards the Smolnyy, where it turns back to its moorings.

### Old Customs House Старая таможня                                                           $$$$$
*Tamozhennyy pereulok 1* **Tel** *327 8980*                                                     **Map** *1 C5*

Conveniently located behind the Kunstkammer at the tip of the Strelka, the House is a good, reliable establishment with a general air of bonhomie. It has a strongly French orientation in its wines and menu, and serves plenty of meat. The vaulted interior is of unplastered brick, and there is an open kitchen, a balcony and a private room.

## PETROGRADSKAYA

### Demyanova Ukha Демьянова уха                                                               $$
*Kronverkskiy prospekt 53* **Tel** *232 8090*                                                   **Map** *1 C3*

The city's first specialist fish restaurant retains its premier position over the competition by dint of hard work and unpretentious, traditional, hearty cooking. Fittingly, the name Demyanova Ukha ("Demyanov's Fish Soup") is a reference to a Russian tale about an over-zealous host forcing ever more food on his guests.

**Key to Symbols** *see back cover flap*

## Salkhino Салхино                                        $$

*Kronverkskiy prospekt 25* **Tel** *232 7891*                    *Map 2 D2*

Generous home cooking is offered at this sister restaurant to Ketino on Vasilevskiy Island, by two Georgian women who know how to tempt. Their *khachapuri* (cheese-filled bread) is arguably the best in town. Try the aubergine (eggplant) stuffed with walnuts. Be wary, however, of allowing the staff to order for you: it is easy to end up with more than you can eat.

## Tbiliso Тбилисо                                          $$

*Sytninskaya ulltsa 10* **Tel** *232 9391*                      *Map 2 D2*

A Georgian eaterie. The waiters wear Georgian dress and suitably impressive moustaches, and the authentic menu includes such dishes as *mamalyga* (ground corn with salted cheese), which will turn a true Georgian's knees weak with joy. Tables are arranged to create booths for privacy – a "true" Georgian man dines only with his lady love and close friends.

## Volna Волна                                             $$

*Petrovskaya naberezhnyaya 4* **Tel** *322 5383*              *Map 2 F3*

One of the cheaper fusion restaurants in town, with an Asian accent on the menu. The Japanese-style minimalist interior complements the cuisine. Try the Italian lettuce with salmon tempura or the grilled white salmon with mint and prawn sauce. Volna is found just behind the Cabin of Peter the Great.

## Yakitoriya                                              $$

*Petrovskaya nab 4, Petrogradskaya* **Tel** *327 7700*         *Map 2 F3*

One of the best sushi restaurants in St Petersburg, Yakitoriya is favourably located near the Cabin of Peter the Great, just a five-minute walk from Peter and Paul Fortress. It's difficult to find good sushi in the city but this restaurant offers not only high quality food but very attractive prices, too.

## Zver Зверь                                              $$

*Aleksandrovskiy park 5* **Tel** *232 2062*                    *Map 2 E3*

Zver means "wild animal" and every hunter's catch imaginable is available here, from wild boar to hare. The place resembles a huge steak house, with long wooden tables and hearty portions, and has a good children's menu. It is set deep among trees; avoid the garish pavilions opposite the Fortress, and plunge further into the park to find it.

## Austeria Аустерия                                       $$$

*Peter and Paul Fortress* **Tel** *230 0369*                   *Map 2 E3*

Location is Austeria's strong point – right by Peter and Paul Fortress – and those who plan to see all the sights hereabouts will certainly need refreshment. The interior re-creates Peter the Great's favourite Dutch style, as does the Fortress Cathedral, while the menu comprises traditional Russian dishes.

## Na zdorovye! На здоровье!                               $$$

*Bolshoy prospekt 13, Petrogradskaya* **Tel** *232 4039*       *Map 1 B3*

Those who have seen and liked Boris Kustodiev's colourful pictures of buxom Russian beauties in the Russian Museum will love the garish interior of Na zdorovye. The name translates as "Your health!", and guests who practise the toast here will soon find themselves clinking glasses, in a whirl of Russian hospitality, to the sound of gypsy songs.

## Aquarel Акварель                                        $$$$

*Near Birzhevoy Bridge, Petrogradskaya Storona* **Tel** *320 8600*    *Map 1 C4*

One of the city's most expensive, this hi-tech fusion restaurant has modern, luxurious decor. Effectively a glass box, it sits on a pontoon on the River Neva, and offers great views. On the first floor is Aquarel itself, but one floor up the prices are nearly halved in the restaurant's second hall, an Italian bistro called Aquarellissimo.

## Moskva Москва                                           $$$$

*6th floor, City Centre Business Centre, Petrogradskaya naberezhnaya 18* **Tel** *332 0200*    *Map 2 F2*

This self-styled "panoramic restaurant" offers great views from its upper platform. Tucked away at the top of a business centre, art rubs shoulders with money here in yet another professionally designed, minimalist interior. Popular for creative events, product launches and exhibitions, Moskva also hosts big-name performers occasionally at weekends.

## Terrace Терраса                                         $$$$$

*Flying Dutchman, Mytninskaya naberezhnaya, Birzhevoy most* **Tel** *336 3737*    *Map 1 C4*

On board the frigate *Flying Dutchman*, this modern restaurant boasts a fireplace and broad views across the Neva to the Winter Palace. European and Latin American dishes are on the menu; there are sushi and salad bars, and a selection of elegant pastries. A nanny is available, and you can halve your bill by dining in the Zebra Bar.

# PALACE EMBANKMENT

## 1913                                                    $$

*Voznesenskiy prospekt 13* **Tel** *315 5148*                  *Map 5 C2*

Named after the last year of Russian imperial greatness, 1913 prides itself on generous portions and outstanding regional dishes such as *draniki* (potato pancakes) with bacon, and sorrel soup, as well as "fine" dishes such as lobster. A warm atmosphere and excellent service compensate for a bland interior. A singer and guitarist perform Russian songs from 8pm.

## Christopher Columbus Христофор Колумб
*Bolshaya Morskaya ulitsa 27* **Tel** *312 9761*

**Map** *6 D2*

Not surprisingly, given the name, at Christopher Columbus both food and decor have a strong maritime theme. Amongst the portholes and ropes, there is even a parrot. There is also a wide choice of fish – try fillet of pike-perch with jasmine rice, or crab with basil and kumquat sauce – and a great willingness to adapt dishes to clients' requests.

## Da Albertone
*Millionnaya ulitsa 23* **Tel** *315 8673*

**Map** *2 E5*

Just behind the Hermitage, this plain Italian restaurant is an oustanding option for those with children. The kids' menu offers animal-shaped pizzas, there is a richly equipped children's room, and a nanny is available every day from noon until late. For added adult indulgence, there are 40 types of pizza and a variety of pasta dishes. No smoking before 11pm.

## Gastronom Гастроном
*Marsovo Pole 7* **Tel** *314 3849*

**Map** *2 F5*

With its fashionable mixture of Italian and Japanese cuisine – plus a dash of Russian in its jellied meats with horseradish and mustard – the menu is aimed at a young crowd. But with a location like this, and tables on the pavement in summer, Gastronom is always going to be popular with tourists of all ages, even just for a beer.

## Krokodil Крокодил
*Galernaya ulitsa 18* **Tel** *314 9437*

**Map** *5 B2*

Krokodil offers easily the best value for money in the St Isaac's area. Small, dark and intimate, it was one of the first restaurants to introduce fresh salads, plentiful vegetarian options and a non-smoking room. There is a second branch at Kazanskaya ulitsa 24, but this is definitely the best.

## Oliva Олива
*Bolshaya Morskaya ulitsa 31* **Tel** *314 6563*

**Map** *6 D2*

This huge taverna, with five airy rooms and its own bakery, offers a healthy and varied Greek menu, with plenty of Greek wines and spirits, an extensive salad bar and range of Mediterranean *hors d'oeuvres*. One room, mainly for families, is non-smoking. Oliva is perfect for a late dinner, after a walk around town during the White Nights.

## Park Giuseppe Парк Джузеппе
*Naberezhnaya kanala Griboedova 2v* **Tel** *571 7309*

**Map** *2 F5*

On the corner of the Mikhaylovskiy Garden, with views across the Moyka to the Field of Mars, this is an ideal White Nights location; a place for eating late and sipping Italian wine as the sun gently dips, but never sets. The menu is Italian, with Neapolitan pizza baked in a wood-burning stove. A terrace is open for summer dining al fresco.

## Senat Bar Сенат-бар
*Galernaya ulitsa 1* **Tel** *314 9253*

**Map** *5 C1*

Senat is known for its "imperial" interior, with portraits and busts of tsars, and 19th-century antiques, and for its elegant Russian and European menu. Despite the fact that women are present and there is dancing in the evenings, the mood is masculine, with lots of business diners – some doing deals, others just relaxing.

## Canvas
*Renaissance Hotel, Pochtamtskaya ulitsa 4* **Tel** *380 4000*

**Map** *5 C2*

The breakfast room in this modern hotel in the quiet area beyond St Isaac's turns into a restaurant later in the day. In an area that is rather deprived of quality restaurants – most emphasise historic interiors to the detriment of the cooking – Canvas concentrates on food and service, and offers fine, traditional European cuisine.

## T-Lounge
*Renaissance Hotel, Pochtamtskaya ulitsa 4* **Tel** *380 4000*

**Map** *5 C2*

The T-Lounge offers delicious sandwiches, salads and pastries throughout the day, with live music in the evenings. Located within the Renaissance St Petersburg Baltic hotel, alongside the Canvas restaurant, it is close to all the sights and is justifiably popular with locals as well as hotel guests.

## Borsalino борсалино
*Bolshaya Morskaya ulitsa 39* **Tel** *494 5115*

**Map** *6 D2*

Borsalino offers an authentic Italian menu of high quality food within the historic Angleterre hotel *(see p174)*. The great food and fabulous interiors attract locals as well as hotel guests and visitors. The restaurant is an especially good place to relax after a day's sightseeing, offering live jazz in the bar most evenings.

## Beau Rivage
*Kempinski Hotel Moika 22, Naberezhnaya reki Moyki 22* **Tel** *335 9111*

**Map** *2 E5*

The Beau Rivage is a fine dining restaurant that serves French/International cuisine, and also offers an excellent choice of fine wines and liqueurs. The restaurant features stylish furniture and a truly unique atmosphere. In the morning it is open for a full buffet breakfast. Worth the splurge.

## Bellevue
*Kempinski Hotel Moika 22, Naberezhnaya reki Moyki 22* **Tel** *335 9111*

**Map** *2 E5*

On the 9th floor, Bellevue offers such superlative views over the city centre, of Palace Square and the Winter Palace, that diners may be tempted to ignore the food. But the French-dominated menu is good, if not cheap. This place charges for the food itself, and not for a merely stylish veneer, the way some other St Petersburg restaurants do.

**Key to Price Guide** *see p184* **Key to Symbols** *see back cover flap*

## GOSTINYY DVOR

### Blinnyy domik Блинный домик
*Kolokolnaya ulitsa 8* **Tel** *315 9915*
**Map** *7 B2*

Full of pine tables and kitsch detail, this modest, bustling pancake house is hugely popular with Russians and non-Russians alike, even though the English menu is sometimes difficult to comprehend. Try pancakes stuffed with local forest mushrooms or fish. For the strong-headed, there is *medovukha*, the Russian equivalent of mead.

### Fasol Фасоль
*Gorokhovaya ulitsa 17* **Tel** *571 0907*
**Map** *6 D2*

*Fasol* means haricot bean, but this is not a vegetarian restaurant. It does, however, have plenty of healthy, relatively low-fat dishes on its restaurant-scale menu. Service is speedy, and the interior is modern, café-style. By virtue of its superb location on the corner of the Moyka, there is nowhere better for filling up while walking the canals.

### La Strada
*Bolshaya Konyushennaya 27* **Tel** *312 4700*
**Map** *6 E1*

Pasta and pizza are made in full view of the diners, in an "Italian courtyard" complete with a fake balcony, set beneath a crystal cupola that comes into its own during White Nights. The food is standard Italian fare, but the management are genuinely child friendly, providing a nanny at weekends from noon to 10pm, and a children's room all week.

### Suliko Сулико
*Kazanskaya ulitsa 6* **Tel** *314 7373*
**Map** *6 E2*

Most central of all the truly Georgian restaurants, tucked away behind the Kazan Cathedral, Suliko is a lot cheaper than the Kavkaz-Bar and popular with Georgians themselves. More meat- than vegetable-oriented, there is no pandering to European tastes here. Try Georgian wines: Saperavi for a sharp red, Mukuzani for a cooling white.

### Vostochnyy Ugolok Восточный уголок
*Gorokhovaya ulitsa 52* **Tel** *713 5747*
**Map** *6 E3*

It is the fact that it is not geared to tourists or rich Russians that makes this *chaikhana* or Azeri "tea-drinking" house so charming. A range of Caucasian meals are served. Try *dushbara* soup with lamb and mint, sitting surrounded by Oriental carpets in a bustling atmosphere. Lots of Azeris and other nationalities from Central Asia come here.

### Aragvi
*Nab Reki Fontanki* **Tel** *570 5643*
**Map** *2 F5*

Aragvi features light, elegant interiors and large windows which offer enchanting views on to the Fontanka river. The restaurant serves authentic Georgian cuisine and you can try almost all the traditional Georgian dishes here, including *satsivi* (walnut sauce), *khachapuri* (baked bread filled with cheese) and pork *shashlyk* (kebabs).

### Kalinka-Malinka Калинка-Малинка
*Italyanskaya ulitsa 5* **Tel** *314 2681*
**Map** *6 F1*

"Kalinka-Malinka" is the Russian folk song that is played whenever a Russian appears in a Hollywood film or on TV. Kalinka-Malinka the restaurant has a rustic, wooden-hut interior and serves traditional Russian meals, with romantic songs and folk music most evenings. It attracts lots of tourists and groups, but is none the worse for that.

### Ket u Mimino Кэт у Мимино
*Karavannaya ulitsa 24* **Tel** *315 3800*
**Map** *7 A1*

A small and comfortable basement restaurant, Ket specializes in European and Georgian dishes; the owner prides himself on being descended from Georgian princes. Rare for the city centre in attracting mainly local customers, and remarkable for its lack of pretension, this is a good place to mix with "old-style" Russians.

### Literary Café Литературное кафе
*Nevskiy prospekt 18* **Tel** *312 6057*
**Map** *6 E1*

This is the former Wolff and Beranger Café, from where the idolized Russian poet Alexander Pushkin set off for his fatal duel. The venue retains its popularity with tourists and lovers of Russian literature, though the experience of eating here is more exciting historically than gastronomically. Traditional, rather heavy dishes are served, with lots of meat in rich sauces.

### Mama Roma Мама Рома
*Karavannaya ulitsa 3* **Tel** *314 0347*
**Map** *7 A1*

One of the city's first authentic Italian restaurants, Mama Roma attracts many middle-class Russians. Like any good Italian restaurant, the interior is light and airy, and children are welcome. There is a junior menu and toys. The excellent Vinarium downstairs is a good place to buy wine for a boat trip.

### Sukawati
*Kazanskaya ulitsa 8* **Tel** *312 0540*
**Map** *6 E2*

One of the few Asian restaurants in the city that gets both setting and food right. The setting is clean, with blond wood furniture and white walls. The food is excellent Indonesian with some Japanese, and saté that does not disappoint. Service is quietly efficient. Sukawati is found just behind Kazan Cathedral, 200 yards from Nevskiy prospekt.

### Erivan Ериван    ✚♥Ⓥ    ⑤⑤⑤
*Naberezhnaya reki Fontanki 51* **Tel** *703 3820*    **Map** *6 F2*

All three rooms are furnished in Armenian style, with rugs and brightly coloured tablecloths and crockery. Ignore the VIP room and head for the Rural Room. All dishes are traditional, with lots of mutton and veal – which are hard to find in Europe today – and rarities such as brains in olive oil.

### Kavkaz-Bar Кавказ-бар    ✚Ⓥ    ⑤⑤⑤
*Karavannaya ulitsa 18* **Tel** *312 1665*    **Map** *7 A1*

Caucasian (Georgian and Armenian) cuisine, and excellent Georgian wines and brandies are on offer here – at a price. Kavkaz-Bar has a superb location close to Nevskiy prospekt, and an intimate atmosphere. It also serves the best vegetarian kebabs in town. A selection of dishes is available in the less formal outer café, overlooking a quiet square.

### Caviar Bar and Restaurant    ♿✚♪♥    ⑤⑤⑤⑤
*Grand Hotel Europe, Mikhaylovskaya ulitsa 1/7* **Tel** *329 6000*    **Map** *6 F1*

Open in the evenings only, this bar-restaurant has the most elegant and varied ways of serving caviar and fish in town. Try caviar in quail's egg, salmon marinaded in vodka, or one of the monthly special Russian regional dishes. The interior is tiny with a small fountain, rather like a grotto in an 18th-century park.

### Count Suvoroff Граф Суворов    ✚♥    ⑤⑤⑤⑤⑤
*Ulitsa Lomonosova 6* **Tel** *315 4328*    **Map** *6 F2*

The Count Suvoroff has an imperial theme. Most dishes derive from pre-revolutionary menus, and the elegant interior is decorated in the style of the early 19th century, with an abundance of candlesticks and polished silver. Across the corridor, the affiliated café-bar Poruchik (Ensign) Rzhevskiy serves similar food in a more lively, informal setting.

### L'Europe Европа    ♿✚♪🍴♥Ⓥ⚡    ⑤⑤⑤⑤⑤
*Grand Hotel Europe, Mikhaylovskaya ulitsa 1/7* **Tel** *329 6000*    **Map** *6 F1*

This cavernous, Art-Nouveau (Style-Moderne) hall with stained-glass ceiling is not a re-creation of St Petersburg's glorious past, but the real thing, beautifully restored. The food is first-class European – lobster soup, steak tartare – but there are regular special events and celebrations of Russian cuisine. Sunday brunch attracts many Russian and ex-pat locals.

### St Petersburg Санкт-Петербург    ♿✚♪Ⓥ    ⑤⑤⑤⑤⑤
*Naberezhnaya kanala Griboedova 5* **Tel** *314 4947*    **Map** *6 E2*

The cost of a meal here is high considering the standard Russian fare on offer (albeit served in abundant portions), but it does include a popular "folk" floor show at 9pm every night except Sunday. Live music begins at 8pm, after which there are Russian dancers and *balalaikas*. It may not be authentic, but it is extremely lively and loud, and great fun.

## SENNAYA PLOSHCHAD

### Apsheron Апшерон    ✚♪♥Ⓥ⚡    ⑤
*Kazanskaya ulitsa 39* **Tel** *312 7253*    **Map** *6 D2*

The meat-oriented cuisine at Apsheron comes from Azerbaijan in Central Asia, and is cooked by an Azeri chef brought in from Baku. There are plenty of vegetarian dishes on the menu, too, and even Azeri wine. To suit the Azeris who flock here, each of the three dining rooms is comfortably warm and colourful. No fashionable minimalism here.

### Olimpos Олимпос    ✚Ⓥ    ⑤
*Ulitsa Dekabristov 22* **Tel** *571 4076*    **Map** *5 C3*

Located just 10 minutes from St Isaac's Cathedral and 5 minutes from the Mariinskiy Theatre, Olimpos looks like an ordinary Russian café, but its extensive Greek menu includes un-Russian quantities of fresh vegetables and salads. Look out for the house specials – Greek seasonal dishes. Service can be a little too relaxed, but the food never fails.

### Kido    Ⓥ⚡    ⑤
*Voznesenskiy prospekt 46* **Tel** *327 2316*    **Map** *6 D4*

Kido is a network of sushi bars in St Petersburg, comprising six venues in different parts of the city. It offers a good selection of sushi, sashimi, and both vegetable and spicy rolls. Two of its specialities are Fudjiyama (spicy crab, salmon and cucumber) and Dragon (crab, avocado, cucumber and eel).

### Lenin's Mating Call Зов Ильича    ♿✚♪    ⑤⑤
*Kazanskaya ulitsa 34* **Tel** *571 8641*    **Map** *6 D2*

This is a great place for those who are fascinated by Russia's Soviet past, with its hundreds of busts of Lenin large and small, and newsreels from the Brezhnev era projected onto screens. It is all good fun, served up with a traditional Russian menu and spiced with a touch of irony. Lenin and Brezhnev look-alikes might drop in of an evening.

### Noble Nest Дворянское гнездо    ✚♪🍴♥Ⓥ    ⑤⑤⑤⑤⑤
*Ulitsa Dekabristov 21* **Tel** *312 3205*    **Map** *5 C3*

Those who love the idea of Russian empire-style dining should note that this is one of the few places where you can truly live the illusion. Housed in the garden pavilion of the Yusupov Palace, it sports columns, chandeliers, portraits of tsars and an outstanding wine list. The menu mixes dishes from the Yusupov kitchens with modern inventions.

**Key to Price Guide** *see p184* **Key to Symbols** *see back cover flap*

## FURTHER AFIELD

### EAST OF THE FONTANKA Lagidze Waters Лагидзе Воды ⬛🚹Ⓥ ⑤
*Ulitsa Belinskovo 3* **Tel** *579 1104* **Map** *7 A1*

Excellently located a short walk from the centre, on one of the city's shortest and best restaurant-lined streets, Lagidze serves Georgian food and wine in a modest but modern interior, at modest prices. Try the *lodka* (hot cheese-filled bread with egg) and the *satsivi* (chicken in walnut sauce), and finish the meal with Georgian brandy.

### EAST OF THE FONTANKA Bufet Буфет ♿🚹 ⑤⑤
*Pushkinskaya ulitsa 7* **Tel** *764 7888* **Map** *7 B2*

Close to Nevskiy prospekt, Bufet's charming interior is made to look like a good, old-fashioned St Petersburg apartment. With only 20 place settings, framed photographs and mementos on the walls, it almost feels like one. The cuisine is Russian and plain, the atmosphere is warm and prices are moderate. A special place.

### EAST OF THE FONTANKA Focus Ⓥ ⑤⑤
*Naberezhnyaya reki Fontanki 40* **Tel** *719 6144* **Map** *2 F5*

Oriental style mixes with classic European in both the decor and the food at this cosy venue in the very heart of the city. It's the perfect spot to meet, chat and relax while enjoying a bite to eat. A special feature of Focus is that it also offers hookah pipe smoking, with a vast range to choose from.

### EAST OF THE FONTANKA Imbir ♿🚹Ⓥ ⑤⑤
*Zagorodnyy prospekt 15* **Tel** *713 3215* **Map** *7 A3*

Originally an oriental restaurant (Imbir means "ginger"), this eaterie now offers an eclectic mix of noodles, sushi, lighter Russian meat and fish dishes (try the poached salmon), and simple but good wines. Its unpretentious, café style attracts a quiet, relatively young crowd, and it is a good place for people-watching. There's a new dish every month.

### EAST OF THE FONTANKA NoName 🚹 ⑤⑤
*Ulitsa Marata 4* **Tel** *315 8574* **Map** *7 B2*

Just off Nevskiy prospekt, NoName offers a mixture of European and Japanese food (mainly sushi and some excellent clear soups). It is aimed, despite its designer interior and fusion menu, at anyone of any age who wants to relax in understated surroundings. There is sometimes live rock in the evening.

### EAST OF THE FONTANKA Palermo ♿ ⑤⑤
*Naberezhnaya reki Fontanki 50* **Tel** *764 3764* **Map** *7 A2*

Pictures of Sicilian landscapes hang in the windows, the walls are painted in sand yellow and olive green, even the chef comes from Sicily. But there is no need to fear the Mafia here: this is simply a good Italian family restaurant, offering a classic Sicilian menu with the addition of a few Russian favourites – mainly heavy meat dishes.

### EAST OF THE FONTANKA Povari Повари 🚹🔁 ⑤⑤
*Bolshoy prospekt 38/40, Petrogradskaya* **Tel** *233 7042* **Map** *1 C2*

Look, no pizza! This Italian restaurant specializes in all kinds of freshly made pasta, such as *fettuccini* with mushrooms and truffle sauce. In winter, tables are tucked away inside the building, but in warmer weather the covered terrace on the square outside sprouts comfortable wicker chairs. This is the perfect place to watch shoppers on bustling Petrogradskaya.

### EAST OF THE FONTANKA Rizhskiy Dvorik Рижский дворик ⬛🚹 ⑤⑤
*Ulitsa Mayakovskovo 34/4* **Tel** *273 1149* **Map** *3 B5*

This small basement café-restaurant is named for Riga, capital of Latvia and a favourite holiday destination during the Soviet period. Guests receive plenty of Latvian hospitality and Riga balsam (a herbal liqueur drunk separately or as part of a cocktail, and supposedly good for one's health). On a cold winter day, try the *draniki* (potato pancakes).

### EAST OF THE FONTANKA Sherbet Шербет 🚹 ⑤⑤
*Ulitsa Vosstaniya 26* **Tel** *716 0874* **Map** *7 C1*

Uzbekistan meets 21st-century cool at Sherbet. The ambience is very laid back, with elegant, candlelit tables and sofas scattered with silk cushions. The menu is not entirely Uzbek (though the *plov* or pilau is definitely worth tasting), but combines the best "Oriental" cooking with some Turkish dishes. Lunchtime discount of 20%.

### EAST OF THE FONTANKA Shinok Шинок 🚹 ⑤⑤
*Zagorodnyy prospekt 13* **Tel** *571 8262* **Map** *7 A3*

This restaurant offers food and folk music from the former Slavic Soviet republic of Ukraine. The elegant minimalism of St Petersburg's coolest restaurants is forsaken here in favour of good, stout food with five kinds of *salo* (salted pork belly), and Ukrainian vodka to wash it down. There is a Ukrainian folk show every evening at 9pm, and lots of jollity.

### EAST OF THE FONTANKA Shury Mury Шуры муры 🚹🔁 ⑤⑤
*Ulitsa Belinskovo 8* **Tel** *579 8550* **Map** *7 A1*

*Shury mury* means "a little of what you fancy", and the restaurant advertises itself with a picture of a romantic couple. Ignore the clichés. This is simply one of the cosiest, least pretentious places in central St Petersburg, with a plain Russian menu and a consistently welcoming atmosphere. A perfect place to dip into out of the cold.

## EAST OF THE FONTANKA Staryy Dom Старый дом

*Ulitsa Nekrasova 25* **Tel** *579 8343* **Map** *7 B1*

Azerbaijanian and Russian food is served in this simple basement café-restaurant furnished with pine benches and tables. Real home cooking is on offer, including meaty *kharcho* soup and vegetarian *chebureki* filled with herbs and grasses rather than meat, as well as excellent Georgian wine served in faience jugs. Very popular with Georgians.

## EAST OF THE FONTANKA Sunduk Сундук

*Furshtatskaya ulitsa 42* **Tel** *272 3100* **Map** *3 C4*

Technically an art café, Sunduk is too good a restaurant to be hidden in the Nightlife section of this guide. It boasts an extensive cocktail list, a filling Russian and European menu, and good live jazz (for which there is a $3 surcharge after 8:30pm). The back room is the quietest. A clown entertains children every Sunday from noon to 5pm.

## EAST OF THE FONTANKA Tres Amigos

*Ulitsa Rubinshteyna 25* **Tel** *572 2685* **Map** *7 A3*

Mexican, Peruvian, Colombian and Ecuadorian cooking are on offer, together with a bizarre mix of decor inspired by Aztecs and beer halls. Tres Amigos deserves a mention mainly for its excellent children's room with slide and swings, its children's menu, and the professional nanny it employs at weekends to entertain the kids while adults down tequila.

## EAST OF THE FONTANKA Xren

*Zagorodnyy prospekt 13* **Tel** *347 8850* **Map** *7 A3*

Guests choose which of three rooms they want to eat in (each has a different look), order stylishly designed food, and sit and watch the world bustling by through windows overlooking the "Five Corners" (an intersection not far from Nevskiy prospekt). The menu includes two-colour gazpacho, duck and couscous. DJs perform every weekend.

## EAST OF THE FONTANKA Demidoff Демидов

*Naberezhnaya reki Fontanki 14* **Tel** *272 9181* **Map** *3 A5*

There are two rooms in this touristy but adequate restaurant, one for elegant 19th-century dining, one for dining in a pseudo "Old Russian" interior (with brightly coloured, painted vaults). However, the pan-Russian menus are the same and include everything from quail's eggs to pancakes and caviar. There is Gypsy music every evening from 8pm.

## EAST OF THE FONTANKA Kolkhida Колхида

*Nevskiy prospekt 176* **Tel** *274 2514* **Map** *8 E3*

This is the place to get a very cheap business-style lunch, and is perfectly located for those visiting the Alexander Nevsky Monastery. The menu offers a wide range of Georgian dishes, such as *tsatsivi* (chicken in walnut sauce), and wines. There is traditional Georgian singing in the evening. The street is a night-time pick-up spot, so book a taxi.

## EAST OF THE FONTANKA Matrosskaya Tishina Матросская тишина

*Ulitsa Marata 54/34* **Tel** *764 4413* **Map** *7 B4*

The advertisement for this restaurant reads "fish fashion", and so it is. Inside there is a real trawler cut into pieces, aquariums stuffed with live lobsters, oysters and crayfish; and tiger prawns and sea scallops, and just the right wines to wash them down. None of the fish or seafood is frozen – everything is delivered fresh and kept cool on ice.

## EAST OF THE FONTANKA Probka

*Ulitsa Belinskovo 5* **Tel** *273 4904* **Map** *7 A1*

This elegant Italian wine bar has the same management as more expensive Il Grappolo next door. Minimalist decor complements minimalist Italian cuisine – with fine sauces rather than the heavy, creamy pastas served in some of the city's other Italian restaurants – and no pizza. On warm days, huge windows open to embrace the outdoors.

## EAST OF THE FONTANKA Troika Тройка

*Zagorodnyy prospekt 27* **Tel** *713 6615* **Map** *6 F3*

Troika is not just a restaurant, but a remainder from the good old Soviet days of floorshows, with circus acrobatics (slender girls doing strange things with hoops), folk songs, Russian dancing, glitz and glamour. There is no erotica, unlike in some more recently opened locations. The menu is unremarkable, but the show is the star.

## EAST OF THE FONTANKA X.O.

*Ulitsa Zhukovskovo 10* **Tel** *719 6542* **Map** *7 B1*

Amongst the city's *haute cuisine* establishments, X.O. has been doing especially well. It received the Best Chef Award in 2005, has a stylish modern interior and offers a mixture of Italian, European and Asian cuisine, with seafood delicacies, an extensive wine list, and an unusually good selection of cheeses. Watch out for the slippery metal stairs at the entrance.

## WEST OF THE CENTRE Russian Fishing Русская рыбалка

*Yuzhnaya doroga 11, Krestovskiy ostrov* **Tel** *323 9813*

This is a stylized fisherman's hut with a pond in which guests can catch their own fish – trout, sturgeon, beluga sterlet – and watch it cooked. The concept is masculine, but the restaurant tends to attract families during the day because of the playground outside and children's room inside. The place is more adult at night, and can get rowdy in the early hours.

## WEST OF THE CENTRE Karl & Friedrich Карл и Фридрих

*Yuzhnaya doroga 15, Krestovskiy ostrov* **Tel** *320 7978*

A taxi is needed to get to and from this restaurant-brewery on Krestovskiy Island near the Gulf of Finland. The venue is aimed at families and employs a nanny from 7pm to 10pm during the week, and two nannies and a clown from 2pm to 10pm at weekends. There is a strong meat orientation to the menu, and great beer.

**Key to Price Guide** *see p184* **Key to Symbols** *see back cover flap*

## WEST OF THE CENTRE Krestovskiy sad Крестовский сад          $$$

*Yuzhnaya doroga 15, Krestovskiy ostrov* **Tel** *320 7978*

Another eaterie in the Karl & Friedrich brewery complex, Krestovskiy sad serves roast lamb cooked on an open spit in the grounds in summer – perfect for the White Nights. Sit at a table outside and watch the sun sink slowly over the Gulf of Finland, or eat at the smaller, seasonal café on the nearby beach.

## NORTH OF THE NEVA 7:40          $$

*Bolshoy Sampsonievskiy prospekt 108* **Tel** *492 3444*

The best known Jewish restaurant in town. Its name (*sem-sorok* in Russian) refers to the well-known Jewish song and dance that gets faster and faster until participants are whirling, which is just the kind of exuberant spirit this friendly establishment aims to emulate. Staff serve a wide range of traditional Jewish dishes in a colourful interior.

## NORTH OF THE NEVA Le Mon          $$

*Kamennoostrovskiy prospekt 64/2* **Tel** *974 4078*                    **Map** *2 D1*

For those taking a walk along Kamennoostrovskiy prospekt to view the Style-Moderne buildings of the Petrograd Side, Le Mon is a dream – smart, but much less expensive than it looks. The "French" menu actually delivers a sort of classy European cuisine, including superb *carpaccio* for *hors d'oeuvres* and some very elegant desserts.

## NORTH OF THE NEVA Pirosmani Пиросмани          $$

*Bolshoy prospekt 14, Petrogradskaya* **Tel** *235 4666*                **Map** *1 B3*

This colourful Georgian restaurant is set out like a Georgian hill village, with wattle and daub houses, a stained-glass window and even real ponds (when booking, ask to sit on a raft). Walls are hung with works by Pirosmani, arguably the best Georgian painter of the 20th century. Try the *lobio* – beans in spicy sauce – washed down with Old Tbilisi wine.

## NORTH OF THE NEVA Staraya Derevnya Старая деревня          $$

*Ulitsa Savushkina 72* **Tel** *431 0000*

One of St Petersburg's first independent restaurants, Staraya Derevnya is still one of the friendliest places in town. A long way from the centre, it is nevertheless perfect for those driving back into town from the Gulf of Finland. Service is personal, the interior informal – like an old-fashioned apartment. Russian, Jewish and Gypsy songs are performed in the evening.

# BEYOND ST PETERSBURG

## NOVGOROD Detinets Детинец          $

*Pokrovskaya Tower, Detinets (Novgorod Kremlin)* **Tel** *(8162) 774624*

Novgorod's most famous restaurant is located inside one of the 17th-century towers of the Detinets (Kremlin). Traditional Russian dishes are served, including *medovukha* (mead) and *sbiten* (spiced tea). There is a bar in the basement (a former women's prison), and in summer food can be served outside. Quite an experience.

## NOVGOROD Yuryevskoye Podvorie Юрьевское подворье          $$

*Yuryevskoye shosse 6a* **Tel** *(8162) 946067*

Especially attractive in summer, this restaurant is the ideal place if you want to avoid the crowds and noisy venues closer to the city. It has two large dining halls as well as a smaller banqueting space for intimate dining. Russian cuisine is served, such as salads, mushrooms, pancakes with caviar, *borsch* and *ukha* (fish soup).

## PAVLOVSK Podvorie Подворье          $$$

*Filtrovskoe shossee 16, Pavlovsk* **Tel** *4668544*

It is worth making a special trip to this re-creation of a 17th-century wooden house, situated by the grounds of Pavlovsk Palace, a short walk from Pavlovsk railway station. The restaurant is kitsch and great fun, with folk songs at lunchtime, and a traditional Russian menu with *pelmeni*, plenty of meaty soups and vodka. In the snow, it is magical.

## PUSHKIN Staraya Bashnya Старая башня          $$

*Akademicheskiy prospekt 14* **Tel** *466 6698*

With its huge menu and wine list, this is something of a find in provincial Pushkin: prices are half what they would be in St Petersburg itself. The restaurant is near the famous district of Fyodorovskiy gorodok, which was built in 1913 to mark the 300th anniversary of the Romanovs.

## REPINO Chaliapin Шаляпин          $$$

*Ulitsa Nagornaya 1* **Tel** *432 0775*

In summer the Gulf is rich in cafés offering *shashlyk* (kebabs), but year round the best place to eat out here is Chaliapin. Do not be put off by the unattractive concrete exterior, and the location over a supermarket (though surrounded by trees), because inside it is charming, with a vast fireplace in winter. In summer, there is a roof terrace.

## SHUVALOVKA Sobranie Собрание          $$

*Sankt-Peterburgskoe shosse 111, between Strelna and Petrodvorets* **Tel** *450 5393*

Set in a stylized Russian tower at the heart of the Shuvalovka Russian Village (a sort of Russian Disneyland on the road to Peterhof), Sobranie is a good place to try traditional Russian rural dishes and listen to folk songs – even for those who have not been sliding down snowhills and riding in a *troika* in the Village.

# Light Meals and Snacks

Despite their plastic chairs and metal tables, Russian and ethnic cafés often serve very tasty food – from simple sandwiches to hefty meat dishes. Look out for the word кафе (café) and try one. Cautious travellers can experiment in one of the restaurants listed opposite, which frequently offer moderately priced meals between noon and 4pm. A number of bars and "art cafés" with live music *(see p205)* also have excellent kitchens. (In the evening these may be filled with people and noise, but at lunchtime they are calmer.) During the summer many cafés add tables outside – which is great for people-watching. In colder weather, the ground-floor cafés of the Moika or Radisson SAS hotels, Jili-bili or Il Patio are almost as good.

## RUSSIAN

Traditional Russian dishes such as *borsch* and *draniki* (potato pancakes) are widely offered. *Pelmeni* (dumplings filled with meat, potatoes or mushrooms) and *vareniki* (dumplings filled with fruit) are in a class of their own. Specialist *pelmeni* establishments are truly "local", with no flashy decor or tourists. Try the **Pelmeni Bar** behind the Peter and Paul Fortress. Russian *bliny* and *blinchiki* (flat pancakes) come in both sweet and savoury varieties at the outstandingly cheap **Russkie Bliny U Natashi**.

Some places listed are quite plain, notable mainly for their location. **Priboy** is behind the Hermitage *(see pp84–93)*, **Sadko** is next to the Mariinskiy Theatre, **Café de Clie** is next to the Peter and Paul Fortress. **The Stroganoff Yard** is in the (heated) courtyard of the Stroganov Palace *(see p112)*. Near St Isaac's Square *(see p79)* is **Idiot**, a vegetarian café popular with ex-pats. **Luna** is cheap, cheerful and crowded. **U Kamina** is known for its cosy fire and generous portions.

## ETHNIC FOOD

Georgian and Armenian foods are popular in St Petersburg. The **Kavkaz-Bar** restaurant *(see p188)* and **Magrib** have small café sections, and many other small cafés offer Caucasian dishes. Filling Uzbek food is on offer at **Asia**, a tiny, bustling and cheap café in the heart of the residential and consulate area.

## FAST FOOD, PIZZA AND PASTA

The first Russian fast food was an open sandwich with cheese or salami, or *pirozhki* (small buns) filled with rice, cabbage or something sweet like apple. The best *pirozhki* come from **Stolle**. A slightly cheaper version is available from the **Bulochnaya** on Bolshaya Konyushennaya ulitsa. Always avoid fried *pirozhki* with meat. Never buy them on the street.

In addition to the well-known fast-food chains, local options include the 24-hour **Layma** and **U Tyoshi Na Blinakh**, where customers choose by pointing. **Teremok** specializes in pancakes. **Green Crest** salad bar and the **Troitskiy Most** chain are good vegetarian options. Pizza and pasta houses are popular. (**Il Patio** caters for children.)

## PASTRIES AND SWEETS

Russians are sweet-toothed, and in private homes tea is never offered without biscuits or cakes. Ice cream – best bought from one of the many street sellers – is enjoyed all year round. **Sladkoezhka** sells an amazing range of fresh cream desserts and pastries, and is probably the city's favourite spot for a hit of sugar. Coffee shops, such as **Albina** and the **Idealnaya Chashka** chain, also offer a variety of cheesecakes and cakes. At **Stirka 40°** customers drink tea while doing their washing (it doubles as a launderette).

## PUBS AND BARS

All bars serve a good range of food. In addition to the standard English and Irish pubs, where food is unadventurous and the clientele is composed mostly of ex-pats, there are now a number of Russian "pubs", such as **Pivnaya 0.5**, that offer a range of excellent local beers. **Argus** and **Tinkoff** make their own beer on the premises.

One of the joys of summer is to drink beer sitting on one of the pontoons that appear with the warm weather on the canals and rivers, particularly around Nevskiy prospekt. Whilst such places do not usually offer food, they do allow customers to linger and watch the sunset on the water.

## SUSHI

An enduring craze for sushi bars – which tend to be quite good – means that there are plenty of good alternatives for quick, healthy lunches in St Petersburg. Menus are easy to understand because they include pictures of each dish. Try **Dve Palochki** or **Planet Sushi**.

## EATING OUT ON DAY TRIPS

More effort is required when seeking a place for a modest lunch outside the city. Pavlovsk *(see pp158–61)* and Peterhof *(see pp148–51)* have reasonable cafés in the palaces, although space is limited in summer. Peterhof's tiny **Trapeza** is always a favourite. At Tsarskoe Selo *(see pp152–5)*, there are several cafés along and around Oranzhereynaya ulitsa, leading off the park. Gatchina Palace *(see p147)* has cafés in the grounds and even Oranienbaum *(see p146)* has a tiny café, too. In general, however, the best option is to take a picnic to Gatchina or Oranienbaum. (Delicious take-away pies can be bought from **Stolle**.) In Novgorod *(see pp162–5)*, the **Golden Ladle** serves many kinds of beer and snacks.

# DIRECTORY

## RUSSIAN

### Café de Clie
Kronverkskiy prospekt 27.
**Map** 2 D2.
*Tel 232 3606.*

### Carusel
Карусель
Ulitsa Kirochnaya 8.
**Map** 3 B5.
*Tel 272 1778.*

### Chaynaya Khizhina
Чайная хижина
Bolshaya Konyushennaya
ulitsa 19 (entrance from
Volynskiy pereulok).
**Map** 6 E1.
*Tel 314 9786.*

### Idiot
Идиот
Naberezhnaya reki
Moyki 82. **Map** 5 C2.
*Tel 315 1675.*

### Jili-bili
Жили-были
Nevskiy prospekt 52.
**Map** 6 F1.
*Tel 314 6230.*

### Luna
Луна
Bolshaya Konyushennaya
ulitsa 5. **Map** 2 E5.
*Tel 312 4260.*

### More
Troitskiy most:
Kamenoostrovskiy
prospect 9/2.
**Map** 2 E4. *Tel 232 6693.*
Zagorodnyy prospekt 38.
**Map** 2 E4. *Tel 312 6810.*

### Pelmeni Bar
Пельмени-бар
Kronverkskiy prospekt 53a
(entry from ulitsa Markina).
**Map** 1 C3. *Tel 498 0977.*

### Priboy
Прибой
Naberezhnaya reki
Moyki 19. **Map** 2 E5.
*Tel 571 8285.*

### Russkie Bliny U
Natashi (pancakes)
Русские блины у Наташи
5-ya Sovetskaya ulitsa 24.
**Map** 7 C1. *Tel 271 5958.*

### Russkiy Pub
Русский паб
Ulitsa Michurinskaya 12.
**Map** 2 E2.
*Tel 346 1762.*

### Sadko
Садко
Ulitsa Glinki 2.
**Map** 5 B3.
*Tel 920 8228.*

### Soiree
Суаре
Ulitsa Zhukovskovo 28.
**Map** 7 B1. *Tel 272 3512.*

### The Stroganoff
Yard
Строгановский двор
Nevskiy prospekt 17.
**Map** 6 E1. *Tel 315 2315.*

### U Kameni
У Камина
Malyy prospekt 29,
Petrogradskaya Storona.
**Map** 1 C1. *Tel 235 0458.*

## ETHNIC FOOD

### Asia
Азия
Ulitsa Ryleeva 23.
**Map** 3 B5. *Tel 272 0168.*

### Magrib
Магриб
Nevskiy prospeckt 84.
**Map** 7 B2. *Tel 275 4470.*

## FAST FOOD, PIZZA
AND PASTA

### Bulochnaya
Булочная
Bolshaya Konyushennaya
ulitsa 15. **Map** 2 E5.
Nevskiy prospekt 66.
**Map** 7 A2. *Tel 314 8559.*

### Green Crest
Грин Крест
Vladimirskiy prospekt 7.
**Map** 7 A2. *Tel 713 1380.*

### Il Patio
Nevskiy prospekt 30.
**Map** 6 E1. *Tel 380 9183.*
Nevskiy prospekt 182.
**Map** 8 E3. *Tel 271 3177.*

### Layma
Лаима
Naberezhnaya kanala
Griboedova 16. **Map** 6 E1.
*Tel 315 5545.*

### Stolle
Штолле
Ulitsa Dekabristov 33.
**Map** 5 C3.
*Tel 714 2571.*
Konyushennyy pereulok 1/6.
**Map** 2 E5. *Tel 312 1862.*

### Teremok (pancakes)
Теремок
Nevskiy prospekt 60.
**Map** 7 A2. *Tel 314 2701.*

### Troitskiy Most
Троицкий мост
Kronverkskiy prospekt 35.
**Map** 2 D2. *Tel 326 8221.*
6-ya liniya 27,
Vasilevskiy ostrov.
**Map** 1 A5. *Tel 327 4622.*

### U Tyoshi Na Blinakh
(pancakes)
У тёши на блинах
Ligovskiy prospekt 29.
**Map** 7 C2. *Tel 275 9782.*

## COFFEE, PASTRIES
AND SWEETS

### Albina
Альбина
Ulitsa Vosstaniya 10.
**Map** 7 B1.
*Tel 273 7459.*

### Denisov-Nikolaev
Confectionery
Ленисов и Николаев
Naberezhnaya kanala
Griboedova 77.
**Map** 6 D3.
*Tel 571 9495.*

### Idealnaya Chashka
Идеальная чашка
Nevskiy prospekt 112.
**Map** 7 B2. *Tel 275 7140.*
Vladimirskiy prospekt 1.
**Map** 7 A2. *Tel 310 3735.*
Kamennoostrovskiy
prospekt 2.
**Map** 2 E2. *Tel 233 4953.*

### Lavka Smirdina
Лавка Смирлина
Nevskiy prospekt 22.
**Map** 6 E1.
*Tel 315 9017.*

### Sladkoezhka
Сладкоежка
Marata ulitsa 2.
**Map** 7 B2.
*Tel 571 1420.*
Sadovaya ulitsa 60.
**Map** 5 C4.
*Tel 310 8144.*
Gorokhovaya 44.
**Map** 6 E3.
*Tel 310 8005.*

### Stirka 40°
Стирка 40°
Kazanskaya ulitsa 26.
**Map** 6 D2.
*Tel 314 5371.*

## PUBS AND BARS

### Argus
Аргус
Bolshaya Konyushennaya
ulitsa 15.
**Map** 6 E1.
*Tel 571 0154.*

### Pivnaya 0.5
Пивная 0.5
44/2 Zagorodnyy prospekt.
**Map** 6 E4.
*Tel 315 1038.*

### Tinkoff
Тинькофф
Kazanskaya ulitsa 7.
**Map** 6 E2.
*Tel 718 5566.*

## SUSHI

### Dve Palochki
Две палочки
Ulitsa Vosstaniya 15.
**Map** 7 C1.
*Tel 335 0222.*

### Eurasia
Евразия
Nevskiy prospekt 3.
**Map** 6 D1.
*Tel 571 8286.*

### Planet Sushi
Планета Суши
Nevskiy prospekt 94.
**Map** 7 B2.
*Tel 275 7533.*

## DAY TRIPS

### Bashnya
Башня
Sankt-Peterburgskiy
prospekt 46, Petrodvorets
(Peterhof).
*Tel 427 7878.*

### Delvig
Дельвиг
Oranzhereynaya ulitsa 20,
Tsarkoe Selo.
*Tel 466 2958.*

### Golden Ladle
Золотой Ковш
Novo-Luchanskaya ulitsa
14, Novgorod.
*Tel (8162) 73 05 99.*

### Trapeza
Трапеза
Kalininskaya ulitsa 9,
Petrodvorets (Peterhof).
*Tel 427 9393.*

# SHOPS AND MARKETS

A trip round St Petersburg's shops and markets provides an insight into local life. Even today, shopping in the city requires flexibility and even a sense of adventure: you can never depend on finding what you set out to find, but may confidently expect to end up buying something you never guessed you needed. In recent years, imported goods have pushed out many local products. Even

**Matryoshka doll**

so, Russian linen, the city's celebrated Krupsksaya chocolates, vodka, caviar, and Russian crafts and toys all make wonderful gifts. Larger shops are concentrated around main streets such as Nevskiy and Bolshoy prospekts, and metro stations, notably Sennaya Ploshchad and Vasilievskiy Ostrov. However, most buildings are occupied by shops or restaurants at ground level. Do venture in.

**Ladies' fashion at one of the numerous up-scale boutiques along Nevskiy prospekt**

## OPENING HOURS

Hours vary, but shops usually open from 10am until at least 7pm, though "fashionable" outlets may open later. A few, mainly cheap food shops, close for lunch. On Sundays department stores remain open, as do other large shops. During the summer, smaller places may reduce their hours and close at weekends. There are 24-hour food shops all over town.

## HOW TO PAY

Shops no longer express prices in "y.e." or "conditional units", but a few restaurants still do so. One y.e. is usually worth about one US dollar or one Euro (check at the restaurant for their exchange rate), but the customer must still pay in roubles. Paying in non-Russian currency is a criminal offence. The only place you might be able to pay in foreign currency is at a tourist market.

There are numerous, reliable exchange offices and automatic teller machines inside metro stations

**Russian box-camera (1920s)**

and outside banks *(see p214)*. Moreover, many stores now accept credit cards. In some shops, customers are forced to peer at goods stacked behind the counter. If you would like a closer look, just point to what you want and say "*mozhno*" ("may I?"). To purchase something, pay for it at the cash desk and then return to collect the item from the counter. Shop assistants will usually realise if you do not speak Russian, and will write down the prices for you to hand to the cashier. Defective goods can be returned provided they are accompanied by a receipt.

## BARGAINING ETIQUETTE

If a set price is displayed at markets, this indicates no bargaining. In all other cases you can usually get some reduction if you haggle, especially since visitors (and prosperous-looking Russians) are likely to be quoted a higher price. Haggling in Russia, however, is a serious matter, so do not bother unless you genuinely intend to buy.

**Second-hand bookshop sign**

## BUYING ART AND ANTIQUES

Under Russian law, all objects made before 1956, and all objects made from valuable materials such as gold, silver, precious stones and fur, are subject to strict export controls. Works of art, including contemporary watercolours, also fall under this ruling, likewise books published before 1946.

Be aware that, although there are now green and red channels at the airport customs, and not all suitcases are x-rayed, there are random checks. In practice, customs officials may turn a blind eye to prints and watercolours without frames, and unless a book is extremely rare you are likely to be able to export it without authorization. In all other cases, strict rules are applied.

Permission to export both books and art objects can be obtained from a department of the **Ministry of Culture**. This process is relatively speedy. The gallery from which or the artist from

EXPORT PERMISSIONS

**Ministry of Culture**
Министерство культуры
Ministerstvo kultury
Malaya Morskaya Ulitsa 17.
**Map** 6 D1. **Tel** 571 0302.
◑ Mon–Fri 11am–5pm.

Tertia *(see p198)* has exportable antiques to suit all budgets

whom the item is purchased should always assist with the paperwork.

If you have not obviously tried to cheat customs, any objects not allowed through can simply be handed over to someone who is remaining in St Petersburg. If, however, there is any hint of foul play, the item will be placed in storage at the airport, for which, if you wish to reclaim it later, there will be a charge. Any objects that remain unclaimed after a year will be confiscated, as will objects which have obviously been hidden to avoid detection. Valuable pieces may be donated to a museum.

## DEPARTMENT STORES

Known as "univermag" or universal shop, Russian department stores generally evolved from the old trading rows, which were literally rows of kiosks owned by different traders. Present-day department stores have altered a great deal and now operate as a complex of boutiques and distinct sections. Even though the goods on sale do not differ much from those that are available in European shops, every visitor to St Petersburg should explore **Gostinyy Dvor** *(see p108)*, the oldest and largest shopping centre in the city, and **Passazh** *(see p48)*, a smaller department store. Despite the glitzy

goods, however, the narrow passages and layout speak of a different age.

The newer department stores such as **Vladimirskiy Passazh** *(see p199)* and Grand Palace are more like Western European and American shopping malls, with up-scale boutiques.

## MARKETS AND BAZAARS

Food can be bought in one of the 11 farmers' markets (*rynoks*) dotted around the city. The most centrally located is **Kuznechnyy** *(see p199)*, just off Nevskiy prospekt, which sells flowers, fruit, vegetables, delicious home-made cream cheese and wonderful natural honey which you can sample. Note that prices at markets tend to be higher than at the super-markets, but buyers do have the option of haggling.

Apraksin Dvor market used to be the most popular for everything from cigars to CDs but in 2009 the market moved from the centre to Rustavelli Street. Another famous market is **Unona**, which is at Avtovo metro station. Keep your valuables well hidden – pickpockets are active here.

Flea markets are perpetually being moved on, though some sellers continue to pop up at the city's main markets. The true seeker of unusual finds amid the trash will set off on a Friday or Saturday morning for Udelnaya metro, where a vast unofficial market sprawls along the railway line.

Souvenir watercolours and prints of varying quality are sold throughout the year at the

open-air market, **Vernisazh** *(see p199)*, outside the Church of St Catherine *(see p48)* on Nevskiy prospekt. The official **Souvenir Market** *(see p199)* near the Church on Spilled Blood *(see p100)*, sells the best and cheapest selection of *matryoshka* dolls *(see p197)*. You are also likely to find handmade chess sets, watches, fur hats, old cameras, t-shirts and military paraphernalia.

Visitors browse the shelves at the Hermitage Museum Shop

## MUSEUM SHOPS

The best museum shop is found inside the **Hermitage** *(see pp84–93)* and sells repro-duction prints and objects, books on the city and its art, jewellery and silk scarves, both inside the museum and online: www.hermitagemuseum.org

The **Russian Museum** *(see pp104–7)* has several outlets, though these are not run by the museum itself. The best is in the Stroganov Palace *(see p112)*.

Of the other shops attached to museums, the best are found in the **Peter and Paul Fortress** *(see pp66–7)* and in the palaces at **Pavlovsk, Peterhof** and **Tsarskoe Selo** *(see pp148–61)*. These tend to sell souvenirs (rather than reproductions of exhibits and other related objects): amber and semi-precious stone jewellery, dolls, lacquered boxes and books on the city.

Souvenirs sold at the tourist market opposite the Church on Spilled Blood

# What to Buy in St Petersburg

**Decorative box**

It is easy to find interesting and beautiful souvenirs in St Petersburg. They range in price from small, enamelled badges, which sell for very little, through to hand-painted Palekh boxes and samovars which can be very expensive. Traditional crafts were encouraged by the state in the old Soviet Union and many items, such as lacquered boxes and bowls, matryoshka dolls, wooden toys and chess sets, are still made by craftsmen and women using age-old methods. Memorabilia from the Soviet era also make good souvenirs and Russia is definitely the best place to buy the national specialities, vodka and caviar.

**Samovar**
*Used to boil water to make tea, samovars come in all shapes and sizes (see p183). A permit is needed to export a pre-1945 samovar.*

**Vodka and Caviar**
*An enormous variety of both clear and flavoured vodkas (such as lemon and pepper) is available (see p182). They make excellent accompaniments to black and red caviar (ikra), which are often served with blini (see p180).*

**Clear vodka**

**Flavoured vodka**

**Red caviar**

**Black caviar**

**Malachite egg**

**Amber ring**

**Semi-precious Stones**
*Malachite, amber, jasper and a variety of marbles from the Ural mountains are used to make a wide range of items – everything from jewellery and chess sets to inlaid table tops.*

**Wooden Toy**
*These crudely carved wooden toys often have moving parts. They are known as Bogorodskiye toys and make charming gifts.*

**Matryoshka Dolls**
*These dolls fit one inside the other and come in a huge variety of styles. The traditional dolls are the prettiest, but those painted as Russian, Soviet and world leaders are also very popular.*

**Chess Sets**
*Attractive chess sets made from all kinds of beautiful materials, including malachite, are widely available. This wooden chess set is painted in the same style as the matryoshka dolls.*

## LACQUERED ARTIFACTS

Painted wooden or papier-mâché artifacts make popular souvenirs and are sold all over the city. The exquisite hand-painted, lacquered Palekh boxes can be very costly, but the eggs decorated with icons and the typical red, black and gold bowls are more affordable.

### Palekh Box

*The art of miniature painting on papier-mâché items originated in the late 18th century. Artists in the four villages of Palekh, Fedoskino, Mstera and Kholui still produce these hand-painted marvels. The images are based on Russian fairytales and legends.*

**Painted wooden egg**

### Bowl with Spoon

*The brightly painted bowls and spoons, usually known as "Khokhloma", have a lacquer coating, forming a surface which is durable, but not resistant to boiling liquids.*

**Russian hand-painted tray**

Tuners　　　Strings

### Russian Scarf

*These brilliantly coloured traditional woollen shawls are good for keeping out the cold of a Russian winter. Mass-produced polyester versions are also available, mostly in big department stores, but these are not as warm.*

### Musical Instruments

*Russian folk music uses a wide range of musical instruments. This gusli is similar to the Western psaltery and is played by plucking the strings with both hands. Also available are the brightly painted balalaika and the bayan (accordion).*

### Soviet Memorabilia

*An eclectic array of memorabilia from the Soviet era is on sale. Old banknotes, coins, pocket watches and Red Army kits, including belt buckles, badges and other items of uniform, can be found alongside watches with cartoons of KGB agents on their faces.*

### Gzhel Vase

*Ceramics with a distinctive blue and white pattern are produced in Gzhel, an area near Moscow. Ranging from figurines to household crockery, they are popular with Russians and visitors alike.*

**Pocket watch**

**Badge with Soviet symbols**

**Red Army leather belt**

# Where to Shop in St Petersburg

The main department stores in the city centre stock everything from souvenirs to vodka and furs, all of a high quality. For some local products, however, it is best to visit specialist shops, most of which are conveniently located in or near the centre. In a city which prides itself on its intellectuals, books and art are appropriately St Petersburg's other main exports. Soviet memorabilia has also become very popular in recent years.

## FOOD AND DRINK

Good vodka is to be had everywhere. Avoid cheaper brands in "amusing" packaging, they are invariably of poor quality. Diplomat and Gzhelka are good, standard brands.

Caviar should be bought only from a food shop or department store. **Gostinyy Dvor** department store and the Supermarket in **Passazh** department store are the most central, reliable places for both vodka and caviar. The many **Liviz** outlets also stock a wide range of alcoholic drinks. All kinds of food shopping can be done at **Kuznechnyy Market**, stacked high with Russian specialities. St Petersburg's **Krupskaya Fabrika** chocolate factory has long been famous across the Soviet Union. The **Chocolate Museum** sells novelties such as famous buildings crafted in chocolate. All kinds of sweets are on sale at the much-loved **Sever**.

## SOUVENIRS AND CRAFTS

In summer, when traders set up stalls by tourist spots, the city is flooded with *matryoshka* dolls, music boxes shaped like a church, painted lacquerware and chess sets. In winter, it can be quiet on the retail front. The **Souvenir Market** and **Vernisazh** market, however, operate all year, and there are good gifts to be found in Gostinyy Dvor and Passazh department stores. Shops in or near museums also stock souvenirs – notably those in the Stroganov Palace *(see p112)* and Tsarskoe Selo *(see pp152–5)*. The shop inside the Hermitage *(see pp84–5)* sells higher range goods and excellent art books. Local porcelain from the **Imperial**

**Porcelain Factory** is much prized. The factory makes everything from gaily painted rustic cups to reproduction revolutionary-era porcelain. **Unona** at Avtovo is a real local market – a must if you want to see what locals buy.

## SOVIET MEMORABILIA

Artifacts from the Soviet era are now produced specifically for the tourist market. Be careful when buying on the street: many apparently genuine articles are modern reproductions. Original pieces can be picked up at the **Souvenir Market**, though **Sekunda** and **Sobiratel** antiques shops are more reliable. Or you could try one of the smaller second-hand shops. Soviet badges are easily transportable. DIY models of Soviet military hardware are available from the top floor of **D.V.K**.

## ANTIQUES AND ART

Although older antiques and many works of art need to be cleared with customs, some pieces, such as small water-colours, may be exempt. Many shops are extortionately expensive, but **Tertia** is an exception, with readily expor-table items to suit all pockets, and the **Antique Centre** is a veritable treasure trove. Only buy an expensive object if you are sure the relevant paper-work and export applications can be obtained *(see p194)*. **Antikvariat** should be able to provide the paperwork for purchases made in the centre.

Paintings all require export licences, but as galleries can provide these themselves it is worth dropping in to **Anna Nova**, **S.P.A.S.** or **Borey** to see

what they have. The **Union of Artists** has exhibitions by traditional local artists. The **Pushkinskaya 10** artists' colony stages shows at weekends, some with works for sale.

## BOOKS, FILM AND MUSIC

St Petersburgers perceive their city as an intellectual focal point, with a great literary and artistic past. The centre has been taken over by book chains such as **Bookvoed**, but there are some smaller new and second-hand bookshops. The best are still **Dom Knigi** *(see p47)* and the **Writers' Bookshop**. If you need a holiday novel in English, try **Anglia**, Dom Knigi or Bookvoed. More unusual, second-hand English books – usually donated by tourists – can sometimes be found in **Akademkniga** and **Na Liteynom**. **Severnaya Lira** sells sheet music – everything from classical to folk songs – as well as instruments, CDs and books on music. Art books can be bought in Dom knigi, or second-hand in **Staraya Kniga**.

Very inexpensive DVDs of English-language films and CDs can be purchased in shops such as **Kailas**.

## FURS AND FASHION

Clothes and other accessories are mainly imported. Elegant boutiques occupy part of Gostinyy Dvor and run along streets such as naberezhnaya kanala Griboedova and ulitsa Zhukovskovo. Some local designers have their own boutiques; notably **Tatyana Parfyonova**, whose garments have been purchased by the Russian Museum.

**Paloma** and the **Hat Shop** offer hats in everything from straw to fur. Furs are sold in **Lena**, Paloma and on the top floor of Gostinyy Dvor. Russian linen is a also a good buy. Elegant shift dresses and the traditional *kosovorotka* (peasant shirt) are found in **Slavyanskiy Stil**. Locally made jewellery of semi-precious stones from the Urals and amber from the Baltic is available in jewellers such as Samotsvety; for rarer works, visit **Ananov**.

# DIRECTORY

## DEPARTMENT STORES

### Gostinyy Dvor
Гостиный двор
Nevskiy prospekt 35.
**Map 6 F2.**

### Passazh
Пассаж
Nevskiy prospekt 48.
**Map 6 F1.**

### Vladimirskiy Passazh
Владимирский пассаж
Vladimirskiy prospekt 19.
**Map 7 A3.**

## MARKETS

### Andreevskiy Market
Андреевский рынок
Bolshoy prospekt 18.
**Map 5 A1.**

### Kuznechnyy Market
Кузнечный рынок
Kuznechnyy pereulok 3.
**Map 7 A3.**

### Souvenir Market
Рынок сувениров
Naberezhnaya kanala
Griboedova, by Church on
Spilled Blood. **Map 2 E5.**

### Unona
Унона
Rustavelli most.
Buses K-60, K-80 from
Avtovo metro station.
*Tel 742 0200.*

### Vernisazh
Вернисаж
Nevskiy prospekt 32–4.
**Map 6 E1.**

## FOOD AND DRINK

### Chocolate Museum
Музей шоколада
Nevskiy prospekt 17.
**Map 6 E1.** *Tel 315 1348.*

### Krupskaya Fabrika
Кондитаерская фабрика
им. Н.К. Крупской
Ulitsa Vosstaniya 15.
**Map 7 C1.** *Tel 346 5532.*

### Liviz
ЛИВИЗ
ulitsa Zhukovskovo 27.
**Map 7 B1.** *Tel 272 1969.*
Liteynyy prospekt 12.
**Map 3 A4.** *Tel 273 6755.*

### Sever
Север
Nevskiy prospekt 104.
**Map 7 B2.** *Tel 273 7436.*

### Supermarket at Passazh
Nevskiy prospekt 46.
**Map 6 F1.** *Tel 315 5257.*

## SOUVENIRS AND CRAFTS

### Imperial Porcelain
Императорский
фарфоровый завод
151 Obukhovskoy
oborony prospekt.
**Map 8 F4.** *Tel 560 8544.*
Vladimirskiy prospekt 7.
**Map 7 A2.** *Tel 713 1513.*
Nevskiy prospekt 160.
**Map 8 D3.** *Tel 717 4838.*

## SOVIET MEMORABILIA

### D.V.K. (Dom Voyennoy Knigi)
Д.В. К. (Дом
военной книги)
Nevskiy prospekt 20.
**Map 6 E1.** *Tel 312 4936.*

### Sekunda
Секунда
(Sovet memorabilia)
Liteynyy prospekt 61
(in the yard).
**Map 7 A2.** *Tel 275 7524.*

### Sobiratel
Собиратель
Sadovaya ulitsa 135.
**Map 6 F1.** *Tel 973 3727.*

## ANTIQUES AND ART

### Anna Nova
ulitsa Zhukovskovo 28.
**Map 7 B1.** *Tel 275 9762.*

### Antikvariat
Антиквариат
Malaya Morskaya ulitsa 21.
**Map 6 D1.** *Tel 571 2643.*

### Antique Centre
Центр антикварной
торговли
3-ya Sovetskaya ulitsa 36/5.
**Map 7 C2.** *Tel 327 8271.*

### Ars Magna
Kamennoostrovskiy
prospekt 26/28, No. 45.
**Map 2 D1.** *Tel 232 4535.*

### Borey
Борей
Liteynyy prospekt 58.
**Map 7 A1.** *Tel 275 3837.*

### Pushkinskaya 10
Пушкинская 10
(The Door Gallery,
Naviuila Artis, Art-Liga,
New Academy of Fine
Arts, Nonconformists'
Museum)
Ligovskiy prospekt 53.
**Map 7 B3.** *Tel 764 5371.*

### Rapsodiya
Рапсодия
Bolshaya Konyushennaya
ulitsa 13 (in courtyard).
**Map 2 E5.** *Tel 314 4801.*

### Russkaya Starina
Русская Старина
Nevskiy prospekt 20.
**Map 6 E1.** *Tel 320 6622.*

### S.P.A.S.
С. П.А.С.
Naberezhnaya reki
Moyki 93.
**Map 5 C2.** *Tel 571 4260.*

### Tertia
Терция
Italyanskaya ulitsa 5.
**Map 6 E1.** *Tel 710 5568.*

### Union of Artists
Союз художников
Bolshaya Morskaya
ulitsa 38. **Map 6 D2.**
*Tel 314 3060.*

## BOOKS, FILM AND MUSIC

### Akademkniga
Академкнига
Liteynyy prospekt 57.
**Map 7 A1.** *Tel 272 3665.*

### Anglia
Англия
Naberezhnaya reki
Fontanki 40.
**Map 7 A2.** *Tel 579 8284.*

### Bookvoed
Буквоед
Ligovskiy prospekt 10.
**Map 7 C2.** *Tel 346 5327.*

### Dom Knigi
Дом книги
Nevskiy prospekt 28.
**Map 6 E1.**
*Tel 448 2355.*

### Kailas
Кайлас
Pushkinskaya ulitsa 10.
**Map 7 B2.** *Tel 764 2668.*

### Na Liteynom
На Литейном
(Books and antiques)
Liteynyy prospekt 61.
**Map 7 A2.** *Tel 275 3874.*

### Severnaya Lira
Северная лира
Nevskiy prospekt 26.
**Map 6 E1.** *Tel 312 0796.*

### Staraya Kniga
Старая книга
Nevskiy prospekt 3.
**Map 6 D1.** *Tel 312 1620.*

### Writers' Bookshop
Лавка писателя
Nevskiy prospekt 66.
**Map 7 A2.** *Tel 314 4858.*

## FURS AND FASHION

### Ananov
Ананов
Nevskiy prospekt 31.
**Map 6 E1.** *Tel 314 1952.*

### Hat Shop
Шляпный магазин
ulitsa Zhukovskovo 11.
**Map 7 B1.**

### Lena
Лена
Nevskiy prospekt 50.
**Map 6 F1.** *Tel 571 7169.*

### Paloma
Палома
Bolshaya Konyushennaya
ulitsa 27.
**Map 6 E1.** *Tel 314 7262.*
Malaya Morskaya ulitsa 8.
**Map 6 D1.** *Tel 315 7912.*

### Russkiye Samotsvety
Русские Самоцветы
Bolshoi prospekt 45.
**Map 1 C2.**
*Tel 232 7856.*

### Slavyanskiy Stil
Славянский стиль
Pushkinskaya ulitsa 3.
**Map 7 B2.**
*Tel 325 8599.*

### Tatyana Parfyonova
Татьяна Парфенова
модный дом
Nevskiy prospekt 51.
**Map 7 B2.**
*Tel 713 3669.*

# ENTERTAINMENT IN ST PETERSBURG

St Petersburg has an impressive and varied choice of entertainment. Its ballet, opera, classical music and theatre are among the best in the world. In addition to the high culture, a thriving and vibrant nightlife is made up of numerous rock and jazz clubs, bars, art cafés, discos, nightclubs and casinos.

Increasingly, international artists are adding St Petersburg to their tours, and mainstream now exists harmoniously alongside underground in music, theatre and cinema. The St Petersburg Philharmonia and the Mariinskiy (Kirov) ballet and opera *(see p119)* deserve their impressive international reputations, though this does mean that they are often away on tour.

St Petersburg's entertainment changes with the seasons. In winter there are concerts and other traditional indoor events. Summer starts with the White Nights, followed by a mass of festivals and outdoor events.

**Folk dancer**

The magnificent, gilded interior of the Yusupov Theatre

## ENTERTAINMENT INFORMATION

St Petersburg can be quite a difficult city to keep up with, as both official and unofficial events are organized at short notice. For example, theatre programmes are not announced more than a couple of months in advance, so it's important to keep alert in order not to miss the fun.

The best (albeit incomplete) listings in English can be found in the Friday edition of *The St Petersburg Times*, a twice-weekly newspaper, and in the monthly magazine *Pulse (see p217)*, both free in hotels, foreign bars and museums. A much broader range of information is provided in Russian in two bi-weekly listings magazines: *Afisha* (www. spb.afisha.com) and *Time Out* (www.spb.timeout.ru).

**Mariinskiy poster pillar**

Tickets can be booked on the Russian-language website www.bileter.ru.

Most traditional theatres and concert halls close down for July, August and part of September because their troupes go on tour. Whilst this may deprive visitors of local performers, some theatres bring in guest troupes from Moscow and abroad. In addition, other venues such as the Hermitage *(see p84)* and Aleksandrinskiy *(see p203)* theatres launch summer programmes that are aimed at tourists. It is worth noting that, although they are fun, their opera and ballet shows are sometimes not of the highest quality.

Matinees start at noon and most evening performances at 7pm. To avoid disappointment check tickets carefully so you know when to arrive.

## BUYING TICKETS

Most people buy their tickets with cash and in person. Theatre ticket offices and kiosks can be found all over town, offering tickets up to a month in advance. They display a full programme (in Russian) of all theatre and classical music performances for the next 20 days and are generally open daily from 10am–1pm and 4–7pm. Offices within theatres usually work from 11am–3pm and 4–7pm and sell tickets for all advertised concerts. Non-Russian speakers should not be nervous: most ticket cashiers will be helpful and patient while you point to the date you want. Tickets can also be booked by your hotel concierge. The Mariinskiy Theatre has an excellent English-language website on which tickets can be bought (www.mariinsky.ru). Similar services for other theatres are offered on www.artis.spb.ru.

A few venues, notably the Mariinskiy Theatre *(see p119)*, have price bands, with some tickets set aside at a cheaper rate and available only to Russian citizens. Non-Russians trying to use these may be refused entry or asked to pay the difference in price. Visitors, however, may obtain tickets for sold-out performances at the Mariinskiy Theatre if they go on the day.

As in most cities, touts sell tickets for major events, but beware of possible fakes and inflated prices.

**Spectacular performance of the famous *Sleeping Beauty* ballet**

## LATE-NIGHT TRANSPORT

The metro closes its doors soon after midnight and buses run until 12:15am (infrequently after 11pm). There is no all-night public transport, so expect to take a taxi late at night. Avoid any taxis which wait outside foreign hotels and bars as they charge extortionate prices (*see p227*).

## CHILDREN'S ENTERTAINMENT

Many theatres put on plays in Russian especially for children. See the children's section of *Afisha* or *Time Out*. Unfortunately, few give English-language perform-ances except at New Year. No language problems occur at the **Circus**, however, or at the **Dolphinarium** on Krestovskiy Island.

Some of the best shows and concerts for children are held at **Zazerkalye**, while the puppet theatres usually have several productions based on well-known fairytales.

For the "real" Russian winter experience, try a *troika* (sleigh) ride. These are offered at Pavlosk (*see pp158–61*) and at

Shuvalovka, a reproduction Russian village. Located 30 km (19 miles) out of town, Shuvalovka is open throughout the year and includes wooden houses in 17th-century Russian style, a skating rink, ice slides, a working smithy and a museum of peasant life. Take any minibus to Peterhof from Avtovo metro and ask the driver to stop at Shuvalovka.

## FESTIVALS

The several White Nights festivals (*see p51*) draw some of the big names of pop and classical music, and ticket prices go up accordingly – as do accommodation rates – during this time. But there are plenty of other worthwhile seasonal festivals. The White Days (taking in Russian Christmas on 7 January, when the city is shrouded in snow) and Shrovetide festivals place the accent on Russian culture.

Numerous jazz festivals (look out for SKIF in April), the long-standing Early Music Festival (Sep and Oct), along with feature and documentary cinema festivals ensure that the city entertainment scene thrives all year round.

# The Arts

For a city renowned worldwide for its rich tradition of ballet and classical music, it is not surprising that St Petersburg has a wide range of cultural events on offer. An evening at the Mariinskiy Theatre, along with its Concert Hall, is a highlight of any visit. It is also well worth venturing into the many other theatres, music halls and churches to absorb the city's cultural diversity. Classical music is vastly popular and local orchestras are much in demand the world over. In addition, there are the evocative sounds of church choirs, the lively ambience of folk cabarets, and numerous festivals *(see pp50–53)* held to encourage young musicians, composers, film-makers and dancers.

## MARIINSKIY THEATRE

The **Mariinskiy Theatre** *(see p119)*, the epitome of the best in Russian ballet and opera, is still waiting for its new stage. However, the venue is open to the public and gives performances regularly. Its Concert Hall, which opened in 2007, is one of the principal venues for the stars of the White Nights festival. For the most up-to-date information on the theatre's plans and to see the current programme, check the website and keep an eye on the listings.

## BALLET

Some of the best dancers in the world come from the **Mariinskiy** *(see p119)*. Tickets for performances by leading ballerinas Ulyana Lopatkina and Diana Vishneva are hard to come by. One of the highlights of the year is the Christmas performance of *The Nutcracker*, danced by children from the Vaganova Ballet School *(see p110)*. Ballet at the **Mussorgsky Opera and Ballet Theatre** and the **Conservatory Opera and Ballet Theatre** *(see p120)* are of more varied quality but still provide good entertainment.

In summer, many troupes perform for tourists in various theatres, but with inconsistent levels of skill. Boris Eifmann's modern ballet company and Valery Mikhaylovskiy's all-male Muzhskoy Ballet are popular with locals, and play at venues like the **October Concert Hall**.

## OPERA

Tchaikovsky's opera *Eugene Onegin* and Mussorgsky's *Boris Godunov* remain stalwarts in any repertory. Operas are performed (usually in their original language) at the **Mikhailovsky Theatre** and at the **Mariinskiy**. Look out for local stars Anna Netrebko and Olga Borodina, or the tenor Vladimir Galuzin. Less common works, including 18th-century chamber operas, are performed by **St Petersburg Opera** on their own stage, and at the **Hermitage** and tiny **Yusupov Theatres**. Look out for sparkling productions at the children's theatre **Zazerkalye** *(see p201)*.

## CLASSICAL MUSIC

The city's classical repertoire is huge. Tchaikovsky, Shostakovich, Mussorgsky and Rimsky-Korsakov lived in St Petersburg and their music is performed here frequently.

**The Great Hall of the Philharmonia** *(see p98)*, the **Small Hall of the Philharmonia** *(see p48)* and the **Academic Capella** *(see p112)* are historic venues for classical concerts. The former is the home of the St Petersburg Philharmonic Orchestra. Other historic locations used for concerts include the Hermitage *(see p84)*, and the palaces of Tsarskoe Selo *(see p150)* and Sheremetev *(see p129)*. Events are adver-tised specially. By contrast, **Dom Kochnevoy** is an intimate space for chamber music.

## CHURCH MUSIC

The music of an Orthodox choir is one of the most evocative sounds in Russia. The best are heard on Saturday evenings and Sunday mornings at the **Holy Trinity Cathedral** in Alexander Nevsky Monastery *(see p130)* and at the **Cathedral of the Transfiguration** *(see p127)*. Services in the **Cathedral of our Lady of Kazan** *(see p111)* are also of a high standard. More formal religious music is performed in the **Smolnyy Cathedral** *(see p128)*.

## FOLK MUSIC

The tourist industry encour-ages visits to concerts of Russian folk music and danc-ing, some of which are very good. The best are found at **Beloselskiy-Belozerskiy** and **Nikolaevskiy Palace**. Many restaurants, such as **St Petersburg** *(see p188)*, have a folk cabaret, though these can be kitsch and loud. **Podvorye** restaurant *(see p191)* in Pavlovsk, however, has an excellent, small ensemble.

## STREET MUSIC

Democracy had the unex-pected effect of allowing many informal activities such as busking, which brought some highly talented musicians onto the streets. Today, as skilled players stake their pitches, the sound of music fills the city's streets. The two underpasses beneath Nevskiy prospekt by Gostinyy Dvor are busy busking spots, while other metro stations are popular sites for old ladies singing Russian ballads of love.

## THEATRE

All performances are in Russian. For non-Russian speakers, productions of classic plays such as *The Cherry Orchard* may be interesting to experience, but more obscure works can prove difficult.

Since the days of the Soviet Union, the leading light in the drama world has been the **Bolshoy Drama Theatre** (BDT). The **Alexandrinskiy**

**Theatre** *(see p110)* is the oldest in Russia; one of the newest is the **Molodyozhnyy (Youth) Theatre**. In recent years, Lev Dodin's direction of the **Malyy Drama Theatre (MDT)** has brought it international fame as the "Theatre of Europe", even though all performances are in Russian.

## CINEMA

Most cinemas now show Hollywood blockbusters, but the majority of foreign films are dubbed into Russian rather than subtitled. **Mirage** holds showings of undubbed films, as do a few Russian cinemas such as **Dom Kino**.

A large number of film festivals are held in the city every year, and these frequently include films in their original language.

The *St Petersburg Times*, *Afisha* and *Time Out* give full coverage of all festivals, including the main **Festival of Festivals** *(see p51)*.

# DIRECTORY

### TICKETS

*Tickets are sold in city kiosks and at individual theatres unless stated otherwise.*

### BALLET AND OPERA

### Conservatory Opera and Ballet Theatre
Театр оперы и балета Консерватории
*Teatr opery i baleta Konservatorii*
Teatralnaya pl 3.
**Map** 5 C3. **Tel** 312 2519.

### Hermitage Theatre
Эрмитажный театр
*Ermitazhnyy teatr*
Dvortsovaya nab 34.
**Map** 2 E5. **Tel** 571 5059.
*(Tickets from city kiosks and hotels only.)*

### Mariinskiy Theatre
Мариинский театр
*Mariinskiy teatr*
Teatralnaya pl 1.
**Map** 5 B3.
**Tel** 326 4141.
**www**.mariinsky.ru

### Mikhailovsky Theatre
Михайловский Театр
*Teatr Mikhailovskiy*
Pl Iskusstv 1.
**Map** 6 E1.
**Tel** 595 4305.
● *late Jul–Aug.*
**www**.mikhailovsky.ru

### October Concert Hall
Большой концертный зал Октябрьский
*Bolshoy kontsertnyy zal Oktyabrskiy*
Ligovskiy pr 6.
**Map** 7 C1. **Tel** 275 1273.

### St Petersburg Opera
Санкт-Петербург опера
*Sankt-Petersburg opera*
Galernaya ul 33.
**Map** 5 B2. **Tel** 312 3982.

### Yusupov Theatre
Юсуповский театр
*Yusupovskiy teatr*
Yusupov Palace, nab reki Moyki 94. **Map** 5 B3.
*Tel* 314 9883, 314 1991.

### CLASSICAL MUSIC

### Academic Capella
Академическая Капелла
*Akademicheskaya Kapella*
Nab reki Moyki 20.
**Map** 2 E5.
*Tel* 314 1058.

### Dom Kochnevoy
Лом Кочневой
Nab reki Fontanki 41.
**Map** 6 F2.
*Tel* 310 2987.

### Great Hall of the Philharmonia
Большой зал филармонии
*Bolshoy zal Filarmonii*
Mikhaylovskaya ul 2.
**Map** 6 F1.
*Tel* 710 4257.

### Small Hall of the Philharmonia
Малый зал филармонии
*Malyy zal Filarmonii*
Nevskiy pr 30.
**Map** 6 F1.
*Tel* 571 8333.

### CHURCH MUSIC

### Cathedral of Our Lady of Kazan
Собор Казанской Богоматери
*Sobor Kazanskoy Bogomateri*
Kazanskaya ploshchad 2.
**Map** 6 E1.
🚻 *9am & 7:30pm daily.*

### Cathedral of the Transfiguration
Спасо-Преображенский собор
*Spaso-Preobrazhenskiy sobor*
Preobrazhenskaya pl 1.
**Map** 3 B5.
🚻 *10am & 6pm daily.*

### Holy Trinity Cathedral
Свято-Троицкий собор
*Svyato-Troitskiy sobor*
Alexander Nevsky Monastery, pl Aleksandra-Nevskovo.
**Map** 8 E4.
🚻 *10am & 6pm daily.*

### Smolnyy Cathedral
Смольный собор
*Smolnyy sobor*
Ploshchad Rastrelli 3.
**Map** 4 F4.
*Tel* 577 1421.

### FOLK MUSIC

### Beloselskiy-Belozerskiy Palace
Дворец Белосельских-Белозерских
*Dvorets Beloselskikh-Belozerskikh*
Nevskiy pr 41.
**Map** 7 A2.
*Tel* 315 5236.

### Nikolaevskiy Palace
Николаевский дворец
*Nikolaevskiy dvorets*
Pl Truda 4.
**Map** 5 B2.
*Tel* 312 5500.

### THEATRE

### Alexandrinskiy Theatre
Александринский театр
*Aleksandrinskiy teatr*
Ploshchad Ostrovskovo 6.
**Map** 6 F2.
*Tel* 312 1545.

### Bolshoy Drama Theatre (BDT)
Большой драматический театр
*Bolshoy dramaticheskiy teatr*
Nab reki Fontanki 65.
**Map** 6 F2.
*Tel* 310 9242.

### Malyy Drama Theatre (MDT)
МДТ – Театр Евролы
*MDT – Teatr Evropy*
Ul Rubinshteyna 18.
**Map** 7 A2.
*Tel* 713 2078.

### Molodyozhnyy Theatre
Молодёжный театр на фонтанке
*Molodyozhnyy teatr na Fontanke*
Nab reki Fontanki 114.
**Map** 6 D4.
*Tel* 316 6564.

### CINEMA

### Aurora Cinema
Аврора
Nevskiy pr 60.
**Map** 7 A2.
*Tel* 315 5254.

### Crystal Palace
Кристал Палас
*Kristal-Palace*
Nevskiy pr 72.
**Map** 7 A2.
*Tel* 272 2382.

### Dom Kino
Дом Кино
Ul Karavannaya 12.
**Map** 7 A1.
*Tel* 314 0638.

### Mirage
Мираж
Bolshoy pr 35,
Petrogradskaya.
**Map** 1 C2.
*Tel* 232 4838.

# Live Music and Nightlife

St Petersburg was at the heart of the underground Soviet rock scene and many of the best Russian sounds originate here. The nightclub scene offers mostly techno music and mainstream pop, in vast complexes with strobe lights, and attracts the well-paid young and *nouveaux riches*. Some smaller clubs featuring an eclectic mix describe themselves as "art" clubs or cafés, and host live music one night and *avant-garde* fashion shows or films the next. Some large clubs and casinos accept credit cards. Where hours are not given, check programmes before heading out. Avoid places that admit foreigners or females free.

## ART AND CAFE CLUBS

**Fish Fabrique** is probably the oldest art café in town, having survived the ups and downs of recent Russian history, but it is facing strong competition from newcomers. **Che** offers a mixture of classical and jazz concerts, with poetry readings as well as family-friendly kids' mornings on Sundays. **GEZ-21** even manages to fit philosophy readings in amongst rock concerts.

## ROCK VENUES

Under the Soviet regime, Leningrad rock was rebellious without being overtly political. Though there is now less emphasis on poetical lyrics that express a spirit of freedom from control and repression, Russian rock still owes much to its rebellious past, while also managing to incorporate the latest in Western music trends.

**Red Club** is the most adventurous club, but **Pyatnitsa**, with its rowdy punk bands, is good for a high. Rockabilly gave birth to **Money Honey** and to the **City Club** upstairs (for older rockers), which in turn led to an explosion of rockabilly groups in the city.

Big-name, massed audience rock and pop concerts are usually held in one of the big concert halls such as the **Oktyabrskiy Bolshoy Kontsertnyy Zal**, or the most prestigious of them all, the **Ledovyy Dvorets**. When Paul McCartney came to town, however, he performed on a specially erected stage in Palace Square.

## JAZZ VENUES

The father of Petersburg jazz is David Goloshchokin, who set up the **Jazz Philharmonic Hall**. As the name suggests, the jazz played in the hall is mainly very traditional, and, sadly, dancing or talking are prohibited. In recent years, **JFC** has led the way for improvisation and innovative jazz. Guests here are often musicians with an international reputation. **Jimi Hendrix Blues Club** comes a close second to JFC by virtue of its mixture of blues and rock, and its good food.

Restaurants such as **Sunduk** (*see p190*) often bring in good live performers. **Street Life** is a classy restaurant-club with room for 150 people.

## BARS WITH MUSIC

Live music is played in many bars around town, but on the whole a lot of the music in such places is awful. It is best to stick with the established, more reliable clubs.

**Liverpool**, for example, hosts live bands, not all of whom play Beatles cover versions. In addition, **Manhattan** sometimes has good jazz acts. The only problem with **Tsinik** is that it is often difficult to hear the music above the noise made by the clientele.

## NIGHTCLUBS AND DISCOS

Big entertainment complexes such as **Metro** (with three floors) cater mainly to the young and upwardly mobile, playing house, techno and Russian dance music. **Havana Club** has Latin evenings, but also plays house and pop, and boasts a pool and chill-out room. Despite its location in the high-rise suburbs of the city, **Prosvet** has a good concert and DJ programme.

**Tribunal** has a policy of playing only mainstream music, and thus manges to attract a huge crowd during summer months, when young tourists stream in.

Smaller, more diverse clubs, such as the underground **Griboedov**, are still very much of the alternative culture trend, playing a variety of the latest hits from Europe, and hosting fashion shows and other cultural events. **Tunnel** – which tends to come and go, but is always good when it is is active – specializes in techno and electronic dance music. **Jakata** has an excellent record, but perhaps some of the strictest "face control" in town. Be cool, or don't bother to come near.

## GAY CLUBS

For some reason, few gay clubs in St Petersburg manage to last more than four or five years. **Greshniki** is, however, an exception, remaining popular while other venues come and go; and **Cabaret** seems to have made a go of it, too. Gay culture in the city is strongly tied into the art world, and events are advertised at Saturday exhibitions in the New Academy of Fine Arts at Pushkinskaya ulitsa 10. The only dedicated lesbian club is **TriEl**.

## CASINOS

In an attempt to increase security for clients, and to get away from a past reputation for sleaziness, all respectable casinos now form part of large complexes incorporating excellent restaurants and bars.

Stand-alone casinos and those further from the centre of the city tend to be high risk for punters. Others offer highly risqué floorshows and attract a less polished clientele. Such establishments are not listed.

# DIRECTORY

## ART AND CAFE CLUBS

### Che
Poltavskaya ul 3.
**Map** 8 D3.
**Tel** 277 7600.
⭘ 24 hours.
www.cafeclubche.ru

### Fish Fabrique
Ligovskiy pr 53.
**Map** 7 B3.
**Tel** 764 4857.
⭘ 3pm–6am daily.
www.fishfabrique.spb.ru

### GEZ-21
ГЕЗ-21
Ligovskiy pr 53.
**Map** 7 B3.
**Tel** 764 5263.
www.tac.spb.ru

## ROCK VENUES

### Arctica
Арктика
Ul Beringa 38.
**Tel** 715 4838.

### Ledovyy Dvorets
Ледовый дврец
Pr Pyatiletok 1.
**Tel** 716 6620.

### Money Honey / City Club
Apraksin dvor block 13,
Sadovaya ul 28–30.
**Map** 6 E2.
**Tel** 310 0549.

### Oktyabrskiy Bolshoy Kontsertnyy Zal
БКЗ Октябрьский
Ligovskiy prospekt 6.
**Map** 7 C1.
**Tel** 275 1300.

### Pyatnitsa
Пятница
Moskovskiy pr 10–12.
**Map** 6 D3.
**Tel** 310 2317.
www.fridayclub.spb.ru

### Red Club
Poltavskaya ul 7.
**Map** 7 C3.
**Tel** 717 1366.
www.clubred.ru

### Yubileynyy Dvorets Sporta
Дворец спорта
юбилейный
Pr Dobrolyubova 18.
**Map** 1 B3.
**Tel** 119 5615.

## JAZZ VENUES

### Jazz Philharmonic Hall
филармония лжазовой музыки
Zagorodnyy prospekt 27.
**Tel** 764 8565.
⭘ 8–11pm Tue–Sun.
www.jazz-hall.spb.ru

### JFC
Shpalernaya ulitsa 33.
**Map** 3 C4.
**Tel** 272 9850.
⭘ 7–11pm daily.
www.jfc.sp.ru

### Jimi Hendrix Blues Club
Джими Хендрикс блюз-клуб
Liteynyy prospekt 33.
**Map** 3 A5.
**Tel** 579 8813.
⭘ 11am–1am daily.
Concerts 8:30pm.

### Street Life
2-ya Krasnoarmeyskaya
Ul 6. **Map** 6 D5.
**Tel** 575 0545.
www.street-life.spb.ru

## BARS WITH MUSIC

### Datscha
Дача
Dumskaya ul 9.
**Map** 6 E2.
⭘ 6pm–6am daily.

### Liverpool
Ливерпуль
Ul Mayakovskovo 16.
**Map** 7 B1.
**Tel** 279 2054.

### Manhattan
Nab reki Fontanki 90.
**Map** 6 E3.
**Tel** 713 1945.
⭘ noon–5am daily.
www.manhattanclub.ru

### Tsinik
Циник
Per Antonenko 4.
**Map** 6 D2.
**Tel** 312 9526.
www.cinic.spb.ru

## NIGHTCLUBS AND DISCOS

### Griboedov
Грибоедов
Voronezhskaya ul 2A.
**Map** 7 B4.
**Tel** 764 4355.
⭘ 6pm–6am.
www.griboedovclub.ru

### Havana Club
Moskovskiy pr 21.
**Map** 6 D5.
**Tel** 259 1155.
⭘ 5pm–6am daily.
www.havanaclub.ru

### Jakata
Ul Bakunina 5.
**Map** 8 D2.
**Tel** 346 7462.

### Metro
Метро
Ligovskiy pr 174.
**Tel** 766 0204.
⭘ 10pm–6am daily.
www.metroclub.ru

### Port
Порт
Per Antonenko 2 (in yard).
**Map** 6 D2.
**Tel** 314 2609.
⭘ 3pm–6am daily.

### Prosvet
Просвет
Ul Bryantseva 11.
**Tel** 594 5000.

### Revolution
Ul Sadovaya 28/30.
**Map** 6 E2.
**Tel** 717 5915, 571 2391.
⭘ 1pm–6am daily.

### Tribunal
Pl Dekabristov 1.
**Map** 5 C1.
**Tel** 311 1690.
⭘ noon–6am daily.

### Tunnel
Тоннель
Corner of Zverinskaya ul
and Lyubanskiy per.
**Map** 1 C3.
**Tel** 233 4015.

## GAY CLUBS

### Cabaret (A.K.A. Matrosskaya Tishina)
Кабаре
Nab Obvodnogo kanala 181.
**Tel** 259 9512.
www.cabarespb.ru

### Greshniki
Грешники
Nab kanala Griboedova 29.
**Map** 6 E2.
**Tel** 570 4291.
www.greshniki.ru

### TriEl
5-ya Sovetskaya ul 45.
**Map** 8 D2.
**Tel** 710 2016.
www.triel.spb.ru

## CASINOS

### Astoria
Казино-клуб Олимпия
Malaya Morskaya ul 22.
**Map** 6 D1.
**Tel** 313 5020.
⭘ 24 hours daily.

### Golden Garden
Vladimirskiy pr 9.
**Map** 7 A2.
**Tel** 572 2244.
⭘ 24 hours daily.

### Olympia
Казино-клуб Олимпия
Liteynyy pr 14.
**Map** 7 A1.
**Tel** 275 5060.
⭘ 24 hours daily.

### Premier
Премьер
Nevskiy prospekt 47.
**Map** 7 A2. **Tel** 703 5370.
⭘ 24 hours daily.

# SURVIVAL
# GUIDE

# PRACTICAL INFORMATION

The street signs and maps of St Petersburg are not as difficult to negotiate as it may first appear when confronted with daunting Cyrillic letters. Not only do hotels, restaurants and all service sectors attempt to compensate by being helpful to foreigners, but in recent times the city has started putting up English signs pointing out major sights and shops. Conventional tourist offices do not exist in the city and information points, along with services such

Logo of the Neva Travel Company

as foreign exchange offices, are often concentrated in hotels and other areas frequented by foreigners. Once out on the street, things will seem unfamiliar, but with patience and determination everything is possible, from making international telephone calls and exchanging money to finding emergency medical treatment. Telecommunications are rapidly gaining ground and, as quality improves, prices come closer to, and occasionally outstrip, Western equivalents.

**Grand Hotel Europe concierge**

## TOURIST INFORMATION

Hotels are the main source of tourist information. In the bigger hotels and mini-hotels the concierge will provide travel and booking services and general assistance. Lesser hotels have a Service Bureau offering similar services, but advice can be indifferent. **Cosmos**, **Neva Travel Company** and the **MIR Travel Company** run reliable, tourist information services as well as booking accommodation and entertainment. Also try www.petersburgcity.com which is a useful English-language website.

English-language newspapers (see p217) give up-to-the-minute useful information.

## EXCURSIONS

Hotels can book guided group tours and day trips in several languages. In addition to city tours and canal cruises, there are day trips to the suburban palaces and

Novgorod (see pp146–65). Both Cosmos and the Neva Travel Company offer several excellent tours. City-run excursions, which gather tourists on Palace Square (see p83) and by the Portik Rusca on Nevskiy prospekt (see p48), tend to be in Russian, as do ordinary river cruises (see p226).

On summer weekends there are helicopter tours operating on a turn-up basis from the Peter and Paul Fortress (see pp66–7). Groups of 20 can book through **Baltic Airlines**.

## ADMISSION CHARGES

Many museums and theatres, notably the Hermitage (see pp84–93), the Russian Museum (see pp104–107) and the Mariinskiy (see p119) charge foreigners more than Russians, although prices are still well below European and American norms. Students and schoolchildren are entitled to discounts. Credit cards are only accepted at some sights.

The ticket office or kassa is often far from the entrance, so look for the КАССА sign.

**Tour helicopter picking up tourists by the Peter and Paul Fortress**

**Sign advertising the MIR Travel Company**

## OPENING HOURS

Most sights open standard hours, 10 or 10:30am to 6pm, with no break for lunch, and close one day a week. They also close one day each month for cleaning; this date varies, so phone to check. Last tickets are sold about one hour before closing. Parks are usually open from 8am to 8pm, later during White Nights.

# ОТКРЫТО

**Sign for open (otkryto)**

# ЗАКРЫТО

**Sign for closed (zakryto)**

## VISITING CHURCHES

Attending an Orthodox service is a fascinating experience. Since services tend to run for several hours, it is generally fine simply to drop in. It is polite to make a donation and certain dress codes must be observed: no shorts; men should remove hats; ladies should cover their shoulders and chest and preferably wear a hat or headscarf. Women in trousers are accepted in town churches, but all monasteries will strictly enforce the no trousers rule. The most important services are on Saturday evening, Sunday morning and on church holidays.

Most major faiths are represented in the city. Churches tend to be open all day from early morning till late. Church service times are published in Friday's *St Petersburg Times (see p217)*.

**Friends greeting with a handshake**

## LANGUAGE

Cyrillic, the alphabet used in the Russian language, is named after the 9th-century monks Cyril and Methodius who invented it. The apparent similarity between Cyrillic and roman letters can be misleading. Some letters are common to both alphabets, others look similar but represent totally different sounds. Various systems of transliteration are in usage, but they do not differ enough to cause serious confusion.

Most people who come into contact with tourists speak some English and passers-by on the street will do their best if asked directions. Knowledge of a few Russian words *(see pp260–4)* is appreciated.

## ETIQUETTE

Despite an ever increasing Westernization of manners and language, the use is still strictly in force of the formal you *(vy)* and the informal *(ty)*.

On public transport, it is accepted that young men should relinquish their seats to children or the elderly.

Smoking is prohibited in cinemas, museums, theatres and on public transport. (Special areas are usually allocated for smoking.) Drinking beer is prohibited in the street.

Russians take great pleasure in smoking and drinking and frequent toasts are required to justify the filling and draining of glasses. At a private home, always toast the hostess *(za khozyayku)* or the host *(za khozyayina)*. Greetings amongst friends involve a handshake (between men) or a kiss, or simply saying – *"privet"* (hi).

**House number and Cyrillic street name**

## PAYING AND TIPPING

Roubles are the sole valid currency in Russia *(see p215)*. All cash payments must be made in roubles only and all prices are given in roubles. Credit cards are accepted in some restaurants and most hotels, as well as larger shops.

Tipping is a matter of choice, but baggage handlers at the airport and the train station may ask for exorbitant sums. Do not lose your nerve, however, and simply pay what you feel is right; a few dollars are usually quite sufficient.

## ADDRESSES

Russian addresses are given in reverse order: index/zip code, city, street name, house number, apartment number and finally name of person.

After 1917, when the city was renamed Leningrad, many streets and sights were renamed to avoid imperial connotations or in order to commemorate Soviet heroes. Since the city resumed its original name after a referendum in 1991, most streets in the centre have officially reverted to their pre-1917 names. The area surrounding the city, however, is still the Leningrad Region. Many people happily use both the original and Soviet names; no offence is caused when one is used in preference to another.

| Index/ zip code | City | Street name |
|---|---|---|

193015 Санкт Петербург
улица Восстания
д. 34, кв. 52
Милане Прекрасной

| House number | Apartment number | Name of recipient |
|---|---|---|

---

**Dvortsovyy most (leading to Vasilevskiy Island), raised to allow ships access along the Neva**

## BRIDGE OPENING TIMES

From early April until mid-November, when navigation is possible on the Neva river, all its bridges but the new Vantoviy Most are raised between approximately 2am and 5am. This timetable is a guide, but variations do occur.

**Dvortsovyy most**: 1:25–4:50am.
**Troitskiy most**: 1:50–4:50am.
**Blagoveshchenskiy most**: 1:40–4:55am.
**Liteynyy most**: 1:10–4:45am.
**Birzhevoy most**: 2:00–4:55am.
**Tuchkov most**: 2:10–3:05am & 3:35–4:55am.
**Bolsheokhtinskiy most**: 2:20–5:00am.
**Most Aleksandra Nevskovo**: 1:30–5:10am.
**Volodarskiy most**: 2:10–3:45am & 4:15–5:45am.

**Information office, offering free advice and literature to visitors**

## VISAS

Visas are required for all visitors to Russia. Package tour companies will organize visas for you, but independent travellers need to arrange their own. This can be a complex, time-consuming process. Document requirements change regularly and it is essential to check these in advance. You will need to show proof of either pre-booked accommodation or an invitation (visa support) from a tour company, business or private individual in Russia. **Cosmos** and the **Neva Travel Company** can fax express invitations directly. Private invitations cannot be faxed and the process of issuing them takes at least one month through **OVIR** (Visa Registration Dept). The easiest option is to pay your travel agency to process the visa for you. The alternative is to go along in person to the Russian Embassy where visas are issued.

The cost of a tourist visa is around £30 for British nationals, and around $100 for US citizens. A visa usually takes ten days, but for an extra fee can be arranged in a single day.

Inside Russia, visa extensions can only be granted by the organization which issued the initial invitation. If you over-stay, expect to be stopped at the airport and turned back until you have either obtained the necessary extension visa or paid a considerable fine.

## CUSTOMS AND IMMIGRATION

Passports and visas are checked thoroughly at immigration. All visitors must fill out an immigration card, which is available in Russian and English. Part of the completed card is retained by travellers for presentation on departure.

Essentially there are no limitations on the amount of money people are allowed to bring into Russia; you are also allowed to export Russian money as long as the value does not exceed US$10,000. Any items of considerable value, such as diamond jewellery and computers, should be noted on a customs form on entry. All such valuables must be re-exported, or import duty will be charged. You should be aware that on arrival and also on departure, all items of luggage may be put through X-ray machines.

Bear in mind that the departure customs are particularly strict when it comes to dealing with works of art and antiques (see p194), but there should be no problem at all with modest quantities of ordinary, everyday consumer goods.

## REGISTRATION

All foreigners must register with **OVIR** within three days of arrival, and obtain a stamp of registration on their registration card. Hotels do this for their guests (as do **Cosmos** and **MIR**), but those staying in private accommodation must register at the branch of **OVIR** where their invitation was issued. For an extended visa an application must be made at the same branch. Visitors who forget to register can be fined and prevented from leaving Russia until all the necessary paperwork is in order.

## EMBASSIES AND CONSULATES

Anyone intending to reside in Russia for longer than three months is advised to register with their consulate or embassy. If visitors are hospitalized, robbed, imprisoned or otherwise rendered helpless, consular officials will help make arrangements, find an interpreter, or at least offer advice. They can re-issue passports and in some emergency cases provide money to get visitors home.

Great Britain, USA, Canada and Australia have consulates in St Petersburg. Visitors from New Zealand or Ireland, however, would have to contact their embassies in Moscow.

## DISABLED TRAVELLERS

St Petersburg has almost no facilities for the disabled. Transport is inaccessible, entrances have steps and narrow doors and there are rarely public lifts. It takes real determination for disabled travellers to get around.

## STUDENT TRAVELLERS

An international student card entitles its holder to discounts in museums, and on rail and air travel if it is booked through Sindbad Travel at the **St Petersburg International Youth Hostel** (see p170).

**HOSTELLING RUSSIA**

**Sign for the St Petersburg International Youth Hostel**

## TRAVELLING WITH CHILDREN

**Men's toilet sign**

Russians adore children, and travellers in the company of under-tens are likely to attract a good deal of attention and many compliments. Russian *babushki* (grannies) also think nothing of telling parents of their failings.

**Women's toilet sign**

The city has many play parks and during school holidays temporary playgrounds are sometimes set up around town.

Museums and public transport are free for under-fives. Schoolchildren pay the full price on transport but pay a reduced price at museums.

**Children playing on temporary bouncy castle in Palace Square**

## PUBLIC TOILETS

The situation is improving, but some public toilets are quite basic, and a few cafés do not have any toilet facilities at all. In such cases, go to the nearest hotel or, if lacking an alternative, use the pay toilets in department stores, for example. The person who takes the money hands out toilet paper rations.

## PHOTOGRAPHY

Photographic restrictions have more or less disappeared, except in the metro. In museums expect to purchase a ticket for the right to photograph or video. Tripods and flashes are prohibited.

## ELECTRICAL APPLIANCES

The electrical current is 220 V. Two-pin plugs are required, but some of the old Soviet two-pin sockets do not take modern European plugs which have slightly thicker pins. American appliances require a 220:110 current adaptor. Adaptors are widely available in St Petersburg.

## TIME DIFFERENCE

St Petersburg follows Moscow time, which is three hours ahead of Greenwich Mean Time (GMT), and eight hours ahead of Eastern Standard Time. In line with the rest of Europe, Russia puts its clocks forward one hour at the end of March and back one hour at the end of October.

## CONVERSION TABLE

**Imperial to Metric**
1 inch = 2.54 centimetres
1 foot = 30 centimetres
1 mile = 1.6 kilometres
1 ounce = 28 grams
1 pound = 454 grams
1 pint = 0.6 litres
1 UK gallon = 4.6 litres

**Metric to Imperial**
1 centimetre = 0.4 inches
1 metre = 3 feet, 3 inches
1 kilometre = 0.6 miles
1 gram = 0.04 ounces
1 kilogram = 2.2 pounds
1 litre = 1.8 UK pints

**Standard Russian two-pin plug**

# DIRECTORY

### TOURIST INFORMATION AND GUIDED TOURS

**Baltic Airlines**
*Baltiyskie avialinii*
Nevskiy pr 7/9. **Map** 6 D1.
*Tel* 710 1676.
www.balticairlines.ru

**Cosmos**
Vasilevskiy Island, 2-ya
Liniya 35. **Map** 1 A5.
*Tel* 327 7256.
www.guide.spb.ru

**MIR Travel Company**
Nevskiy pr 11. **Map** 6 D1.
*Tel* 325 7122.
www.mir-travel.com

**Neva Travel Company**
Ul Prof Popova 28.
*Tel* 234 0082.
www.nevatravel.ru

### VISA FORMALITIES IN UK AND US

**Go Russia Limited**
Boundary House, Boston
Road, London, W7 2QE.
*Tel* (020) 3355 7717.

**Visit Russia**
257 West 39th St, Studio
39, New York, NY 10018.
*Tel* (1800) 755 3080.

### VISA FORMALITIES IN RUSSIA

**OVIR**
Овир
*(Tsentralnyy district)*
Foreign department,
Pereulok Krylova 5.
**Map** 6 F2. *Tel* 315 7936.
◻ 10am–6pm Mon–Fri.
*(Central)* Ul Kirochnaya 4.
**Map** 3 B5. *Tel* 278 3486.
www.visatorussia.com

### EMBASSIES AND CONSULATES

**Australia**
Moscow, Podkolokolny
pereulok 10/A2.
*Tel* (495) 956 6070.
www.russia.embassy.gov.
au

**Canada**
Moscow, Starokonju-
shenny per 23.
*Tel* (495) 925 6000.

**Ireland**
Moscow, Grokholskiy per 5.
*Tel* (495) 937 5911.

**New Zealand**
Moscow, Povorskaya ul 44.
*Tel* (495) 956 3579.

**UK**
Pl Proletarskoy Diktatury 5.
**Map** 4 E4. *Tel* 320 3200.

### US
Furshtatskaya ul.15.
**Map** 3 B4. *Tel* 331 2600.
*Fax* 331 2852.

### DISABLED TRAVEL

**RADAR**
Unit 12, City Forum, 250
City Road, London EC1V
8AF. *Tel* (020) 7250 3222.

**SATH (Society for Accessible Travel & Hospitality**
347 Fifth Ave, Suite 605,
New York, NY 10016.
*Tel* (212) 447 7284.

### STUDENT TRAVEL

**St Petersburg Int. Youth Hostel**
3-ya Sovetskaya ul 28.
**Map** 7 C2. *Tel* 329 8018.
www.ryh.ru

# Personal Security and Health

Despite lurid media reports worldwide about the activities of the mafia, St Petersburg is still a relatively safe city. Petty crime should be the only concern for tourists, and even this can generally be avoided if the usual precautions are taken. Make copies of your passport and visa, note traveller's cheque and credit card numbers and, for language reasons, keep a card with your Russian address on it.

Medical insurance is essential, as local healthcare compares poorly with Western standards, and English-speaking services or medical evacuation via Finland are very expensive. Many medicines are readily available, but it is best to bring specific medicines needed.

**Traffic policeman checking papers**

## PROTECTING YOUR PROPERTY

Every visitor to Russia is seriously advised to take out travel insurance. Once in St Petersburg, simple rules should be observed, such as not displaying large sums of money; carrying cash in a concealed money belt; and keeping passports, tickets and all valuables in the hotel safe whenever possible. Security in Western-run hotels is very high, but in all hotels it is advisable to place valuables in the safe. Traveller's cheques (see p214) may have an insurance policy but are expensive to use and are easily laundered in Russia.

Avoid the "gypsies" who occasionally group on Nevskiy prospekt, apparently begging. If they do approach, do not stop for them and keep a firm hold of your possessions.

If you have property stolen, report it to the local police station for insurance purposes. They are unlikely to have an interpreter, so ask your hotel for assistance.

## PERSONAL SAFETY

The greatest danger faced by foreigners is that posed by pickpockets and petty thieves because there is a danger that they

might use violence if they meet with resistance. As in any country, it is advisable to hand over belongings that are demanded with menace.

The supposed mafia, an organization that is largely overrated by the media, has no contact with tourists, who are generally much less wealthy than Russian businessmen these days.

Women on their own are unlikely to encounter sexual harrassment, though they should ignore kerbcrawlers and avoid taking a cab alone at night. Of course, there is no such thing as a completely safe place, so always be alert and make sure that you take responsibility for your own safety. The main threats on the streets come from local drivers, who see all pedestrians as a nuisance, and from manhole covers, which tend to rock or even collapse under your feet. This can be hilarious to watch on a movie screen, but is not so funny if it happens to you in real life.

**New-look police fleet car**

**Free, state-run ambulance service**

**Fire engine**

## POLICE

Several kinds of police operate on St Petersburg's streets. Their uniforms change according to the weather, with the very neccessary addition of fur hats and big overcoats in the winter. The street officers or militia *(militsya)* wear dark blue-grey combat-style uniforms

**Militsya policeman**

and many carry guns. Their uniform is very similar to that worn by the riot police or OMON, the only obvious difference being in the badges.

Separate from both these are the traffic police, whose uniforms carry the logo ДПС (DPS) on the chest and shoulder. They have the authority to stop any vehicle to check documents.

Both the militia and traffic police supplement their low income by fining people for minor infringements of the law, notably for crossing Nevskiy prospekt between signals. It is best to pay the moderate "fine" imposed – about 100 roubles – but object if more is demanded.

## PHARMACIES

The best pharmacies *(apteka)*, are located along Nevskiy prospekt. These sell many imported medicines, some with Russian instructions, others in their original language. Strong medications can be bought over the counter, so prescriptions are not necessary. Every assistant is a trained pharmacist and can advise alternative drugs. If you have specific requirements, particularly insulin, bring sufficient supplies for your stay.

## MEDICAL TREATMENT

If you fall ill, seek advice at your hotel, which should have its own doctor. Several companies, notably the **Medem International Clinic** and **Euromed**, specialize in dealing with foreigners. They cover everything from dental care, X-rays and pre-natal care to medical evacuation. Their charges are fairly high, but they are used to dealing with foreign insurance policies. They all have English-speaking Russian doctors, and can deal competently with minor emergencies.

For those in need of immediate attention, the casualty department of the **Trauma Clinic of the Central District** is just off Nevskiy prospekt. English is not spoken here, but basic care involving stitches or injections can be administered.

If you are taken to a local hospital and require further treatment, it is best to contact either your consulate or one of the above medical centres. They can either have you moved or they can oversee your treatment in the hospital.

A good dentist can be fiendishly expensive in St Petersburg. The medical clinics listed opposite are good and are covered by insurance policies. Others such as the **Dental Palace** are also good, but costs will not be reimbursed.

## HEALTH PRECAUTIONS

Neither visitors nor residents should drink tap water, which contains heavy metals and *giardia*, a parasite causing stomach problems. To be safe drink bottled water only. If you do pick up *giardia*, it can be treated with metronidazole.

Russian food, on the other hand, is unlikely to do much harm. Avoid the meat pies sold on the streets.

On the rise are syphilis, HIV and other sexually transmitted diseases, so all due caution should be exercised.

## MOSQUITOES

Mosquitoes *(komari)* are rife between June and late September. Repellents are available locally but to avoid missing any sleep it is best to come well equipped. Burning oils or plugs which heat chemical tablets are recommended for use at night time.

**АПТЕКА**

**Sign for pharmacy or** *apteka*

# Banking and Local Currency

St Petersburg is moving into the credit card age, and major European debit and credit cards can now be used in hotels, as well as in some restaurants and shops. In all other places, however, cash remains the norm, and roubles are the only legal currency. The city is well provided with exchange points and cash dispensers where visitors can turn their currency (US dollars and euros are still the most popular) into roubles. It is wise to do a little personal research or to visit a few exchange points before exchanging money, as commission rates offered do vary.

## CHANGING MONEY

Roubles are difficult to obtain outside Russia, but there are numerous exchange offices throughout St Petersburg, including at the airport.

Some exchange offices are open for 24 hours a day. A passport has to be shown when changing money. Any visible defect on foreign bank notes, especially vertical tears or ink or water stains, makes them extremely difficult to exchange. Travellers should make sure that all the bank notes they bring into Russia are in good condition, and that any US dollars were issued after 1990.

Because bank rates are so good in St Petersburg, visitors should never be tempted to change their money on the streets, however appealing the rates on offer from individuals appear to be. The unpleasant truth is that street-changers will try to cheat anyone willing to take the risk.

**Automatic cash dispenser**

**CURRENCY EXCHANGE**
**ОБМЕН ВАЛЮТЫ**
Принимаем старые и ветхие купюры $US, DM

**A sign for a currency exchange office (obmen valyuty)**

## BANKS AND EXCHANGE OFFICES

A few of the foreign banks in St Petersburg offer over-the-counter services. The most reliable Russian bank is **Sberbank.**

Exchange offices are plentiful in St Petersburg. They are often branches of banks, offering both cash currency exchange, and cash advances on credit or debit cards. Larger branches also cash travellers' cheques. Exchange offices often work long hours. Sberbank exchange rates are not particularly high, but there are branches conveniently located all over the city.

A fast and safe, but expensive, way of transferring cash to Russia is by Western Union, which has offices in most banks now.

## CREDIT CARDS

It is possible to obtain both roubles and US dollars with a credit card through the larger banks and from the automatic cash dispensers that are springing up all over town. The local commission is between 2 and 5 per cent, plus credit card charges. (This can work out as cheap as or cheaper than bringing cash to change.) The most accepted cards are VISA, MasterCard and Eurocard. Diners Club and American Express are less

widely recognized. Cash dispensers at **Alfabank** and in the Hermitage offer more cash per transaction than others. Less commission is charged for cash in roubles.

Lost or stolen credit cards should be reported immediately to the credit card company.

## TRAVELLERS' CHEQUES

Banks charge at least 3 per cent to cash travellers' cheques. However, only large banks, such as Alfabank and Sberbank, offer this service. The cheapest alternative is American Express cheques, with a 2 per cent commission if cashed at the American Express office. Travellers' cheques can only be used as payment for goods or services in a few large hotels, and are acceptable only in US dollars and euros. You will need to present your passport whenever exchanging or paying with travellers' cheques.

## LOCAL CURRENCY

The Russian currency is the rouble (or ruble), written рубль or abbreviated to p or руб. The higher denominations of roubles are currently available in banknotes, which all bear images of well-known Russian cities, the lower denominations in coins. The kopek, of which there are 100 in a rouble, is issued in coins.

Take note that bank notes and coins issued before 1997 (that is, before the rouble was revalued owing to its stronger value and lower inflation) are not legal tender.

### Banknotes
*There are 6 denominations of notes, with values of 10, 50, 100, 500, 1,000 and 5,000 roubles. They have the same design as their pre-revaluation equivalents. When changing money check that the notes correspond to those shown here.*

### Coins
*The revaluation of the Russian rouble in 1998 led to the revival of the long-redundant but much-loved kopek. Traditionally, the rouble had always consisted of 100 kopeks. As well as coins for 1, 2 and 5 roubles, there are now coins for 1, 5, 10 and 50 kopeks. Any coins which were issued before 1997, prior to revaluation, are essentially valueless and you are perfectly within your rights to refuse to accept them if they are given to you in your change.*

10 roubles

50 roubles

100 roubles

500 roubles

1,000 roubles

1 rouble

2 roubles

5 roubles

1 kopek

5 kopeks

10 kopeks

50 kopeks

# Communications

**International telephone sign**

Telecommunications is one of the biggest growth areas in northwest Russia. A once-antiquated phone system has rapidly been brought up to date, with satellite and digital lines, and direct dialling worldwide. The same period has seen an explosion of magazines, newspapers and TV channels. Unfortunately, the everyday postal service is not improving at the same rate, but St Petersburg offers many inexpensive and efficient alternatives.

## TELEPHONE SERVICES

The local system, Petersburg Telephone Network (PTS or, in italic Cyrillics, "ПТС") is reliable and relatively cheap. PTS phone boxes are green and located on the streets and in some metro stations. Calls abroad can be made directly from a card-operated PTS phone. PTS phonecards are available from kiosks, post offices and branches of Sberbank *(see p214)*. Inter-city and international calls are cheaper between 10pm and 8am and at weekends. Non-card PTS phones have been almost totally phased out. They can be used for local calls only. To use a PTS coin phone, check that you have a tone before dialling. Drop the 1, 2 or 5 rouble coins into the slot at the top of the phonebox and then dial the number. Most phoneboxes have instructions in Russian only.

Local calls made from private phones are free of charge, although this may change in the near future.

International calls are much cheaper with a pre-paid card such as the Zebra card; these are available from kiosks and brances of Sberbank and also serve as internet pay-as-you-go cards.

**Emergency services** can be reached by dialling two-digit numbers free of charge: for the fire service dial 01, for the police dial 02 and for the ambulance service dial 03.

To find out if a mobile phone will work on Russian networks, check with your local service provider before travelling. GSM subscribers should not have any trouble using their mobile phones, but visitors should be aware that "roaming" in Russia is very expensive.

### REACHING THE RIGHT NUMBER

- To phone **Russia** from abroad, dial 007 followed by the local area code and individual number.
- To phone **St Petersburg**, dial 812 followed by the individual number.
- To phone **Moscow**, dial 495 followed by the individual number.
- St Petersburg directory enquiries, dial 09.
- There is no international directory enquiries.
- Inter-city call booking, dial 07.
- International call booking, dial 315 0012.
- To phone the **UK**, dial 8 (tone) 1044 followed by the number, omitting first 0 from area code.
- To phone **Canada** or the **US**, dial 8 (tone) 101 followed by the number.
- To phone the **Irish Republic**, dial 8 (tone) 10353 followed by the number.
- To phone **Australia**, dial 8 (tone) 1061 followed by the number.
- To phone **New Zealand**, dial 8 (tone) 1064 followed by the number.
- To phone **South Africa**, dial 8 (tone) 1027 followed by the number.

## USING A PTS CARD-OPERATED PHONE

**2** Wait until the display tells you to insert your card.

**3** Insert your card in the slot, where it should remain for the duration of the call.

**1** When using a PTS card phone, begin by lifting the handset.

**4** When your card has been cleared, dial the number. PTS phones require you to press the star button when there is an answer.

**5** When you have finished your call, hang up, and only remove your card when instructed to by the display.

**A PTS phonecard**

## POSTAL SERVICES

The state-run, international postal system is generally slow and unreliable. Efficient and cheap services are run by **Westpost** and **Post International** who offer ordinary, express, courier and poste restante services. American Express *(see p214)* also operates a poste restante service for cardmembers. The Europe and Corinthia Nevskij Palace hotels *(see p176)* run cheap and remarkably quick postal services, taking three days to the UK via Finland, which costs about $2 per letter. Ordinary post offices, such as the **Main Post Office**

**Westpost on Nevskiy prospekt**

*(see p122)* and those in hotels, sell normal and commemorative Russian stamps, postcards, envelopes and local phonecards. Russian postboxes are marked Почта *(Pochta)* and are most plentiful in the city centre. Tourists should use the small pale blue boxes. The yellow ones are used for special local services only.

## FAX AND E-MAIL SERVICES

Most of the city's hotels offer fax services. (Note there are plans for the Main Post Office to stay open round the clock.) Post International and Westpost offer fax and e-mail services. Internet access is available at cafés and clubs such as **Cafe Max** and **5.3 GHz**, as well as at the **Information Centre of the**

**Russian National Library**, and inside the Hermitage museum *(see p84)*.

## COURIER SERVICES

St Petersburg is well supplied with courier services. **DHL** and **Fedex** take three days to Europe and four to Australasia and the US.

A cheaper service is provided by local companies Westpost and Post International. Westpost also offers door-to-door next-day delivery to Moscow. Anything other than papers must go through customs, which can add an extra day.

## TELEVISION AND RADIO

Russian-language television is dominated by soap operas, local game shows and talkshows. The best news in Russian is on NTV, Rossia and Channel One (formerly ORT).

Most hotels in St Petersburg have satellite television and receive many other Western programmes.

The best English-language radio broadcast to the city on shortwave is still the BBC World Service.

## NEWSPAPERS AND MAGAZINES

There are three English-language newspapers and magazines available in the city, which are distributed free to all hotels, major restaurants and most fast-food chains. *The St Petersburg Times* appears twice weekly with international and sporting news and coverage of local events. The Friday edition provides detailed listings and reviews. The monthly *Pulse* is leisure oriented, and its listings section is worth perusal. *Neva News* has a pull-out map of the city and its major sights.

Foreign papers can be picked up at highly inflated prices from the major hotels.

**St Petersburg local newspapers**

# DIRECTORY

| TELEPHONE SERVICES | POSTAL SERVICES | INTERNET CAFES | COURIER SERVICES |
|---|---|---|---|
| **Peregovornyy punkt (Call Centre)**<br>Nevskiy prospekt 85.<br>**Map** 7 C2.<br>*Tel* 740 1849.<br>⬚ 7am–11pm. | **Main Post Office**<br>Главпочтамт<br>*Glavpochtamt*<br>Pochtamtskaya ul 9.<br>**Map** 5 C2.<br>*Tel* 315 8022.<br>⬚ 9am–9pm Mon–Sun.<br>● public holidays. | **Cafe Max**<br>Кафе Макс<br>Nevskiy prospekt 90–92.<br>**Map** 6 E1. *Tel* 273 6655.<br>⬚ 24 hours daily. | **DHL International Centre**<br>Nevskiy prospekt 10.<br>**Map** 7 B2.<br>*Tel* 326 6400.<br>*Fax* 326 6410.<br>⬚ 9am–9pm Mon–Fri, 10am–4pm Sat & Sun. |
| **MOBILE PHONE SERVICES** | **Post International**<br>Nevskiy prospekt 34.<br>**Map** 6 E1.<br>*Tel* 570 4472.<br>⬚ 10am–7pm Mon–Fri, 11am–4pm Sat. | **Information Centre of the Russian National Library**<br>Информационно-Сервисный Центр<br>Российская библиотека<br>Sadovaya ul 20.<br>**Map** 5 A5. *Tel* 310 9676.<br>⬚ 10am–8pm Mon–Sat. | **DHL International Centre**<br>Izmaylovskiy pr 4.<br>**Map** 5 C5.<br>*Tel* 326 6400.<br>*Fax* 326 6410.<br>⬚ 9am–9pm Mon–Fri, 10am–4pm Sat & Sun. |
| **Megafon**<br>Мегафон<br>Artilleriyskaya ul. 1.<br>**Map** 3 B5.<br>*Tel* 960 0555.<br>www.megafon.ru | **Westpost**<br>Nevskiy prospekt 86.<br>**Map** 7 B2.<br>*Tel* 275 0784 or 336 6352.<br>*Fax* 275 0806.<br>⬚ 9:30am–8pm Mon–Fri, noon–8pm Sat.<br>www.westpost.ru | **5.3 GHz**<br>Nevskiy prospekt 63.<br>**Map** 6 E1. *Tel* 314 6009.<br>⬚ 24 hours daily. | **Fedex**<br>Per Grivtsova 6.<br>**Map** 6 D2.<br>*Tel* 325 8825.<br>⬚ 9am–8pm Mon–Thu, 9am–7pm Fri. |
| **MTS**<br>МТС<br>Kazanskaya ul 45.<br>**Map** 6 D2.<br>*Tel* 380 0000.<br>www.mts.ru | | | |

# GETTING TO ST PETERSBURG

St Petersburg is slowly regaining its popularity as a tourist destination, after the severe drop in numbers during the early 1990s. Now, as the number of businessmen regularly travelling in and out is also rising, the number of flights and alternative means of transport is on the increase. Flying remains the most popular way of travelling to St Petersburg, both for individuals and groups, with the train from Moscow or Helsinki a close second.

Aeroflot plane landing in St Petersburg

Independent travel in Russia is difficult as well as costly and for this reason it is worth considering a package tour. British companies run a variety of tours with specialist guides, which often incorporate St Petersburg and Moscow. Since overall tourist numbers are still fairly limited, package tours are not among the cheapest. Shopping around can uncover some good deals, particularly on flights with stopovers in Europe or low-season packages.

Stalinist architecture at Pulkovo 2, St Petersburg's international airport

## ARRIVING BY AIR

Direct flights from the UK to St Petersburg run seven days a week on British Airways and three days on Pulkovo. There are connecting flights on other airlines every day and these are often a much cheaper option. **Scott's Tours** in London are particularly good for budget fares. The plane journey from London takes around three-and-a-half hours, or about six hours with a stopover in a European city.

Direct flights to St Petersburg from Ireland, US, Canada, South Africa and Australasia are either extremely limited or simply do not exist. The usual route from these destinations is to fly via a European city (often Helsinki) or via Moscow from where you can transfer to another flight or continue by road or rail.

During the winter the number of direct flights to St Petersburg from all international destinations is

significantly reduced. Certainly, you should not expect to find a direct flight from Canada or Australasia.

It is worth noting that travelling from Australasia can be fairly complicated. The most usual route is to pick up a European carrier in Singapore, with a stopover in Europe.

On landing, passengers are sometimes required to confirm onward flights. You can do this through the airline you are travelling with or the **Central Air Communication Agency** on Nevskiy prospekt.

## ST PETERSBURG AIRPORTS

International flights arrive at **Pulkovo 2** which, although recently modernized, is still small and relatively primitive. Its separate arrival and departure buildings each have a small duty-free shop. Arrivals also has a

foreign exchange office. On arrival, the longest wait is likely to be for passport control. Departures on the weekend can be hectic and it is best to arrive at least 90 minutes before a flight in high season.

**Pulkovo 1** is for domestic flights only. The 1970s building is cramped and dark, but those using commercial flights to and from Moscow have a separate arrivals and departure lounge. On the first floor, this has its own entrance which cannot be reached from inside the main terminal building.

## GETTING INTO THE CITY

Both airports are located 17 km (11 miles) south of the city centre. The major hotels operate cars to pick up individual tourists for a cost of around $45. The service, which can be charged to

Limousine transfer service from the Grand Hotel Europe (see p185)

Ordinary yellow taxi waiting outside the domestic airport, Pulkovo 1

**No. 13 bus from Pulkovo 2 to Moskovskaya metro station**

**Minibus or *marshrutnoye taksi***

the hotel bill, should always be requested when making a hotel booking. The taxis waiting at the airport only tend to undercut hotel cars by about $5 while ordinary yellow cabs, rarely found at the international airport, are a great deal cheaper, charging around $30 in roubles.

Anyone on a more limited budget, and who has already changed money at the airport, can take the No. 13 bus (from Pulkovo 2) and No. 39 (from Pulkovo 1) to Moskovskaya metro station. Minibuses, known as *marshrutnoye taksi*

or route taxi, travel the same route and charge a minimally higher fare *(see p227)*.

## TRAVELLING BY TRAIN

Rail is a relatively cheap way to travel from Finland to Moscow and within Russia in general, although European student discount passes provide little or no reduction in fares.

More than 10 trains a day run in each direction between Moscow and **Moscow Station** and **Ladozhskiy Station**, and between Helsinki and **Ladozhskiy Station**. For those with time and some sense of adventure, it is possible to travel by train

**Ticket office or *kassa* at Central Train Ticket Office**

between London and St Petersburg via Central Europe (Warsaw, Prague, Berlin). It takes about three days and is generally more costly than flying. The trains are comfortable and usually run on time, but unfortunately carriages can be overcrowded and thefts are not uncommon. Transit visas may also be necessary for countries such as Ukraine and Belarus (Belorussia). All visitors to Russia need a visa and obtaining one can be a complicated procedure. For information on visa acquisition see page 210.

Trains travelling from Eastern Europe arrive and depart from **Vitebsk Station**. Tickets for train journeys from St Petersburg should be bought from the **Central Train Ticket Office** or **Moscow Station**, or from an agent such as **Okdail** *(see p220)*. Taxis from train stations can be overpriced, but all have efficient transport connections.

**Finland Station, the departure point for local trains to Repino and the Gulf of Finland**

## TRAVELLING BETWEEN MOSCOW AND ST PETERSBURG

Many visitors fly in to Moscow and out of St Petersburg, or vice versa. The most popular form of transport between the two cities is the train, of which there are ten or more a day. Daytime trains take about five hours, while faster night-time trains take eight and a half hours. Prices vary according to the class of the train – the Red Arrow being most expensive – and the choice of seat. All trains have a choice of *SV* (two-person compartment), *coupé* (four-person), *platzkart* (open seating), or *sidyachyy* (open seating). All except *sidyachyy* are

**St Petersburg – Moscow sign in train carriage**

sleepers. For daytime travelling *sidyachyy* is more comfortable and cheaper than *platzkarte*. One-way prices range from the equivalent in roubles of around $100 for *SV* to $30 for *sidyachyy*. Prices do not always include bed linen, for which there is an additional charge when you purchase your ticket. On cheaper trains, the *provodnik*, or carriage attendant, will issue and charge for bed linen. Food may be available but it is best to travel with your own supplies.

Regular commercial flights connecting the two cities take 50–90 minutes. These are run by Aeroflot and independent companies such as Pulkovo and Transaero. Prices are modest, at around $90 for an economy class one-way ticket, and $140 for business class. Tickets are sold at the airport, or at the **Central Air Communication Agency**. In summer, travel by boat to and from Moscow is also possible *(see p220)*.

**SV compartment on the luxurious Red Arrow train from Moscow**

One of Finnord's coaches

## TRAVELLING BY COACH

Comfortable coaches run to and from Helsinki in Finland, offering a cheaper alternative to the train. **Finnord** runs one daytime coach and one overnight in each direction; the journey takes around eight hours. Coach companies do not always use the city's inconvenient coach stations but will drop off instead at various locations in St Petersburg. Finnord's final stop is by the Pulkovskaya Hotel. Advance booking is advised with this company as many Russians take advantage of these coaches to go shopping in Lappeenranta, just over the border, or in Helsinki itself.

## TRAVELLING BY BOAT

Arriving by boat can be one of the most exciting and novel ways to approach St Petersburg. However, ferries and cruises operate irregularly and it is best to check with a travel agent for details.

Ferries from Scandinavia usually dock at the **Maritime Passenger Terminal**, on the west side of Vasilevskiy Island. Trolleybus No. 10 and bus No. 7 run from here to the centre or, heading in the other direction, to Primorskaya metro station.

In summer, river cruises between Moscow and St Petersburg are run along the Volga and across Lake Ladoga. The trips last about two weeks and make a very pleasurable way to see more of Russia. The cruises are bookable in the UK through **Noble Caledonia** or

**Voyages Jules Verne**, and in the US through **Visit Russia**. Ships dock at St Petersburg's **River Terminal**, ten minutes' walk from Proletarskaya metro. Cruise companies run buses to and from the city centre.

Luxury cruise ships from London, the US and elsewhere arrive at the city's cargo port, 5 km (3 miles) southwest of the centre. Access to the port is restricted, so the ships have their own coaches to carry tourists into town and back.

Ferry moored at Maritime Passenger Terminal on western edge of Vasilevskiy Island

# DIRECTORY

## UK AND US TOUR COMPANIES

**Noble Caledonia**
2 Chester Close,
Belgravia,
London SW1X 7BE.
*Tel* (0207) 409 0376.

**Scott's Tours**
141 Whitfield Street,
London W1T 5EW.
*Tel* (0207) 383 5353.
*Fax* (0207) 383 3709.

**Visit Russia**
257 West 39th St, Studio 39, New York, NY 10018.
*Tel* (1800) 755 3080.

**Voyages Jules Verne**
21 Dorset Square,
London NW1 6QG.
*Tel* (0207) 616 1000.
*Fax* (0207) 723 8629.

## AIRPORT INFORMATION

**Pulkovo 1**
Пулково 1 *Tel* 704 3822.

**Pulkovo 2**
Пулково 2 *Tel* 704 3444.

## AIRLINE OFFICES

**Austrian Airlines**
Nevskiy pr 32. **Map** 7 B2.
*Tel* 8 800 700 8080.
*Tel* 346 8101 *(Pulkovo 2).*

**British Airways**
Malaya konyushennaya ulitsa 1/3A. **Map** 6 E1.
*Tel* 380 0206.
*Tel* 346 8146 *(Pulkovo 2).*

**Central Air Communication Agency**
Nevskiy pr 7/9.
**Map** 6 D1.
*Tel* 315 0072 *(inter).*
*Tel* 571 8093 *(dom & CIS).*

**Finnair**
Malaya Konyushennaya ul. 1/3A.
**Map** 6 E1.
*Tel* 303 9898.
*Tel* 324 3249 *(Pulkovo 2).*

**KLM**
Malaya Morskaya ul 23.
**Map** 6 D1.
*Tel* 346 6864.

**Lufthansa**
Nevskiy pr. 32.
**Map** 6 F2.
*Tel* 320 1000.
*Tel* 325 9140 *(Pulkovo 2).*

**Rossiya**
Pulkovo-Express, 1-ya Krasnoarmeyskaya ul 4.
**Map** 6 D5. *Tel* 777 0550.

**SAS**
Nevskiy pr 22.
**Map** 6 F2. *Tel* 326 2600.
*Tel* 324 3244 *(Pulkovo 2).*

**Transaero**
10-ya Sovetskaya 4–6.
**Map** 8 D1.
*Tel* 331 5570.

## TRAINS

**All Train Enquiries**
*Tel* 055.

**Central Train Ticket Office**
Центральные железно-дорожные кассы
*Tsentralnye zhelezno-dorozhnye kassy*
Nab kanala Griboedova 24.
**Map** 6 E2. *Tel* 067.

**Finland Station**
финляндский вокзал
*Finlyandskiy vokzal*
Pl Lenina 6. **Map** 3 B3.

**Ladozhskiy Station**
Ладожский вокзал
*Ladozhskniy vokzal*
Zanevskiy pr 73.

**Moscow Station**
Московский вокзал
*Moskovskiy vokzal*
Pl Vosstaniya. **Map** 7 C2.

**Okdail**
Moscow Station (24 hrs) & Central Train Ticket Office.
*Tel* 335 9807, 740 1324.

**Vitebsk Station**
Витебский вокзал
*Vitebskiy vokzal*
Zagorodnyy prospekt 52.
**Map** 6 E4.

## COACHES

**Finnord**
Italyanskaya ulitsa 37.
**Map** 6 F1. *Tel* 314 8951.

## BOATS

**Maritime Passenger Terminal**
Морской пассажирский вокзал *(Morskoy passazhirskiy vokzal)*
Pl Morskoy Slavy.
*Tel* 322 6052.

**River Terminal**
Речной вокзал
*Rechnoy vokzal*
Prospekt Obukhovskoy Oborony 195. *Tel* 262 0239.

# GETTING AROUND ST PETERSBURG

Although public transport in the city is abundant, efficient and very cheap, the most enjoyable way to get around and fully appreciate St Petersburg is on foot. A glance at a map reveals that some attempt was made to bestow the city with a rational, organized layout, which makes it considerably easier to negotiate. When exhaustion sets in, however, a boat cruise along the waterways can be a wonderful way to become acquainted with the city.

**Sign indicating pedestrian crossing**

Nevskiy prospekt is where many of the city's transport routes and main roads meet. Metro lines, tram, bus and trolleybus routes radiate out from here, criss-crossing the city with a network of rail tracks and overhead wires. It is possible to travel without too much difficulty to almost anywhere in town from this main avenue.

Driving is not recommended due to the combination of poor road conditions, aggressive Russian driving and over-efficient traffic police.

## WALKING

In some areas, particularly around Palace Embankment, sights are situated so close together that using public transport from place to place is pointless. A few of the more scattered sights are at some distance (20 mins on foot) from the nearest transport and walking the last stretch is often the most practical option. Apart from the ease, getting around on foot can be a most rewarding way to explore the city, allowing you to soak up the atmosphere and appreciate the fascinating architectural and sculptural detail on many of St Petersburg's buildings.

As soon as the sun appears, in winter as well as in summer, people of all ages emerge onto the streets and into the

**Street sign for Nevskiy prospekt**

parks. Locals are very fond of walking, whether it be promenading up and down Nevskiy prospekt, or ambling around the Neva at 2am during the White Nights (see p51). The Summer Gardens (see p95) and Mikhaylovskiy Gardens have long been popular with Petersburgers. For longer walks mixed with some architectural interest, two good areas to try are Kamenniy and Yelagin islands (see pp136–7), with their official residences and dachas, many dating from the early years of the 20th century.

For a romantic stroll around the city away from the traffic, walk along the Moyka or Griboedov canals (see pp134–5). To the south of Nevskiy prospekt, majestic buildings gradually give way to smaller, 19th-century residential blocks, complete with rows of trees by the waterside and leafy squares and courtyards.

Drivers have little respect for pedestrians and traffic is the main hindrance to walking. Cars drive on the right-hand side, so look left first when crossing the road. If there is an underpass, use it and, if not, look for a light-controlled crossing with red and green figures indicating pedestrian right of way. Crossings without lights are marked by a blue sign showing a pedestrian, but

**Street signs indicating street directions and major shops**

these are simply recommended crossing sites and drivers are not obliged to stop. Be warned that if you are caught crossing a road where there are no marked crossings, you may be fined by a traffic policeman (see p213).

There are few bicycles on the roads, but cyclists tend to ignore traffic lights and signs of all descriptions, causing an additional hazard for the unwary pedestrian.

On the main city streets, dark blue sponsored nameplates give street names in Russian and English. Elsewhere, black-on-white street names

**Sign showing a pedestrian underpass**

are in Cyrillic only. Many maps, like the free pull-out in Neva News (see p217), give the main street names in Cyrillic and in transliteration. If you get lost, a dual-language map can be helpful when asking passersby for assistance.

Excellent walking tours in English, can be booked through **Peter's Tours** via the International Youth Hostel (see p171). For timings, log on to www.peterswalk.com

**Mikhaylovskiy Gardens, behind the Russian Museum (see pp104–107)**

# Travelling by Metro

**Blue neon metro sign**

Since overland transport is the most efficient means of getting around the city centre, the metro is used mainly to get to and from the outskirts of the city. As a tourist attraction, however, the metro's stunning stations, intended by Stalin to be "palaces for the people", should be high on your itinerary. The metro is extremely safe and runs a full service until after midnight. Travelling in the late evening will avoid most of the two million people estimated to use the metro each day. The main setback is that signs are mostly in Cyrillic but, with just five lines, negotiating the network is still fairly straightforward.

**Steep escalators to platforms**

**Exterior of Ploshchad Vosstaniya metro station**

The metro now has 63 stations, ranging in style and ambience from the dim lighting and memorial atmosphere of Ploshchad Muzhestva (Courage Square, 1975) near Piskarovskoe Memorial Cemetery *(see p126)*, to the 1980s vulgarity of Udelnaya and the cool of Komendantskiy Prospekt (2005).

## THE METRO AS A TOURIST ATTRACTION

The Soviet Union's best architects were employed to design St Petersburg's metro stations. Thousands of tonnes of marble, granite and limestone were used to face the walls, and sculptures, mosaics and chandeliers were commissioned from leading artists. The first line opened in 1955, its eight stations connecting ploshchad Vosstaniya with the new Stalinist blocks of flats in the southwest and the city's largest factory, the Kirov Factory. This line is one of the most fascinating, being the supreme embodiment of Stalinist style and ideals. The station at Kirovskiy Zavod is a fine example, a vast basilica, a temple to the factory workers. The line's crowning glory has to be Avtovo, incorporating a wealth of style and detail, even down to the moulded glass columns.

## THE NETWORK

The metro is vital for getting to and from the further afield hotels and the airport.

The four lines run from the outskirts through the centre, where they intersect at one of six main stations.

Trains run every few minutes during the day and every five minutes late at night and, although doors into stations close at midnight, the last trains leave

the centre ten minutes after this. There is no rush hour as such but the metro tends to be full at most times of day, which makes it very safe. Platforms are not staffed, but there is an attendant in a booth at the bottom of each escalator who can call for assistance.

Because of the many waterways in the city, stations are buried deep underground and long escalators lead down to the platforms. Passengers are required to stand on the right, leaving the left side free for those who prefer walking.

New stations are still being added to the St Petersburg metro, the latest ones being Krestovskiy Ostrov, Staraya Derevnya and Komendantskiy Prospekt on the yellow line.

**Directional sign listing all stops on this line in Cyrillic**

**Interchange sign listing all stations on the other line**

## FINDING YOUR WAY

Before setting foot in St Petersburg's metro, ensure you have a network map with the Cyrillic and transliterated names to hand. Signs inside the metro are mainly in Cyrillic and wall maps have become rare in station ticket halls and on the trains. Inside a station, the name is only written on the far wall of the platform which means that, if the train is in the station, or if you are on the train itself, it is not possible to see the sign.

**Mosaics and unusual glass columns at richly decorated Avtovo metro station**

**Metro platform sign showing
stations and interchanges**

Busy stations in the city centre
have a central concourse with
safety doors between this and
the trains. When the train
stops, these doors open, and
only then do the train doors
open. At these stations, a map
of the line you are on is to be
found on the concourse. Other
stations have platforms and the
map of the line is on the wall
on the far side of the tracks.

Before the train doors close,
the driver will announce,
*"Ostorozhno. Dveri zakryva-
yutsya"* (Be careful. The doors
are closing). As the train
approaches a stop, he will
say the name of the station
and mention if you need to
change here for another line,
followed by the name of the
next station. It is always best
to keep count of the stops,
in case you do not catch
the announcements.

To change to another line,
follow the interchange signs
for переход (*perekhod* –
crossing). The exception is at
Tekhnologicheskiy Institut,
where the two southbound
lines are on parallel platforms,
as are the two northbound
lines: thus to continue
in the same direction
on another line you
simply cross the
central concourse.

Exits are marked
выход (*vykhod*). Some
stations, such as
Moskovskaya (for the
airport) and Gostinyy Dvor,
have two or more exits.

## TICKETS AND
## TRAVEL CARDS

The most common means of
paying for the metro is the
token (*zheton*), purchasable
only from metro stations.
Magnetic cards, which can be
topped up with as many trips
as needed, are also available.

Barrier machines are installed
at the top of the escalators;
most take both cards and
tokens. Cards must be inserted

**Metro token**

with the magnetic strip
facing up. If you try
to go through a
machine without
paying, an
automatic barrier
closes in front of you.
At the far right an
attendant checks
passes and allows you to put
your token in a machine
which does not have automatic barriers. Those with magnetic cards cannot pass
through this machine.

Monthly magnetic passes for
the metro or for all forms of
public transport are valid for 70
metro journeys and an infinite
number of journeys on overground transport during a calendar month. They can only be
purchased from the 10th to
the 20th of the current month,
and are valid until the 15th of
the next month.

Visitors who plan to stay in
the city for a while may find
it worthwhile to purchase a
personal "smart" card bearing
their photograph, to which
they can transfer credit to
fund future journeys at any
metro station. Such cards are
not inserted into the barrier
machines that check tickets
and tokens, but placed briefly
onto a sensor marked with a
white circle. There are no
further ticket checks once past
the barriers, inside the station.

**Card with magnetic strip, for travel
on the metro system**

---

## ST PETERSBURG'S METRO

Комендантекий Проепект
Komendantskiy pr

Старая деревня
Staraya derevnya

Крестовский остров
Krestovsky ostrov

Чкаловская
Chkalovskaya

Спортивная
Sportivnaya

Приморская
Primorskaya

Василеостровская
Vasileostrovskaya

Гостиный двор
Gostinyy Dvor

Адмиралтейская
Admiralteyskaya
*(under construction)*

Сенная пл
Sennaya Pl

Садовая
Sadovaya

Звенигородская
Zvenigorodskaya

Технологический инст
Tekhnologicheskiy Inst

Технологический инст
Tekhnologicheskiy Inst

Балтийская
Baltiyskaya

Нарвская
Narvskaya

Кировский завод
Kirovskiy Zavod

Автово
Avtovo

Ленинский пр
Leninskiy Pr

Пр Ветеранов
Pr Veteranov

Парнас
Parnas

Пр Просвещения
Pr Prosveshcheniya

Озерки
Ozerki

Удельная
Udelnaya

Пионерская
Pionerskaya

Черная речка
Chernaya Rechka

Петроградская
Petrogradskaya

Горковская
Gorkovskaya

Невский пр
Nevskiy Pr

Слассская
Spasskaya

Владимирская
Vladimirskaya

Достоевская
Dostoevskaya

Пушкинская
Pushkinskaya

Пиговский пр
Ligovskiy Pr

Обводный Канал
Obvodnyy Kanal
*(under construction)*

Волковская
Volkovskaya

Бухарестская
Bukharestskaya
*(under construction)*

Фрунзенская
Frunzenskaya

Междунаробная
Mezhdunarodnaya
*(under construction)*

Моск ворота
Mosk vorota

Проспект Славы
Prospekt Slavy
*(under construction)*

Электросила
Elektrosila

Елизаровская
Elizarovskaya

Парк Победы
Park Pobedy

Московская
Moskovskaya

Пролеаарская
Proletarskaya

Звездная
Zvezdnaya

Обухово
Obukhovo

Купчино
Kupchino

Рыбацкое
Rybatskoe

Пл Восстания
Pl Vosstania

Маяковская
Mayakovskaya

Пл Александра Невского
Pl Aleksandra Nevskovo

Пл Александра Невского
Pl Aleksandra Nevskovo

Новочеркасская
Novocherkasskaya

Ломоносовская
Lomonosovskaya

Ладожская
Ladozhskaya

Пр болшевиков
Pr Bolshevikov

Ул дыбенко
Ul Dybenko

Девяткино
Devyatkino

Гражданский пр
Grazhdanskiy Pr

Академическая
Akademicheskaya

Политехническая
Politekhnicheskaya

Пл Мужества
Pl Muzhestva

Песная
Lesnaya

Выборгская
Vyborgskaya

Пл ленина
Pl Lenina

Чернышевская
Chernyshevskaya

# Travelling by Tram, Bus and Trolleybus

**Tram-stop sign, seen hanging over the rails**

Overground transport is crowded during the day, particularly at rush hour, but it is still the best way to make short trips around the city or simply to sightsee. In the centre of town, an array of overhead tram and trolleybus cables crisscross many roads. Trolleybuses are frequent and conveniently routed but overcrowded; trams are less busy but noisy; buses are usually sporadic. On all forms of public transport you are unlikely to get a seat during the day. More frequent and comfortable, and slightly more expensive, are the commercial bus and minibus routes. Note that the outlying areas are often accessible only by bus, and that during rush hour it is often faster to walk. For more information on public transport routes, see inside back cover.

**People getting on a tram**

## TRAMS

Trams offer a marvellous way to see St Petersburg and are less crowded than trolleybuses. Tram stops are marked by red and white signs suspended on wires above the tram rails. Separate islands for people to embark are found only on wide roads outside the centre; elsewhere passengers wait on the pavement. When the tram doors open, the oncoming traffic is obliged to wait and let passengers cross to and from the pavement. In practice, there is always one car which cannot wait, so take care before stepping out.

At various crossroads along the route, the driver may need to change points on the rails. He will open his door or the front passenger door to do this. Do not attempt to board or exit a tram when it has stopped for this purpose.

**Stop for buses and minibuses near the Mariinskiy Theatre**

## GENERAL INFORMATION

Trams, buses and trolleybuses start at around 5:30am, and a little later along the middle of the routes. The services operate with rather arbitrary frequency during the day and very infrequently after 11pm, grinding more or less to a halt around midnight. Only a few of the city bus routes display timetables. Each form of overground transport has its own separate stops, and distances between them can be great.

Queueing is not standard practice, so be prepared for an unruly rush to get on first. Trams, buses and trolleybuses can be boarded at the front, middle or back. The front eight seats are reserved for the disabled, the elderly and people with children, all of whom have precedence getting on and off at the front. On board, a conductor collects the fares.

As a stop approaches, people near an exit may be asked *Vy vykhodite?* ("are you getting out?"), which really means "could you move aside?". At busy times, head for the exit well before your stop, or prepare to do some pushing.

Good for sightseeing is the No. 10 trolleybus, which runs from ploshchad Vosstaniya through the centre and across Vasilevskiy Island *(see pp56–63)* to Primorskaya metro station. Other scenic routes are the No. 46 bus from the Field of Mars *(see p94)* to the Chernaya Rechka metro station, the No. 22 bus from the Smolnyy Institute *(see p128)* via St Isaac's Square *(see p79)* and the Mariinskiy Theatre *(see p119)* towards the Stalinist architecture in the southwest, and the No. 46 or 76 bus from the Field of Mars up Kamennoostrovskiy prospekt *(see p70)* and to Kamenniy Island *(see pp136–7)*.

**Sign for a bus stop, showing name of stop and bus numbers**

## BUSES AND MINIBUSES

All services run about every 20 minutes, sometimes less often. Bus stops in the city centre are marked by white and yellow signs with a red letter "A" for *avtobus*, placed by the side of the road or attached to lamp-posts. These are slowly replacing the old-style yellow signs.

**Side view of a single section tram**

**City trolleybus on Nevskiy prospekt**

**A commercial bus on Vasilevskiy Island**

Many routes are now duplicated by commercial buses, marked with a "k" before the number, or minibuses.

Fares on these buses are 50 per cent higher than those on non-commercial equivalents, and are paid to the driver when getting on or off – just follow what other passengers do. These buses can be hailed or requested to stop anywhere along the route.

## TROLLEYBUSES

Trolleybuses still run along the city's main artery, Nevskiy prospekt – unlike trams. They offer convenient routes and stops around the city but are often overcrowded. Ticket inspectors are most often on patrol on trolleybuses. Trolleybus stops are marked by small blue-and-white signs suspended from wires or lamp-posts, indicating the trolleybus numbers. On main roads, stops are also marked by other signs on building walls. These show what seems to be a flat-topped blue "M", but is in fact a Cyrillic "T" for *trolleybus*, on a white background.

The power rods on the roofs of the trolleybuses are known familiarly as "horns" *(roga)* or "little whiskers" *(usiki)*. Occasionally these become detached from the overhead cables and the trolleybus lurches to a halt. It is the driver's responsibility to reattach them, causing a slight but generally negligible delay.

**Trolleybus-stop sign on building wall**

## TICKETS AND TRAVEL CARDS

A flat fare is payable on all forms of transport, what-ever the length of the journey. Tickets are purchased from the conductor (who wears a blue-and-yellow jacket) or, on commercial transport, from the driver. The ticket must be bought before the next stop after you got on, and large items of baggage must be paid for separately. Fines for non-payment can be imposed on the spot by plain-clothes inspectors. Check the inspector's identity document. Fines should not come to more than 100 roubles.

The cheapest way to travel in St Petersburg, if you are staying a few weeks or more, is to buy a monthly or half-monthly card for all forms of transport, including the metro *(see pp222–3)*. The magnetic monthly card, or *yedinyy bilet*, is valid from the 16th of the current month until the 15th of the next, and can be bought from the 10th to the 20th of the current month. Half-monthly *yedinyy bilety* run from the 1st until the 15th of the month, and can be purchased from the last day of the current month to the 5th of the next month. Separate monthly cards are also sold for each form of transport. Travel cards are valid for trips to Tsarskoe Selo and Pavlovsk, but not Peterhof, Gatchina or Oranienbaum *(see pp228–9)*.

**Waiting at a trolleybus stop on Nevskiy prospekt, near ploshchad Vosstaniya**

# Canal and River Cruises

**Sign for water taxi**

St Petersburg's numerous natural waterways were adapted and added to, to make it resemble Peter the Great's beloved Amsterdam *(see pp20–21)*. Indeed, it would be true to say the city vies with Amsterdam for the title "Venice of the North".

A wide selection of cruises, for small and large groups, in open and closed boats, depart from bridges along Nevskiy prospekt. They offer marvellous opportunities to see more of the city, especially for those unable to walk long distances. Forming part of any cruise are the broad Fontanka river with its Neo-Classical palaces, the leafy Moyka river with its ironwork bridges, and the Griboedov canal which twists and turns its way through southwest St Petersburg. Bring a bottle of champagne, a picnic and a warm jumper and just relax.

**Canal cruise on the Moyka**

## GENERAL INFORMATION

The weather plays a vital role in determining the exact time of year canal cruises start and finish. Most boats operate daily from mid-May to late September. Their routes also vary because regular construction work, reinforcing the granite embankments, sometimes prevents movement along small parts of the canals.

The Gulf of Finland is tidal and this affects the Neva and inland waterways. Strong winds can cause the water level to rise significantly and all boat trips may then be cancelled.

## GUIDED CANAL TRIPS

Large, covered cruise boats depart every 30 minutes, between 11:30am and 8pm, from the Anichkov Bridge on Nevskiy prospekt *(see p49)*.

Tickets for the next available boat should be purchased from the kiosk on the embankment, although, if the queues are long, tickets may be sold in advance for later cruises on the same day. The trip lasts 70 minutes and takes in the Moyka, Griboedov and Fontanka. Weather permitting, the boats usually go out onto the Neva, from where there are superb views of the whole city.

**Ticket kiosk for canal trip, Anichkov Bridge**

Foreigners pay around $15–30 in roubles for these trips, slightly more than Russians. The guided tour is in Russian only. Large groups are advised to book in advance, through the kiosk or by phone, especially during school holidays. Boat trips providing guided tours in English can be booked through any of the major hotels.

During hot weather, it can get very stuffy and confined inside the boats. The visibility through the scratched perspex windows can also be less than perfect at times. If you wish to stand outside to see more, there is a platform at the back of the boat for which there may be an extra charge. Take your own soft drinks and sandwiches, as these are rarely available on board these cruises.

## DIRECTORY

**City Excursion Bureau of St Petersburg**
Sadovaya ul 28–30. **Map** 6 E2.
*Tel* 312 0527.

**MIR Travel Company**
Nevskiy pr 11. **Map** 6 D1.
*Tel* 325 7122. **www**.mir-travel.com

**Russkiye Kruizy**
Nevskiy pr 51. **Map** 7 B2.
*Tel* 325 6120. **www**.russian-cruises.ru

**Taxi Reservations**
*Tel* 600 0000, 068 320 0200.

## NEVA CRUISES

A variety of boats cruise up and down the Neva between the Gulf of Finland and the River Station *(Rechnoy vokzal)* to the southeast. The trips, operating hourly between 10am and 10pm, last an hour. Foreigners pay more than locals, but the tickets are not expensive and can be bought on the landing stage or on the boat. The boats leave from the landing stage opposite the Bronze Horseman on Decembrists' Square, and from the one near the main entrance of the Hermitage *(see p75)*.

These boat trips are a pleasant way of passing the time rather than a serious sightseeing opportunity. Food and drink are usually served and, in the evenings, alcohol is available on some of the boats.

Luxury catered cruises can be booked in advance. **MIR** and **Russkiye Kruizy** offer a variety of routes along the Neva and along a number of the city's many canals.

**Cruise boat on the Neva with the Hermitage and Palace Embankment in the background**

Water taxis moored on Griboedov canal near
Kazanskiy most by Nevskiy prospekt

## WATER TAXIS

Water taxis are similar to
private motorboats, carrying
anything from 4 to 20 people.
During White Nights, boats
run late into the night.

For a small boat, wait at the
landing stage on the north side
of Zelenyy most where
Nevskiy prospekt *(see pp46–9)*

crosses the Moyka,
or alongside the
Gostinyy Dvor
metro station on the
Griboedov canal
close to Kazanskiy
most. Larger boats
may need to be
negotiated at least a
couple of hours in
advance to ensure
their availability.

Prices are negoti-
able, but generally
range from about
$40 to $70 an hour,
depending on the
size of the boat and
the route you decide to
follow. One hour takes you
along the inland waterways,
but an extra half hour
includes the Neva,
crossing over to go
round the Peter
and Paul Fortress
*(see pp66–7)* and
giving a good
view of all the

**Water taxis on the Moyka
by Politseyskiy most**

waterfronts. Most drivers can
at least point out major sights
in English, others can give
you a basic guided tour. If
you ask in advance, it may be
possible to find an English-
speaking guide. Boats can be
booked in advance on pay-
ment of a small deposit, but
are generally plentiful and are
best picked up spontaneously.

Since the boats are open and
it can be cold on the waterways, particularly at night,
warm clothing is necessary,
even during the summer
months. There is usually at
least one blanket on board for
anyone who is unequipped.
Pilots allow you to do more
or less as you like on board
the boat as long as it
is safe, and tend to
be undisturbed
by the noise of
popping cham-
pagne corks or
other sounds
of merrymaking.

---

# Taxis

St Petersburg's official yellow taxis are gradually being
replaced by private cabs in a variety of colours. Most
locals use the cheaper alternative of catching a *chastnik*,
effectively hitching a ride in any passing vehicle.

**St Petersburg's bright yellow taxi**

## OFFICIAL TAXIS

The city's distinctive yellow
official taxi fleet has in recent
years faced tough competition
from private taxi firms which
run imported modern cars.
Drivers of private taxis may
charge a flat fare agreed in
advance. Never get into a taxi
parked in front of a hotel,
restaurant, airport or sight –
the fare will be extortionate.
Move a short distance away,
and hail a cab.

Whatever type of taxi you
choose to take, always name
your destination before getting in. Taxis are not obliged
to take you, and they may
well refuse, or simply drive
away if they do not wish to go

in the same direction as
you. Taxi fares are
relatively cheap.
Newer cabs are
fitted with modern
meters, which indicate the
sum to be paid, but meters in
the older taxis are unreliable
or simply switched off. For
this reason it is wise to agree
on a price before starting out
on the journey to avoid
unnecessary confusion. If you
feel you have been over-
charged however, it is worth
disputing the matter.

In some areas, official taxis
are not readily available, and
you must either book one by
phone or hope for a *chastnik*.

## CHASTNIKI

For many years Russians
have been used to flagging
down the drivers of private
cars, which are easier to
locate and often cheaper to
use than official taxis. Thus,
as soon as you stick your

hand out to hail a taxi, as
likely as not, a private car will
stop. Some of the cars are not
overly salubrious, but the
driver is likely to be more
willing with baggage than
official taxi drivers. Exercise
reasonable caution by not
getting into any car with more
than the driver already in it.
Private cars, and taxis that
have not been pre-booked,
are not recommended for
those who are travelling
alone at night.

As with ordinary taxis, name
your destination and, if the
driver agrees, be sure to settle
a price before setting off.

**St Petersburgers flagging down a
*chastnik*, or private car**

# Travelling Beyond St Petersburg

Every weekend during the summer, and even in winter, many locals leave the city. They head for their *dacha* or for the woods, to gather seasonal fruits and vegetables, go cross-country skiing or visit one of the former imperial summer residences. Buses and suburban trains operate frequently throughout the year and are the usual means of transport to sites out of town. Peterhof is the unique exception in being accessible by hydrofoil across the Gulf of Finland. Foreigners tend to take coach excursions out of town but, with planning, travelling independently can be part of the fun.

Passengers boarding suburban train at Vitebsk Station

Interior view of one of St Petersburg's suburban trains

## SUBURBAN TRAINS

Train travel is the most romantic way to visit most of the outlying sights. Tickets can be bought from the local cash desks *(prigorodnyye kassy)* at each station, where a timetable is displayed. Return tickets are no cheaper than two singles. Note that smoking is prohibited and that, between the hours of 10am and midday, there is often a break in the timetable.

Style-Moderne architecture in Vitebsk station restaurant

## GETTING TO TSARSKOE SELO AND PAVLOVSK

Trains for Tsarskoe Selo (Pushkin) *(see pp152–5)* and Pavlovsk *(see pp159–61)* depart every 20 minutes from **Vitebsk Station**. The line was originally built for the royal family to reach their summer residences and the station is a marvellous example of Style-Moderne architecture. The ticket office is on the right of the main building. All local trains take about 25 minutes, stopping first at Tsarskoe Selo (Detskoe Selo), then Pavlovsk.

At Detskoe Selo station, the 382 and 371 buses go to Tsarskoe Selo, stopping near the palace.

At Pavlovsk, the train station is opposite the entrance to the park, through which it is a pleasant half-hour walk to the palace.

A host of minibuses run to Tsarskoe Selo (Pushkin) and Pavlosk from Moskovskaya metro station in St Petersburg. They provide a reliable and convenient alternative means of transport to the train.

## GETTING TO PETERHOF AND ORANIENBAUM

There are suburban trains for Peterhof *(see pp148–51)* and Oranienbaum *(see pp146–7)* departing every 20 minutes from **Baltic Station**. The trains that reach Oranienbaum are those destined for Kalishche, or Oranienbaum itself.

For Peterhof, get off the train at Novyy Petergof (40 minutes from town), from where it is ten minutes to the palace on bus 348, 350, 351, 352 or 356.

During the summer, take a hydrofoil from the Hermitage. Fares are the equivalent of about $15 in roubles.

At Oranienbaum, turn right out of the station and walk about 200 m (650 ft) to the main road. Almost directly opposite is the entrance to the park, and from here it is only a five-minute walk to the Great Palace or into the heart of the park.

An efficient minibus service runs passangers to both Peterhof and Oranienbaum from Avtovo metro station in the city.

## GETTING TO GATCHINA

Trains run approximately every half hour from **Baltic Station** to Gatchina *(see p147)* and the journey takes an hour.

Opposite Gatchina train station is a short road leading directly to the square in front of the palace.

Alternatively, there is a bus No. 431 as well as regular, fast minibuses running from Moskovskaya metro station. On this particular suburban route, city bus tickets and monthly passes are not valid.

## GETTING TO REPINO AND THE GULF OF FINLAND

For Repino *(see p146)* and the Gulf of Finland, trains depart every 20 minutes or so from **Finland Station**. Tickets should be bought at cash desks within the main building. Avoid any train marked Beloostrov or Krugovoy.

At Repino, cross the main road, head down the hill towards the Gulf of Finland and turn left onto the asphalt road until you reach Penaty.

Bus No. 211 also runs to Repino and stops right outside Penaty. The bus leaves from Chernaya Rechka metro.

**Coach to Novgorod**

## GETTING TO NOVGOROD

Coaches leave for Novgorod *(see pp162–5)* every two hours from the **Coach Station**. Although it has been known for these rather old coaches to break down en route, they are nevertheless more reliable than trains. The journey takes four hours.

A simpler alternative is to book a tour *(see p208)*.

## DRIVING IN ST PETERSBURG

Car hire is still not widely available in Russia. Cars and minibuses in St Petersburg can often be hired only with company drivers. **Hertz** and **Europcar** are the exceptions to this rule, but their prices are much higher than in Europe, and they only accept payment by credit card.

For the few who do find themselves at the wheel, there are a number of things to bear in mind. An international licence is obligatory, as well as international insurance and documents proving you have the right to be driving the car: for example, registration documents or a hire agreement bearing your name. Traffic policemen *(see p213)* have the right to stop you and check your documents. They may not issue on-the-spot fines for minor infringements – such as having a dirty number plate, not having a first-aid kit, or more serious offences such as drink-driving. (Drivers are not allowed to drink any alcohol.) The proper procedure is to issue a ticket requiring payment within a month at the State Bank (Sberbank). The traffic police are active as they use fines as a means of increasing their income.

Local drivers tend to ignore rules of the road and do more or less as they like, so be on your guard. Drive on the right and make no left turns on main roads unless a road sign indicates that it is permitted.

In winter conditions, driving requires studded tyres as chains can be damaged on tram lines and vice versa. It is also advisable not to use your handbrake in cold weather as it has a tendency to freeze.

Unleaded petrol is rarely available and you should use nothing lower than grade 95 petrol. There is no charge for parking in most parts of the city centre. The Nevskij Palace and Europe hotels *(see p176)* have 24-hour security parking.

**Road sign in Russian indicating driver must stop**

## DIRECTORY

### TRAIN AND COACH STATIONS

**All train enquiries**
*Tel 055.*

**Baltic Station**
Балтийский вокзал
*Baltiyskiy vokzal*
Nab Obvodnovo kanala 120.

**Coach Station**
Автобусный вокзал
*Avtobusnyy vokzal*
Nab Obvodnovo kanala 36.
**Map** 7 C5. *Tel 766 5777.*

**Finland Station**
Финляндский вокзал
*Finlyandskiy vokzal*
Pl Lenina 6. **Map** 3 B3.

**Moscow Station**
Московский вокзал
*Moskovskiy vokzal*
Pl Vosstaniya. **Map** 7 C2.

**Vitebsk Station**
Витебский вокзал
*Vitebskiy vokzal*
Zagorodnyy pr 52. **Map** 6 E4.

### CAR HIRE

**Europcar**
Pulkovo 2 Arrivals. *Tel 7 (911) 987 2956.*

**Hertz**
Pulkovo 1 Arrivals. *Tel 326 4505.*

## THE HYDROFOIL TO PETERHOF

**Hydrofoil arriving at the Hermitage landing stage**

The most enjoyable and by far the most scenic way to reach the imperial summer palace of Peterhof is the 45-minute trip across the Gulf of Finland by hydrofoil. The service runs from early June until early October and sets off from the second landing stage outside the Hermitage *(see p75)* where a weekly timetable is posted. Generally hydrofoils operate every hour from 9:30am with the last boat returning at 6pm. Buy your return ticket on arrival at Peterhof. A fee is charged to enter the lower park and this ticket is needed to get back into the park to return by hydrofoil.

# ST PETERSBURG STREET FINDER

The key map below shows the areas of St Petersburg covered by the *Street Finder*. The map references given throughout the guide for sights, restaurants, hotels, shops or entertainment venues refer to the maps in this section. All the major sights have been clearly marked so they are easy to locate. The key below shows other features marked on the

**Pausing on the steps of Kazan Cathedral**

maps, such as post offices, metro stations, ferry stops and churches. The *Street Finder* index lists street names in transliteration, followed by Cyrillics (on the maps, Cyrillics are only given for major roads). This guide uses the now reinstated old Russian street names, rather than the Soviet versions *(see p209)*. Places of interest are listed by their English name.

0 kilometres   1
0 miles   1

## KEY TO STREET FINDER

| | | | | |
|---|---|---|---|---|
| ▣ Major sight | | ⛴ River boat pier | | ⊠ Post office |
| ▣ Place of interest | | 🚕 Taxi rank | | ═ Railway line |
| ▣ Other building | | ✚ Hospital | | «45 House number (main street) |
| 🚆 Train station | | 🚓 Police station | | |
| Ⓜ Metro station | | ✚ Orthodox church | | **SCALE OF MAP PAGES** |
| 🚋 Tram stop | | ✚ Church | | |
| 🚎 Trolleybus terminus | | ✡ Synagogue | | 0 metres   300 |
| 🚌 Bus terminus | | ☪ Mosque | | 0 yards   300 |

# Street Finder Index

## ABBREVIATIONS & USEFUL WORDS

| | | |
|---|---|---|
| ul | ulitsa | street |
| pl | ploshchad | square |
| pr | prospekt | avenue |
| per | pereulok | lane |
| | most | bridge |
| | sad | garden |
| | shosse | road |

# General Index

# Acknowledgments

Dorling Kindersley would like to thank the following people whose contributions and assistance have made the preparation of this book possible.

## Main Contributor

Christopher Rice holds a PhD in Russian history from the University of Birmingham. He and his wife Melanie, also a writer, first visited Russia in 1978 and have been returning regularly ever since. Together they have written numerous travel guides to the city, and to a variety of other destinations, including Prague, Berlin and Istanbul, as well as the *Eyewitness Travel Guide to Moscow*.

Catherine Phillips is an art historian who arrived in Russia in 1985 and has lived there ever since, moving to St Petersburg in 1989. She covered major events for British and American TV and radio during the early years of *perestroika* and authored and contributed to some of the first guides to the new Russia. Today she concentrates on translating and editing scholarly texts and writing for works of reference.

## Additional Contributor

Rose Baring began to study Russian at the age of 12. She has an MA in Modern History and divided her time between London, Moscow and St Petersburg for much of the early 1990s. She has written guides to St Petersburg, Moscow and other destinations, including the *Eyewitness Travel Guide to Istanbul*.

## Special Assistance

Dorling Kindersley would like to thank Marc Bennetts (walks writer), Anastasia Makarova (factchecker), Hilary Bird (indexer), Ian Wizniewski (food and drink consultant), Valera Katsuba (photo permissions), Marina Maydanyuk (researcher), Oleksiy Nesnov (language consultant), Victoria Rachevskaya (language consultant), Agency Information Resources for helping with research, Yuliya Motovilova (St Petersburg Tourist Company) and the staff of Peter TiPS.

## Proofreader

Stewart J Wild.

## Design and Editorial Assistance

Gillian Allan, Douglas Amrine, Liz Atherton, Andrei Bogdanov, Laurence Broers, Lucinda Cooke, Vivien Crump, Dawn Davies-Cook, Hannah Dolan, Alexandra Farrell, Claire Folkard, Freddy Hamilton, Paul Hines, Leanne Hogbin, Vicki Ingle, Kathryn Lane, Sam Merrell, Fiona Morgan, Jane Oliver, Helen Partington, Marianne Petrou, Amir Reuveni, Ellen Root, Luke Rozkowski, Alison Stace, Ingrid Vienings, Veronica Wood.

## Additional Illustrations

Claire Littlejohn, John Woodcock.

## Additional Photography

Valentin Baranovsky, Andrei Bogdanov, Victoria Buyvid, Andy Crawford, Erich Crichton, Neil Fletcher, Steve Gorton, Paul Miller, Ian O'Leary, Clive Streeter; KOMMERSANT Photo Agency: Yevgeny Pavlenko, Sergey Semyenov.

## Photography Permissions

The publisher would like to thank all those who gave permission to photograph at their establishments, including hotels, museums, churches, shops and other sights, too numerous to thank individually.

## Picture Credits

t = top; tl = top left; tlc = top left centre; tc = top centre; trc = top right centre; tr = top right; cla = centre left above; ca = centre above; cra = centre right above; cl = centre left; c = centre; cr = centre right; clb = centre left below; cb = centre below; crb = centre right below; bl = bottom left; b = bottom; bc = bottom centre; bcl = bottom centre left; br = bottom right; d = detail.

The publisher would like to thank the following individuals, companies and picture libraries for their kind permission to reproduce their photographs:

AISA, BARCELONA: 18t, 44t, 55 (insert), 106tr; AKG, LONDON: 16, 17t, 20bl/cl, 20–21c, 25tl, 26cl, 27c, 28br, Erich Lessing 28bl, 29c, 37b, 42cl/bl/br, 43br, State Russian Museum, St Petersburg 105crb; ALAMY IMAGES: Art Kowalsky 10cl; brt Russia 81tc; Medioimages 10br; Robert Harding Picture Library Ltd 10tc, 138cr; Robert Harding Picture Library Ltd/ Sylvain Grandadam 180cl, 181tl; Peter

Titmuss 138br; ANCIENT ART & ARCHITECTURE COLLECTION: 45cr; APA: Jim Holmes 93tl; AXIOM: Jim Holmes 153b; VALENTIN BARANOVSKY: 84bl, 85tl, 201t; IAN BAVINGTON-JONES: 130t; YURI BELINSKY: 31t; BRIDGEMAN ART LIBRARY, LONDON/NEW YORK: 153c; Forbes Magazine Collection 28–9c; State Hermitage, St Petersburg 21cb, 24–5c, 25cl, 86t/b, 87t/b, 88b, 89tr/b, 90t/b, 91t/c, *La Danse,* Henri Matisse (1910) © Succession Henri Matisse/DACS 2006 87c; Private Collection *20th Century Propaganda Poster 1920,* D Moor © DACS 2006 29tr; State Russian Museum, St Petersburg *The Cyclist,* Natalya Goncharova (1913) © ADAGP, Paris and DACS, London 2006 40b, *Portrait of Princess Olga Konstantinovna Orlova,* Valentin Alexandrovich Serov (1911) 104clb; Tretyakov Gallery, Moscow 19t, *The Circus,* Marc Chagall, 1919 © ADAGP, Paris and DACS, London 2006 45tl.

CAMERA PRESS: Roxana Artacho 85bl; DEMETRIO CARRASCO: 2–3, 6b, 15b, 36t, 53bl, 80bl, 93cr/br, 102–103; CENTRAL STATE ARCHIVE OF PHOTOGRAPHS AND FILM DOCUMENTS, ST PETERSBURG: 42t, 72c, 110c, 118bl; JEAN-LOUP CHARMET: 23t; CHRISTIE'S IMAGES: 82b; CORBIS: Dean Conger 52tr, Antoine Gyori 139t; E. O Hoppe/Bettmann 118cr; Rob Howard 181c; Bob Krist 201b; Library of Congress 28tl; Michael Nicholson 152t; Gianni Dagli Orti 8–9, 119bl; Steve Raymer 31crb, 118br, 138cl; Gregor M. Schmid 138tl; State Hermitage, St Petersburg 24bl; State Russian Museum 25bl; E T ARCHIVE: Bibliotheque Nationale, Paris 17cl; Hermitage, St Petersburg 88t, 89tl.

GETTY IMAGES: Hulton Archive 43tr, 118cl, 121c, 182tr; The Image Bank/Harald Sund 11br; GIRAUDON: State Russian Museum 43cr, 105cr; Tretyakov Gallery, Moscow 165cr.

MICHAEL HOLFORD: 18c, 19c, 21bl; HOTEL DOSTOEVSKY: 173cb; INTERIOR ARCHIVE: Fritz von der Schulenburg 161c; KATZ PICTURES: 167 (insert); KEA PUBLISHING SERVICES: Francesco Venturi 92 (all three); DAVID KING COLLECTION: 29tl, 30t, 45b, 69b, 129c; LONELY PLANET IMAGES: Jonathan Smith 11tr, 139crb; MARY EVANS PICTURE LIBRARY: 9 (insert), 19b, 21br, 22c, 23c, 24cl/br, 25br, 26t, 29br, 62b, 141 (insert), 161bl, 207 (insert); PAUL MILLER: 51cr; MIR TRAVEL COMPANY: 208tc; NOVOSTI (LONDON): 20br, 21tl, 26b, 27t, 30cl, 31c, 43tl, 50c, 51b, 78b, 165t/l; ORONOZ, MADRID: 22t, 43bl.

PARK INN PRIBALTIYSKAYA: 168cl; PLODIMEX AUSSENHANDELS GMBH, HAMBURG: 178cr/bl; NATASHA RAZINA: 152b, 153t; RENAISSANCE ST PETERSBURG BALTIC HOTEL: 172c; REX FEATURES: V. Sichov/SIPA Press 30cr; ROBERT HARDING PICTURE LIBRARY: 84br; ROCCO FORTE HOTELS, ST PETERSBURG: 169br; ELLEN ROONEY: 53t, 79t, 83b, 140–41; GREGOR M SCHMID: 50br; SCIENCE PHOTO LIBRARY: CNES, 1989 Distribution Spot Image 11cr; VLADIMIR SIDOROPOLEV: 182br; STATE RUSSIAN MUSEUM: 7cr; *Blue Crest,* Wassily Kandinsky (1917) © ADAGP, Paris and DACS, London 2006 39br; 93tr, 104bl/br, 105tl, 106tl/b, 107 (all three), 110b; TRAVEL LIBRARY: Stuart Black 85br; VISUAL ARTS LIBRARY: 44b; State Hermitage, St Petersburg *L'Homme aux bras croisés,* Pablo Picasso (1905) © Succession Picasso/DACS 2006 91b; 123c.

Jacket: Front – Alamy Images: Jon Arnold Images c; DK Images: John Heseltine clb. Back – Demetrio Carrasco: bl; DK Images: Demetrio Carrasco clb, cla; John Heseltine tl. Spine - DK Images: Demetrio Carrasco b; Front Endpapers: DK Images: Valentin Baranovsky crb.

All other images © Dorling Kindersley. For further information see: **www.dkimages.com**

## SPECIAL EDITIONS OF DK TRAVEL GUIDES

DK Travel Guides can be purchased in bulk quantities at discounted prices for use in promotions or as premiums. We are also able to offer special editions and personalized jackets, corporate imprints, and excerpts from all of our books, tailored specifically to meet your own needs.

To find out more, please contact:
(in the United States) **SpecialSales@dk.com**
(in the UK) **TravelSpecialSales@uk.dk.com**
(in Canada) DK Special Sales at **general@tourmaline.ca**
(in Australia) **business.development@pearson.com.au**

# Phrase Book

In this guide the Russian language has been transliterated into Roman script following a consistent system used by the US Board on Geographic Names. All street and place names, and the names of most people, are transliterated according to this system. For some names, where a well-known English form exists, this has been used – hence, Leo (not Lev) Tolstoy.

In particular, the names of Russian rulers, such as Peter the Great, are given in their anglicized forms. Throughout the book, transliterated names can be taken as an accurate guide to pronunciation. The Phrase Book also gives a phonetic guide to the pronunciation of words and phrases used in everyday situations, such as when eating out or shopping.

## GUIDELINES FOR PRONUNCIATION

The Cyrillic alphabet has 33 letters, of which only five (а, к, м, о, т) correspond exactly to their counterparts in English. Russian has two pronunciations (hard and soft) of each of its vowels, and several consonants without an equivalent.

The right-hand column of the alphabet, below, demonstrates how Cyrillic letters are pronounced by comparing them to sounds in English words. However, some letters vary in how they are pronounced according to their position in a word. Important exceptions are also noted below.

On the following pages, the English is given in the left-hand column, with the Russian and its transliteration in the middle column. The right-hand column provides a literal system of pronunciation and indicates the stressed syllable in bold. The exception is in the *Menu Decoder* section, where the Russian is given in the left-hand column and the English translation in the right-hand column, for ease of use. Because of the existence of genders in Russian, in a few cases both masculine and feminine forms of a phrase are given.

## THE CYRILLIC ALPHABET

| | | |
|---|---|---|
| А а | a | **a**limony |
| Б б | b | **b**ed |
| В в | v | **v**et |
| Г г | g | **g**et (see note 1) |
| Д д | d | **d**ebt |
| Е е | e | **ye**t (see note 2) |
| Ё ё | e | **yo**nder |
| Ж ж | zh | lei**s**ure (but a little harder) |
| З з | z | **z**ither |
| И и | i | **s**ee |
| Й й | y | **bo**y (see note 3) |
| К к | k | **k**ing |
| Л л | l | **l**oot |
| М м | m | **m**atch |
| Н н | n | **n**ever |
| О о | o | **r**o**b** (see note 4) |
| П п | p | **p**ea |
| Р р | r | **r**at (rolling, as in Italian) |
| С с | s | **s**top |
| Т т | t | **t**offee |
| У у | u | **b**oo**t** |
| Ф ф | f | **f**ellow |
| Х х | kh | **kh** (like loch) |
| Ц ц | ts | le**ts** |
| Ч ч | ch | **ch**air |
| Ш ш | sh | **sh**ove |
| Щ щ | shch | fre**sh sh**eet (as above but with a slight roll) |
| ъ | | hard sign (no sound, but see note 5) |
| Ы ы | y | l**i**d |
| ь | | soft sign (no sound, but see note 5) |
| Э э | e | **e**gg |
| Ю ю | yu | **yo**uth |
| Я я | ya | **ya**k |

## Notes

1) Г Pronounced as *v* in endings -oro and -ero.
2) E Always pronounced *ye* at the beginning of a word, but in the middle of a word sometimes less distinctly (more like *e*).
3) Й This letter has no distinct sound of its own. It usually lengthens the preceding vowel.
4) О When not stressed it is pronounced like *a* in across.
5) ъ, ь The hard sign (ъ) is rare and indicates a very brief pause before the next letter. The soft sign (ь, marked in the pronunciation guide as ') softens the preceeding consonant and adds a slight *y* sound: for instance, *n'* would sound like *ny* in 'canyon'.

## In Emergency

| | | |
|---|---|---|
| Help! | Помогите! *Pomogite!* | pama**geet**-ye |
| Stop! | Стоп! *Stop!* | stop! |
| Leave me alone! | Оставьте меня в покое! *Ostavte menya v pokoe!* | asta**vt**'-ye mye**nya** v pa**koye**! |
| Call a doctor! | Позовите врача! *Pozovite vracha!* | paza**veet**-ye vra**cha**! |
| Call an ambulance! | Вызовите скорую помощь! *Vyzovite skoruyu pomoshch!* | **viz**aveet-ye **skoru**-yu po**mash**'! |
| Fire! | Пожар! *Pozhar!* | pa**zhar**! |
| Call the fire brigade! | Вызовите пожарных! *Vyzovite pozharnykh!* | **viz**aveet-ye pa**zharnikh**! |
| Police! | Милиция! *Militsiya!* | mee**leet**see-ya! |
| Where is the nearest... | Где ближайший... *Gde blizhayshiy...* | gdye blee**zhaysheey**... |
| ...telephone? | ...телефон? *...telefon?* | ...tye**lyefon**? |
| ...hospital? | ...больница? *...bolnitsa?* | ...bal'**neetsa**? |
| ...police station? | ...отделение милиции? *...otdelenie militsii?* | ...atdyel**yenye** mee**leet**see-ee? |

## Communication Essentials

| | | |
|---|---|---|
| Yes | Да *Da* | da |
| No | Нет *Net* | nyet |
| Please | Пожалуйста *Pozhaluysta* | pa**zhalsta** |
| Thank you | Спасибо *Spasibo* | spa**seeba** |
| You are welcome | Пожалуйста *Pozhaluysta* | pa**zhalsta** |
| Excuse me | Извините *Izvinite* | eezveen**eet**-ye |
| Hello | Здравствуйте *Zdravstvuyte* | **zdra**stvooyt-ye |
| Goodbye | До свидания *Do svidaniya* | da sveed**anya** |
| Good morning | Доброе утро *Dobroe utro* | **dobra**-ye **oo**tra |
| Good afternoon/day | Добрый день *Dobryy den* | **dobree** dyen' |
| Good evening | Добрый вечер *Dobryy vecher* | **dobree vye**chyer |
| Good night | Спокойной ночи *Spokoynoy nochi* | spak**oy**nay **no**chee |
| Morning | утро *utro* | **oo**tra |
| Afternoon | день *den* | dyen' |
| Evening | вечер *vecher* | **vye**chyer |
| Yesterday | вчера *vchera* | fchye**ra** |
| Today | сегодня *sevodnya* | syev**odnya** |
| Tomorrow | завтра *zavtra* | **za**ftra |
| Here | здесь *zdes* | zdyes' |

| There | там *tam* | tam |
| What? | Что? *Chto?* | shto? |
| Where? | Где? *Gde?* | gdye? |
| Why? | Почему? *Pochemu?* | pachyemoo? |
| When? | Когда? *Kogda?* | kagda? |
| Now | сейчас *seychas* | seychas |
| Later | позже *pozzhe* | pozhe |
| Can I...? | можно? *mozhno?* | mozhna...? |
| It is possible/allowed | можно *mozhno* | mozhna |
| It is not possible/allowed | нельзя *nelzya* | nyelzya |

## Useful Phrases

| How are you? | Как Вы Поживаете? *Kak vee pozhivaete?* | kak vee pozhivaete? |
| Very well, thank you | Хорошо, спасибо *Khorosho, spasibo* | kharasho, spaseeba |
| Pleased to meet you | Очень приятно *Ochen priyatno* | ochen' pree-yatna |
| How do I get to...? | Как добраться до...? *Kak dobratsya do...?* | kak dabrat'sya da...? |
| Would you tell me when we get To...? | Скажите, пожалуйста, когда мы приедем в...? *Skazhite, pozhaluysta, kogda my priedem v...?* | skazheet-ye, pazhalsta, kagda mi pree-yedem v...? |
| Is it very far? | Это далеко? *Eto daleko?* | eta dalyeko? |
| Do you speak English? | Вы говорите по-английски? *Vy govorite po-angliyski?* | vi gavareet-ye po-angleeskee? |
| I don't understand | Я не понимаю *Ya ne ponimayu* | ya nye paneema-yoo |
| Could you speak more slowly? | Говорите медленнее *Govorite medlennee* | gavareet-ye myedlyenye-ye |
| Could you say it again please? | Повторите, пожалуйста *Povtorite, pozhaluysta* | paftareet-ye, pazhalsta |
| I am lost | я заблудился (заблудилась) *Ya zabludilsya (zabludilas)* | ya zabloodeelsya (zabloodeelas') |
| How do you say... in Russian? | Как по-русски...? *Kak po-russki...?* | kak pa-rooskee...? |

## Useful Words

| big | большой *bolshoy* | bal'shoy |
| small | маленький *malenkiy* | malyen'kee |
| hot (water, food) | горячий *goryachiy* | garyachee |
| hot (weather) | жарко *zharko* | zharka |
| cold | холодный *kholodnyy* | khalodnee |
| good | хорошо *khorosho* | kharasho |
| bad | плохо *plokho* | plokha |
| okay/fine | нормально *normalno* | narmal'na |
| near | близко *blizko* | bleezka |
| far | далеко *daleko* | dalyeko |
| up | наверху *naverkhu* | navyerkhoo |

| down | внизу *vnizu* | fneezoo |
| early | рано *rano* | rana |
| late | поздно *pozdno* | pozdna |
| vacant (unoccupied) | свободно *svobodno* | svabodna |
| free (no charge) | бесплатно *besplatno* | byesplatna |
| cashier/ticket office | касса *kassa* | kasa |
| avenue | проспект *prospekt* | praspyekt |
| bridge | мост *most* | most |
| embankment | набережная *naberezhnaya* | nabyeryezhnaya |
| highway/motorway | шоссе *shosse* | shasse |
| lane/passage | переулок *pereulok* | pyeryeoolak |
| square | площадь *ploshchad* | ploshat' |
| street | улица *ulitsa* | ooleetsa |
| flat/apartment | квартира *kvartira* | kvarteera |
| floor | этаж *etazh* | etash |
| house/block | дом *dom* | dom |
| entrance | вход *vkhod* | fkhot |
| exit | выход *vykhod* | vikhot |
| river | река *reka* | ryeka |
| summer country house | дача *dacha* | dacha |
| swimming pool | бассейн *basseyn* | basyeyn |
| town | город *gorod* | gorat |
| toilet | туалет *tualet* | tooalyet |

## Making a Telephone Call

| Can I call abroad from here? | Можно отсюда позвонить за границу? *Mozhno ostyuda pozvonit za granitsu?* | mozhna atsyooda pazvaneet' za graneetsoo? |
| I would like to speak to... | Позвоните, пожалуйста... *Pozovite, pozhaluysta* | pazaveet-ye, pazhalsta... |
| Could you leave him/her a message? | Вы можете передать ему/ей? *Vy mozhete peredat emu/ey?* | vi mozhet-ye pyeryedat' yemoo/yay? |
| My number is... | Мой номер... *Moy nomer...* | moy nomyer... |
| I'll ring back later | Я позвоню позже *Ya pozvonyu pozzhe* | ya pazvanyoo pozhe |

## Sightseeing

| castle | замок *zamok* | zamak |
| cathedral | собор *sobor* | sabor |
| church | церковь *tserkov* | tserkaf |
| circus | цирк *tsirk* | tseerk |
| closed for cleaning "cleaning day" | санитарный день *sanitarnyy den* | saneetarnee dyen' |
| undergoing restoration | ремонт *remont* | remont |
| exhibition | выставка *vystavka* | vistafka |
| fortress | крепость *krepost* | kryepost' |
| gallery | галерея *galereya* | galeryeya |

| garden | сад | sad |
| | *sad* | |
| island | остров | ostraf |
| | *ostrov* | |
| kremlin/fortified | кремль | kryeml' |
| stronghold | *kreml* | |
| library | библиотека | beeblee-atyeka |
| | *biblioteka* | |
| monument | памятник | pamyatneek |
| | *pamyatnik* | |
| mosque | мечеть | myechyet' |
| | *mechet* | |
| museum | музей | moozyey |
| | *muzey* | |
| palace | дворец | dvaryets |
| | *dvorets* | |
| park | парк | park |
| | *park* | |
| parliament | дума | dooma |
| | *duma* | |
| synagogue | синагога | seenagoga |
| | *sinagoga* | |
| zoo | зоопарк | zapark |
| | *zoopark* | |

## Shopping

| open | открыто | atkrita |
| | *otkryto* | |
| closed | закрыто | zakrita |
| | *zakryto* | |
| How much does | Сколько это стоит? | skol'ka eta stoeet? |
| this cost? | *Skolko eto stoit?* | |
| I would like to | Я хотел (хотела) бы | ya khatyel (khatyela) |
| buy...... | купить... | bi koopeet'... |
| | *Ya khotel (khotela)* | |
| | *by kupit...* | |
| Do you have......? | У вас есть...? | oo vas yest'...? |
| | *U vas yest....?* | |
| Do you take credit | Кредитные | kryedeetnye |
| cards? | карточки вы | kartachkee vy |
| | принимаете? | preeneemayetye? |
| | *Kreditnye kartochki* | |
| | *vy prinimaete?* | |
| What time do you | Во сколько вы | Va skol'ka vy |
| open/close? | открываетесь/ | atkrivayetyes'/ |
| | закрываетесь? | zakrivayetyes? |
| | *Vo skolko vy* | |
| | *otkryvaetes/* | |
| | *zakryvaetes?* | |
| This one | этот | etat |
| | *etot* | |
| expensive | дорого | doraga |
| | *dorogo* | |
| cheap | дёшево | dyoshyeva |
| | *deshevo* | |
| size | размер | razmyer |
| | *razmer* | |
| white | белый | byelee |
| | *belyy* | |
| black | чёрный | chyornee |
| | *chernyy* | |
| red | красный | krasnee |
| | *krasnyy* | |
| yellow | жёлтый | zholtee |
| | *zheltyy* | |
| green | зелёный | zyelyonee |
| | *zelenyy* | |
| dark blue | синий | seenee |
| | *siniy* | |
| light blue | голубой | galooboy |
| | *goluboy* | |
| brown | коричневый | kareechnyevee |
| | *korichnevyy* | |

## Types of Shop

| bakery | булочная | boolachna-ya |
| | *bulochnaya* | |
| bookshop | книжный магазин | kneezhnee magazeen |
| | *knizhnyy magazin* | |
| butcher | мясной магазин | myasnoy magazeen |
| | *myasnoy magazin* | |

| camera shop | фото-товары | foto-tavari |
| | *foto-tovary* | |
| chemist | аптека | aptyeka |
| | *apteka* | |
| delicatessen | гастроном | gastranom |
| | *gastronom* | |
| department store | универмаг | ooneevyermag |
| | *univermag* | |
| florist | цветы | tsvyeti |
| | *tsvety* | |
| grocer | бакалея | bakalye-ya |
| | *bakaleya* | |
| hairdresser | парикмахерская | pareekmakhyerskaya |
| | *parikmakherskaya* | |
| market | рынок | rinak |
| | *rynok* | |
| newspaper stand | газетный киоск | gazyetnee kee-osk |
| | *gazetniy kiosk* | |
| post office | почта | pochta |
| | *pochta* | |
| record shop | грампластинки | gramplasteenkee |
| | *gramplastinki* | |
| shoe shop | обувь | oboof |
| | *obuv* | |
| travel agent | бюро путешествий | byooro |
| | *byuro puteshestviy* | pootyeshestvee |
| bank | банк | bank |
| | *bank* | |

## Staying in a Hotel

| Do you have a | У вас есть | oo vas yest' |
| vacant room? | свободный номер? | svabodnee |
| | *U vas yest* | nomyer? |
| | *svobodnyy nomer?* | |
| double room with | номер с | nomyer s |
| double bed | двуспальной | dvoospal'noy |
| | кроватью | kravat'-yoo |
| | *nomer s dvuspalnoy* | |
| | *krovatyu* | |
| twin room | двухместный | dvookhmyestnee |
| | номер | nomyer |
| | *dvukhmestnyy* | |
| | *nomer* | |
| single room | одноместный | adnamyestnee |
| | номер | nomyer |
| | *odnomestnyy nomer* | |
| bath | ванная | vana-ya |
| | *vannaya* | |
| shower | душ | doosh |
| | *dush* | |
| porter | носильщик | naseel'sheek |
| | *nosilshchik* | |
| key | ключ | klyooch |
| | *klyuch* | |

## Eating Out

| A table for two, | Стол на двоих, | stol na dva-eekh, |
| please | пожалуйста | pazhalsta |
| I would like to | Я хочу заказать | ya khachoo zakazat' |
| book a table | стол | stol |
| | *Ya khochu zakazat* | |
| | *stol* | |
| The bill, please | Счёт, | shyot, pazhalsta |
| | пожалуйста | |
| | *Schet,* | |
| | *pozhaluysta* | |
| I am a vegetarian | Я вегетерианец | ya vyegyetareeanyets |
| | (вегетерианка) | (vyegyetareeanka) |
| | *Ya vegeterianets* | |
| | *(vegeterianka)* | |
| breakfast | завтрак | zaftrak |
| | *zavtrak* | |
| lunch | обед | abyet |
| | *obed* | |
| dinner | ужин | oozheen |
| | *uzhin* | |
| waiter! | официант! | afeetsee-ant! |
| | *ofitsiant!* | |
| waitress! | официантка! | afeetsee-antka! |
| | *ofitsiantka!* | |
| dish of the day | фирменное блюдо | feermenoye |
| | *firmennoe blyudo* | blyooda |
| appetizers/starters | закуски | zakooskee |
| | *zakuski* | |

| | | | | | | |
|---|---|---|---|---|---|---|
| main course | второе блюдо *vtoroe blyudo* | ftaroye blyooda | | капуста *kapusta* | kapoosta | cabbage |
| meat and poultry dishes | мясные блюда *myasnye blyuda* | myasniye blyooda | | картофель *kartofel* | kartofyel' | potato |
| fish and seafood dishes | рыбные блюда *rybnye blyuda* | ribniye blyooda | | квас *kvas* | kvas | kvas (sweet, mildly alcoholic drink) |
| vegetable dishes | овощные блюда *ovoshchnye blyuda* | avashshniye blyooda | | клубника *klubnika* | kloobneeka | strawberries |
| dessert | десерт *desert* | dyesyert | | колбаса *kolbasa* | kalbasa | salami sausage |
| drinks | напитки *napitki* | napeetkee | | кофе *kofe* | kofye | coffee |
| vegetables | овощи *ovoshchi* | ovashshee | | красное вино *krasnoe vino* | krasnoye veeno | red wine |
| bread | хлеб *khleb* | khlyeb | | креветки *krevetki* | kryevyetkee | prawns |
| wine list | карта вин *karta vin* | karta veen | | курица *kuritsa* | kooreetsa | chicken |
| rare (steak) | недожаренный *nedozharennyy* | nyedazharenee | | лук *luk* | look | onion |
| well done (steak) | прожаренный *prozharennyy* | prozharenee | | малина *malina* | maleena | raspberries |
| glass | стакан *stakan* | stakan | | минеральная вода *mineralnaya voda* | mineral'naya vada | mineral water |
| bottle | бутылка *butylka* | bootilka | | мороженое *morozhenoe* | marozhena-ye | ice-cream |
| knife | нож *nozh* | nosh | | мясо *myaso* | myasa | meat |
| fork | вилка *vilka* | veelka | | огурец *ogurets* | agooryets | cucumber |
| spoon | ложка *lozhka* | loshka | | осетрина *osetrina* | asyetreena | sturgeon |
| plate | тарелка *tarelka* | taryelka | | пельмени *pelmeni* | pyel'myenee | meat or fish dumplings |
| napkin | салфетка *salfetka* | salfyetka | | персик *persik* | pyerseek | peach |
| salt | соль *sol* | sol' | | печенье *pechene* | pyechyen'ye | biscuit |
| pepper | перец *perets* | pyeryets | | печёнка *pechenka* | pyechyonka | liver |
| butter/oil | масло *maslo* | masla | | печёный *pechenyy* | pyechyonee | baked |
| sugar | сахар *sakhar* | sakhar | | пиво *pivo* | peeva | beer |
| | | | | пирог *pirog* | peerok | pie |

## Menu Decoder

| | | | | | | |
|---|---|---|---|---|---|---|
| абрикос *abrikos* | abreekos | apricot | | пирожки *pirozhki* | peerashkee | small parcels with savoury fillings |
| апельсин *apelsin* | apyel'seen | orange | | помидор *pomidor* | pameedor | tomato |
| апельсиновый сок *apelsinovyy sok* | apyel'seenavee sok | orange juice | | морепродукты *moryeprodukty* | moryeproduktee | seafood |
| арбуз *arbuz* | arbooz | water melon | | рыба *ryba* | riba | fish |
| белое вино *beloe vino* | byelaye veeno | white wine | | салат *salat* | salat | salad |
| бифштекс *bifshteks* | beefshtyeks | steak | | свинина *svinina* | sveeneena | pork |
| блины *bliny* | bleeni | pancakes | | сельдь *seld* | sye'ld' | herring |
| борщ *borshch* | borshsh | borsch (beetroot soup) | | сосиски *sosiski* | saseeskee | sausages |
| варенье *varene* | varyen'ye | Russian syrup-jam | | сыр *syr* | sir | cheese |
| варёный *varenyy* | varyonee | boiled | | сырой *syroy* | siroy | raw |
| ветчина *vetchina* | vyetcheena | ham | | утка *utka* · | ootka | duck |
| вода *voda* | vada | water | | фасоль *fasol* | fasol' | beans |
| говядина *govyadina* | gavyadeena | beef | | форель *forel* | faryel' | trout |
| грибы *griby* | greebi | mushrooms | | чай *chay* | chai | tea |
| груша *grusha* | groosha | pear | | чеснок *chesnok* | chyesnok | garlic |
| гусь *gus* | goos | goose | | шашлык *shashlyk* | shashlik | kebab |
| джем *dzhem* | dzhem | jam | | яйцо *yaytso* | yaytso | egg |
| жареный *zharenyy* | zharyenee | roasted/grilled/fried | | слива *sliva* | sleeva | plum |
| икра *ikra* | eekra | black caviar | | фрукты *frukty* | frookti | fruit |
| икра красная/кета *ikra krasnaya/keta* | eekra krasna-ya/ kyeta | red caviar | | яблоко *yabloko* | yablaka | apple |

## Transport

| | | |
|---|---|---|
| north | север *sever* | **sy**ever |
| south | юг *yug* | yook |
| east | восток *vostok* | va**sto**k |
| west | запад *zapad* | **za**pat |
| airport | аэропорт *aeroport* | aera**po**rt |
| aeroplane | самолёт *samolet* | samal**yot** |
| traffic police | ДПС *DPS* | day-pay-**ess** |
| bus | автобус *avtobus* | af**to**boos |
| bus station | автобусная станция *avtobusnaya stantsiya* | af**to**boosna-ya stantsee-ya |
| bus stop | остановка автобуса *ostanovka avtobusa* | astan**of**ka af**to**boosa |
| car | машина *mashina* | ma**shee**na |
| flight | рейс *reys* | ryeys |
| metro (station) | (станция) метро *(stantsiya) metro* | (stantsee-ya) myet**ro** |
| no entry | нет входа *net vkhoda* | nyet f**kho**da |
| no exit | нет выхода *net vykhoda* | nyet **vi**khada |
| parking | автостоянка *avtostoyanka* | afto**sto**yanka |
| petrol | бензин *benzin* | byen**zeen** |
| railway | железная дорога *zheleznaya doroga* | zhel**ye**zna-ya da**ro**ga |
| railway station | вокзал *vokzal* | vag**zal** |
| return ticket | обратный билет *obratniy bilet* | o**bra**tnee bee**lyet** |
| seat | место *mesto* | **my**esta |
| suburban train | пригородный поезд *prigorodniy poezd* | pr**ee**garadnee po-**yezd** |
| straight on | прямо *pryamo* | **prya**ma |
| taxi | такси *taksi* | tak**see** |
| ticket | билет *bilet* | bee**lyet** |
| token (for a single metro journey) | жетон *zheton* | zhe**ton** |
| to the left | налево *nalevo* | nal**ye**va |
| to the right | направо *napravo* | na**pra**va |
| train | поезд *poezd* | po-**yezd** |
| tram | трамвай *tramvay* | tram**vay** |
| trolleybus | троллейбус *trolleybus* | tral**ye**yboos |

## Numbers

| | | |
|---|---|---|
| 1 | один/одна/одно *odin/odna/odno* | a**deen**/ad**na**/ad**no** |
| 2 | два/две *dva/dve* | dva/dvye |
| 3 | три *tri* | tree |
| 4 | четыре *chetyre* | chye**tir**-ye |
| 5 | пять *pyat* | pyat' |
| 6 | шесть *shest* | shest' |
| 7 | семь *sem* | syem' |
| 8 | восемь *vosem* | **vo**syem' |
| 9 | девять *devyat* | d**ye**vyat' |
| 10 | десять *desyat* | d**ye**syat' |

| | | |
|---|---|---|
| 11 | одиннадцать *odinnadtsat* | a**dee**natsat' |
| 12 | двенадцать *dvenadtsat* | dv**ye**natsat' |
| 13 | тринадцать *trinadtsat* | tree**na**tsat |
| 14 | четырнадцать *chetyrnadtsat* | chye**tir**natsat' |
| 15 | пятнадцать *pyatnadtsat* | pyat**na**tsat' |
| 16 | шестнадцать *shestnadtsat* | shest**na**tsat' |
| 17 | семнадцать *semnadtsat* | syem**na**tsat' |
| 18 | восемнадцать *vosemnadtsat* | vasyem**na**tsat' |
| 19 | девятнадцать *devyatnadtsat* | dyevyat**na**tsat' |
| 20 | двадцать *dvadtsat* | d**va**tsat' |
| 21 | двадцать один *dvadtsat odin* | d**va**tsat' a**deen** |
| 22 | двадцать два *dvadtsat dva* | d**va**tsat' dva |
| 23 | двадцать три *dvadtsat tri* | d**va**tsat' tree |
| 24 | двадцать четыре *dvadtsat chetyre* | d**va**tsat' chye**tir**-ye |
| 25 | двадцать пять *dvadtsat pyat* | d**va**tsat' pyat' |
| 30 | тридцать *tridtsat* | **tree**tsat' |
| 40 | сорок *sorok* | **so**rak |
| 50 | пятьдесят *pyatdesyat* | pyad**ye**s**yat'** |
| 60 | шестьдесят *shestdesyat* | shes'd**ye**s**yat** |
| 70 | семьдесят *semdesyat* | s**yem'**dyesyat |
| 80 | восемьдесят *vosemdesyat* | **vo**syem'dyesyat |
| 90 | девяносто *devyanosto* | dyevy**a**nosta |
| 100 | сто *sto* | sto |
| 200 | двести *dvesti* | dv**ye**stee |
| 300 | триста *trista* | tree**sta** |
| 400 | четыреста *chetyresta* | chye**ti**ryesta |
| 500 | пятьсот *pyatsot* | pyat'**sot** |
| 1,000 | тысяча *tysyacha* | **ti**syacha |
| 2,000 | две тысячи *dve tysyachi* | dvye **ti**syachi |
| 5,000 | пять тысяч *pyat tysyach* | pyat' **ti**syach |
| 1,000,000 | миллион *million* | meelee-**on** |

## Time, Days and Dates

| | | |
|---|---|---|
| one minute | одна минута *odna minuta* | ad**na** meen**oo**ta |
| one hour | час *chas* | chas |
| half an hour | полчаса *polchasa* | polcha**sa** |
| day | день *den* | dyen' |
| week | неделя *nedelya* | nyed**yel**-ya |
| Monday | понедельник *ponedelnik* | panyed**yel'**neek |
| Tuesday | вторник *vtornik* | f**to**rneek |
| Wednesday | среда *sreda* | sryed**a** |
| Thursday | четверг *chetverg* | chyet**vy**erk |
| Friday | пятница *pyatnitsa* | **py**atneetsa |
| Saturday | суббота *subbota* | soo**bo**ta |
| Sunday | воскресенье *voskresene* | vaskry**esy**en'ye |